THE COLONIAL PRESENT

THE COLONIAL PRESENT

THE RULE OF IGNORANCE AND THE ROLE OF LAW IN BRITISH COLUMBIA

BY

KERRY COAST

CLARITY PRESS, INC.

AND

INTERNATIONAL HUMAN RIGHTS
ASSOCIATION OF AMERICAN MINORITIES
(IHRAAM)

© 2013 Kerry Coast

ISBN: 978-0-9860362-3-1
E-book: 978-0-9860362-2-4

In-house editor: Diana G. Collier
Cover: R. Jordan P. Santos

Library of Congress Cataloging-in-Publication Data

Coast, Kerry.
  The colonial present : the rule of ignorance and the role of law in British Columbia / by Kerry Coast. -- First edition.
    1 online resource.
  Includes bibliographical references and index.
  Description based on print version record and CIP data provided by publisher; resource not viewed.
  ISBN 978-0-9860362-3-1 () -- ISBN 978-0-9860362-2-4
  1. Indians of North America--British Columbia--Government relations. 2. Indians of North America--Civil rights--British Columbia. 3. Indians of North America--Land tenure--British Columbia. 4. Indians, Treatment of--British Columbia--History. 5. British Columbia--Race relations. 6. British Columbia--Colonization. 7. British Columbia--Politics and government. I. Title.

E78.B9
323.1197'0711--dc23

2013017180

Clarity Press, Inc.
Ste. 469, 3277 Roswell Rd. NE
Atlanta, GA. 30305 , USA
http://www.claritypress.com

IHRAAM
101-5170 Dunster Rd., Ste. 117
Nanaimo, BC V9T 6M4
Canada
http://www.ihraam.org

TABLE OF CONTENTS

INTRODUCTION / 11

Chapter 1.
A POOR TO MIDDLING CONSPIRACY / 13

Chapter 2.
GEE, EH? GENOCIDE AWARENESS /26
    A Few Meaningful Cases /28
    The Convention on the Prevention and Punishment
        of the Crime of Genocide, 1948 /32
    War / 41

Chapter 3.
$10 BILLION, OR, THE CASH OF THE MATTER /43
    Buying Justice / 44
    The Value of Denying Title / 49
    No One Left To Pay / 51

Chapter 4.
STUDYING INDIFFERENCE / 55
    Sinking Out of Sight / 56
    Texts and Reference Books / 59
    The Rise of Historiomythology / 67
    Inbreeding Academia / 74
    The Academic Oath / 85

Chapter 5.
ON RESERVE / 91
    How Reserves Came to Be / 92
    How the Reserves Were Fought / 100
    Agents in Right of Canada / 114
    Off Reserve / 116

Chapter 6.
EXTINGUISHMENT WITH CONSENT / 119
    The BC Treaty Commission: Negotiating Extinguishment / 120

Chapter 7.
ASSIMILATION OR CRIMINALIZATION / 142
    Savages in a Chrstian Empire / 142
    Resistance: Criminalization / 151

Capitulation: Assimilation / 162
Indigenous Academics / 173

Chapter 8.
IMMIGRATION, OR ESCAPEMENT / 178
Who Were We Then? / 178
From Henry Hudson's Bay to Simon Fraser's River / 197
The Colony as a Province / 202

Chapter 9.
THE ROLE OF LAW / 206
Chicanery Today / 211
The Frozen Right / 218
Royal Commissions / 223

Chapter 10.
THE RULE OF IGNORANCE / 231
The Corporate News Disservice / 232
Freedoms of the Press / 234
A National Broadcasting Corporation / 249
The Fickle Nature of Stupidity / 253
Satisfied Confusion / 257
Keeping It Simple / 260

Chapter 11.
TESTING THE NEW MYTHOLOGISTS / 264
Improvement / 264
Separating Business and Politics /266
Landing Suspended Disbelief / 271
Political Migrations on Unceded Lands / 274
Lawyers / 279
Culling the Other Lawyers / 282

Chapter 12.
WHO ARE WE NOW? / 286
After Law / 292
Superiority and Schizophrenia / 294
Post-Historic Man / 300
The New Deal / 304
Beyond Insincerity / 307
Reconciliation / 308

ENDNOTES / 341

INDEX / 339

FOR ALL OF US

ACKNOWLEDGMENTS

O, Nk'ultenlhkálha,

Kúk'wstum'kacw.

Tákem i saq'w, tákem i matq, tákem i tsáylec, tákem i nq'áylec, tákem i rip: kuk'wstum'kál'ap.

Without knowing where to start or where to stop, I would simply like to offer my thanks to all those people who believed in me, those who made me doubt myself, and those who were completely indifferent and made me realize that it's necessary to listen to one's own heart.

For sharing with me their profound humanity, for being so very brave and refusing to become something less, I thank Tsemhúqw, Láhalus, Yáoqus, Nák'sten, Pau Tuc La Simc, Wénemqen, Sweláops, Pást'sa, Bill Lightbown, John Shafer, Wolverine, Flora Samson , Shelagh Franklin, Felípe, Favianna, Aka, Lémya7, Freddy, Saw't and the guy I met on the bus at Lytton when I was twelve. For helping me so much to understand the meaning of this story I thank Arthur Manuel, Russell Diabo, Nicole Schabus, Qwatsinas and Lyn Crompton. For giving me this chance to share my view I thank Diana Collier Kly.

Thank you all.

Tákem i nsneq'wnúq'wa.

Nák'sten (Arnold Williams) and Tipta, Líl'watmc, 1990

INTRODUCTION

But I fear we have seen the end of history. Who now would posit thoughts on our origins, our causes, or any time since them, as being relevant to what we are now? As if we could be liable for the past? We who left our own homelands in war and impoverished, colonized and barren, overpopulated or overcome by dictatorship: we have come through too much, we say; we don't need history to hold us back. And now, when all we have of recorded history has been exposed for the ethnocentric tool it is; now, when history is inconvenient to a global consciousness. Now, when so much of history has been hopelessly obscured, and while we frantically bury the evidence of our own recent events: it worries us. Could we uncover authentic pieces and discover ourselves less than at liberty to write the definitive version - not the victors? Even the victims?

Now, when we individuals and families are no longer part of *a people* - with land and language, as we used to be before we came here. Now, when there is no other "we," only those of us who are here. "We" have little in common but this history here, just this making our new selves out of someone else's homelands.

Already archaeologists and all manner of students of humanity refer to a time they call "pre-history." And certainly anything since then and up to a comfortable place in the not-so-distant past is "history," but we believe we are separated from it. We look at some of the things we have done, things our grandparents, aunts and uncles did to tilt the world in our favour - actions that have never been resolved; and we select the irritating aspects and say: "*that* is history." As if those changes are beyond reversal. And to what we have been and that which continues to define us, to our footprints which lead to our present wealth and security, we claim no connection.

Now we are up to our ankles in the rise of post-history. No more a people making history, satisfying it, but merely sharp human edges on the machines of an all-consuming Empire. We are merely detailing a foregone conclusion, the same conclusion and the same conditions which made us abandon our homes and histories in the first place. We will remove and replace the peoples of the land, at the same time as saying this was done many years ago and it's over now. Who will we be when history has ended without *us,* and what we have done? Who are we now?

Chapter 1

A POOR TO MIDDLING CONSPIRACY

It's not that a grand strategy was brilliantly executed and a progressive modern province was hewn from the wilderness to join Canada. That sort of mastery will not settle nicely on the shoulders of the subjects of this book. What has happened in British Columbia is a long series of colonizing violence against dozens of indigenous nations, followed by bumbling, over-confident lies and ensuing cover-ups. This series leads to the present day, to the present page of the present chapter, being written now. If it wasn't, this sort of book would be impossible: the evidence would be more carefully disposed of—the participants too; the "official version" would be free of so many stretched seams.

As for that record: there were a few possibly strategic office fires, like at Indian Affairs headquarters in Williams Lake in the 1920's.[1] And fires destroyed several unoccupied cabins that served as storage for important communications between companies like BC Electric and the leaders of indigenous communities whose lands were desired; communications documenting promises like free electricity in exchange for use of plots of land for generating stations and safe passage for transmission lines.[2] Communications which confirmed that the newcomer needed an invitation to proceed; that he needed permission. The most informative historical governmental memos, for instance those which encouraged the dispersal of indigenous societies by criminalization and punishment of indigenous culture, have long since been relegated to the bin.[3]

What has happened is a protracted series of disobedient, actually illegal, assumptions and assertions, on the parts of individual politicians, judges, corporate officers, civil servants and individuals at large. They have produced a winding web of legal inconsistency and duality, with apocalyptic indigenous casualty rates, and led to the juridical and social quadriplegic that is the province of British Columbia today. BC, or rather 26 indigenous nations, was made a British colony in 1858, and a Canadian province in 1871. They had the benefit of instructive histories in colonization already carried out by Great Britain in India, Kenya, China, Nigeria, Ireland, the Thirteen Colonies (later the USA) and South Africa. British Columbia is the youngest of the many unconquered frontiers of the late British Empire.

The haphazard and trial-by-necessity-or-fire nature of colonial development in British Columbia, Canada, is nothing more sophisticated than a brutal land race determined by the advantage that a gun takes over an arrow; that a built-up resistance to small pox, tuberculosis and flu takes over an unaccustomed immune system; that the remaining majority newcomer holds over the remnant minority populations of its victims. It's nothing morally more than what influence a gunboat takes over beach-front cedar plank villages, or an entire Ministry of Justice takes over outlawed and criminalized peoples. It is nothing socially more than the settlers' ability to deny law and even common decency for a century and a half. And it is nothing less.

Matthew Bailie Begbie was a lawyer with the unproven but accredited capability of arguing British common law, a status which might today be equivalent to an articling clerk. In 1858 the new "judge" Begbie arrived in what he instantly proclaimed the colony of British Columbia on behalf of his new employer, Queen Victoria. Here he discovered a fur trading ring run by a band of frontier men operating under martial government, delivered bloodily by the Hudson's Bay Company, and a lot of grubby and desperate Americans streaming in from the empty California gold fields to the Fraser gold rush. Thirty thousand American miners, to be precise. The Bay Company's Chief Factor and Governor of Vancouver's Island, James Douglas, had asked his superiors in London to send for the job of Chief Justice a man with "physical endurance, courage, and the ability to withstand the financial temptations offered by the conditions in the gold fields…"[4] The lawman had these and the advantage of aristocratic parents.

Begbie arrived by boat and, within twenty yards of the water at Fort Langley, announced the creation of the colony. He named James Douglas its Governor. Governor Douglas turned back to him and named him the Chief Justice.

Begbie made only one known dabble in insider trading related to the goldfields, but he did not withstand other temptations associated with monarch-delegated powers backed by a navy whose admirals sat "in the seat of Neptune."[5] Rather than going about meeting with the leaders of the indigenous nations to talk treaty, or even with the British Colonial Secretaries to discover the nature of his jurisdiction or the laws that he should enforce, he took up shop issuing accordances that would provide the otherwise skint new colony with revenue from gold mining licenses attached to lands his new government did not own.

In effect, Begbie engineered the interception of tariffs that were due to the indigenous nations: monies they would surely have collected if the advancing miners had not felt free to shoot to kill them instead. The Indians were unaware of the new government's sworn allegiance to the rule of law and of the resultant judicial remedies which Begbie had at his disposal to enter to enter into international agreements with them and to enforce British law on the miners—certainly neither the Hudson's Bay Company nor the new imperial authorities had done anything to suggest the newcomer lived by any sort of consistent law whatsoever, unless self-interest. Rather than introducing himself and the venue of justice which he was meant to represent, the Chief Justice allowed for the miners' theft of indigenous caches, homes, properties and the occupation of critical fishing areas. He failed to mitigate the conduct of those who had come from all over the world to buy mining licenses from his government. The indigenous peoples had no agreements with Begbie or his Colony for defense from or recourse against the oncoming bearers of the plague of gold fever,[6] which resulted in violence such as at Grouse Creek, one of the "Gold Rush Wars," where native militias had few options and drove miners back towards the ocean via the Fraser current.

Begbie then assumed juridical jurisdiction, purporting to drag all twenty six of those nations—and fighting fit—under British rule. On November 18, 1858, the law of the land belonged to the nations who had lived on it from time immemorial. On November 19, 1858, Begbie and the Governor addressed a few dozen desperately assembled whitefolk in Fort Langley and spoke the greatest sort of lie that is possible in human languages: the Chief Justice declared that the power of law on these unconquered, unsolicited, unceded, unsurrendered—and very much occupied—lands belonged to him in right of a foreign power: Great Britain. Without so much as a notice to the affected parties that he planned to do so. The following February, Governor Douglas declared that every right in the soil belonged to BC in right of the Crown.[7] The winter of 1858-59 claimed a great number of indigenous souls by starvation.

And that is how the "Indian land question" in modern British Columbia was posed: the original peoples have never sold or in any way released claim to their lands, but Canada and the province behave as if these territories are now crown land. They wonder, do indigenous peoples have any rights at all which may have survived Britain's appetite for their homelands? Can those rights have possibly survived colonization over a century and a half? These are not really the most important questions, however the colonizer might present the situation. So ludicrous to the indigenous was the assertion of control made by the newcomer, who was apparently lost and obviously totally dependent on them, that they did not take his ambitions seriously enough until they were outnumbered. They underestimated the inhumanity of the Briton, but by 1850 he was himself the result of some millennia of violent displacement and dispossession, notably accentuated in 1066, living in a culture of servitude and conformity.

The question facing BC now is: how can the newcomers acquire legal title to enough land to carry on existing, or, failing that, how can they maintain the present patently extra-judicial business? The question with which this book is concerned, however, is whether the people of British Columbia today can turn around two centuries of a genocidal approach, before it's too late. Their work today in this respect is unfortunately comparable to their founding moments.

Not only did Begbie decline to meet with the indigenous nations over whose territories he went on to assume legal and economic jurisdiction, in the decades that followed he refused to admit, much less discuss, the facts and the growing liabilities of his indefensible assertions.

Instead, he sent Surveyors. These men assured the various Chiefs, on a community-by-community basis within the various indigenous nations, that they, the Surveyors, were going about the business of limiting their colonial colleagues' (the miners and settlers) illegal use of and settlement on untreated land. They said they were there to map and respect the communities' outer boundaries which were set by the Chiefs, promising to respect the boundaries which were set by the Chiefs in those early consultations. They announced the Queen's law and proclaimed the justice of their work. Begbie did a bit of surveying himself, of a different sort: one of his official tasks early on the job included something of a reconnaissance mission for Douglas, surveying the lay of the land in the interior and assessing the likelihood of mineral deposits.[8]

In truth, the Indian Reserve Surveyors' assigned job was to limit the land scope of the original indigenous nations to a few seasonal areas that would prove convenient to the requirements of settler expansion and Missionary purpose. This they accomplished by telling the Chiefs one thing and the settlers another, and the colonial and imperial governments something else again. Some of the maps from the Douglas era still exist, depicting a likeness of the great valleys which the various Chiefs pointed out as the lands they could not live without and which should be entirely reserved for their use and free of settlers. As the settlers' requirements increased, the Reserves shrank from the outer limits of whole valleys and watersheds down to menial parcels defined by fences that followed potato patches or an outcrop of fishing rocks along the river. The great nations were forced to take the shape of many tiny, scattered communities, their trade routes were overrun, their travel was restricted and their commerce interrupted.

The old surveys of the first Indian Reserves, when they can be found, do not match the Indian Reserves which now show up as mere pinpoints on a map of British Columbia. It seems that whether the Surveyors' account of the "Reserves" they were demarcating coincided with the Chiefs' directions mattered little in the end. The provincial government has simply forcibly, or at best coercively, removed indigenous people from sought-after lands. Within the last hundred years many Reserves have disappeared, notably Kitsilano, Pemberton and Neskonlith.

Because Begbie did not engage the nations in his settlement scheme, not so much as a broken promise to them remains to substantiate the crown's claim to their title. One does not simply wash up somewhere and say the place belongs to them. Not without a fight.

The peculiar aspect of BC colonization is that the actual colonizers and the crown made no such challenge nor equally honest offer. Instead, they waited morbidly for the germs they brought to do the job for them and avoided all discussion in the interim. A Líl'wat Elder in the 1970s recalled to ethnographers' recording machines the experience of Hudson's Bay Company men ("King George men") wearing gloves to distribute blankets which infected the recipients with smallpox.[9]

They also waited for a few settlers to run amok in the indigenous populations and be killed. Then they carried out retaliation. "Strategic retaliation," using British naval gunboats to raze coastal villages; public hangings, ordering the whole village out to see the execution of whoever the villagers had relinquished as guilty parties in exchange for the safety of their structures.[10] Apparently it was these "disciplinary" actions which were meant to indicate that a transaction for the lands and resources had taken place.

In the late nineteenth century, white colonists were very much labouring under the mistaken belief that the native peoples would soon die out. That confidence was surely inspired by their active determination to achieve such a result. When there were still indigenous nations by 1923, the anthropologist Diamond Jenness said there certainly wouldn't be any by the end of the 20th century.[11] That ultimately mistaken belief, however, was probably the most significant flaw throughout their proceedings. Indigenous peoples are here today. And they have the same strength of claim to land title, juridical superiority and national preservation that their great, great grandparents had. In a few cases, there are people still living who were directly and personally displaced from their family lands; that's how fresh this wound still is. There are Elders alive today who were raised out in the cabins along the river routes, who were kidnapped right from their parents' alpine homes by the Indian Residential School recruiters.

And that is why aboriginal title to the land exists throughout British Columbia. The government's courtrooms cannot address it because they are partial to the outcome. They will not even permit the matter of continuing indigenous jurisdiction in their own homelands to be raised in the courtrooms, unless couched in terms of application for recognition of rights, including title, which will be delegated and described by Canada. For all the judicious posturing, there was not even an attempt by the colony or the province to purchase the land, except the few hectares around Victoria which were supposedly relinquished to Governor Douglas for blankets and the odd cap and coat. The fact of unextinguished aboriginal title and the absence of treaties is enough to challenge any layer of Canada's actions to dispose of indigenous lands and resources, to administer their affairs, determine their family, cultural and governmental systems.

When a court lacks impartiality, it loses jurisdiction to rule on the question at hand. This is a foundational precept of the rule of law. British Columbia never gained jurisdiction over the Indian Lands, as they are called in Canada's Constitution, because it never bought them or made a treaty with the people who have jurisdiction and could have shared it: BC has always functioned as a military occupation. Their courts are, arguably, still at the level the Hudson's Bay Company was endowed with when it was chartered by the King of England in 1670: a sort of military tribunal for urgent matters. This level, a military occupation, will not satisfy international mores nor the rights of human beings. The governance of the province today has not matured through such actions as would lead it to become legitimate in a foreign land through some arrangement with the local nationals, and its courts are still biased in the interests of preserving the viability of the occupation.

British Columbia's problems with respect to its actions against the indigenous are several and drag into the 21st century without any indication of a human rights based resolution in development. BC did not complete treaties with the indigenous nations to lawfully acquire the lands it now claims. This obligation is made clear by an Executive Order (the Royal Proclamation of 1763) demanding such purchases before settlement. The Colony of British Columbia ignored that Order, and so does the modern province, as part of Canada. The 1763 Proclamation, which requires purchase and treaty before settlement or entry, is part of Canada's Constitution.

As well as being in contravention of its own domestic legal basis, BC is in violation of international human rights laws related to genocide, having flagrantly and continuously carried out genocidal acts against every single indigenous nation whose land it claims. This can most easily be recognized in reference to the Indian Residential Schools which indigenous children throughout BC were sent to, on pain of their parents' imprisonment, which achieved the intended result of interrupting inter-generational cultural transmission among indigenous nations to the extent that most of the people are unable to speak the languages of not just their forefathers, but their parents.[12]

This situation is not "history," it is an unresolved and ongoing problem today raising the specter of international trials for charges under the 1948 International Convention on the Prevention and Punishment of the Crime of Genocide. Canada does nothing to reprimand BC's flat refusals to respect or appropriately respond to Supreme Court of Canada rulings which have found that aboriginal title continues to exist,[13] discrediting BC's claims to the contrary and prompting international credit agencies to insist[14] that the province show how it is going about acquiring the lands now. Multi-national corporations wishing to work in BC create their own agreements with the indigenous:[15] the province obviously cannot guarantee corporate interests.

The climate of racial discrimination in the province, and the resulting general approval of policies devised to extinguish aboriginal rights and title, has been so extreme as to have rung alarm bells and calls for reform in every United Nations human rights committee the complaints have been addressed to. There are neither clean hands nor good faith in BC's proposed solution: a series of conflict-of-interest-ridden negotiations that the province has commenced with the Band Councils, elected members of a federally regulated *Indian Act* governance structure imposed on indigenous nations by Canada, who are personally dependent upon it for their authority. The BC Treaty Commission, which has no legal standing to negotiate what are recognized in international law to be "treaties," is put forward by the government as "the unbiased arm" of negotiations over the land, even as it places ads in newspapers exhorting the financial benefits to BC of settling the land dispute in its manner. Then there is the obvious and easily documented problem of a nasty culture of coercion[16] dominating whatever pre-determined "negotiating" processes that the governments, provincial and federal, finance for the deliberately and dramatically impoverished nations and their representatives.

These insidious activities might continue as long as there is no clear victor to finally complete these chapters of history. Because BC hasn't won yet.

Indigenous peoples are bringing home ancestral remains from museums to rebury them; they are demanding an account of the failure of the fisheries; they are owed compensation for expropriation of lands and resources. They are demanding reparations, not just compensation to individuals, for the damages done their nations by the infamous Indian Residential Schools. And many are conscious and cognizant of their legitimate claims to self determination in their homelands, increasingly recognized internationally, in spite of endless attempts to assimilate, criminalize and scatter their people. They report to international Committees and Fora. Never in the colonial imagination, which placed indigenous peoples amid the wildlife, did such a scenario arise.

The British Columbia government is slack-jawed. And then verbose. And it is not only the politicians who recite inventive nationalist poesy at a desperate pace, but the entire academic profession—frantically rewriting history; the colonial lawyers and judges bent on usurping jurisdiction and, not least, the media. All of these leaders of public political thought scramble to add detail to the patchy myth of newcomer superiority and the inevitability of their domination that is taught and discussed in place of what actually went down in history. None of them is conversant in the equivalent indigenous laws, languages, traditions or spiritual cultures, but these are pronounced inferior to the new way of life. Perhaps British Columbians can invent a past, a colonial creation story, which does not feature wiping out indigenous nations—but it continues to carry out the actions which will effect just that result.

The spur-of-the-moment provisions made by a nineteenth century Victorian colony for its future generations were lackluster at best, and at worst, and more accurately, have led an ignorant, desperate and self-interested public into complicity with crimes of genocide. This invites discussion of the non-descript origins of the emigrated population of the colony. The province was and continues to be populated mainly by refugees fleeing war, famine, economic disaster and tyranny in Europe, Asia, South America, the Orient, the United States, the Pacific Islands and Africa. In other words, the displaced and dispossessed of other European countries and colonies have now come to the north west Pacific coast to take a place for themselves.

They perhaps should not have put their faith in the same imperial movement that jarred them loose from their homelands overseas. The settlers have been hoodwinked, and an eclipsing lien is staid on their acreages and city lots. They have bought into a vicious cycle of resource-rich boom— subsidized by denial of the indigenous—and the plunderers' leftover bust; a cycle possibly unsurpassed around the world. Decade after decade, the gold, salmon and timber have been liquidated and exported by the workers, and the public government, subsidizing private ventures by policing the indigenous out of the way of this progress, has fallen deeper in debt.

The natural wealth is gone. The corporations and their Boards are certainly culpable, but not bankable. Just as fluidly as millions of dollars worth of gold left the province in every year of the 1860s, the equivalent in modern currency has steadily escaped the provincial public—and the indigenous coffers—annually since then.

And that is why the jurisdictional question, and indeed the question of whether the rule of law applies in an overgrown British colony, is the most important question of the west. If it is to be answered honestly, indigenous peoples might stand a chance.

Today an indigenous individual is faced with the dilemma of abandoning most whatever is left of their born nationality to enter the world of the colonizer / conqueror, or embracing a life of desperate struggle for their people: to preserve their homeland and language, their nation and its precious future. Indigenous languages are dying out, plants and animals are daily dropping through the jaws of industry into the bottomless tract of extinction, and the communities are coming apart at the seams under the pressure. Communities are extinguishing themselves through the "modern day treaty process" just for the relief of not being targeted as the incarnation of every non-native taxpayer's woes. The statistics of poor health and poorer prospects among aboriginal people in Canada are closer to third world conditions than the top standard of living indicated by Canada's place in the United Nations human development index. And most non-native people do not care that this is their fate; most non-native people are not even aware. They certainly do not seem moved by the fact that it is their elected government's policies that are the cause of it.

But then how could they know? Canadians and British Columbians have produced a small canon of mythology and rhetoric in place of their history. The news media ardently shields its subscribers from the actuality of and reasons for indigenous poverty, ill-health and disintegration, as well from the citizenry's day to day connection with the causes of it. Public schools teach children that First Nations belong to the past. The mass media and the official record sides with the settler, the imperialist and the industrial colonist in acting as if these unnatural and untimely national indigenous deaths *should be* occurring, and are a function of their progress. This is the media which, in British Columbia, was hatched by the politically ambitious with founding prose to the effect of "get the Indians out of our forests."[17] The same cry reverberates in the metal news boxes of the same newspaper, *The Colonist*, here today. It was nearly repeated verbatim by Premier Mike "get the fucking Indians out of the park" Harris in Ontario in 1995, just before Dudley George was shot to death in Ipperwash; and at the same time by BC Attorney General *and* Minister of Human Rights Ujjal "terrorist catcher" Dossanjh, just before 77,000 rounds of government ammunition rained down on a dozen Sundancers camped in defiance of the BC government at Ts'peten, or Gustafsen Lake.

The academics, media and politicians maintain the public mood of indifference to attacks on indigenous nations and their citizens. That is, when choice radio, television and print sources are not inciting or rationalizing those attacks. The situation of a rapidly climbing number of missing or murdered indigenous women on a northern BC highway and in the slums of Vancouver took over twenty years to become the subject of a government inquiry.

It is impossible to grasp the moral and legal realities of what are maligned as "Indian land claims," meaning the unsurrendered indigenous land titles, by relying on commentary circulating in the mainstream media or texts in government-run schools within the province. Politicians banter in malevolent racial slurs.

Recently in the news, reporters have drawn the public's attention to the results of surveys which show that aboriginal issues are not very high on the list of things which most concern them. The reporters then opine that this is not looking too good for First Nations progress. It is a strange choice for headlines, though; it's not news that British Columbians and Canadians are indifferent to the fate of indigenous peoples. This is media development of the theme that the indigenous nations can't look to protections enshrined in the Canadian constitution because they enjoy no favour in Canadian public opinion; that native claims are insignificant simply because so many think so.

Are they starting a rumour? That public opinion could lead to a Constitutional amendment, something along the lines of repealing the need to make treaties with Indian nations before trespassing on lands "not having been purchased"?[18] In practice, successive colonial governments and their electorates ignore the Constitution anyway, possibly informing the Everyman view that both the government and he, himself, can do whatever he wants to indigenous people. That message comes through clearly: "native people are not as important as we, the more worldly descendants of more ancient and more advanced societies, are." Elected leaders and the judges they appoint are still largely and deliberately ignoring aboriginal title and rights, wherever the Supreme Court of Canada keeps finding and then narrowly defining them.

Aboriginal people who defend their homelands and cultures are criminalized, even as case after government-backed court case fails to prove that extinguishment of aboriginal title has taken place. And while the indigenous right to self-determination is enshrined and made explicit in the United Nations Declaration on the Rights of Indigenous Peoples,[19] as well as Covenants on Civil, Political, Economic and Social Rights, the champions of that right are never vindicated in the press. Instead the very assimilated are hoisted on pedestals and used by news media as beacons of success.

Assimilation is asked—capitulation is demanded by the invader. That is the real law. The consequences of not doing so are public humiliation and a mark against a person which indicates the unlikelihood of survival, while the rewards for heading up the assimilation process are equally extreme—like having a new well-funded and handsomely-staffed Federal Board to chair. There are no "Aboriginal Canadian" heroes held up for their perseverance in fighting for the right of their nation to continue to exist as such and to determine their own collective future—for their right to self-determination, a human right enshrined in internationally binding legal conventions signed by Canada. There is no reward for demanding the government back off from man-handling the small communities into position, and insisting on progress with internationally supervised reparations payments. Indigenous individuals who advocate for the opposite—for the surrender of their lands, for the catchy slogan "separate business from politics," for economic integration at the expense of their people's survival as a nation or even their economic viability as a community, for social and cultural integration as an ethnic minority within the Canadian body politic, for the indemnification of British Columbia, Canada and "anyone else" for all past harms to them, these are the few indigenous people who are celebrated, promoted and rewarded in the dominating society.

Acceptance by indigenous people of the resulting and elaborately wrought historio-mythology, the popular culture, is considered a pre-requisite to all forms of their survival: genial social relations with what self-preserving colonials call "the broader society;" a child's success in school; employability.

Surrender their future, and they too can emigrate to Canada. It's true that there is more room now than ever in the "broader society's" view for a place of dignity for First Nations' ancestors, as long as their political power is fixed in the past.

It is a fight of might versus right. The industrial province harvesting valuable resources has grown to outnumber the many peoples whose homelands those materials are taken from. In BC, those who might be lawful and "right" have little visible might.

New immigrants today are faced with the same historical dilemma of confronting the realities of their adopted country that every other European, Asian, American or Oriental person faced when they came here, usually after abandoning an over-populated or dictatorial unfeasibility elsewhere, usually their homes. But they may not be so immediately aware of it today. Still, should they accept the position of oppressor here, comfortable as it is? Or should they align themselves with the nation whose territory they are actually living in, maybe Tsilhqot'in or Okanagan; Sto:lo, Haida or Musqueam? Would the newcomer even know the name of that nation? What is their identity now, as colonizers? Are they aware of the importance of this question, and that the indigenous are looking for a good answer?

Today's British Columbians can act on the truth, on the law, or condemn indigenous nations off the earth by simply continuing the federal and provincial policies of extinguishment. The result of that policy is what others elsewhere have termed a Final Solution. Here in BC, that solution presently has the broad, if tacit, support of the non-native majority. The decision to continue with it would result in the loss of vital, essential and intrinsically meaningful expressions of humanity: the peoples that are indigenous to *this place*.

The results of previous Canadian decisions in this respect are gruesome.

It is undeniable that human beings have, throughout history, fought each other ruthlessly for control of territories, but who are we now, carrying out these last tasks of extinguishing indigenous peoples? We are descended from those who have already lost most everything to this same cause. We are those who have fled it when it overtook our own natural homelands. We are those who have named a new country in honour of our willingness to carry on in such circumstances, and even perpetuate them. We concentrate on the tangible gains we have made, and yet it seems the simple presence of people still walking the earth their ancestors sprang from is a threat. But what we have gained in doctors and Medicare we have lost in health. What we have gained in education we have lost in compassionate intelligence. What we have gained in security we have lost in freedoms of every kind. What we have gained in order we have lost in law. What we have gained in communication technologies we have lost in meaning. What we have gained in passports, drivers licenses and credit cards we have lost in identity.

Canada still clutches at the velvet hem of the monarch stamped on the currency and holding the position of Head of State. Canadians are like the lost children who partially built the country—the orphans of Industrial Britain, the "Home Children," who provided ballast for otherwise empty cargo ships returning to the resource-rich shores of eastern Canada in the 19th and 20th centuries: children who are the parents of 12% of today's population.

Those child slaves' descendents have the opportunity to save themselves from what will be understood as a bone chilling historical legacy and racist identity, and, in so doing, free indigenous peoples. In that same opportunity would come liberation for both to build a future worth having. They and their heirs and their refugee-come-colonial colleagues have the opportunity to fail to continue as ballast, as fleshy frontlines, and insist on their freedom to be good and right. They have the opportunity to insist on the truth. Is that worth fighting for? For that, is it worth fighting one's own self as one knows it? Is it worth giving up ignorance?

Many are content not to know who we are now. For those of us with any curiosity, there are some court transcripts, bits of colonial correspondence that survived burnt-down Indian Agent offices, the odd diary and the financial statements. Unfortunately, the evidence has been all too frequently interpreted, rubbed out or presented unrecognizably by state supporters who can muse over the injustices of the past centuries and calmly regret them, but who cannot admit to the continuance of that history to the present date on the calendar: the present debate in Parliament, the present news headlines. That was history, they say.

That is how the rule of law is held captive by political forces. The outstanding and unresolved matters that should require some application of truth to affairs—the dissolution of entire human cultures, attacks on families, the stealing, the killings—these are merely treated as curiosities of our past history and not an urgent present concern.

There is the chance—and the reason—to reignite a movement to dignity, to pursue truth, justice, peace, legal pluralism, cooperation, equality and justice, and even spiritual reckoning. Certainly the world is thirsty for such a refreshing tonic. It will not, however, be sparked by the impotent speeches of BC politicians who parrot school textbooks written to conceal history; who make up new words, new relationships and new codes which can quickly be cracked to reveal the same attitudes of exploitation, dehumanization and submission to economic elites.

British Columbians need education in the history of the place they inhabit, its peoples and themselves, the late comers from elsewhere. The popular new brand of *reconciliation* with the indigenous, if it is to stick, to be genuine and not another media stunt to boost Canada's reputation elsewhere, will require more than an indigenous cooperator who Canada has put in place to show up at the United Nations Permanent Forum on Indigenous Issues and wield the phrase like a club. In recognition of their problem, British Columbia may have added "and Reconciliation" to the name of its "Ministry of Aboriginal Affairs" but there is no place within BC government offices where it is recognized that you cannot have reconciliation while outstanding grievances are filed, officially, in the past.

Why address those grievances now?

Why indeed. At this time, the BC Treaty Commission, the "independent and impartial (government financed and politically mandated) facilitator " of Final Agreements on "land claims" is overseeing the coercion of small, isolated First Nations into treaty settlement capital packages which extinguish aboriginal title and replace indigenous nations with municipal governments (this is the promised "self government") which remain under the thumb of British Columbia and Canada. Today, Canada broadcasts and markets these solutions to "The Indian Problem" in places as far-flung as Pakistan, Israel and Guyana. This is a companion policy to the "Section 35 Solution": Section 35 of the Constitution of Canada acknowledges the indigenous have aboriginal and treaty rights and then the government effectively declares, "We don't know what those are." Case after multi-million-dollar case ensues, and gradually those rights are examined, tested and defined one by one out of all meaning or practicability.

It is a timely cause, understanding history, understanding who we are—if "humanitarian" is ever again going to mean something good; if the post-history world is to include the only connection to "pre-history" in living memory; if memory is courage and reason; if everyone comes from and still desires a place in this world that affords an identity, a legal right, and a history. That memory is still tangible, in spite of everything, in indigenous peoples all over the world and in British Columbia, where it is securely connected to the land. The memory is an infectious, life-infusing and spirit bucking tonic: this is the gift that colonizers worldwide are welcomed to receive in exchange for arresting their progress at the point of *attempted* genocide.

Chapter 2

GEE, EH? GENOCIDE AWARENESS

"We have always been here on this land we call Turtle Island,
on our homelands given to us by the Creator, and we have a
responsibility to care for and live in harmony with all of her creations.
We believe that the responsibility to care for this land
was given to us by our Creator, the Great Spirit.
It is a sacred obligation, which means the first people must
care for all of her creation in fulfilling this responsibility.
We have carried this responsibility since long before
the immigrants came to our homeland.
Our elders remember agreements with the people...
The flag of BC is one of them."
—O. J. James (Eyabay) Pitawanakwat from *This Is My Defense*,
entered as defense during the Gustafsen Lake trial, April 25, 1997

Most British Columbians cannot identify with the genocidal actions of their governments. Many of them have been sheltered from the seriousness of the situation by politicians, educational institutions and media, which often work closely to preserve and promote the interests of the colony's resource-driven masters. Once it became apparent that native people were not going to simply die out and disappear by the 20th century, British Columbia's policy has always been to get title to the land by any and all means necessary. They have exploited many such means, mainly along the lines of promoting the dying out and disappearing.

There are possibly more than thirty individual indigenous nations within and straddling British Columbia's borders today. They range in size from something like Lebanon to something like Poland. The west coast was so rich in its sea resources before modern days that it was capable of supporting a large population in a way that is now almost out of memory.

It isn't possible or fair to put a certain number on the indigenous nations surviving in British Columbia today because several of the nations are struggling to maintain identity within themselves, which happens every few hundred years in human societies, and they do not have the autonomy to deal with such national emergencies as whether to separate from each other or cling together against the odds. The divide and conquer strategies of the federal and provincial governments have whittled once mobile and interactive peoples into small villages bordered by an alien "federal" policy and per-capita funding shortages. These nations are splintered and overrun and have much more compelling problems even than national unity: they have the problem that foreign powers, the most sophisticated colonizers, are trying to annihilate them completely.

The very foundation of their self-determination—their land—is the price exacted for any "reconciliation" sought by Canada or BC. There is no "reconciliation" process in practice today that does not end prescriptively in extinguishment of a nation's aboriginal title—a title which exists in spite of every effort by Canada to deny and destroy it. Canada and BC are not trying to resolve the problem they have caused in a way that would respect the self-determination and futures of the many indigenous nations. Instead, they launched a deceptively titled "treaty" process, with full knowledge that "treaties" are international agreements reached between states, which sub-state units cannot claim to enact. And the end goal of each is the extinguishment of aboriginal title.

This process of extinguishment, in its many historical and modern forms, fits the description of the crime of genocide in each of its five internationally defined articles.

"Extinguishment," as it is characterized in the modern day BC treaty Final Agreements, is the exchange of "existing aboriginal title and rights," as affirmed in Section 35 of the *Constitution Act*, 1982, for a determinate suite of rights to be guaranteed by Canada and BC in the Final Agreement. This is called "the modified rights model," and has been identified by United Nations human rights committees as the same in effect as extinguishment; they mean "cede, release and surrender."[1] The "treaties" require that a First Nation agree that there will be no more "lands Reserved for the Indians," and that their Indian Band will no longer exist, upon ratification. Instead, the community—usually remote, impoverished and without capacity for economic development within its numbers—is required to accept lands in fee simple title, as per the land selection process, with the underlying title becoming the property of the Province as a result of the Final Agreement.

In almost every case, a "First Nation" in BC is not actually an original nation but one community of a much larger nation. The community-by-community approach taken by the governments, lessening the numbers of each First Nation concerned and making each one appear less viable and less worthy of sustaining a claim on nationhood than were the original indigenous nations, had they been addressed in their entirety, has made a national cohesion or national approach impossible for almost every indigenous nation. Furthermore, in the BC treaty process, each First Nation to ratify will "release and indemnify Canada, British Columbia and *anyone else*," in perpetuity, for any past harm and from all claims related to their aboriginal title and rights.

These are treaties of capitulation: of cede, release and surrender—not the equitable, sustaining arrangements described by the governments. They are assigned the lofty but misleading moniker of "self-government" agreements, but in actuality they simply force approval of policies made by Canada. They do not approach the kind of scope that would allow self determination. These treaties at no point contemplate a land base, a schedule of restitution, reparations and skilled assistance that would allow any single nation to restore its national character in a modern context, to say nothing of the health of its people, land, language and culture, and their future development. The process is discussed in Chapter Six, *Extinguishment with Consent,* but it is important to note at this point that the BC Treaty Commission is the pinnacle of government interaction with the indigenous nations whose lands it occupies: nations that have won the following cases in Canadian courts. The BC treaty approach is called a "political solution" to a legal problem that the province will not admit it has.

A Few Meaningful Cases

At the center of the conflict is resource-rich lands and who has the right to use, occupy and benefit from them. An ironic situation emerges: British Columbia and Canada base their appalling conduct towards the indigenous entirely on their insistence that the indigenous do not own the land and their demands are unjust, and yet the very reason that the governments reject no opportunity to discredit and diminish the indigenous is because they know perfectly well that the indigenous *do* own the land. The governments know this because they have never bought the land from the indigenous nations, but all efforts go to denying that and making up alternative explanations for the indigenous demands for justice, while attempting to finally disintegrate and dissolve those nations. These facts are incontrovertible and are gaining widespread recognition—but not in the popular British Columbian conscience.

At an extradition hearing in a county circuit court, Oregon, USA, the American judge agreed with the aboriginal defendant that he was a political prisoner in Canada. She refused his extradition, which was requested by Canada. The case, *Pitawanakwat, 2000,* remains unchallenged by Canada. James Pitawanakwat left Canada fleeing sentencing incurred as a result of his participation in the Gustafsen Lake stand-off near 100 Mile House in Secwepemc in 1995. His situation was compared successfully with Irish exiles involved with Sinn Fein and the Irish Republican Army, who were spared extradition to England by courts in the USA and Spain on the basis that their "crimes" were to resist the occupation of their country which was being controlled by a foreign power. Judge Stewart decided similarly in *Pitawanakwat* that the "defendant's crimes for which he was convicted and later paroled were "of a political character" and therefore may not provide the basis for extradition of defendant to Canada. Extradition Treaty, Art. IV(1)(iii)."[2]

That international legal event was reported in BC only once, in two column inches, deep in the folds of a daily newspaper. The media teaches us that this is not important. The United States government recognized a general state of political persecution of people who defend their right to occupy their aboriginal title land in Canada, and Canadians and British Columbians do not.

In 1973, three Supreme Court of Canada judges agreed with Frank Calder that the Nisga'a have continuing title to their homelands. But another three of the seven judges, all seven allegedly under the discreet influence of Prime Minister Pierre Trudeau, decided alternatively that the Nisga'a right to their homeland had been ended by the simple fact of the existence of a colony named British Columbia and the British monarch's claim to sovereignty over the lands.

The seven judges were well divided. The seventh declined to decide based on a technicality, which caused the case to be dismissed: there was no ruling. There was no policy change, there was no investigation of the implications, there was no change to the Indian Act. BC's position was that there had never been any right or title to extinguish. Both sides of the *Calder* decision have been relied on to decide subsequent cases. Ultimately, the lack of decision in *Calder* served to confirm local judicial approval of BC's jurisdiction to dispose of lands and make Acts and regulations to control them.

While it did not answer the question put before it, the court in *Calder* had provided three Supreme Court judges' opinions that aboriginal title in BC continued. It was the first time this acknowledgement had happened since the early days of the colony, when Colonial Secretaries dispatched numerous urgent pleas for the BC Governor to treat with the indigenous nations: to buy *their* land.[3]

In the late 1980s, seventeen indigenous family houses, the main form of their authentic government, went to BC court to establish that they had never sold their lands to the province and that they were still the legal owners. The original *Delgamuukw* ruling in BC Supreme Court in 1992 by

Judge Allan McEachern described pre-contact native life as "nasty, brutish and short"—one of the characterizations of others furnished by a British culture rich in slanderous imperial insults. His ruling stated neatly that there was no Gitxsan or Wet'suwet'n title to be concerned with, as those "groups" had never exercised such a thing before contact with the British explorers, and that all Great Britain had to do was declare its sovereignty across the lands to collect the titles to them. This is of course untrue.

When *Delgamuukw* was successfully appealed and the judgment came out in 1997, the Supreme Court of Canada (SCC) ruled for the house of Delgamuukw, and the 16 other tribal houses pleading under the same case, that nothing British Columbia had done since it was founded could have extinguished, pre-empted or otherwise modified their aboriginal title. There was no record of a transaction between the Gitxsan, Wet'suwet'n and the colony to that effect; none had taken place. On top of this, the SCC reasoned that the province could not have extinguished aboriginal title at any time since 1871, when BC joined Confederation and allowed Canada to take responsibility for "Indians and lands Reserved for Indians."[4] The court declared, in a UN Committee's interpretation, that "…if an Aboriginal group can establish that, at time of sovereignty, it exclusively occupied a territory to which a substantial connection has been maintained, then it has the communal right to exclusive use and occupation of such lands."[5] The indigenous have a proprietary right to their lands, which according to the Supreme Court of Canada, includes the rights to use them, choose how to use them, and benefit economically from any such use. Finally, the government must consult with aboriginal title holders over its use of aboriginal title lands.

Since then, the governments of Canada and British Columbia have ignored that actual Supreme Court ruling, returning instead to the lengthy and unsparing dissident opinions in *Calder*, although Delgamuukw proved them erroneous, as they continue to wage the many-headed war of delay, denial and dismissal against indigenous sovereigntists. The governments accept the recent legal invention that aboriginal title is *"sui generis"*—an idea that neither native nor newcomer had ever contemplated before contact. The Canadian legal infrastructure had to invent the special use of this concept to solve its land problem, since the term has no international usage. Saying that the indigenous have no concept of governance and land ownership, Canada dismisses their nations—which have managed their affairs since time immemorial—as incompetent to exercise jurisdiction.

Three years later, the neighbours of the *Delgamuukw* appellants would ratify the first modern-day extinguishment treaty. The Nisga'a Final Agreement was approved by Parliament in 2000, but is contested in court to this day by Nisga'a people and their neighbours. The Nisga'a are now owners of about 8% of their traditional land base, holding the title in fee simple, having sold the rest to BC for a Settlement Transfer amounting to about $22/

hectare, payable over ten years, plus some financial, governance and sustenance gathering rights arrangements covered in the Agreement. The negotiations were not undertaken on the basis of acknowledgment of aboriginal title, but the Agreement extinguished it.

In 2004, the Haida nation had received an SCC ruling that acknowledged the provincial crown must not permit or license any activity on Haida land when it so much as anticipates that action may have adverse effects on the exercise of their aboriginal title. The government must consult with the perceived aboriginal title holder and accommodate their interests before carrying out the desired action "…when a Crown actor has knowledge, real or constructive, of the potential existence of aboriginal right or title and contemplates action that that might adversely affect it."[6] The Haida have never received a declaration of aboriginal title in court, and the 2004 ruling in their favour is worded so that government can use aboriginal title land merely by making accommodations for the "potential existence" of it—rather than being held to positively identify aboriginal title land.

Ten years after *Delgamuukw* established that British Columbia could not have unilaterally deprived the Gitxsan and Wet'suwet'n nations of their homelands, the Tsilhqot'in people received the opinion of BC Supreme Court Justice Vickers that they had proven exclusive title to at least half of their traditional homelands. This judgment prompted the established native rights lawyers in BC to advise indigenous national leaders, in conferences and web-cast forums, to act like landlords. Even though the case had not been won on the exact pleadings, which was for a Declaration of Tsilhqot'in title to 100% of their homeland, Vickers wrote 500 pages—most of it a non-binding opinion—of substantial, gravitational support for the juridical competitiveness and accompanying clear title of the Tsilhqot'in nation. This was the *Williams* decision, in 2007. It has recently been appealed by both sides.

And none of that has really affected anyone, native or non-native, in recognition of indigenous peoples' right to their lands and self determination, and the reality of aboriginal title. These are incredibly significant landmark legal decisions which should see native peoples spring back from oppression, but they don't.

Official maintenance of the position that aboriginal people have no title until they prove it in court; the corralling of the exercise of proven rights into provincial and federal programs; uneven, insincere and inconsistent application of such "consultation and accommodation" requirements as are spelled out in *Haida*; all these reprehensible behaviours should be a fairly difficult agenda for the government to defend—even in light of just these few rulings. That is, the suppression of the indigenous would be hard to keep up if the peoples impacted by these policies and practices were not also reeling from the maintenance of a genocidal campaign against them.

The Convention on the Prevention and Punishment
of the Crime of Genocide, 1948

Article 2 of the International Convention on the Prevention and Punishment of the Crime of Genocide defines genocide as any of the following acts:

(a) Killing members of the group;
(b) Causing serious bodily or mental harm to members of the group;
(c) Deliberately inflicting on the group conditions of life calculated to bring about its physical destruction in whole or in part;
(d) Imposing measures intended to prevent births within the group;
(e) Forcibly transferring children of the group to another group.

Anyone even dimly aware of the history, old and new, of British Columbia must be able to pick out at least two examples of genocide occurring today. Each of the thirty-odd indigenous nations within British Columbia fulfills the criteria of being a "group" against whom genocidal acts could be perpetrated. The fact is that every single act of genocide defined in the international Convention has been carried out repeatedly against every nation since the colony's inception, and every single act continues today with no sign of abating.

Ultimately it is the genocidal acts which enable the modern practices of denial and extinguishment to continue—while the denial and extinguishment lead to genocidal results. It is important to remember that genocide refers to acts committed against members of a group *because they are members of that group*. Although the evidence of the collective intention of the colonizers of British Columbia to completely destroy all the indigenous nations is often not in the form of direct testimonials or affidavits, those types of documents certainly exist. In 1924, Ronald Campbell Campbell-Johnson made the following entry in this particular ledger:

Where the Catholic priests control the tribe, they fervently teach them that all these old-fashioned Indian customs are the works of the devil, and so have already persuaded their congregations in all cases, to publicly burn every one of these ancient possessions. The Ottawa Indian Department, having entirely forbidden potlatches (giving-away-feasts), are now demanding, through their local agents, the confiscation of old Indian regalia, dresses, masks, insignia and every instrument of music, cedar bark ropes, and all things having any connection with these feasts, and are shipping these articles wholesale to the Museum there, having already procured seventeen cases from Alert Bay alone, as the Indians, in fear, bring them in.

So the impossibility of obtaining any more of these particularly valuable treaty-bowls or totems, has now become a fact.[7]

The treaty bowls were the critical tools used in international agreements between many of the coastal people; their equivalent to the Vienna Convention on the Law of Treaties; one of the lead vehicles by which self-determination moved. Such monumental assaults on the nationhood of the indigenous as a whole are rivaled by those carried out on the individuals.

a) Killing members of the group.

There are simply too many names to mention. The numerous deliberate strategies to kill the people ranged from outright shootings and show-trials of people suspected of theft from the Hudson's Bay Company forts to unnatural deaths in prison custody to biological warfare to the apprehension and neglect of children.

In earlier days, the shooting deaths of native people by Hudson's Bay Company factors and traders, loosely formed posses of American miners, and homesteaders are only occasionally recorded, and very rarely include a victim's name.

Baptiste Ritchie, a Lil'wat elder who died in the 1990s, recorded a story that had been entrusted to him by his parents about small pox coming to his village. He retold how the fur traders had visited and given out blankets to the people while wearing gloves.[8] There are well-known results of the small pox epidemic in that territory. The small pox burial grounds there have been the site of at least two roadblocks in the last few decades: the people have successfully prevented logging and hydroelectric development at the center of the burial place.[9]

Still others can retell the visit of Chief Factor Todd of Fort Kamloops, when he rode towards the Fountain trading center in about 1850 and warned of an imminent (but nonexistent) smallpox outbreak, and demanded 10,000 dried salmon in exchange for vaccinations.[10] The Lillooet had been unwilling to trade the amount of salmon required by the Fort, as it left them without enough for themselves, but they did so when the threat of smallpox was presented. The

Chilcotin War of 1864 was prompted by the actions of individuals to arrest progress of a road being built from the coast into their territory. They feared the deliberate introduction of smallpox, among other things.

Officially there is something of a myth around the impact of the smallpox epidemic among indigenous peoples. Scholars in BC universities and government remarks on the subject teach that perhaps a third of the indigenous populations died in the 1962 outbreak. Indigenous record keepers and more thorough, very recent, research points to a more likely average of 90% mortality to this disease at that time.[11]

In Indian Residential Schools, some children had the assigned chore of digging graves for their classmates who died there. According to recent research carried out under the auspices of Canada's Truth and Reconciliation Commission, the Missing Children Project, at least 3,000 children are known to have died while in Indian Residential Schools. The new research is the preliminary result of the first systematic search of government, school and other records. Deaths were, according to surviving witnesses and this new report, mainly the result of neglect during critical illness or assault by school staff members.

Fred Quilt was a Tsilhqot'in man. When he was driving home one day, in the winter of 1971, he was stopped by police and dragged out of his car and beaten and kicked in the stomach. He died of his injuries. The police were cleared in two inquiries into the death.[12] In 1976, Coreen Thomas from the Stoney Creek Reserve was run over and killed in Vanderhoof when she was eight months pregnant. The evidence given in the resulting inquiry made it clear the hit could have been avoided if the non-native driver slowed down, or swerved, but it also showed that the contempt local non-natives felt towards Indians would have made it unlikely for this precautionary measure to have crossed the driver's mind.[13] In 1979, eleven year old Renee Smith died of a ruptured appendix some time after having been admitted to the village hospital at Alert Bay. The non-native doctor on duty was drunk. The non-native nurse did not inspect her when she was admitted. After she died, her body was taken to the morgue and the non-native mortician completed the embalming procedure although he did not have a signed death certificate specifying the cause of death.[14] What is unusual about these cases is that there were inquiries, and people wrote books which mentioned them.

Ron George, Wet'suwet'n, became leader of the United Native Nations and then the Native Council of Canada. That was long after one of his brothers was found in the local dump, a year after he had been killed by torture. He was not a gang member. Rusty Machell, a Lillooet man suspected of driving while intoxicated, was pursued in his vehicle by a policeman along the West Pavilion road to his home. Rusty, unarmed, was shot to death outside the porch steps of his house, and the police vehicle the officer drove was later assessed to reveal that police-issue rounds were fired from inside the vehicle, through the windshield, and those bullets were the cause of Rusty's death.

A BC Inquiry was recently held under the name of Frank Paul, a native man who was brought into custody by Vancouver police for appearing drunk in public. He was stripped, hosed down, released by way of being deposited in an alley at night in January, and died of exposure. The Inquiry was called because of so many other similar deaths.

An Inquiry has still not been called into the uninvestigated highway murders of hundreds of native women in British Columbia, after two decades of protest and demonstration by those women's family and friends.

b) *Serious bodily or mental harm.*

RCMP violence to Indians walking home is simply incalculable. Women have had their wrists broken while handcuffs were applied, for no reason other than their having no acceptable reason to be in public. What is an acceptable reason for a non-native woman to be in public alone? Should she need one?

For thirty years, between 1927 and 1957 at least, indigenous people would be arrested on their front porch for drinking alcohol, and transported to lock-up. Native men, particularly those who are well-known for their involvement in road-blocks, are beaten in jail cells and threatened with lethal injections to provoke made-up confessions.

Many nations have built their own institutes to buffer their people's vulnerability to colonization. Bill Mussell, as Chair of the Salishan Institute's Mental Health Association, wrote:

> From an Aboriginal perspective, mental wellness is holistic. Holism includes consideration of physical, emotional, cognitive and spiritual health with particular attention to congruence between the mind and body encompassed by the spirit. Individual wellbeing is strongly connected to family and community wellness.
>
> In the 1983 Round Table discussion of the Royal Commission on Aboriginal Peoples, Dr. C. Brant, a Mohawk psychiatrist, identified poverty, despair, poor housing and political alienation as the root causes for the traumatic mental health problems that plague many Aboriginal communities. He identified suicide and depression, violence, sexual abuse, substance abuse, and child neglect and abuse as the most serious mental health outcomes of these conditions.

As caregivers and policy analysts become informed about colonial history, they do not view Aboriginal mental health problems as medically defined disorders. Instead, they contend that suicidal and other self-destructive behaviors are primary by-products of the colonial past with its layered assaults on Aboriginal cultures and identities. They see these as serious threats to the survival and health of Indigenous communities."[15]

Criminalization of the indigenous in the mainstream and publicly-subsidized press is such an extravagance of British Columbian media that it warrants a chapter later in this volume. The mental and physical harm of these regularly libelous characterizations is not documented by any existing study, but it is hardly debatable. As Maurice Switzer, Mississauga of Rice Lake First Nation, director of communications for the AFN, put it:

> Scant few newspapers will publish native affairs columns, although writers espousing stridently anti-Indian viewpoints have little difficulty finding media platforms. Do *Globe* editors understand that such media finger-pointing has been known to jeopardize the safety of Aboriginal people in the streets and schoolyards of BC communities?[16]

That indigenous nations have suffered serious mental harm is reflected in the disproportionate numbers of aboriginal suicides. "Suicides among aboriginal young people are the result of the history of injustices that they have suffered and continue to suffer... To prevent young aboriginal people from taking their own lives there must be a commitment to end the tyranny that dominates and destroys their lives." These lines are part of the Report of the Honourable John Reilly, Alberta Provincial Court, following a public inquiry pursuant to the *Fatality Inquiry Act* in the town of Cochrane, Alberta, 1999, after the suicide of Sherman Laron Labelle.[17] A suicide among people aged 15-24 in British Columbia is five times more likely to have been committed by a native person. In some years, it is ten times more likely.[18]

During the Royal Commission on Aboriginal Peoples, 1990-96, Dr. Alan Crews submitted that "the first step towards achieving better health for native Indians would be to settle land claims. Destruction of culture has created despair and a sense of hopelessness that has led to alcohol and drug abuse."[19] The previous year, the BC Medical Association passed a resolution calling on federal and provincial governments to settle outstanding land claims with natives.

Twelve-year-old girl protesters are treated to excessively weighted police chiefs kneeling on their ribs and breaking them during arrests at peaceful road blocks.[20] Even aboriginal people who are not part of blockades suffer for them, like in 1995 at the time of the Gustafsen Lake stand-off, where people reported: "Our children have been taunted and bullied, members of our communities have been beaten up and we have received serious threats personally."[21]

The Indian Act, first amalgamated from existing statutes in 1876, eventually listed 200 offenses that could only be committed by Indians. Many of these referred to cultural and economic activities and legal pursuits, which were still outlawed after the ratification of the Genocide Convention in 1948. When such cultural activities as were the social economy of the people were banned, people were prevented from occupying recognizable positions within their communities. The South African Nationalist Party came to power in 1949 on a platform of implementing apartheid, for which they are said to have used the Indian Act template. There is extensive reportage of the forms of mental harm caused by the outlawing of one's cultural identity provided by testimonies given in their Truth Commission. The same can be expected from the Truth and Reconciliation Commission's proceedings presently underway in Canada in relation to Indian Residential Schools.

c) Deliberately inflicting conditions of life calculated to bring about physical destruction.

The confinement of indigenous people to Reserves so small that today less than half of the natural population actually fits on them is such a condition. The depopulation of Indian Reserves is effected by inadequate housing, barriers to employment in the rural areas that most Reserves are located in which are characterized by racial prejudice, a lack of access to capital in the inability to mortgage a house owned on a Reserve—even through the Indian Band office, the restriction of access to food-gathering, which was effective until 1970 in most backwards places in BC, and a longer list of conditions that would fill a book themselves. The criminalization of social gatherings, political organizing, fund raising and whole economies—which require freedom of access to resources and freedom to transport and trade them—are easily documented conditions, having been legislated in the Indian Act.

The imposition of Christian church participation to the exclusion of traditional spiritual practice was the result of the government's support for the self-promoting work of missionaries, be they Anglican or Catholic, French speaking or English, and whether they too apprehended children who had been orphaned by parents who died of disease (a large number) or merely patrolled for more direct cash subsidies—collecting fines from the indigenous for drunkenness or other non-Christian forms of behavior exhibited by their intended converts.[22] The Christians' insistence that god must be worshipped in a single building contributed importantly to bringing the considerable and economically paramount mobility of the land-based peoples to a halt.

Today, satisfactory conditions of life imply employment and business opportunities. Unemployment on Indian Reserves is often north of the 80% mark, according to exhaustive statements on the subject by aboriginal leaders as well as surveys and studies. Off-Reserve, studies show gaps in employment rates between aboriginal and non-aboriginal individuals: in 2001, 35% of urban aboriginal women aged 15 to 24 were employed, in contrast to 57% employment in the same non-native demographic.[23] There are 40 year old employees of treaty-negotiating teams that have never had a job outside the BC treaty-making process. In every treaty-negotiating community, economic conditions are mitigated by treaty payments to Elders for their participation in treaty gatherings, where their appearance is then construed as support for the supposedly consensual extinguishment process.

What is worrying is that the measures BC and Canada are using could reasonably be said to be succeeding in bringing about the physical destruction of the whole. Forested areas are now on their way to desertification or overgrowth since clearcutting has scoured the province. This practice, along with impacts from the massive hydroelectric dams and mines, has emptied or rotted out the traditional breadbaskets of the nations. While aboriginal people in BC amount to some 3% of the general population, prisons here are populated 50% by aboriginal people. Seventy percent of children in state custody in BC are aboriginal. The recently attained 50% graduation rate for aboriginal students— only in some areas—is considered a great leap forward. Youth suicide, gang involvement and addiction outstrip rates in the general population by seven to twenty times. The incidence of diabetes in native communities is at least ten times that in the general population. Average life expectancy of aboriginal people is officially reported conservatively at 7-10 years shorter for men and women than what it is for non-native people.[24]

d) *Measures intended to prevent births.*

Priests raped and impregnated pubescent girl students of Indian residential schools at a serial rate and the ad-hoc abortions left many unable to bear children. Later gynecological treatments included sterilization programs. At one point, sterilization was a routine procedure for any native woman who happened to be in hospital. At Coqualeetza, a hospital specializing in the treatment of tuberculosis, which was rampant in native communities throughout the early decades of the 20th century, many Indian men and women graduated from treatment without their ability to bear children intact.[25]

e) Forcible removal of children to another group.

On June 26, 1997, at a meeting of indigenous Chiefs in Vancouver, John Watson, the Director-General of the Department of Indian Affairs' Pacific region, was the first government of Canada representative to admit that residential schools were part of an assimilation policy of the Canadian government.[26] That is, since Duncan Campbell Scott put it to his government in 1920, when he was Superintendent General of Indian Affairs and proposing an amendment to the Indian Act which made indigenous children's attendance at the residential schools compulsory. Scott said, "I want to get rid of the Indian problem. Our objective is to continue until there is not a single Indian in Canada that has not been absorbed into the body politic and there is no Indian question, and no Indian Department, that is the whole object of this Bill." As of 1920, attendance at an Indian Residential School was mandatory for aboriginal children under the age of fifteen. That is to say, if a parent was found guilty of harbouring their own child from the Indian Residential School recruiters, and misinforming the local priests as to the child's whereabouts, they faced jail sentences. This Canada-wide legislative amendment to the Indian Act followed closely on the heels of a pan-indigenous plea to protect and preserve a reasonable amount of Indian land in BC.

In the 1960s, colonial well-wishers of the child-apprehension variety combed the Canadian countryside for native children, even kidnapping them from playgrounds.[27] These children were placed in white homes, for the most part, and with no usual or formal grounds for doing so. It's known as The 60's Scoop. Today, of the approximately 60,000 children apprehended by state agents and placed in out of home care across Canada, half of them are native children.[28] The IHRAAM Petition to the Inter-American Commission on Human Rights from which these statistics are drawn challenges Canada and British Columbia's right to exercise jurisdiction over Líl'wat children. The matter was brought to the UN Regional Court in 2007 because it is not possible to address the issue in Canadian courts.[29]

In one of very few existing grass-roots surveys of rural indigenous life in 1980s British Columbia, journalist Terry Glavin noted the usual procedure, in Tsilhqot'in territory, which followed hospital births of native babies. The mother was advised to go on home while the doctors gave some extra care to the baby, whom they insisted was healthy but could use a little further treatment. When the mother, who in some cases spoke little English and still believed that any refusal to whites in authority might result in a hanging as it did for five of her Chiefs in 1865 at the end of the "Chilcotin War," went back to pick up the baby, it was gone. It had been placed in an "improved situation": with a non-native family.[30]

The present day criteria for BC's Ministry of Children and Families to remove an aboriginal child from her home are singularly vaporous, and entirely subjective. Considering that so many decision makers in the BC Ministry continue to recommend the forcible removal of so many of these children, without so much as a protocol with their community leadership or otherwise willing and able family assistants in the community, the bureaucrats appear to be comfortable with the racist motives of the institution. Young babies are taken from their families while the mothers are in hospital; young children are taken from their homes by police assisting social service helpers. Parents are offered such catch-22 ultimatums as: you can apply for subsidized housing once you have your children back, and you can have your children back once you have got proper housing. This to people who live on Reserves where the wait list for housing is backed up fifteen to twenty years, and the available housing is often so rotten or condemnable that even if they got into it, it would not meet Ministry standards for getting their kids back.[31] It is often precisely this quality of housing which served as justification for the removal of children in the first place. Infants are apprehended purely on the basis that their older siblings were apprehended.

Statistically, one in seven aboriginal children in British Columbia will be seized from his or her parents and placed under Ministry of Children and Family Development care. In 1998, 30 native children had been taken from Carrier Chilcotin families in the space of two months.[32] Case for case, the majority of these children would not have been apprehended from a non-native family in the same circumstances. When the aboriginal children's aunts, grandparents or cousins attempt to use Ministry processes to get custody of their young relations, with the parents' support, they face a nearly impenetrable screen of code language, never-ending impossible tasks and expensive trips to the urban centers where the children have been removed to.[33]

Canada ratified the Genocide Convention in 1953. However, instead of simply implementing it and making it part of the Canadian criminal code, they altered it. Of the five acts listed as constituting genocide in Article II of the UN Convention, (b), (d) and (e) were omitted. No one in Canada can appeal for relief under these sections because they are not present in the criminal code.

While the Genocide Convention's definition of genocide also includes "(c) Deliberately inflicting on the group conditions of life calculated to bring about its physical destruction in whole or in part," this is addressed in the criminal code of Canada under Article 318, and is titled "*Advocating Genocide.*" This narrow tailoring of the crime is an effective barrier to litigation: (1) "Every one who advocates or promotes genocide is guilty of an indictable offence and liable to imprisonment for a term not exceeding five years."[34] Remarkably, sentencing for a crime intended to "bring about the destruction in whole or in part" of an entire people is actually limited to much less extensive punishment than a single murder. But the cleverness appears to be that actually *accomplishing* genocide is not punishable, whereas *advocating* it is. The Canadian government does not openly advocate genocide, it just continues to carry it out under other names.

War

Canadians think of themselves as peacekeepers. In places really far away. Few would think of themselves as belonging to a nation that has been at war since its inception, one that is still at war today on its claimed soil. In fact Canadians are still fighting to assert dominion over what they arrogantly think of as their national territory.

If it were incontrovertibly theirs, they wouldn't still today be seizing native children; arresting road blockers; sponsoring corrupt and invasive DIA regimes on "lands Reserved for the Indians;" trying to extradite indigenous sovereigntists from countries where they've fled; running propaganda machines to incite civilian aggression against Indians; manufacturing the contradictory appearance of resolutions in the broader public interest; incarcerating for psychological evaluation a lawyer who attempted to raise the resulting jurisdictional question in their court rooms; launching ground assaults on Sundancers' camps at a scale not deployed since the Korean War; arming Fisheries Officers with tanks and also having them jump onto gill nets in rivers during high-speed boat chases (where the Department's boats are dubbed *Nina, Pinta* and *Santa Maria* by the radio communications) to cut the lines.[35]

If these modern practices were really an anomaly, there would not be such a consistent history of targeting only indigenous peoples with land title. There would not be the history of delivering small pox blankets to Reserves; arming largely American posses with badges to push back natives from gold mining areas at the origin of the colony;[36] endorsing the wholesale plunder of indigenous food caches by never punishing it or even identifying the practice as unacceptable; blowing up petroglyphs and sacred sites to destroy evidence of title; imposing curfews, travel restrictions, gun, alcohol and other restrictions; controlling trade with Indians by licensing the Hudson's Bay Company exclusively to engage in it; enforcing attendance at Indian Residential Schools run by victim graduates of institutions which harboured the most criminally insane forms of violence—many imported from the Christian Brothers of Irish industrial school infamy; criminalizing every expression of traditional life by an Indian Act which by 1927 listed over 200 such acts as being illegal; conditional enfranchisement, the condition being renunciation of native status; the unconcluded court cases that were thrown out by a judge who had just heard the native Chiefs' defense: "Tell us when and how you got the right to control our people?"[37]

If Canada was not at war with native people today, there would not be Indian Reserves serving as concentration camps, where nothing can be owned but everything can be fought over. There would not be a single elected

Chief in each Reserve who is accountable to Canada's Department of Indian Affairs[38] before the people of the community, after the fashion of the colonial governors in Nigeria and Puerto Rico. If Canada was not at war with native people today, there would be no point in coercive programs like Forest and Range Agreements where an indigenous community specifically, and without precedent, declares that it has been consulted and accommodated and gives up its interests in the traditional territory to undefined alien logging activities in exchange for a (piteously low) per capita payment.

If there was no war, the so-called First Nations, actually imposed and restricted villages of the previously expansive nations now occupied by BC, would not be "negotiating" modern day treaties / Final Agreements / land claims settlements (as they are called interchangeably, according to provincial negotiator Trevor Proverbs[39]) under their present day duress. The bottom line of all these Agreements is extinguishment of the aboriginal title presently in place across all untreated land—which is all of BC, excepting now the Nisga'a, Tsawwassen and Maa-nulth territories, graduates of the BC treaty process; the broken Treaty 8; and possibly a few Cowichan acres treated for by Governor Douglas in 1854.

And it is duress which impels First Nations to engage in that Treaty Commission. The First Nations are under duress as surely now as Piapot was when he was overwhelmed by the North West Mounted Police and forced to sign a treaty he viewed with skepticism. For First Nations in BC, treaties take the form described above; they will not be international documents between nations like Piapot's was, but Final Agreements jointly crafted with British Columbia, a province, to surrender, plain and simple.

British Columbians have a history of being at least as pleased to withdraw from these negotiations, provoke the militants and shower them with live bullets. In 2005, support for the BC New Democratic Party skyrocketed when the Attorney-General persistently stated, "Gustafsen Lake has nothing to do with aboriginal land-claim issues," and unleashed 400 cops, eight tanks, helicopters, fixed-wing aircraft and 77,000 rounds on the indigenous militants who were prepared to die to show that the land on which they stood was both sacred space and part of a larger unceded Shuswap territory.[40]

In this context, First Nations accept federal program funding allocations under the Indian Act which amount to an exercise in re-distributing the poverty rations provided by the federal government as it fulfills the self-prescribed fiduciary obligations to the indigenous whose lands are plundered and developed for the benefit of the newcomers. But these payments are turned upside down by media and politicians and made to appear one of the improving effects of western society on indigenous life—even an attractive alternative to national survival, self-determination and freedom.

Chapter 3

$10 BILLION

"...should the present elaborate and cumbersome mode of dealing with the Indian lands be continued until the entire number and extent of the reserves throughout the Province be determined and appropriated, many years will necessarily elapse before the work can be completed; whilst the costs to both Governments must be excessive, and entirely disproportionate to the results attained."
**—A C Elliot, Provincial Secretary (BC)
to the Minister of the Interior, Canada, 1877[1]**

"There are about 1,000 Indians in the Valley distributed among five villages. ...Private individuals, unable to obtain any title from the Government to portions of these reserves, pursue the reckless policy of dealing with the natives themselves. This, fostering the idea of a right existing where the Government recognizes none, will give the Indians a conviction that there is some fabulous value in their land, and will render it altogether impossible for the Government to obtain a settlement with them on anything like reasonable terms. I allude especially to a case in which a contract has been entered into with a chief by which he is paid fifty dollars for allowing a white the privilege of cutting hay upon a certain specified portion of the reserve. Let this but become an established practice and the settlement of Indian titles will require more gold than the Crown lands Revenue will easily spare for the purpose."
**—The Reverend Alex C. Garrett, Anglican clergyman and
Superintendent of Indian Missions for Vancouver Island, in a
letter to B.W. Pearse, Acting Surveyor General, 1865[2]**

> *"They save billions of dollars by not making settlements. They do these negotiations, but that's cheaper for them than settling."*
> **—Chief Robert Louie, Westbank First Nation, November 25, 2009**

Buying Justice

The cash of the matter has largely replaced the facts of the matter for most Canadians. They are brought to the point of outrage by the mass media when the figure of $10 billion is pronounced as the annual cost of the Department of Indian Affairs, DIA, or Aboriginal Affairs and Northern Development Canada, as the Department has recently been re-named. Or, Indian and Northern Affairs Canada, which is what it was called at the time the "$10 billion" myth was manufactured. While the Gross National Income on these lands reaches $1.37 trillion annually, Canadians can be made to feel their colony is under siege by the welfare demands of about a million Status Indian people: or about $10,000 per person. The outrage speaks mainly to their ignorance.

Perhaps the average citizen cannot put $10 billion into context, perhaps they have nothing to compare it to. It is close to the amount that the spread of noxious weeds cost the Canadian economy in 2010: $7.5 billion.[3] It is about the same amount that Canada spent on subsidies, in the form of corporate tax incentives, to private companies in 1984[4]—just a historical pinpoint on a spectrum indexed to inflation. It's less than the total of 172 separate federal programs to assist and support the private sector: $11.2 billion, identified in the Nielsen Task Force report on Services and Subsidies to Business of 1985.[5] $10 billion could be just "an accounting gap" in the purchase price of a fleet of new F-35 fighter planes.[6] One of the 650 First Nations in Canada is suing federal and provincial governments for $10 billion because that's how much revenue from oil and gas production it has been denied.[7] The $10 billion among 1.7 million aboriginal people in Canada is worth $1,870 less per-person per-year than Canada's Old Age Security payments to the elderly recipients.[8] The OAS program is a cash-to-end-recipient structure, not an umbrella program like Aboriginal Affairs which does not simply send out cheques to each individual but includes on-Reserve education and housing; Band administration; infrastructure and maintenance, Ministry administration, etcetera.

In 1993, aboriginal organizations tasked with building housing for off-Reserve natives showed that the Canada Mortgage and Housing Corporation received $2 billion per year to provide housing units for off-Reserve native Indians. The groups that built, maintained and managed the housing, that is, the organizations that did the entire work of building the houses, received only $130 million per year to carry out the program.[9]

The federal 2012 budget has nipped over $5 billion from 2012-13 federal program spending, "less than 2.0 per cent of federal program spending in 2016–17, or 0.2 per cent of Canada's gross domestic product (GDP) in that same year."[10] The national deficit was reduced by $37 billion between 2006 and 2008.

"But those are our tax dollars," the settlers say. In the case of British Columbia, taxes come from resource-based industries. They come from service industries that rely on clientele from the resource industries. As Canada's 2012 Budget put it: "Canada's resource sector is an asset that will increasingly contribute to the prosperity of all Canadians. Some $500 billion is expected to be invested in over 500 major economic projects across Canada over the next 10 years, driven in part by demand from emerging economies."

Popular calculations around the $10 billion in DIA funds do not reflect the top-heavy administration of it, most of which goes to non-native people: consultants, bureaucrats, administrators, lawyers and contractors, before anything gets into the Indian Band accounts. In fact, the native communities cannot hold on to any of the money because they are not in business, they do not have banks, and they are prohibited from doing so and making them by a web of legal, social and institutional barriers from meaningful or sustaining industry. The money goes right back into the Canadian economy—which is owned and managed by non-natives. It's like a transfer payment to all the other Canadian businesses, to Canada Mortgage and Housing Corporation, to ICBC, to local schools and hospitals and dentists, to the corner store and the service providers.

The Assembly of First Nations did a little research on social spending on aboriginal people in 2007. It formed the basis of a "Make Poverty History" campaign in Canada. They discovered that on-Reserve per capita expenditures for basic services declined by 6.4% since 1996-1997. In contrast, Canadians receive health and social programs through direct federal transfers to provinces and territories at an average rate that's growing by 6.6% per year. The AFN brought to light the Auditor General's remark that "Indian and Northern Affairs Canada's funding increased by only 1.6%, excluding inflation, in the five years from 1999-2004, while Canada's Status Indian population, according to the Department, increased by 11.2%". They found that only $5.4 billion of the $9.1 billion of federal Aboriginal spending, at that time, actually ever reached First Nations.[11]

The popular mythology is quite different: native people get free education—as much of it as they want! Native people get free medical attention— anywhere they choose! Native people get free houses—as many as they can live in! The reality is that Indian Reserve administrations get a per capita lump sum for these necessaries. It amounts to housing wait lists that put most young people, who might want to start a family in one, past child bearing years; a slice of medical budget that might get certain patients to the first in a series of treatments – unless treatment is still at the experimental stages, in which case participation is deeply encouraged; and a share of education dollars which, as of 2010, was some $20 million short of tuition fees requested by eligible aboriginal students in British Columbia.[12]

Few Canadians can claim to have done the math to calculate just how much Medicare, welfare, emergency services, etc, comes from their tax dollars for the average aboriginal person or community. For instance, the annual budget for Health Canada is about the same as the total budget for the aboriginal people. And yet many seem to know that native poverty has created an alarming series of statistical anomalies, with rates of diabetes and addiction being separated by orders of magnitude, between the native and non-native populations of their beloved home. Still Canadians feel the tax payer money that goes to the indigenous population is really unjustifiable, without understanding that it is actually less per-capita than what they themselves receive in social program dollars.

The belief that benefits under the *Indian Act* are adequate is somehow prevailing. Seventy-four percent of British Columbians polled in a 2012 Ipsos Reid survey believe that "Canada's Aboriginal People's receive too much support from Canadian taxpayers." Fifty-six percent of Canadians between the ages of eighteen and thirty-four agreed with the statement "Canada's aboriginal people are treated well by the Canadian government." Interestingly, agreement decreased with age: 75% of respondents aged 35 to 54 agreed, and 67% over the age of 55 agreed.[13]

And the Indian Department doesn't spend ten billion dollars on aboriginal people every year, anyway. The Minister of Indian Affairs, Chuck Strahl, liked to say so, and he made many inflammatory statements in 2008 which do not appear to be based on his own Department's information available at that time, or from that time. He used the words "ten billion dollars" almost every time he spoke about the aboriginal peoples under his Ministry. If it was true that he cobbled together percentiles of provincial spending on urban aboriginal people and subtracted that from federal transfers to provinces, it's still not true that $10 billion really was spent by the DIA. And even if it was, it amounts to less than one half of one percent of Canada's Gross Domestic Product. What Strahl's Department says, according to the Budget, is:

> Over the period from 2008-2009 to 2012-2013, Aboriginal Affairs and Northern Development Canada's expenditures increased from $7.0 billion to $7.8 billion.
>
> According to the 2012-2013 Main Estimates, tabled in Parliament on February 28, 2012, AANDC will spend approximately $7.8 billion. Of this, approximately 83 per cent goes directly to recipients [i.e., Band administrations] through transfer payments. Much of this funding ensures that Aboriginal people have access to basic services comparable to those provided to other Canadians through provincial, municipal and territorial governments. These services

include education, housing, community infrastructure (water and sewage systems), social support services and other benefits. In addition to expenditures for basic services, the department promotes economic development, negotiates and oversees the implementation of comprehensive and specific claim settlements, and implements practical forms of self-government.[14]

Given that Canada's public program spending is in the order of $264 billion per annum, it doesn't seem likely that indigenous people on overcrowded Reserves living under the *Indian Act* would be able to finance any service "comparable to those provided to other Canadians" with the budget they have to use. And they're not. This is not a source of concern for the Canadian Commission on Human Rights. A case launched in 2007 and pertaining to chronic under-funding of aboriginal children and families was thrown out by the Commission in 2011. They reasoned that you can't argue aboriginal children are less funded when in state care than non-aboriginal children under provincial care, because there is no other federally-run program for non-aboriginal children in care to compare it to, hence no discrimination.[15] And that argument might suffice when comparing housing, health and employment standards as well. You can't argue that people living on Indian Reserves are less-funded than non-aboriginal people in Canada, because there is no specific state-run fund for the latter which lumps social spending, to which it can be compared.

Indian Affairs Minister Chuck Strahl announced plans in 2008 to overhaul fiscal management and accountability measures on Reserves. He didn't highlight the fact that this was the result of three years of mulling by DIA since their own Aboriginal Horizontal Framework report had been received, giving information on how to reduce overlapping services and increase Department efficiency. The Horizontal Framework was just another program review looking for ways to cut spending, something the federal Conservatives will do to 2.9 million Aboriginal and Northern Affairs dollars in 2012-13.[16] He also didn't mention anything about fiscal responsibility and the 1999 report which stated that "Documents released by the Finance Department recently indicate that aboriginal and comprehensive land claims totalling $200 billion are on the government books as contingent liabilities."[17]

When Canadians bitterly describe native people as welfare bums, which they do, it is certainly ironic that this demographic was the very last one to receive such social consideration in the eventual post-World War II economic buoyancy experienced by Canada.[18] These regular transfer payments did have a significant cumulative value, albeit not for the aboriginal people. In 1975 the Union of BC Indian Chiefs organized a rejection of funds campaign, where every Band in BC refused these transfers on the principle that they would not be made to appear complicit in the unilateral welfare-for-lands trade that Canada insists on. That rejection of funds campaign was eventually busted, in no small part by pressure from the non-native business owners and townspeople that had inherited the rural Forts, which had become Gold Rush Trail roadhouses, which became Indian Agent villas nearest the Reserves. The message from them was: "You guys should go and get your monies again; we're starving here, we've got to pay mortgages too—go get your welfare money so we can get some too."[19]

When politicians and their devoted media reporters extrapolate on a handful of oil-rich First Nation Chiefs paying themselves $200,000 salaries, that somehow becomes $300,000—since they "don't pay taxes," and it is deliberately misunderstood by the public representatives to mean that *most* First Nation Chiefs make that kind of salary. This salary is hardly as usual for the job as the incessantly outraged Canadian bigot insists on making it seem, and it is hardly unreasonable—not when compared to the public purse gaping at a few recently retired Members of the Legislative Assembly from British Columbia. Pensions for eleven of them will amount to $13.7 million – if they live to be 80,[20] and that's for when they're *not* working. There are no such government pensions for retired Chiefs, just welfare. Most Chiefs of First Nations do not receive salaries, and the invention is a recent one.

Canadians are out of touch with aboriginal people. Their preferred hang-out is to chastise Indians for being unemployed and challenge them to get a job. Presumably in a Canadian industry. Employment opportunities for aboriginal people are limited. A university only needs one or two Elders to meet the abysmal criteria of "pro-aboriginal;" a Reserve only needs one Chief; there are no working native journalists in BC, unless they are freelancing for the Aboriginal Peoples' Television Network. Corporations literally need only a "token Indian" to receive extra grants and subsidies. BC forestry companies can get subsidies for their businesses through the "Forests For Tomorrow" program by employing just one Status Indian. Wage disparity between aboriginal and non-aboriginal Band employees who do the same job in the Band office was most recently surveyed at gaps reaching 88%.[21] Researchers from the Canadian Centre for Policy Alternatives estimated a sixty year lag time before the gap is closed.

Corruption among indigenous players here is as high as it has ever been in any British colony where the dispossessed are left to fight for their "turn to eat"—as different indigenous peoples in Kenya have called elected power since "independence." Incidentally, present day Kenyan exports of Orange Pekoe tea leaves, cashews and coffee are brokered at advantages reminiscent of the 500% profit enjoyed by fur traders using the Pacific Northwest Coast in the 19th century.[22]

It should give everyone pause when they read that an entire Band

Council decided to pay themselves a $300,000 monthly stipend for a year upon sealing a benefits-sharing deal with a gold mining company.[23] Who could do that? Living in a community of maybe 100 people, many of whom those Councilors are related to, who could just take the money and close their ears to such ongoing Elder recriminations as, "You have displayed selfishness and very little respect for the rights of your traditional territory, membership, elders, neighbours and future generations."[24] The RCMP did not find any evidence of wrongdoing or the alleged betrayal of trust. The money transfers, like so many others before them – supervised by non-native accountants, were an act of straightforward desperation. No amount of statistics can improve on the clarity of a picture where people act on their *belief* that they have no financial chance of survival outside of abject poverty. And they have been initiated into a larger view: this is how the Europeans do business everywhere. People in positions do not "betray their countries" when they sell off lucrative sectors under pressure to privatize: no, they call it sales commissions, or some other similar business term, to reinterpret what is in actuality bribery and corruption.

While the 2012 budget features program funding for aboriginal education and violence-prevention strategies, all meant to improve aboriginal participation in the Canadian economy, it doesn't mention anything about recognizing aboriginal title to lands which would then restore to the nations sufficient resources to redevelop their own economies as they see fit—in a climate of self-determination.

The celebrated buyout of aboriginal interests in their lands has been nothing more than a cover-up. The crimes against humanity wrought by Canada against the indigenous challenge those of any post-industrial nation. Suffice it to say that welfare payments are not a competitive modern settlement for those crimes, if it were the case that the victims wanted only cash compensation, which it is not.

The Value of Denying Title

> *"We won't agree to anything that affects our economy."*
> **—Ken Gorsline, provincial negotiator at BC / First Nation**
> **government to government protocol table, 2007[25]**

The World Trade Organization and NAFTA have considered the suggestion that Canada's denial of aboriginal title is a direct subsidy to its economy. During the softwood lumber dispute between Canada and the USA, an intervention was submitted by the Indigenous Network on Economies and Trade,[26] based in British Columbia and led by Arthur Manuel of Neskonlith, Secwepemc. That submission described the value of the forest resources to many indigenous witnesses, and the criminalization and incarceration of native people who either attempt to use the timber on their own territory, or prevent provincially licensed corporations from removing it without their consent. British Columbia collects billions of dollars in stumpage and license revenues from forestry annually.

The value of mining in the province is estimated at $8 billion annually, since 2008. The commercial salmon fishery on BC's coast and in the mouth of the Fraser has brought uncalculated billions to the provincial economy: to private businessmen, independent fishermen and canneries. Until the first undeniable collapse of that fishery in 1994, the commercial fishery harvested 80% to 90% of the runs returning in numbers of 20-30 million. Since then the commercial salmon fishery has become so worthless that the government has bought back many licenses and fishing vessels and is attempting to use these in treaty negotiations with First Nations. An anomalous return of Fraser sockeye in 2010 numbered over 30 million, it is quite inexplicable and the largest run since the 1930s, but it made for a $500 million commercial fishery in BC that year.

The rock on which the province was initially founded was gold. In 1864, six years after the initial flood of miners into the Fraser Canyon and the accompanying designation of British Columbia as a colony, the Cariboo Gold Fields peaked at an annual production of $3.7 million worth of gold.[27] In the same year, incidentally, BC registered a debt of over one million dollars, and the separately managed Colony of Vancouver Island was in the red by a quarter million dollars. The expense of administration—if not the inability of the colonies to hold on to the resources they were tapping—prompted Britain to amalgamate the two. Miners took $20 million in gold from Williams Creek alone, in 1860s dollars.[28]

The extreme cycles of boom and bust in BC have risen and crashed over gold mining, timber, salmon, and building hydroelectric infrastructure. One hundred and fifty years later the BC economy is still in a deficit. Here are some figures from a good year before 1936:

> British Columbia: Mills - 371; Employees: 15,430; Output in board feet - 3 billion; Value - $64 million; Reserves of Timber in board feet - 352,834,000,000. Pacific halibut landings in a recent year throughout BC amounted to 29.2 million pounds. About 400 whales were harvested each year at a value of $1.5 million.[29]

There may be some taxpayer issues with the BC economy that are unrelated to the Indian welfare payments. After all these generations of subsidizing the resource companies by keeping the indigenous title holders out of the way, BC's economic plans still primarily feature resource extraction, but next-level forms of extraction like tar sands, industrial salmon farming and hydro-electric development, showing that the land is almost barren. Can the depleted indigenous lands really be negotiated over, without consideration of compensation and restoration? Would anyone reasonably begin negotiations for an average 2 - 4% of their own barren territory, and in so doing release *anyone* for past infringements, as the BC treaty process requires they do?

Greg McDade, QC, of Ratcliff and Company, spoke at a conference in Westbank about the implications of the *Tsilhqot'in* decision of 2007.

> In my opinion, the best thing we can do to follow up the win in *Tsilhqot'in* is to have four or five more such cases. If you do own the land, and you do have jurisdiction, you will be able to place that tax on all the following developments as well. You need to act as if you know what you own, and they know what you own. How much should you charge? That's a developing science, changing with every court case. The court says the proper amount of accommodation monies depends on the strength of the claim to title and the degree of impact. You need expert advice on that, and you need to be stubborn on what you want. Act as a landowner would act. Act as a responsible government would act.
>
> If you don't want the project to go ahead, then just say "no." But if you do want it to go ahead, you need to have a price that is reasonable as a landowner and a good government.
>
> There are currently 700 big projects listed with BC Ministries to go ahead in the next ten years. They are worth about $148 billion. $5 - $10 billion would be probably your percentage of that.
>
> *Tsilhqot'in* didn't change who owns the land. It just shows what happens when you stand up for the land.[30]

Unfortunately, *Tsilhqot'in* didn't change the way the province encourages business as usual, either.

No One Left to Pay

If money is the highest good, and colonizers feel it's reasonable to withhold and delay justice and basic human rights while substituting them with welfare, they may eventually be unable to meet their ideas of seeing justice to be done—when and if they change their collective mind dramatically and that day does come when they want to pay restitution, restoration and compensation. There may be no one left to pay it to. British Columbians currently believe that they have taken care of *their* Indians by confining them on Reserves and giving out welfare payments. Some think this is an improvement. They think that combined with access to hospitals (where the blatant racism and experimental bent of the doctors can be quite unsafe), and schools in English (where racially motivated bullying leads to defensive gangs, experiences of isolation and feelings of inferiority), western society's moving here has saved the Indians from themselves.

Radical British Columbians will go on the march, albeit rarely, to demand policy changes that will save salmon, whales, trees, and occasionally endangered birds' nesting habitat, but it has never yet crossed their minds to demand protections for the people. There has never yet been a blockade of a Reserve where the young and old non-native dissidents demand, for instance, that the language of that nation be protected; that the children be left alone and the parents not punished for keeping them out of school so they can learn from the Elders, as the Elders desire. There have been plenty such roadblocks by the indigenous themselves, but this is by now a predictable string of events: letters, petitions and demonstrations followed with no response from the governments; threats of roadblock and media escalation of hatred; roadblock; court injunction; police drag people away; a halt to media interest; incarcerations in pre-trial; court dates that drag on for years; the carrying out of the disputed development which impacts land and culture. More often than not the media does not actually figure at all in the latter stages of the progression.

British Columbians do not perceive indigenous societies to be endangered. This even while one of their last remaining unique possessions occasionally makes the news on its way to oblivion: the languages. Indigenous languages in British Columbia are the most endangered in the world.[31]

The newcomers seem unable to understand that loss of homeland and sovereignty over it would endanger a people. They do not agree that a human being needs a homeland, a language and a culture in order to survive. After all, the settlers don't have those things, and they are still alive. Sometimes the wildlife species that once were the mainstay of the indigenous nations have more rights and reserved lands to ensure their survival than the endangered peoples.[32]

A small minority of Canadians and British Columbians will argue, with the support of leading scientists but not of profitable corporations, that they must protect lands, waters, fish and wildlife in order to have an environment worth living in. When indigenous nations insist on this, they are accused of being Neolithic.

On top of the welfare payments to these "historical 'might have beens',"[33] many Canadians are stricken to learn that their governments propose further compensation. If reconciliation along the lines of the Prime Minister's 2008 apology for Canada's use of Indian Residential Schools to subdue and assimilate the indigenous, combined with delayed and shockingly small payouts to victims of sexual, physical and other residential school abuses, is to really solve things and can be given out at any future time once colonial requirements are made certain, it requires the thinker to believe that cultures and languages survive indefinitely, regardless the prevailing conditions. This is, however, not true. And the conditions in British Columbia are prevailing against the native peoples.

It is not too onerous a task to add up the value of these very occasional compensation packages, tack them on to the usual welfare and buy-out schemes such as the Forest and Range Agreements, compare them with the value of the land theft to the successful thief, and see that BC comes up with a fiscal award that is to the victim, in light of his shattered viability, as one bone of a salmon—the whole river having been consumed by the perpetrator.

Is money a substitute for a legal remedy? Is Benefits Sharing in a clearcutting operation as good or better than a forest, with its trout bearing streams, its inexhaustible mushroom patches, its berries and mink? Presently communities are rammed into provincial court slipknots where they are forced to be consulted and then forced to abide by the company's decisions about accommodating the values identified, in the way that is most "practicable" for the company. Non-native society gets to make all the choices about what is fair and appropriate.

Many people will declare their outrage at "paying for" the crimes against humanity which delivered into their hands the country with which they now identify, Canada, as if those crimes are in the past. These people seem completely unaware that even as they "pay" for those "past" crimes, they are actually *still carrying them out*. At this point they are amassing a kind of debt that can not be repaid.

By their logic, welfare payments and subsidized housing to the tune of one tenth of what is required should create the firm foundation of a thriving and sustainable culture. Either they think that or they have never even thought at all about whether the indigenous nations will survive. Or, put another more likely way, they either know nothing about the subject or abhor it past intelligent discussion. The facts are that welfare dependence, a prohibited economy, inadequate "relief" housing, all lead to a gripping cycle of poverty, displacement, family breakdown, social disorder, addiction and a statistical nightmare: not a safe haven for language and culture.

Beyond welfare dependence, the next offers on the table are partial or national extinguishment. Benefits sharing arrangements in industrial activities and one-time historical impacts settlements, like for hydroelectric impacts, require the indigenous recipients to release the governments and everyone else from further obligations, and effectively surrender the use of the lands or resources at issue.

Modern day treaties along the line of BC Treaty Commission deals will not save people either—quite the opposite. Not enough land base, not enough rights, not enough money, not enough capacity, not enough potential. The modern day Treaty Commission is no different than the original Reserve Commission of 1912: twenty acres per family of five—unless it's an urban treaty.

The best economic recognition that all First Nations in British Columbia have ever received was paltry. Under the Forest and Range Agreement scheme, after 2004, there was a per-capita payback to a community for the certainty—in advance—that all economic interests of that First Nation in all forestry activities in the next five years had been accommodated. It was usually signed before any Forest Stewardship Plan was completed, and was intended to fulfill obligations identified in *Haida*. Perhaps the scheme would also eliminate further submissions like INET's when international trade was concerned. The same per-capita deal was offered to a community in active logging areas on the coast where big cedars were the target, to those in interior areas where only pine-beetle kill was available, and to urban First Nations with no forest left. In 2010 the Chehalis Indian Band shattered even this cellar threshold with an agreement that their economic interests had all been accommodated, in exchange for 3% of the province's stumpage revenues from their territory.[34]

This is how money, in any amount, is confused with justice—easy to do when the confusion is a requirement of going ahead with business-as-usual. In a culture where money is the highest value, the oppressor will pretend he cannot understand when the underdog wants something more important than money.

Chapter 4

STUDYING INDIFFERENCE

*"We find ourselves practically landless, and that in our own
country, through no fault of ours, we have reached a critical point,
and, unless justice comes to the rescue, we must go back and
sink out of sight as a race."*
**A statement delivered to Sir Robert Borden, Prime Minister,
by James Teit on behalf of a delegation of nine BC Chiefs,
Ottawa, 1912.[1]**

In the following hundred years, this statement elicited nothing but indifference from British Columbians. Ottawa's response to that notice at the time, jointly fashioned with British Columbia, was to instigate a Reserve Commission that would reinforce that "practical landlessness" among the thirty indigenous nations—ideally, once and for all. The indigenous were of course not parties to that Commission. And the most crucial details, the details pertaining to whether and how the Indian Land Question would be addressed, were not picked up by the print news services of the day in spite of their importance in the BC context. The importance of the Reserve Commission to the BC settler lay in its capacity to silence the Indians with whom they competed for control of land – not in its capacity to do right by the Indians, to purchase land equitably and come to mutually agreeable arrangements about its use.

The 1912 Commission into the issue of Reserve sizes was struck some forty years after Joseph Trutch, Chief Commissioner of Lands and Works for BC, had assured the Colonial Secretary that all the lands required by the Indians had been reserved for them. Today, a hundred years later, there is still a Reserve Commission at work in BC. The most recent incarnation started in

1992, and it is called the BC Treaty Commission. The government and select native negotiators continue with a schedule of discussions to identify Treaty Settlement Lands: the transformation of Lands Reserved for the Indians, Indian Reserves, into meager fee-simple-title estates, the supposedly consensual Final Agreement on the subject of Indian land. The new Commission is carried out by elected Chiefs and their appointed negotiators, and the process is funded by Canada and the province of British Columbia, while the public remains quite oblivious to the means, method and outcomes in play.

The peoples whom Chiefs predicted would disappear have been, to update the record, "sunk out of sight." They are not gone, but neither are they clearly visible. They have been cloaked in obscurity by popular caricatures; demonized by a ruthless and violent greed; otherwise cut out of the picture altogether.

Sinking Out of Sight

Growing up in the interior, say in Kamloops, a typical non-native child does not know that when the place they live is called Shuswap, that is actually the name of a people. They certainly will not know the proper name is *Secwepemc*. Perhaps there is some awareness of the existence of First Nations, but that is literally a world apart from the child's reality and is only a distant concept. Children are probably more aware of the idea of unicorns, for example. The idea that there are people of that country alive today, who have a claim to the land, who speak another language, who have ideas and aims of their own, has never been raised for him. Not in school, certainly not by his parents in any typical scenario, and it is unlikely that his friends, if he has native friends, would be mentioning their community's political aspirations or unique ways of being. It's not popular with the other kids. If we examine the non-native child who lives in a more rural area, we will discover even less empathetic interest. This child, probably with parents in direct conflict over land use with native people, working in industries like logging, mining and agriculture, will cuss openly about "Indian bullshit" and discuss how lazy and unreliable Indians are, even at such a young age that he himself does not have any responsibilities beyond making his bed. He is aware that Indians are not like other people, he is not entirely sure they are people at all.

The fact that settlers are delusional is only unknown to the settlers; it is certainly no secret to native people. It is quite unnecessary to find a new way to say it. Michael A. Dorris writes,

> 'I' isn't for Indian; it is often for Ignorance. In the Never-Never land of glib stereotypes and caricature, the rich histories, cultures, and the contemporary complexities of the indigenous, divers peoples of the Western Hemisphere are obscured, misrepresented,

and rendered trivial. Native Americans appear not as human beings but as whooping, silly, one-dimensional cartoons. On occasion they are presented as marauding, blood-thirsty savages, bogeys from the nightmares of "pioneers" who invaded their lands and feared for the consequences. At other times they seem preconcupiscent angels, pure of heart, mindlessly ecological, brave and true. And worst of all, they are often merely cute, the special property of a child.[2]

In the documentary film, *Reel Injun,* the popular indigenous actor, Adam Beach, remarked on stereotypical roles for native actors and, by contrast, why he loved his role in *Flags of our Fathers*: "I just got to be a human being."[3]

Books have been self-published by the exceptional non-native person who proves, by breaking it, the rule of distortion and degradation in portrayals of indigenous people. A collection of portraits and short biographies of 31 indigenous people, most from BC, was put out in 1990 by Patricia Richardson Logie, "In response to an enormous amount of frustration and anger toward the depiction of First Nations peoples in art, media, the schools and other areas of society...."[4]

In *Through Indian Eyes*, *The Native Experience in Books for Children,* edited by Beverly Slapin and Doris Seale and printed in the USA, those attitudes being broadcast are neatly undone and exposed for what they are: ignorance and fear. Unfortunately, there are not many critical books in print to recommend— certainly none from BC.

Young non-native opinions are formed early on. They are not formed by their contact with indigenous people who live around them, because there is still very little social mixing of native and non native families in BC. The opinions are formed by story books, Western movies and perhaps by the very occasional First Nations cameo in a TV program.

Canadian Heroes, a Scholastic Canada effort, tells the story of a white French Canadian girl who saved her people from an Iroquois attack.[5] This anomaly is not balanced by the tale of any native child who led his people safely from a miner's attack, a police raid, or through an army ambush. There are no native heroes in that book, despite the numberless Indian struggles for self-determination and their intermittent victories under threat.

Some books written for children are simply historical revision. "… they trusted you with the earth, the water, the air," writes David Bouchard in his poem "The Elders Are Watching."[6] The story is based on coastal people now within BC's borders, but who are not identified. In this story "they" are the indigenous and "you" are the newcomers. The very foundation of the problems which indigenous peoples are trying to have resolved is that no such trust was ever granted to the newcomer. They have had to vigorously reject every newcomer attempt to appropriate indigenous responsibility for the earth, and return themselves to their place of right and responsibility. *That* book does not get published in plain language.

Children learn that the indigenous nations were warlike. "…but all young Indian men fought like heroes in the never-ending wars."[7] They learn to count: "one little, two little, three little Indians; four little, five little… Indian braves…" That picture book was only discarded from one provincial elementary school in 2011.

When children's books do feature native people, they are as a figment of the past, wreathed in the smoke of campfires long out of use. "A Child's Christmas in Yekooche," for instance, or something contemporary like it, has never been attempted. Alternatively, non-native writers have sold many books depicting or improvising on ancient legends, or quite recent ones they have made up themselves and illustrated in the native fashion.[8] However, a handful of children's books by indigenous writers have begun to be published in the 21st century. But *Shin-Chi's Canoe* by Nicola Campbell and *The Gathering Tree* by Larry Loyie depict such themes as residential school and HIV. These are the very few exceptions which involve native children or communities placed in a modern context. However, these and the few others like them do not contemplate the most relevant issues facing those children and their communities, starting with the land title debacle and the resulting dilemma the communities are in.

Otherwise the non-native children understand that native peoples are a thing of the past. "Eleven-year-old Laura Marchak of Golden convinced us: 'The raven *was* a special symbol for the natives…'"[9] Christopher Plummer narrated the following fairy tale for an audio production, "In the Dawning, A Story of Canada:"

> When the earth was ice, the first dawning of Canada's destiny came through the glittering northern lights when Asian nomads trudged across the Alaskan land bridge. These stone age immigrants drifted with the snow, restless hunters drawn by the scent of fresh food, driven by hunger, They followed the animals… that sustained each generation edging ever southward until their tribes clustered in the rough forests and roamed the plains… centuries before the white man ever glimpsed the new land.[10]

And that's it for the Indians' part in *The Story of Canada.* The teacher of Social Studies 9, "First Nations Group Project," 2012, instructs the students: "For this project you will be… given a first nations group to research. …your project must tell us where your group lived, what they lived in, what they ate for food and wore for clothing, what kind of art they created…." As if they no longer eat, dress or make art.

Texts and Reference Books

The public school history curriculum in British Columbia suffers from the minor oversight of neglecting to include very much of it. Graduates won't know why places along the coast have Spanish names like Quadra or Juan de Fuca. The name of Meare's Island does not call to mind that late eighteenth century sailor and his exploits which brought Spain and Britain to the point of war. Young, perhaps aspiring, pirates know nothing of those who harboured on the BC coast in the 19th century, pirates from Spain, England, Portugal and the United States. They all sailed for Canton on unruly seas in unlicensed pursuits while keeping a weather eye out for the British navy. They competed with Russians who had a roaring fur trade along the north coast before men with British Charters, and many without, arrived in what's presently BC to do business.

Students are quite unaware that the interior of the modern province was mostly built up first by American gold prospectors, and the roads and railways were built by the same Americans, and Indians and Chinese; but they will learn about the Royal Engineers who determined the route. British Columbians have the idea that their province evolved in some form of Splendid Isolation from the American mid-west, but the vast majority of original settlers were people who had crossed America in 1849 for the California gold rush, and then moved north in 1858 for the Fraser River gold rush. Thirty thousand of them – then outnumbering other colonists in BC by at least 30-1 for a few years, after which most returned to the USA. The students won't learn about the Nlaka'pamux and their greatest modern chief, Spintlum; nor of Ned Gowan and his posse who rode up the Fraser River to take on the Indians that had sent the headless bodies of their fellow miners back down the river. Spintlum's peace-making probably averted a course of confrontation which would have made the colonization of BC skip tracks.

They don't know that the first Governor of the Colony was himself from the West Indies, Trinidad, and his mother was visibly African; or that he married a woman who was half French and half native, daughter of one of his bosses in the fur trade. James Douglas was actually described as a "canny old Scot" in Victoria's correspondence education branch "1971 Centennial Course." Otherwise, in less official tomes, he is called "black Douglas."[11] The new citizens of BC still shop at the Hudson's Bay Company—something most would probably choose to avoid if they did know its history.

As we become more familiar with the true history of British Columbia, the reasons for such conspicuous absence in books for children become clear. BC history is not the type of material typically thought to be appropriate for children and youth. True accounts would also not suit the modern trend for identity-in-hindsight along the fabulously detached philosophical lines of

"British liberalism," which the students will be expected to believe in when they're older. That is, that even while whole peoples had been subdued in Imperial conquest, eventually they would receive the gift of liberty – an equal vote, the right to private property, and so on.[12] The subdued people will theoretically receive this gift in a manner according to British law and whether they want it that way or not.

British Columbians have accepted the prospect of a whole race of people quitting the face of the earth quite readily, and have demonstrably skipped to the conclusion with an "out of sight, out of mind" approach. First Nations histories are taught firmly in the past tense. It is nowhere required that school children be exposed to the twenty-six names of the different indigenous languages within BC borders, or to the proper name of the indigenous nation on whose territory they live and go to school, or to a map of British Columbia which shows the locations of all the different nations. No school projects contemplate the future of indigenous nations, and few even acknowledge the present.

In the public schools, teaching Kindergarten to Grade 12, there are few courses which include First Nations content in the course objectives, or prescribed learning outcomes. Two of them are elective: First Nations Studies, Grades 11 and 12. The two most substantial are chapters in Social Studies books for Grades 4 and 9 students. In Grade 4 the students learn that the Beothuck of Newfoundland are extinct, and they learn about the defunct traditional economy of the Inuit. In the Grade 9 textbook, there is a partial map of the province showing half a dozen nations. The soft content is questionable, "they covered the floors of their homes with spruce boughs" (ouch!), and it's stuck in the pre-contact past. The First Nations Education Steering Committee, a task force mainly meant to assist Band schools, has produced the First Peoples text for optional high school English classes in Grades 11 and 12. In Grade 10 Social Studies, students in BC learn about the fur trade in eastern Canada but not how it connected to BC, and content pertaining to the indigenous equation of the fur trade is at the discretion of the teacher.

In the words of one longtime BC School District Superintendent, inclusion of aboriginal content in curriculum requires "a perfect storm"[13] of cooperation. The production in 2001 of the textbooks *Sto:lo Coast Salish Historical Atlas,* and *I Am Sto:lo,* and *You Are Asked to Witness* are evidence of one such social weather event. The Chilliwack District, with some 50% aboriginal student population and almost $1.5 million in targeted aboriginal funding each year, partnered with Band schools and Sto:lo communities in the 1990's – an unprecedented adventure. It also brought the teachers who cared to join, which was almost all of them, on a day trip to visit special Sto:lo sites. This District is in the uncommon position of being within the borders of only one indigenous nation: some School Districts' catchment areas span three nations at the corners. Chilliwack produced a First Nations Kindergarten in consultation with the local Bands, a class which incorporated language and culture and produced good students.[14]

Such anomalies as the Chilliwack example, and perhaps the Gold Trail, School District 74, example – where St'át'imcets language classes are taught Kindergarten to Grade 12 and meet university entrance requirements for a second language, are extremely isolated. Individual teachers and principals are free to invite native guests or performers to the schools, but there is no province-wide mandate to include indigenous subject matter, outside the two Social Studies classes. "Aboriginal Education Enhancement Agreements," present in every District now, are devised to ensure academic success by aboriginal students – not necessarily to include those students' relevant social, cultural, economic or political material.[15]

The advent of the "Aboriginal Principal" for each School District is part of the Enhancement Agreements and, in many cases, a funding sink which fulfills cosmetic requirements and keeps bureaucracy thick enough to repel interested parents or would-be participants. In District #48, Howe Sound, James Louie of Líl'wat made appointments to speak to the Líl'wat students there. He wore his special identity tag provided by the non-governmental organization which helps advance his international petition: he is a Human Rights Defender. Louie told the students they are Líl'wat, not Canadian. The planned speaking series was abruptly discontinued. The Enhancement Agreement, by contrast, produces such spin-off positions as the "Aboriginal Support Worker and Alcohol and Addictions Counselor."[16]

When a student goes to college or university specifically to find out about indigenous peoples in BC, when they enroll in First Nations Studies classes, the texts and course material may only be a great improvement in terms of quantity.

Olive Dickason's work, *Canada's First Nations: A History of Founding Peoples from Earliest Times,* is the most widely-used text in First Nations Studies in Canadian universities. Dickason, a Métis woman from Manitoba who apparently did not know she was Métis until in her twenties, began her book by explaining that indigenous peoples in North America arrived via the Bering land bridge. She was almost 70 when she wrote the book, published in 2002. A brand new essay at the end of the most recent edition, by David Mackay, sweeps recent Canadian politics and ignores the near-massacre of indigenous sovereigntists at the Gustafsen Lake stand-off of 1995; he heaves a sigh for former Prime Minister Paul Martin's $5 billion solution to the Indian problem, the Kelowna Accord of 2005 (apparently relying solely on government press releases for his analysis); and fails to inject any potent consideration of the conflict between Canadians and their Constitutional obligations to buy indigenous lands before settling.

Canada's First Nations runs 450 pages, without the endnotes. This book addresses the divided parts, not the entire nations, and there are 650 First Nations in Canada—a First Nation is an Indian Band, or community. None of them belong to Canada, and none of their recent histories, much less their histories from earliest times, can be captured in less than one page.

The university text book *History of the Canadian Peoples, Beginnings to 1857*, has been revised and re-released five times since its original publication in the year 1993. Had 300 year old history changed so drastically by the Fifth Edition in 2009? Was it being freshly reinvented, reinterpreted and reassigned meaning? Inching toward the politically correct while retreating from the historically correct? Two of only nine references cited for a *Canadian Peoples* chapter were original documents, and the rest were published within a decade of the 2002 version of the book itself. With the removal of original sources, such pre-digested statements as the following are possible: "As beaver in the interior plains became more scarce, the Nor'Westers began to seriously pursue the idea of trading in the British Columbia interior."[17]

This simple statement is so disorienting in its complete indifference to the complexity of the situation, it's hard to agree that it is even true and hard even to respond with the relevant correction because, in the context of the book, the crucial details of the "exploration" of British Columbia do not appear. But it is one of the most elaborate references to BC. Pursuing an overland route to the Pacific Ocean, Alexander Mackenzie of the North West Company arrived at salty Kingcome Inlet in 1793. He wasn't pursuing the dearth of beaver skins, he was pursuing a competitive agenda to reach the western coast by land. Perhaps Canada is too big to really bother with such details.

Then at the CONCLUSION of the chapter: "While the West continued to provide homelands for a variety of First Nations in 1821, much of the region had also become an area of European exploitation of beaver furs and sea-otter pelts. The Natives were partners in the fur trade...." Much of the region? The interior plateau, and the coast. There were only eleven forts west of the Rockies in 1821, and six of them were below the 49th parallel, which was soon to become the border between Canada and the United States. Although that line was not relevant at the time, BC is still millions of hectares big. It contains many meaningfully distinct regions, in fact five different climatic zones, and an accompanying diverse set of histories. The text is inaccurate here and throughout.

When the text says "Partners" in the fur trade, really the situation was that the indigenous had the land, the ability to get the animals, the stability of living in complex societies with the long established trade routes and international cooperation, peace and relationships to use them. And the new fur traders came at a time when competition with tribes who had access to sea-going Russian rifles and iron was becoming relevant. It was never the intention of officials or any Europeans to be business partners with native people. They wanted everything, and relied on the assistance, generosity and tolerance of the native people to get established independently so they could take it.

In fact the native fur providers were intimidated, harassed and otherwise pursued to provide the traders with furs, according to Father Morice, a missionary in the northern interior of the province of that time.[18] Describing native people as "partners in the fur trade" is not a good likeness, and yet all the textbooks do it. A better example of the HBC and NWCo policy is found in an older book: "The traders robbed the Indians blind and the factors at the Hudson's Bay Company forts were particularly adept at short-changing them."[19] Such frank statements were made and published at a time in the last century when the future of indigenous peoples and therefore the political reality of their claims was considered unlikely.

None of the modern text books correctly characterize the HBC regime as operating like a military government in foreign territories. They don't reference the incidents and the international situation that would properly contextualize fur trade activities as such: James Douglas used his judicial powers, conferred on him by Great Britain within the HBC Charter, to simply shoot native men suspected of theft.[20] Just as the British military patrolled and controlled Canada from 1760, the end of the Seven Years War with France, to 1763, the date of the related Treaty of Paris resolving their disputes, so Britain patrolled and controlled what they then called the Oregon Territory—part of which is now BC. But there is no treaty to signal the end of the occupation.

As for the HBC's "partners" on the Pacific coast: who takes a gunboat out to raze their partners' villages? Who trades in obsolete technology, just because they have a monopoly on supply, and calls the client "partner"? The long-barrel rifle persisted in BC, long after it had been proven dramatically inferior to shorter models, because guns were traded to natives for the price of the pile of pelts that was as tall as the gun, or alternatively for the gun's full barrel of gold nuggets. Father Morice described axe heads that were half an inch thick on the "sharp" side. Coastal traders were giving "a few nails" in exchange for otter furs that would fetch enough pounds sterling on the other side of the Pacific to make the journey worthwhile for many a ship's crew and captain. That was not partnership, that was exploitation and subjugation; racketeering and extortion; and it was enforced by gunboat.

Unfortunately, the fur trade partners are not meaningfully considered in the most-used university texts canvassing Indians in Canada. The treatment of British Columbia history is superficial and is a resulting lie of omission. One wonders to what extent, when reporting on such a geographically massive subject as Canada, and of such diverse peoples and languages, histories and mythologies, the rest of the stories are patched together just as crudely?

It's also notable that all standard Canadian textbooks purporting to tell indigenous history in university courses today were not written by indigenous people.

The textbooks always use the word "group" to sometimes describe native villages and sometimes nations, and sometimes affiliations. The use of that one word in all kinds of scenarios is a good indication that the so-called "historians" are painfully unaware of the actual history, and worse, must be actually disinterested or disparaging, since they are either unable or unwilling to note what would be very different implications depending on whether a fur trading crew was fighting with a war party, a certain renegade village, or an inter-tribal alliance… "Maquinna was the chief of the Mowachat people—a Nuu'chah'nulth group that numbered about 1,500"[21] Was he head of a legendary warriors' society? What does "Mowachat" mean – a village, a nation, a region, a spiritual sect? Are the Nuu-chah-nulth a "group" related by blood, language, or defined by international relations? Are the Nuu-chah-nulth a larger group of the same type, and the Mowachat a subset? The text does not say. The implication is that "groups" were highly permeable, not well-defined nations with pride and distinction. The reality is that the different indigenous nations had ancient and dignified ways of belonging and relating to one another which deserve and reward respectful inquiry – not haphazard translation into English designations which neither fit nor inform. An improved approach might be to use indigenous terms for the appropriate designations, and thereby enrich English at the same time as honouring others.

Single university courses are called "Indigenous Peoples of the Americas." This is the title of a 400 level class at the University of British Columbia. Such a generic title, if it were in the field of, say, botany, would read "Shrubs of North America." If this comparison helps, it is to prove unrealistic the suggestion that anything at all of indigenous peoples in North America could be learned in a single 3 credit course beyond possibly memorizing their names, linguistic affiliations and general geographic territories. Simon Fraser University has something similar, "History 326 – History of Aboriginal People in North America, 1850 to the present." There is no near-expert lecture called, "People(s) of Europe." There are, however, maybe twenty times the number of classes available at the University of British Columbia's Faculty of Arts which retrieve the minutia of European countries' pasts as there are classes dealing with BC's history. Where would one go to learn BC history? Where, then, to learn of the unfathomable riches of Tsimshian or Kootenay history, or even that of the entire Interior Salish? There is no history class available in BC that has for a subject heading a single indigenous nation's name. There are actually only a handful of books printed in BC which bear a single indigenous nation's name, which are not catalogues of artwork, and most of them are out of print. But then, there are no universities promoting the study of indigenous self-determination; no program funding to invite research on the transitive moments between the colonial period and a pluralistic era of respect and reconciliation. The institutions train new generations in assimilation.

The North West Company and HBC fur traders, factors and Governors did not generalize about aboriginal nations. They made a point of recording vital information, such as borders between them and significant counties and leaders within them, in their journals and letters back to headquarters. They hired interpreters of an especially benign repute to travel between the nations, indicating their appreciation of the meaningful international relations they were navigating. Ethnographers were later hired to go out and discover 800 words in each language and find out about each nation's worldview and lore. This was not, however, out of scholarship in the humanities: the Department of Archaeology, commissioner of this reconnaissance, was then a branch of the Department for Mines.

Unfortunately, the general study of indigenous peoples does not investigate nations, in recognition of the ancient historical boundaries they have, and the separate languages which have passed the linguistic test to indicate a social development isolated from interference for at least several thousand years, and the markedly distinct appearances and lands of the different peoples.

Indifference to indigenous nations is accomplished mainly by absorbing, modifying and appropriating their stories, by writing about them as if they no longer exist, and by strictly avoiding them. A first-ever *Encyclopedia of British Columbia* was produced in the year 2000. Alan Twigg, publisher of *BC Bookworld,* said "if there is a more important book about British Columbia, I haven't read it," and that statement is quoted on the title page. This book does not feature an entry for *Indian Act.* Neither are there entries for *Aboriginal Title; First Nations Summit; BC Treaty Commission; United Native Nations; Inter Tribal Fishing Treaty; Assembly of First Nations; National Indian Brotherhood; BC Association of Non-Status Indians;* or *Indian Rights Association.*

The *Encyclopedia*'s 113 word summary on the Union of BC Indian Chiefs (UBCIC) characterizes that organization and its history simply as to "pursue a land claims settlement in BC." Although British Columbians might accept this out of ignorance, it is about equal in accuracy to suggesting the suffragette movement sought fairer prices for knitting needles. George Manuel, who started that Union by raising the cry for Indian Government, gets his own entry. The most famous picture of him, as UBCIC president, shows him talking on a phone that has the words "Indian Government" stuck to the receiver in huge letters. That photo isn't used in the *Encyclopedia.* Grand Chief Manuel is mentioned, but not the fact that he was nominated three times for a Nobel prize, or that he co-founded the

UBCIC and the National Indian Brotherhood. About the Native Brotherhood of the coastal nations, the authors say: "because it was prohibited by law from pursuing land claims, the Brotherhood concerned itself mainly with fishing." In reality, gathering for any purpose was illegal—except to do business wanted by whites. The coastal people used the fishy cover story to create the Brotherhood, under which pretenses they met to further discuss the land issue and raise funds to strengthen their newly illegal political aims. Summing up the Allied Indian Tribes, the *Encyclopedia* says: "In 1927 a special parliamentary committee in Ottawa considered the Allied Tribes' arguments and ultimately rejected them." This is not even true, as we will see in the next chapter, and does nothing to tie the AIT directly to the McKenna-McBride Reserve Commission, which is why it formed. It also doesn't mention why the AIT dissolved—because of the same *Indian Act* amendment in 1927 which made it illegal to have gatherings about land issues, the same reason the Brotherhood was formed.

But the omission of the Indian Act—the most ghastly piece of racist legislation written in English since the Catholic Laws, the Poor Laws, the Corn Laws, and still in effect!—from a catalogue of events of the province that caused its creation, is truly illuminating. The Indian Act, which was imposed on indigenous people across Canada, either prescribing or criminalizing their every move and retiring so many to their incarcerated deaths, instead of making treaties with the tribal nations in the would-be colony, belongs in any history of British Columbia. This matter will come up in the next chapter as well, as it answers the question of how Indian Reserves could have been successfully implemented without treaties.

Unfortunately, Indian histories are not considered as the histories of individual peoples, but as the homogenized events of individuals who happen to belong to the same race. The *Indian Act* should be reviewed for its contribution to this dehumanizing approach as well; the many books and articles which remark on "Indians generally" are legitimized in their unfocused surveys by this insult to the very distinctly different nations and peoples. The colonizer forces indigenous nations to unite in opposition once his cunning and treacherous plans are finally revealed, a difficult and so far impossible feat in BC, and then he smears the different peoples with one brush.

The surgical omission of critical and nation-specific history enables the now trendy denigration of aboriginal nationhood. The facts of economic, social and political legacies which constitute the many different nations are dismissed as "legal fiction".[22] Such depravity in research gives license to all manner of tenured professors to publish the most wildly misleading and irresponsible works since it was discovered that Swift's *A Modest Proposal* was satire.[23]

The Rise of Historiomythology

> *"Since the early 1970's there has been an upsurge in the production*
> *of print and audio-visual materials dealing with historical and*
> *contemporary experiences of North American Indians."*
> ### The NESA Bibliography for Native Studies,
> ### Green and Sawyer, 1983

The indigenous were swept from the record up until about 1973. Since then, a sort of controlled reintroduction of the subject has been led by key academics.

The vernacular of aggressive indifference, of total academic snobbery that feels licensed to avoid accuracy, can clearly be traced to the cataclysm that was the *Calder* decision in 1973. Three Supreme Court of Canada judges had declared, in that case, that aboriginal title is a real interest in the land: an economic, social and political interest, and that nothing Britain, Canada or BC had ever done had extinguished that title; it exists today.

Green and Sawyer's observation that the incidence of publications about native people had spiked immediately after that is by no means inaccurate. It's as if, once it was obvious that the courts couldn't make aboriginal title disappear – and *Calder* was the first time the question of aboriginal title in British Columbia had been admitted to a Canadian court of any description in the history of colonization—an entire profession stepped up behind the soiled government and declared itself the champion of the lawless colonist. They began to re-write their history, and the battlefield for the land moved into the minds and memories of Canadians.

Earlier texts had not minced words about the desired progress of colonial development, and the acceptable costs to the indigenous. A candid local account of settlement on Vancouver Island simply noted that, "In the nineteenth century it appeared as if all problems connected with the Indians would resolve themselves through the extinction of the Indian race."[24] Every reference to indigenous peoples in *A World Geography For Canadian Schools,* "Authorized for use in the schools of British Columbia and Saskatchewan" in 1936, is in the past tense and merely refers to nomadic activities which have ceased.

The usual histories made little attempt to disguise the true shepherding, or relocating, purpose of missionaries in BC: "Great numbers of the Songhees (at Fort Victoria) had been converted to Christianity… but the work had long been discontinued and the Gold Rush now provided a great stimulus for Christian endeavor among the Indians…"[25] Christian endeavor was one of the most helpful agents in pacifying and making stationary the indigenous clans. As late as 1972 the most influential textbook publishers were minting BC histories which referred to indigenous nations, in passing, as late and lamented. *The Rush for Spoils, The Company Province 1871-1933,* by Martin Robin, put out by McLelland and Stewart Limited, is an example of how books devoted to the province of BC – even to its sordid and corrupt style of progress— strike indigenous peoples from the record. In fact, the word "Indian" is not in the index, and neither is any Indian figure, event or issue. From whom, then, were the titular "spoils" won?

In 1983 came the compilation *As Long as the Sun Shines and Water Flows: A Reader in Canadian Native Studies,* a UBC Press product and the first of its kind. It was such a departure from the previous tone of Canadian histories and such an abrupt lurch into a new place which would be called "First Nations Studies," that one suspects a missing link. It truly is missing; the about-turn was never fully manifested beyond the one line of *The Constitution Act,* 1982, Section 35 (1), "aboriginal and treaty rights are hereby affirmed." But the new writers had a steely grip on the end of straight history and announced an age where the past is fermented in a hog's head of sugar, the resulting mash is squeezed through a press very delicately, and anyone who gets of a whiff of it loses their sense of reason in a kind of vainglorious intoxication that foments post-historical societies.

The leading experts in the fledgling field of "native studies," at least those who contributed to *As Long as the Sun Shines,* were obviously seconded from reliable places in a way that is reminiscent of the use of retired British military personnel as Indian Agents. Such literary efforts are themselves important moments in history. The reader, a series of essays, had a single purpose: to introduce Canadian post-secondary students to a national history which had swallowed, digested and completely absorbed Indian history as part of its own. First Nations Studies assign a place to the indigenous which is usually little better than having assisted with the early days of building Canada. To deal with anything more recent would lead to disillusion, perhaps dissolution.

The indefatigable truth is that the events of removing Indian peoples from coveted lands—of shattering promises about suns and rivers—is only a fraction of a generation away. That is to say, only decades ago BC settlers were bodily removing Indian people from pre-empted claims. This is probably why it is now so acceptable, if not imperative, to make up stories about native people instead of simply adding notes in the margins of older published epitaphs. This must be especially so in British Columbia, where suddenly "aboriginal title exists" according to three judges of the highest court in the land.

Academics publishing in the genre of First Nations pseudo-history have done a remarkably thorough job of keeping such illustrious and ubiquitous ancestors as the Indian-clearing rancher out of their books. References to the more candid histories are also dropping off. The settlers have been amassing an extensive collection of literature around themselves instead, little of which pertains at all, or honestly, to their engagements with native people.

We might coin a phrase to name this re-history: historiomythology. This is the product of academic indifference to truth as compared to career and political advancement. It is politically advantageous to capture the indigenous in unflattering and unusual words, and especially good career material if they can be relegated to somewhere in the past so the page can be turned and the chapter on "moving forward together" can be enjoyed. As a result of many fantastic feats of historical and social engineering, entire Bering land bridges begin to appear across the gulf between what Canadian heritage is and what they wish to make it seem.

Historiomythology is born to the Mother of Invention, Necessity, at the moment in which a society can't deny that its true history is a solid series of genocidal events. That moment occurred when Frank Calder and every single Nisga'a person, all included as appellants in the case, received the minority opinion that they held continuing title to their ancestral lands. The birth has exacted a dreadful price from those of the country's intellectuals willing to sacrifice their integrity. It seems to have brought along an unexpected twin: a schizophrenic vocabulary for British Columbians, if not Canadians as a whole, to explain away their most racist beliefs today by events which did not happen and forefathers who appear to have changed their attitudes and intentions posthumously.

Textbooks in use today in universities are five generations removed from source material. In the laboratories of the ivory tower live old white men, who, when they come down to join a discussion panel with indigenous Chiefs, clearly have no jaw. It's the genetic engineering. Modern day traits in the vast majority of publications in First Nations Studies can be traced to one place.

Osgoode Hall is the pre-eminent Canadian institute for studies in law. Brian Slattery is a tenured professor at that place, and apparently an undisputed authority on aboriginal title in Canada. In fact, he was elected to the Royal Society of Canada in 1995 for his "contributions to the development of the law relating to aboriginal rights."[26] Note that he is not a judge or a politician—his contribution would appear to be in *making up* an acceptable interpretation of the legal history of Canada as it pertains to the Indian land question.[27] What Slattery has accomplished in his writing and teaching is the creation of a language in which to speak about the wholesale annexation of hundreds of indigenous nations without actually using those words or admitting the realities. He has created the sort of rear-view-mirror account of Canadian land law so desperately required to maintain the cultural schizophrenia Canadians enjoy in the field of naming themselves and creating their own historiomythology.

From a survey of Supreme Court and other judgments, Slattery has patched together a leaky tub with which to transport the undiscriminating mind in its 'moving forward' on aboriginal rights The learned professor has handpicked key excerpts and given interpretations of them which create the appearance of logic in today's government behavior and denial. He has also ignored some key excerpts in achieving his goals. Perhaps he was welcomed to do the chore since no one else before had ever tried to create the appearance of a legal thread winding through the dank imperial Minotaur's lair. Some might suggest the scholar has not quite arrived outside the labyrinth.

But he may yet find himself in a position more like that of Bluebeard's eleventh wife upon finding the black and bloody secret closet, than of Hercules. And without sisters to come to his aid. For all the assistance such Privy Council recommendations as those exhumed from the 19th century Southern District of Nigeria may afford, and which Slattery relies on, any vindication-seeking colonial in Canada is really very much alone. Nigeria is no longer a colony. The British indirect rule and accompanying administrations and Districts were objectionable, and the Igbo, Yuruba and Hausa, along with others, threw them off – if unevenly. Canada must have very few friends indeed if it must measure its activities according to policies in play in military governments long since overthrown.

Brian Slattery has published many papers on the subject of aboriginal title. One of his more summary papers is most useful for qualifying objections to his essential points. It was published in the year 2000, under the name *The Nature of Aboriginal Title.* It was commissioned by the most conservative and anti-indigenous institute in Canada that still allows its name and address to be posted in the public view: the Fraser Institute.

Slattery begins with his intended ending: aboriginal title is a *sui generis* concept. No one has ever heard of Indians owning land before, not even the Indians, therefore Canada must invent a meaning for the idea to satisfy them because they were indeed here first. In this way, he blacks out the fact that the real crux of the land issue is that Canadians and particularly British Columbians are not operating in a legal vacuum which can draw in completely random or made-up legal theories. The most clear and powerful instructions they possessed, in any law they could have claimed to be sanctioned by, were that the King told them to buy the Indians' land. That does not meet the requirement for a *sui generis* concept. *Sui generis* refers to an abstract legal concept invented to name a situation that has never existed in law before. Land title existed in the indigenous peoples' laws and it existed in England—there is no mystery here. But then neither Slattery nor any of his contemporaries speaks an indigenous language, so perhaps he hasn't heard.

The British King was quite aware that the Indian nations were "in possession of their homelands" and should not be "disturbed or molested"[28] there. The Indian nations were at least as aware that they should not be challenged in their homelands—hence the presence of able warriors, on which the King relied in his wars abroad with France and then the USA.

Slattery has helped to undefine the meaning of title to that land. He has gone back and misunderstood such basic talk as was spoken by the judge in *St Catherine's Milling,* 1898, where it was said that aboriginal title is "a personal and usufructuary right," and that Indian title is "dependent upon the good will of the Sovereign." He worries that this latter statement "was not explained," but it appears quite straight forward; Indians have no rights other than whatever the newcomer condescends to institutionalize. So indigenous rights do indeed depend on the whims of Colonial Secretaries, Chief Commissioners of Lands and Works, Royal Commissions and Premiers. Slattery says, however, that this unexplained phrase has "bedeviled" understandings of Canadian law.

Unfortunately, the phrases to which Slattery draws our attention in *St. Catherine's Milling* are not the most important ones. In that case, the Judicial Committee of the Privy Council reasoned that Section 109 of the *British North America Act* applied to the provinces to mean that they cannot take and use and benefit from lands which are subject to "Other Interests" – the Indian interests. In *St. Catherine's,* the Indian interests had been purchased in treaty, and this, according to the learned judges, is what left the province in possession of the lands in question. This is particularly relevant to British Columbia. This is the coherent thread; since the lands in question were supposedly purchased by the crown, whether that's true or not, they say they did, then the aboriginal right becomes "personal and usufructuary," within the rest of the traditional territory which was not reserved to the Indians in the treaty.

Maybe Slattery is letting the treaty out with the bathwater because Canada never upheld its side of the bargain. But aboriginal rights in general, where there is no treaty, like in BC, are not personal and usufructuary - they are yet only defined by the aboriginal people themselves because there is no treaty, no constitutional Canadian presence on their lands.. Certainly, if you can ignore that Proclamation of 1763, and the first constitution, the *British North America Act,* 1867, then maybe you can start to make up imaginary constructs that don't fit the rules.

He makes it simple for us: "First, under British law, the Crown gained the ultimate title to the lands held by aboriginal peoples, as it did to all lands in newly acquired colonial territories." No citation follows this pivotal remark. We are, unfortunately, not sure *how* the crown got the title: that is the exact point at issue. If the English had their own laws that they could have title from any aboriginal people just by saying so, then that might be very nice for them but it does not actually solve the problem that they simply did not purchase those titles as they had promised the Indians they would, or otherwise respected them as they were. There is no precedent, no explanation for the assertion that Britain got title to the land just by arriving on it. The Doctrine of Discovery, on which Slattery is perhaps relying, merely provided that the first European to arrive in a given land won the priority right—against other Europeans—to buy the land or make treaties with the indigenous.[29] If they had really believed they inherited North America by landing there, the numbered Treaties, the instructions to BC Governor James Douglas to buy the Indian lands, the Royal Proclamation would all have been quite unnecessary. It is indefensible to suggest that the British believed at that time that they were the legitimate owners of the vast Indian territories.

Slattery's challenge was also to fill in the indigenous back-story to convince the reader, or scholar, of the utter incompetence of indigenous societies at law and every other cultural or political institution but war, and he does so. He takes the next step indicated by his silent partner, *Terra Nullius*: he denies that indigenous nations were human beings who had been engaged in ancient and elaborate forms of organization and that they viewed themselves, as they were viewed by their neighbours, as nations. In papers otherwise heavily burdened by footnotes, he lightly drops convenient but undocumented hypotheses thus: "The identities of the groups themselves changed, as communities dissolved or coalesced and new ones emerged." Perhaps one day a Cree scholar will sum up European history so succinctly.

The geo-political demographic of Europe is demonstrably more mobile in the last millennia than that of North America, where to this day people are named after direct ancestors who survived a flood thousands of years ago by anchoring their few chosen people to the top of the mountain the community still lives under.[30] They are named after great, great, great, great grandfathers who lived near the Black Dome mountain political mecca – one of several geographical indigenous versions of the Versailles Palace, a place for treatying; and fed it faithfully on a special diet of spiritual plants designed to maintain an atmosphere conducive to constructive political deliberation.[31] They are named after the first of their people, dropped down from heaven.[32] That kind of continuity has, for Europe, long since been eroded by the types of land wars and helpless inability to maintain identity that Slattery accuses indigenous peoples of—without so much as qualifying his remarks.

Many quasi-legal solutions are here cobbled together to try to make the contradictions into one seamless whole. Aboriginal title is "inalienable:" it can only be surrendered to the crown. Certainly this restriction precludes any normative exercise of the right of title. That is why it is necessary to invent "Aboriginal Title" as a special and as yet unfinished concept. Indian Reserve lands have been catalogued as "inalienable" – because they supposedly belong to the crown which then allocated them for the use and benefit of the Indians, but they can't be sold by them and – equally – no one else can buy them.[33] But then the matter of Indian Reserves is a Canadian invention, unlike indigenous title to lands. The crown itself, on the other hand, has alienated plenty of aboriginal title land – land which it never bought, but which it was happy to sell and tax. Britain never had any power to stop the Indians selling their land; the exercise in question was to prohibit British settlers from attempting to buy it, as it is stated in the Royal Proclamation.

Not a hint of self-consciousness slows the legal expert as he rolls out suddenly contradictory statements arising from more recent courts than those of colonial Nigeria: "Aboriginal title... gives aboriginal groups the right to the exclusive use and possession of their lands..." He is, judging by his choice of words, referring to *Delgamuukw*, 1997, but what an inexplicable remark, otherwise. What then is the meaning of case after case arising in British Columbia over this matter? Is there no Indian land question? Slattery says, "Prior to the Supreme Court's decision in *Delgamuukw*, some courts had expressed the view that an aboriginal group is permanently limited in its use of aboriginal lands to customary practices followed at a distant historical period, such as the time the Crown first acquired sovereignty." In 2010, both Canada and British Columbia maintain this criteria, in such cases as *Nuu chah nulth*. That's why the practice of denying development to indigenous peoples has earned a contemporary moniker: the frozen right.

Indigenous people would surely be surprised to hear Mr. Slattery's casual statements about how compensation must naturally be given in the event of injury or infringement of the aboriginal title. Especially when their own legal counsel apparently so often advises them that this is not a realistic goal.[34] If what he is describing really is the law of Canada, as he so diligently expounds, then British Columbians are certainly behind on the rent. The Fraser salmon fisheries have been decimated. Most of the province has been clear-cut logged. Extinction of birds, wildlife and vegetation; pollution of the environment—all these are injuries and infringements of title, and they are not the subject of compensation schemes.

Slattery insists: "...under the shelter of aboriginal title, customary land systems remained in force within aboriginal communities and governed the relations of their members among themselves." No "customary land systems" are in force in British Columbia, only *Indian Act* interpretations of them, and their original existence is denied by the courts—which have not acknowledged one square inch of aboriginal title land in the province with a declaration to that effect.

The *deus ex machina* comes finally. Aboriginal title possesses all these attributes, he says, but infringement may be made "with appropriate legislation" and compensation given. What was all that confusion about the 1898 court stating that the Indian title is dependent on the good will of the sovereign? Well naturally, Slattery is applying the Supreme Court's findings in *Sparrow*, 1990 and *Van der Peet*, 1996, and *Delgamuukw*, 1997, to justify the Privy Council court's findings in 1898. Now it is possible, in his worldview, for the judges to have said that the Indians had personal and usufructuary rights—but only because now those can be infringed with the proper legislation. And legislation, Slattery must have us believe, can be enacted to override the constitution.

The whole exercise in creating this supposedly hitherto non-existent concept of "aboriginal title" which only the imperial nations brought into being is merely a meandering way of retroactively inventing, defining and limiting that to which we will then return and seek to extinguish with the stroke of a pen, and heavily armed policemen. But we do, of course, acknowledge as supreme this construct of ours, this generous and noble designation of *aboriginal* title which we extend liberally to those who can afford a twenty year court case to prove they have had it since time immemorial. Once we define "time immemorial." And then we can feel confident that we, the newcomer, can infringe the invented title at will.

This legal argument is based on a fiction: the fictitious and now infamous assertion that indigenous peoples did not enjoy rights to the soil before a "more civilized" people named it in a "more civilized" language. These lines which Slattery has been rewarded for composing are the finer strokes on an elaborate historiomythology designed to pacify colonizers who are not sure how to explain to themselves the glaring problem that they have moved into someone else's homeland and are prospering while the original peoples are disappearing. And yet, when the odd Canadian wonderer needs to reassure himself that his polity does mean something superior, he turns to intellectuals such as this with a grateful sigh of relief. It does not seem to be an immediate worry that the most renowned legal historians in Canada are actually purveyors of self-supporting gobbledy-gook: it remains a case of the emperor's new clothes being too fine for the average person to see. But the average person sleeps easy knowing those clothes are being skillfully cut for active dress, and that if they themselves can't understand it, never will the Indians.

Inbreeding Academia

Slattery describes a foregone conclusion of unstoppable indigenous suffering and extinguishment at the hands of colonizing oppressors going forward, and every academic text pertaining to First Nations cites him as the authority on aboriginal peoples' legal reality. When the books that pre-date him are invariably re-released with a new name (for instance, *Native Peoples and Cultures of Canada* becomes *First Peoples in Canada*), they update the bibliography to include him and modernize their jargon to suit his lexicon.

Before the mid-seventies there were no references in history books to "sui generis" titles. Discussion of a "usufructuary right" had been confined to an earlier age, that of and before 1898, when such terms were required to describe the rights of serfs, including Caucasian serfs in Canada.

The twisted terminology, although it was applied to Indians, did not confer change at the ground level. In 1969, anthropologist Wilson Duff put it clearly: "Should the day come for the non-treaty Indians of British Columbia to negotiate the extinguishment of their aboriginal title, one had better expect that the bargaining will be tougher, and the price-tag will be higher."[35] He was following up a stint as an expert witness, as an anthropologist and ethnographer for the *White and Bob* and *Calder* cases.

The modern academic apologist; the blithe, bush-whacking intellectual who can differentiate between the birthright of the settler and the birthright of the indigenous person without pausing or finding contradiction; the poorly defined terms which make oxymoron teachable; the law professor who contributes half-page opinions to BC dailies on why indigenous legal rights should be the subject of political negotiations; all the tools contributing to this legal architecture are of comparatively recent origin.

A few of these academics warrant individual mention, as spectacular examples of how misrepresentation and obfuscation in the indigenous area is rewarded with academic prestige. Paul Tennant, a longtime professor of politics at UBC, now Professor Emeritus, has lent his expertise to defining indigenous nations out of all realms of privilege or preorogative. Such dismal councils as those pursuing certainty of colonial jurisdiction in BC and the Yukon have used him in expert panels to guide their progress to foregone conclusions. The Yukon Settlement Agreement and the BC Treaty Commission, both extinguishment-with-consent models that have transmogrified indigenous nations into municipalities, each have at their core the objective of coercing the aboriginal title out of the hands that hold it, and at considerably less than market value.

Tennant's great publication was sketched up on index cards as he traveled the province over two years with a handful of native guides. Those particular traveling companions, incidentally, went on in their existing trajectory to become great advocates of the BC treaty process and other wedges in the coastal/interior divide which sapped the unified movement for Indian title in BC. He says he attended "meetings and assemblies of more tribal councils, forums, and Indian organizations in the province than did any other person, Indian or non-Indian." Such an experience might have humbled him by its vast scope, but no matter for one possessed of a formidable gift for summary. As he explains in the Foreword, "The first chapter describes the Indian peoples themselves, discusses aboriginal rights and land claims, and outlines the common Indian and non-Indian perceptions of those rights and claims." The first chapter is fourteen pages long, and the book is not exactly printed on broadsheet.

In this small book, *Aboriginal Peoples and Politics: The Indian Land Question in British Columbia,* Tennant posits many tenuous and often insulting suggestions. Two of them constitute essential untruths, cornerstones of denial carried forward by subsequent professors. "The system of Indian schooling had profoundly important consequences for pan-Indianism and Indian political organization in British Columbia. ... they could not have formed and maintained organizations had they not had the lingua franca that English provided, had they not been able to read and write, and had they not had networks of personal contacts composed of former schoolmates."[36] He is talking of course about the introduction of Indian Residential Schools among nations who used trade routes over a thousand kilometers long, at least when measured outward from five intersecting centers in the interior; nations who held meetings among themselves in eights and nines to "mark how we are joined" at such places as Black Dome mountain and spanning a geography equivalent to one that would encompass Germany, Norway and Ukraine.[37] He is referring here to interior nations like the Okanagan and Secwepemc, who sent away to Hopi land, almost a thousand miles to the south, to bring back a famous peace maker in their time of exhaustion by war.

As well as these examples, there is much more evidence which contradicts the assertion that Indian Residential School increased communications. One hundred and nine leaders met in 1874 and produced a joint statement on their dismissal of the government's Reserve scheme. They represented at least nine languages, and the agreed statement was translated into English. By at least 1880, copies of the Royal Proclamation of 1763 were posted in the Nass Valley. People of the 19th century traveled for days and weeks to meet each other and strategize in the many languages that leaders spoke in those days. They each spoke several languages because they had essential political and economic business with the other nations. The Memorial to Wilfred Laurier, 1910; the Memorial to Frank Oliver, 1911; the Petition of the Cowichan Tribe, 1906: these all preceded the spread of residential schools and enforced attendance, and they all quickly became known by the geographically extensive participants of an existing "pan-Indianism" which did not rely on English.

The Professor Emeritus, at the time of writing, troubled himself with the naming of the indigenous polities. This after apparently rejecting that the Indians "themselves refer to the groups as 'tribes,' 'peoples,' 'nations,' or 'tribal groups,'... 'Nation,' which was commonly used in the last century by colonial officials, missionaries, and other white observers, does remain suitable... 'Tribal group' is perhaps the best..." The Professor will not identify the subtle interactions between these levels of political infrastructure, while getting on with the task of "the description of the indigenous peoples themselves." However, he permits himself the use of fifteen other terms for "Tribal group"—none of them defined—in the ensuing five paragraphs. He then relies on Indian and Northern Affairs Canada—perhaps the colonial group with the most interest in obscuring those identities—for the proper names of these Tribal groups.

Then he tackled the problem of naming the newcomers. White? Non-native? Writing some twenty years after the first English publication of *The Colonizer and the Colonized,* by Albert Memmi in Algeria, for all of his biographic experience studying political science in the United States he did not have the benefit of the much more straightforward and accurate classifications already existing among other such colonized nations as the ones about whom he chose to write. "To agree on a convenient terminology, let us first distinguish between the colonial, the colonizer and the colonialist," wrote Albert Memmi, in French, in 1957 Tunisia.

There are many other insincerities, some accessible only to those who know the territory. Tennant notes a wonderful and profound frame of reference for the coastal societies: that they are what they are because of the cedar tree, and that their culture is even synonymous with it. This statement should be referenced, because it is certainly not an original observation. The connective tissue between the coastal identity and the cedar is ancient, sacred and revealing of the worldview of these people. Instead of honouring his coastal guides into this territory, Bill Wilson, George Watts, and Joe Matthias, who either pointed out this marvelous and sustaining imagery or led him to the person who did, he omits their mention. This is a typical form of colonial scholarship, the kind that recounts Simon Fraser's "explorations" of the interior without mentioning the fact that Fraser and his men were all but packed from Fort St. James through the Fraser canyon to the Pacific Ocean by Indians.

Professor Hamar Foster of the University of Victoria is a lecturer on legal history with the extra qualification of having studied in South Africa. He is a Crown prosecutor as of 2010, since earning a law degree forty years earlier.[38] He also claims residential schools precipitated the legal developments of the second and third decades of the 20th century, and then goes on to contradict himself by situating his key events at times when very few Indians in BC were attending those schools—certainly long before 1920 when it became mandatory. The leaders, usually aged north of 40 when engaged in the legal battles he describes, surely did not have the "benefit" of attending one. Foster's scholarly article "We Are Not O'Meara's Children," was published in 2003 but did not make use of 20/20 hindsight.

Even when tackling such obviously native subjects as the petitions for declaration of Indian title in the early 1900s, Foster can discuss the legal dilemma without a single emotional line. He turns the titular focus of "We" in "We are not O'Meara's Children," to O'Meare himself and begins a sensitive vindication of the white lawyer—retreating immediately from the subjects in his chosen title. The story is actually of poor Edward O'Meare, a lawyer ostracized by his colleagues at law for venturing to find the legal keyhole in which to insert the facts of Indian title and undo the state attitude of denial towards it. The actual legal problems of the province of BC, regarding their failure to gain jurisdiction in indigenous homelands, which O'Meare spent a career trying to point out, are not scrutinized in Foster's writing: just the early lawyer's *approach*. Neither does Foster expand on the implied point in his paper's title about indigenous resistance to colonization being informed by missionaries rather than their own intelligence. This idea, that missionaries originally advised the indigenous that they had rights and should defend them, and that the indigenous would not have realized it otherwise, is a point of adoration among such professors. Even native students seem eager to latch onto it recently.

It is in this paper that the pitiful remark at the start of this chapter can be found. Isn't it marvelous how the author can fix his attention to the career and thinking of a white lawyer, and make the clinging, falling destitute indigenous peoples merely the backdrop?

Foster published *Letting go of the Bone: The Idea of Indian Title in British Columbia, 1849 -1927,* in a collection of essays about law for Osgoode Hall[39] – the fifth in their "magnificent" catalogue of development in Canadian law, particular to BC and the Yukon. The first section is called, "Claims more or less fictitious." Foster starts with this offensive quotation, just as part of the title is a quotation, and then builds an argument to support it, picking his way around and through a historical period which is well recorded to be very dangerous to the conclusion he will arrive at. He gets there simply by refusing to reference the indigenous evidence, the indigenous side of the laws and compacts that were being made. After all, that side was not written into the "law."

"…the question of whether the rule of law protects the colonized or facilitates their oppression, legitimizing what would otherwise be naked usurpation, has long been a matter of debate." Does the rule of law provide for naked usurpation? Isn't that actually against the law? The professors are cherished for their ability to bend it back and forth until the exact point of discussion, which has launched such philosophical debate, has been avoided: and enter the logic of convenience.

This article delves into questions as to why or why not treaties were made in British Columbia at the beginning of the creation of the colony; whether Governor James Douglas knew that the form he got from New Zealand to make his agreements official was affirming native title to all the lands—contrary to his own ideas about the fourteen treaties he was making on Vancouver's Island—and whether Douglas or his contemporaries actually knew anything at all about what Indian title law was, and had the law regarding Indian title accidentally dropped from the pigeon's mouth between Britain and BC, and thereby become null and void?

Foster investigates law as if it were a children's game: somebody is "it" and they make the rules, and whatever they say is good information. "It" in this game seems to be the statute books themselves, the physical paper and ink, but then "it" sometimes morphs into the players, like Governors or Colonial Secretaries or even BC Reserve Commissioners. Then there are people who are "not it"—that's the Indians, and if they viewed the giving of HBC blankets as an acceptable price for the white men to buy their way into the territory, and they would then take the relationship from there and see how things worked out, then this and all the "not it" contributions are completely irrelevant. When "it" decrees that the Hudson's Bay Company lease on Vancouver's Island has expired and title "reverted" to the crown of England, then that is a fact because "it" said so—regardless of the fact that the crown had never ever gotten title to it before. When a fourteenth treaty between Douglas and the indigenous of southern Vancouver Island is discovered to be incomplete, in that the paper form only says, "this treaty is just like the other ones," and then has Xs on it, Foster feels that this has nullified the compact because the paper document does not conform to the letter of "it's" usual code. Foster imitates the Canadian politicians of the ages, who simply dismiss whatever "not it" says and sing the song "I can't hear you" increasingly loudly. Is this really the vision of western society's legal tradition?"

He has been quite prolific, writing essays about indigenous peoples. Many of those papers offer very interesting information, Foster is a legal historian, but they are written with arrogance and disdain for the indigenous, and to the exclusion of the concept that indigenous nations are quite capable of thinking things through together, deciding what to do and managing the realization of their goals for themselves. The "idea" of Indian Title in BC? Is it just a dog's idea? Should he let it go to his master, like a good boy? He makes use of the fragment about letting go of a bone, part of a conversation between Peter Kelly and a member of the Joint Committee appointed to reject the assertions of indigenous title, and attaches it directly to Indian title in a way that approves of and promotes the slander.

Foster provided expert testimony at the *Tsilhqot'in* trial, and wrote a paper about his experience: *One Good Thing: Law, Elevator Etiquette and Aboriginal Rights Litigation in Canada.* His inability to refrain from insulting the people around whose rights he has spun a career is profound. This title, along with all Foster's papers, are removed from the accessible forums where his academic colleagues post their writing.

The Grand Experiment[40] is what Canadian and other colonial writers are able to call the human tragedies that are, and were meant to be, the result of imperialism—and are still ongoing. Foster is one of these writers and one of three editors of the so-named tome of collected neo-colonial reflection. The simple fact is that places were re-named "New France," and "New England" and "New Caledonia" and "New Zealand" because they were intended as colonial feed lots for the "old" France, Caledonia, etc. *The Experiment* authors, however, muse over judges' interpretations of the Waitangi Treaty in New Zealand, at least the one written by the British—not the one written immediately before by the tribal leaders and their independent sea-faring business partners—but never allow their considerations to feel the harsh, rancid light of the present day continuation of those approaches to conquer. This is history of which they are writing: history which is over, and merely a curiosity for the elite to interpret. Academics specializing in indigenous histories appear to be licensed to print death certificates for indigenous peoples.

A complementary and illustrative instance of publishing new type cleaner than the old is the UBC Press publication in the same year as *Experiment*, 2008: *Makúk: A New History of Aboriginal-White Relations*. Here, the story is about BC and exchange, *makúk,* between very different peoples in times of their first contact and how what is given is not necessarily what was received: a truly quaint approach to aggressive colonization.

The author, John Lutz of University of Victoria tenure, begins his story by declaring that the first European to set foot on "what is now BC" was Captain Cook. What of Perez and his visit two years before that? Why then the Nootka crisis between Spain and Britain? What of the Oregon Territory? What of the Russian fort mid-way down the California coast that dates to the eighteenth century?[41] These tendencies to oversimplify, or better ignore, the difficult and complicated existing relationships of the non-native developers of this modern province, who were intimately bound up back home in controversy over its ownership, serve to sever this place from the world.

The "clean and simple" approach denies debate or inquiry, and leaves more than a few things out. If both Cook and Perez noted signs of smallpox among the people of the northwest coast, which Lutz ignores, how did it get there?[42] If a decaying, ax-hewn cedar fort was found in Keremeos in 1863, where no HBC or North West Company traders had built before, and Spanish tools and armour—as well as the story of their coming, generations ago—were found among the local people, what then?[43] If settlers on Vancouver Island used "bits"—an eighth piece of a Spanish coin worth 12.5 cents (and we still use the term "two bits" to refer to a quarter)—until the 20th century,[44] how and why did they do so?

Lutz's research is largely concerned with suggesting explanations for features of colonial lore which are fabrications in the first place. One of these features is the reputation Indians have, among non-natives, of being 'lazy at the workplace.' Lutz explains this (manufactured) laziness is because of their socially egalitarian indigenous roots. He does not question whether or not they were lazy.

In actuality, the indigenous peoples' "anti-capitalist" societies featured work habits that outstripped those of Lutz's supposedly exasperated Protestant whip crackers. That's why the Indians were the fur trappers, the pilots for the 'explorer' canoes, the packers for the gold miners (of course, natives could rarely get mining licenses or claims), the fishermen and processors for the canneries, the farm labourers and cowboys at the gold rush roadhouses and ranches of "free land" that starving Europeans came and took, the ferrymen for settlers up Vancouver Island. Because of their energetic and skilful work, indigenous societies existed for thousands of years without iron, feudal landlords or a back-breaking religious imperative. They were not lazy.

What seems to have happened in the construction of this essential "lazy" myth, where the academics are positing explanations for how non-native workers and industrialists were more successful than native entrepreneurs, is that our historians have neglected to note that indigenous men and women did not set up competition to the whites' capitalist concerns because *they were not allowed to do so.* Indians could not even own property – they would have to be enfranchised for that, in which case they would no longer be Indians. Often the result of overlooking the most basic elements of colonizing history produces truly elaborate, and inaccurate, explanations for things.

There are 19 images of whites in this book, and 95 illustrations (photos) of Indians. But with each white picture, all male except one, there is accompanying it the name of the person and a quotation of what they say or think or did. With the native pictures, there are few quotes, unless they are by a white guy, and mostly the images are just generic work pictures, or soldiers posing but not named. Mute. Lutz states: "I try to engage in dialogue with aboriginal people;" "I... include and compare aboriginal views of the colonial process." To the contrary, all referenced quotes are from whites; all the views and tractable thoughts are white. The Indians are simply in the pictures by chapter 3, where these lines are taken from.

The absurdity and inadequacy of purporting to remark on "Aboriginal-White Relations" in a province occupying 26 separate languages and some 30 nations, not to mention newcomers from all over the world, should be immediately obvious, but it is accentuated wonderfully by the two full chapters which investigate the specific circumstances, at least as regards post-contact work for pay, of two of those nations. It's fair to suggest that there might well have been 28 more chapters in the book to consider colonial relations with the rest of the indigenous nations. And perhaps another two chapters to describe "Aboriginal-Chinese relations," and one for "Aboriginal-Indian relations," both of which colonizing nationalities make up a chunk of history that has been at least as well vanished by the successful, or claiming, white colonizers as that of their native co-exiles.

Not only do generalizations and historical vagrancy suffice for BC's intellectual elite; generalizations and random selection are required. British Columbia's situation is much more complicated than the professional students care to admit. They are not interested in that kind of homework – they need to demarcate an over-simple field of study. Relationships between the many

Chinese immigrants and the native communities, where they tended to live much more closely than whites did, are, incidentally, quite productive and mutual in many memories. Considering that Chinese immigrants outnumbered whites at several times in the early history, it is difficult to accept their exclusion from this account of *Makúk.*

A couple of further examples from the Lutz variety of over-simplifying the problematizing will suffice. Consider the whaling nations whose prime economic offer was train oil (whale oil), and those whose was eulachon oil—what did they do when the Grease Trail, their market place, was overrun? That trade route had run thousands of kilometers in many directions and seen goods moved from the Great Plains to the coast and back again;[45] it was interrupted by Hudson's Bay Company forts who intercepted the cargo and seconded the carriers to their own purposes. What of the crude oil wells in the north east, where sour wells now exude their reek across a pock marked and utterly polluted land that can barely support caribou anymore? 'What kind of an exchange was that?' courts have been asked during the struggle for a part of oil revenues for the signators to Treaty 8, two dozen First Nations covering a land mass of hundreds of thousands of square kilometres, large as France, and including northern Alberta, northeastern British Columbia, northwestern Saskatchewan and a southernmost portion of the Northwest Territories. Interactions between the colonizer and the different nations were necessarily unique, and ignoring that diversity is unhelpful. Today massive modern rifts exist between the interior and coastal nations, some of them are direct results of differences in policies foisted on them.

Our guide to a new history operates in oxymorons such as "peaceable subordination," as he termed the removal of access to fisheries from Indian rights—a feat that was actually accomplished by armed police, who seized the property and fish of the indigenous fishermen and jailed many. He concludes his tale with a chapter titled: "Subordination without Subjugation."

In pursuing the thematic notion that what was offered in trade is not necessarily what was received, there is, however, the unfortunate neglect of many meaningful instances of giving and receiving exactly the same thing, understood equally well by both parties. Newcomers gave natives smallpox and sent them away from the only center with a doctor, Victoria, under armed transport and with the extra encouragement of bombing and burning their settlements around the fort town. The "crop of ruin," as De Cosmos accurately predicted the smallpox of 1862 would sow, was most certainly received as delivered.[46] If the whites hadn't meant to give it that way, they could have taken it back, i.e., vaccinated and quarantined the affected individuals just as they did to their own kind. Whites gave natives Reserves: menial parcels of hopelessly inadequate size and productivity—this was received with full appreciation of the meanness. Whites gave the original societies and their citizens devastating restrictions on their activities, double fines and jail time: all accepted with due heartbreak and resulting incapacity. The women along the gold rush trails received venereal disease and the resulting barren generation slowed population growth for two decades.[47] Can one, by excluding these articles of Makúk, arrive at the otherwise impossible conclusion of "peaceable subordination"?

Surprisingly, we eventually realize that this book is about how Indians contributed to growing the BC economy. We then begin to suspect the author's underlying motive, which is to assimilate indigenous labour history into the larger morass of "development" in the province. This successfully places citizens of independent indigenous nations as intentional co-founders, co-conspirators in the advent of BC – not members of distinct nations for the viability of which they applied the cash benefit of their labouring successes. Another academic coup.

"Integrating aboriginal voices with non-aboriginal voices turns history into dialogue… that can help rematerialize Aboriginal Peoples who have been disappeared from our history." Indicating the underlying premise, that this is British Columbia and it belongs to the public, 97% of which are non-native, this statement betrays the author's stated equivocal or altruistic purposes. Who is doing the integrating? Who is the "us" of "our history," and since when has that "our history" included aboriginal people? The elite, authoritative voices which are published to speak of BC history do not belong to the indigenous. Maybe this unilateral integration seeks to make it look like the indigenous no longer have a future history of their own as peoples. They are still not peoples here, in this book, but ethnic minorities in a colonial enterprise.

The individuals who wrote the back-cover recommendations for *Makúk* were also referenced and quoted severally in the book, and are also associated with UBC. Is publication of this sort of thing less a testament to its relevance and more the fulfillment of an unwritten promise to people who attain tenure as BC professors of history? Or just evidence of the attempt by BC presses to overwhelm any student of the indigenous in BC by contradictory and incorrect printed quantity? Or is it less – just a surrender to the academic norm of publish or perish, with the UBC Press surrendering to the need for venue. This publication points to a complete lack of tension in the study area: to the absence of oversight and ready criticism, and, ultimately, to the complete exclusion of importance in this field. Colonial scholars of indigenous peoples' worlds can get away with saying whatever they want, because no one among their readership cares whether a citation is worth its ink, as long as they pass the class. If someone does care, it is probably because they have an interest in the certain decomposition and appropriation of indigenous history. The native peoples who do care do not have such a well-subsidized voice, nor the ear of media.

It is insincere for these interpreters of history to first presume the existing perspective in the field—that of their society—is right and superior, and then create the appearance of investigating the claims and condition of the other. Anyone who comes to an inter-cultural conversation with books like this in their back pocket is in for a bit of a surprise. Graduates from First Nations Studies programs in BC universities cannot be equipped to improve on the situation if this is what they are relying on for information.

Canadian university presses publish books rife with error. The unmistakable appearance is that "First Nations Studies" is merely one of the luxuries a majority democracy affords its more creative subjects. Anything can be printed, even this:

> As a result, they were either exterminated in genocidal wars, or forcibly relocated to unproductive reserves when the fur trade declined. Native people were *repressed* by indifference to their uneven development and lack of respect for their humanity, not for their labour power. And although raw materials were extracted from areas inhabited by aboriginal peoples, their Neolithic technology had made them previously unable to turn these resources into commodities. Therefore, unlike blacks, nothing of value was taken from them. [emphasis in the original]
>
> Lacking the power that comes from being needed for labour, aboriginals have had to rely on the formulation of legal arguments by the Aboriginal Industry.[48]

In this marvelously whimsical and wholly inappropriate use of *Class Counts* by American Erik Olin Wright, new authors Frances Widdowson and John Howard reveal their shameful ignorance of BC history while going about making pronouncements on it and drawing conclusions from whatever mismatched shreds of historical anecdote they may have bumped into. In *Disrobing the Aboriginal Industry*, an unfortunate title, we have a naked assassination attempt.

It was not until fifty years after its founding that the BC colony had enough manpower to begin to build its own labour force, and given that indigenous Elders today come entirely from families who were maintained by men working in forestry and building hydroelectric facilities and women working as cooks, cleaners and farm labour, the colonials obviously didn't have enough of it to exclude indigenous workers until very recently indeed. Frances Widdowson is coordinator of Political Science, Policy Studies, at Mount Royal University. Her book *Disrobing* was shortlisted for the Donner Prize – the award for the best public policy book by a Canadian.

While such astonishing statements as the above quote from Widdowson's own fiction are now emerging as popular modern "thinking" about BC or Canadian history and its relevance to today's conditions, the public, to whom tidbits are broadcast for their very sensationalism, is helpless to think critically about them. The average high school graduates have nothing in their armory of social studies from required schooling that would allow them to reflect critically on such content. The broadcasters and journalists of the media do not challenge the most recent authors on the pivotal points of their scholarship. Or perhaps they also cannot, having no more special expertise in the subject than the average high school graduate.

As further publications show, indifference to indigenous peoples is clearly succeeding in producing a settler culture which is simply oblivious to the historical and present realities of the place they inhabit. An excerpt from a 2002 BC publication reads, "Pictographs in the Stein Valley bear witness to a native presence predating the appearance of Europeans by hundreds of years."[49] In a 1999 book: "… Indigenous people arrived in this harsh and lovely land some 2,000 years before the Europeans."[50] Both of these assessments are inaccurate by yawning gulfs – the first by orders of magnitude, the second by perhaps ten times.

The Academic Oath

> *"… that organized amnesia which so often obscured discreditable episodes in Britain's imperial history."*
> **Piers Brendon,**
> **The Decline and Fall of the British Empire**[51]

> *"Colonialism is never satisfied with having the native in its grip but, by some strange logic, it must turn to his past and disfigure and distort it."*
> **Steven Biko, South Africa**

Successful BC academics shroud, cloak and otherwise conceal a specific list of inconvenient truths. The published authors are nearly unanimous in their presentation of Indian Residential Schools as mostly beneficial and without alternative. They say that aboriginal title lands just haven't been found yet. According to the majority of scholars, native nations were scattered, sparsely populated and "subsistence" cultures. British Columbians are made to believe that these nations existed almost by accident: there is little reference to the radical differences in language, culture and spiritual practice, and the complex trading and international relationships resulting. Above all, whatever the indigenous may have been, their reality is in the past.

If, as Slattery and his contemporaries are known to suggest, "we know that aboriginal title exists, we just don't know where it is," then we are also clearly not very interested in finding out. The oath that no one knows where aboriginal title lands are is merely a clever play on a transitional legal moment where the Supreme Court of Canada has never reasoned for a map with a shaded area marked "aboriginal title" in the legend. Of course we know where aboriginal title lands are: everywhere. What would be more difficult to find are lands which no indigenous nation has ever used, fought for, or claimed.

If the non-native British Columbian can really only study records produced by non-native British Columbians and early colonials – as opposed to the readily available histories which each indigenous nation possesses for themselves, that is still no excuse. Historians and ethnographers of early colonial times recorded extensive essential points which provide cast iron proof of title, borders and occupation. These records have been buried under new titles which ignore them while the original written sources are left in archives and treated as if they are invisible.

James Teit worked for the Ministry of Mining, Anthropology Division, for twenty years just at and after the turn of the 20th Century. Teit produced reams of detailed, sensitive and accurate information about tribal boundaries, languages, comparative charts of similar dialects; he photographed extensively, sketched and pondered, spoke several Salishan dialects, bought countless objects from collectors, and named, dated and mapped them. He mapped trade routes and interviewed for creation stories and ceremonial rituals. These lie dormant in the form of microfilm in the BC archives, with none of the politically relevant material ever having been published – perhaps with the exceptions of the meeting minutes and native Declarations of Title which he helped to translate. James Teit is possibly the most significant source of native and non-native recorded history in British Columbia, certainly one of three, and his name is entirely unknown to any graduate of BC public schools. The non-native society is not looking for documentation which meets its rather exclusive and bizarre standards, it is looking to *not find it.*

The unwritten oath, apparently requisite upon entering the colonizers' institutions for the purpose of studying the indigenous condition, is of allegiance to the insulating fabric of fraternity, impunity, and most importantly the discourse must pledge itself to irrelevance. Residential schools were necessary because there the native children learned to read and write English. Most leading First Nations Studies professors in British Columbia have published books that say so.[52] Unfortunately for this position, the world is peopled with many multi-lingual folk, most of whom never went to a residential school, and very few of whom are residential school survivors. These successful masters of two or more languages share a conspicuous trait, which is that they first mastered their own language very well, or even two simultaneously. With that basis, that solid world view, they were then able to proceed to learn other languages by drawing them in to their existing first vocabulary and translating. Instead of the alleged great and pivotal residential school success in this area, we find averages of 80% illiteracy in English among the graduates. And since having had their first language beaten out of them with the fist, the branding iron, or the needle under the tongue, they don't speak that very well either.[53] Most indigenous people over the age of 40 in BC are residential school survivors.

Those academics who uniformly approve of the Indian Residential School program demonstrate a curious lack of inquiry into or mention of the best authorities on the reasons for the legally required attendance at these schools at the time: "Kill the Indian in the child," as D.C. Scott, Superintendent of Indian Affairs, explained in Ottawa. For an academic writing in the modern day to state the virtues of the residential school as exceeding the rampant forms of violence is unsupportable. Widdowsen and Howard refer to "incidental sexual abuse" in the schools, and wonder, "what would have happened if they didn't learn English?" That kind of abuse was not incidental, but rather estimated by former students using personal knowledge at an incidence affecting 80% of the students.[54]

The essential oath of irrelevance is repeated at the conclusion of any of the willfully blind forays into impressionist historical sculpture—whatever may have happened in the past, we have dealt with that. The professors conclude by saying something like, "...but all that was before aboriginal title was recognized...." Then they say something like, "...and now that is all being fixed by the BC Treaty Commission and such-and-such good faith sharing arrangements." At least Foster, Lutz, Tennant, Cole Harris, Douglas Harris, Arthur J. Ray, in fact most university-published authors writing about the BC land question, have those lines in the last paragraph or two of their publications. Foster, a legal historian, spoke in support of the political negotiations at a conference hosted by the BC Treaty Commission.[55]

Successful academics must study indigenous British Columbia as if it had been peopled by one homogenous human mass. They write long treatises on the province that feature the spatter gore of colonial lore from 30 individual nations as if racial, linguistic and land borders were indistinguishable; as if the colonial border of British Columbia was an irresistible historical eventuality waiting to happen, and that no future with any other shape than that of British Columbia today is or was thinkable. What they can't do is connect the names of the nations which they carefully learn, and the names of the people they meet there, to the present day. What they won't do is treat the subject as if it has a future—at least not one outside the BC treaty process! What they also will not do is academically treat the individual and unique history of just one of those nations: this would run cross-current to the essential premise that those nations are defunct or never existed, or were such "transients," "nomads" and "fugitives" that nationhood is a recent "fiction," and the same of the people – they don't exist anymore. Their studies are what "a brief history of Europe" would be like if Napoleon had actually succeeded in uniting Eurasia, with the former tribes and nations featured as bug splat on the windshield of superior progress—their languages unrecognizable, their peoples scattered.

The myth that smallpox decreased the indigenous populations across BC by one third in 1862 is a standard which is not even investigated, but apparently accepted as "established" history and repeated without reference, unless to the "established" historians. The indigenous account is quite different: "Possibly 90% of the population was wiped out by smallpox in 1862 and 1863," wrote Joanne Drake-Terry, a historian who married in to the Lillooet community and wrote *The Same As Yesterday* in consultation with Elders and with materials from the BC archives. The researching author, Mel Rothenburger, found testimonial from Francis Poole, an English mining company employee in 1862, who had apparently been on the mission to find minerals which introduced smallpox to Bella Coola. On Poole's return a year later the population of those villages had dropped from 4,000 to a few dozen.[56] Many other testimonies accord with these.[57]

It could be that the white settlers made considerable use of the terror which the threat of this disease instilled in the indigenous. There are few accounts committed to writing, and fewer still have been published, but one elder recalled to ethnographers how "The Indian people were hungry," and so his grandfather got a job washing dishes at a hotel. He accepted as compensation scraps of food and the dregs in the dishwater – and pieces of camphor with instructions to use it in the prevention of smallpox, and it may have worked because his family did not get the disease.[58]

British Columbians believe that indigenous nations were always sparsely populated. That's because their historians have buried the evidence to the contrary. In 1997, professor of geography Cole Harris published what he noted was a little known fact: that there had already been a smallpox epidemic among the north west coast indigenous before Captain James Cook and Captain Juan Perez arrived. This pivotal observation was not the subject of any further scrutiny, just a line or two about how the sailors remarked on telltale scars they noticed and also how unlikely they thought the small populations, considering the richness of the lands and waters.[59] Realizing that the coastal peoples were already substantially diminished by disease by 1778, the decline yet to come can be put in a larger context. Writing in 1923, the historian Diamond Jenness assessed all the population numbers of the different nations in BC at the time. He said of the Nootka, "Their present population is 1,500, as compared with perhaps 6,000 at the end of the eighteenth century."[60] Jenness relies on Cook for the earlier number and, as we finally realize, the number of Nootka or Nuu-chah-nulth people was then at a low that had probably not been seen for centuries at least.

It is an essential academic pillar that the indigenous peoples were always poor and few. The flaw in that particular assertion is so glaring that the idea can only have been constructed deliberately to conceal a greater truth.

The idea that the Nuu-chah-nulth nation, or any other, developed over the millennia at an average number of 6,000 souls at any one time is preposterous.

The anthropological approach to First Nations Studies, to treat people from a chosen culture as raw material, demands that there is no value to original indigenous material until a western perspective or interpretation is added, and the importance of that material is assigned in terms of its value to western society. The soliciting, recording and publishing of what cannot be but sensitive intellectual property, like the histories of Clans and Houses and the details of potlatches and participants,[61] discounts and attempts to replace indigenous peoples' oral histories, as if they were not in fact histories, as if the peoples had been incapable of reflecting on themselves and were therefore fit to occupy the position of a subject race. An example from another discipline is *The Autobiography of James Sewid*—actually a collection of journals written by the Kwagiulth Chief at the request of researchers from the University of Washington's psychiatric and anthropology departments. He was singled out by UBC in 1955 as an entrepreneur and invited to the research because of his exceptional demonstrations of adjusting to "culture conflict." The Hereditary Chief provided them with "an autobiography of a non-Western individual who had successfully adapted to culture conflict and to investigate the complex relationship between rapid culture change and such an individual."[62]

If the "groups" of people who make such interesting raw study material were not organized societies, if they did not have territorial possessions and the intent to defend them, if they did not govern themselves in a clearly recognizable fashion, the likes of which John Jewitt learned quickly and documented sensationally,[63] it would not have been necessary or indeed possible to outlaw those capabilities by outlawing meetings or governing structures such as the potlatch. It would not have been necessary to break up the larger system of communal ownership by introducing the location ticket system, also called Certificates of Possession, which divided up Reserves to private individuals. It would not have been necessary to insist that the hereditary chiefs and family head leaders should be retired in favour of elected Chiefs and Councils, which were legally required by 1925 though the Superintendent General of Indian Affairs had gained the power to impose them back in 1880 in an amendment to the *Indian Act* required in eastern Canada. It would not have been necessary to outlaw gatherings for political purposes of pursuing the land question or raising funds to hire lawyers to do the same, activities that were criminalized in 1927 by another amendment to the *Indian Act*. If indigenous nations did not have such a fortified sense of their individual identities and homelands, it would not have been necessary for priests and nuns to try to erase those in Indian Residential Schools. There would have been no work for those ethnographers of the late 19th and earliest 20th centuries who are rarely cited meaningfully by the academics.

But they do and did have all these things, and the earliest white documentation of the colonial experience here illuminates those essential aspects of nationalism. There is ample evidence in the journals of Judge Matthew Baillie Begbie and HBC Governor James Douglas; in the correspondence and diaries of the countless missionaries, including A.G. Morice and Peter Kelly; and in the records of explorers like Captains Cook and Perez, David Thompson and Simon Fraser, and from BC Land Surveyors, notably G.M. Sproat.

Outside of the heavily armoured academic realm, it is easy to find references to the intricate nature of indigenous society, law and economies in books written by more local and less cultivated historians. *The Fort Langley Journals 1827-30*, by Moragh Maclachlan; *Women of British Columbia*, by Jan Gould; *Tales of Conflict*, by B.A. McKelvie; *Wisdom of the Elders: Native Traditions on the Northwest Coast*, by Ruth Kirk. Countless BC books detail complex and ancient cultures, often incidentally, but somehow those records – produced straight from the sources—are overlooked by academics who must surround history with mystery if they are to retain their elite, expert, and billable status.

There are even books, few and far between, by social justice groups which make an attempt on the broad side of the academic stable, like *Nation to Nation*, published by Citizens for Public Justice. And studies from other countries, like *The Real Poverty Report*, by Ian Adams: "Canada's natives, for example, are much more vulnerable to disease and early death than other Canadians." "... almost all Indians, Eskimos and Métis spend their lives in a world of complete degradation."[64] Adams was published in the USA. The Anglican Book Center produced *This Land Is Not For Sale, Canada's Original People and Their Land: A Saga of Neglect, Exploitation and Conflict* in 1975.[65] These books are not referenced by the mainstream historians.

Mainstream discussion of indigenous peoples is housed in places with very low ceilings. One must actually stoop to enter them.

This painfully protracted discussion of the prevailing methods of teaching indifference to the Indian land question is nevertheless timely and necessary. British Columbians could become aware of and take action against the calm, quiet, paper executions of whole societies which is going on in their names and with the support of their tax dollars. It is, arguably, not the informed consensus of the settler people to carry out this genocide. It is certainly not legal, no matter the construction of this crude, uneven and largely hypothetical rail line through the last 25 decades. The final station at the end of this historical timeline is being built, it is being christened Fort Blissful Ignorance, it will not feature a departing schedule, and the flowery, attractive name will eventually be a stark reminder that people were hoaxed. They just won't know what happened.

Chapter 5

ON RESERVE

"Many of us were driven off our places where we had lived and camped from time immemorial, even places we cultivated, and where we raised food, because these spots were desirable for agriculture, and the Government wanted them for white settlers. This was done without agreement with us, and we received no compensation. It was also in direct opposition to the promises made to us by the first whites, and Government officials, that no white men would be allowed to locate on any place where Indians were settled or which were camping stations and gardens. Thus were we robbed by the Government and driven off many of our places by white settlers (backed by the Government), or coaxed off them with false promises."

—Memorial to Frank Oliver, Minister of the Interior and Superintendent of Indian Affairs, May 10, 1911. The affidavit was signed by some 80 representatives of Carrier, Talhltan, Lillooet, Secwepemc, Nlakapamux, Okanagan, Tsilhqo'tin and Sekani.

Today, Indian Bands are known, if at all, as First Nations. Largely because of the indifference to their situation one way or another, most British Columbians are still completely inarticulate on the subject of why there are Indian Reserves in the first place, or why the name change. They are most certainly unaware of how Reserves came to be located where they are, or why indigenous nations continue to insist that when they talk about their title they are referring to the whole territory of their nation, not the places that were demarcated for them arbitrarily. If today's Reserves are unknown, awareness of the traditional territories borders on the esoteric.

Reserve sites were usually somewhat near settler towns and roadhouses, or as close to them as the whites who came and took over those settlement-ready sites would allow them to remain. But British Columbians are similarly unfamiliar with the miners and homesteading characters so many of the communities are named after, at least in the interior: Yale, Boothroyd, Lytton, Anderson Lake, Pemberton, "Oregon Jack," Williams Lake, Port Douglas. Contrary to the mysterious nature of early BC labour history as it is proposed by the circus variety acts of the historical illusionists, there are ample local records of the cheap native labour which financed the successful operation of those early road houses and their gardens and livestock between Langley and the Cariboo gold fields.[1] Villages had been made at those sites for good reasons, and indigenous people continued to live there, if a little to the left, for those same reasons, especially fishing.

The Bulkley Valley became the site of a scramble for the goldfields in the Cariboo rush; the arable lands of the Kootenays, Fraser Valley, and Okanagan were soon re-populated, and coastal estuaries that had been home to as many as thirty different villages sites, in the case of Bella Coola, were also preferred by the colonists and promptly taken over. The fields and shores of the "Pemberton Band," the Kitsilano, Skohomish, Neskonlith, Saanich, Lillooet, Musqueam, Katzie, Comox, Nadleh Whuten, Kwikwitlem, Penticton, Cowichan, and so many others were taken out from under those people, or rather they were pushed from the ideal locations in any manner that was expedient. Menial cash settlements, interference in Band elections to reinstate a cooperator who had been ousted since accepting a 90% reduction in Reserve size,[2] and aggressive re-settlement with World War I veterans all assisted with the removal of ancient communities, backed of course by the BC Provincial Police, established in 1858.[3] Every city in British Columbia today is built on a much older city.

How Reserves Came to Be

When "Vancouver's Island" was made a colony in 1849, mainly to further discourage American notions of pushing north, the Colonial Secretary in England sent instructions to Governor Douglas to make as many treaties as possible. He did, but the result was poor. The few acres here and there that he treated for, with blankets and HBC credits given in exchange, were very soon in the way of the settlers' expansive appetites and in many cases the treated lands were simply absorbed back under settler fences and structures, or larger provincial corridors like the H&G Rail. It wasn't until exactly 110 years after those exchanges, in 1964, that they were recognized as treaties in the Supreme Court of Canada, in *Bob and White*, along with the accompanying rights "guaranteed" by Douglas—rights hopelessly impossible to exercise given the extermination of most forms of life that would have made those provisions meaningful. At the time, Douglas did not stand up for the treaties he made when the indigenous parties to them were denied their part of the bargains – there is a single letter on record where Douglas clarified his intentions to respect the demarcated treaty areas and protect the rights enumerated in the agreements. Those treaties were sealed with a transfer of pocket change and credits at HBC stores.

Further up the coast and sometime later, the Fort Rupert Factor's daughter, half Haida, helped collect Xs in relation to the sacred Kwakiutl site of Tsaxis, a place where survivors of the Great Flood first emerged again. The HBC had not failed to spot the ideal location and built on it, calling it Fort Rupert. The daughter in question went door-to-door among the villagers with blankets, shirts and trade items, saying that the Chief of white men was "potlatching." People made an "X" to show they had been the recipient of a blanket. Governor Douglas then claimed to own the area outright, saying he had paid three thousand pounds for it, and the HBC moved the Kwakiutl villagers along.[4] This transaction has not subsequently been designated a treaty by modern courts.

When British Columbia made itself indispensable to the crown by yielding up promising gold deposits in 1858, it was made a colony. It was joined together with Vancouver Island in 1864, but no treaties were made with the indigenous peoples on the mainland. Britain refused Douglas' written requests for money to attempt them, saying it was unfair on the British people to pay for such extravagances as Indian welfare when they would get nothing in return.

Douglas was then in the position of making it up as he went along, most pretense of tacking down developments by legal transaction having been utterly abandoned in the urgent effort to keep stirring an international stew boiling over into as yet unmapped gold-producing areas. The Americans had not fully yielded their interests in the northern end of the Oregon Territory. Governor Douglas sent out surveyors to map areas which would be reserved to the indigenous as they instructed, and would be protected from colonial development. He wrote to his colonial overseers:

> I also explained to them [the Indians] that the Magistrates had instructions to stake out and reserve for their use and benefit, all their occupied village sites and cultivated fields, and as much land in the vicinity of each as they could till, or was required for their support; that they might freely exercise and enjoy the rights of fishing the Lakes and Rivers, and of hunting over all unoccupied Crown Lands in the Colony; and that on their becoming registered Free Miners, they might dig and search for Gold, and hold mining claims on the same terms precisely as other miners:...[5]

This sort of next-best idea became Douglas's government policy with the Colonial Secretary of England: to demarcate as much land as any Indian community should recommend to be their Reserve. The Lil'wat, for example, decided on the entire Pemberton Valley, and that was mapped as their Reserve. The Neskonlith marked out a place that was a hundred miles around, and that was mapped for them. One of the Sto:lo communities gave corner landmarks which contained about a thousand square kilometers, and that was mapped as their Reserve.

Perhaps attracted by the scope offered in a new colonial government that didn't particularly require qualifications, an associate of the gold rush, Joseph Trutch, succeeded Douglas in the area of making Reserves. He quickly assumed a power he most certainly did not have: the monarch's prerogative to make Imperial policy, and he embarked on a practice of renegade realpolitik that has seen the province through to the present day. By 1871 the new colonial administration had taken the approach of reducing Indian Reserves to ten acres per family head, or adult male.

Joseph Trutch was one of the first land surveyors in the 1870s to be tasked with marking off minimal plots of land where the Indians should live. The plots should get the Indians out of the way of the settlers. Soon Trutch was Chief Commissioner of BC for Land and Works. By 1874, Trutch responded to the continuing correspondence from the Colonial Secretaries, who were responding to the continuing protests and petitions being undertaken by the tribal nations' leaders, by saying that all the Indians in BC now had Reserves that were quite to their satisfaction. What is remarkable about this is not only that the Reserves were categorically unsatisfactory and an 1874 petition signed by over a hundred Chiefs stated so, but that the northern interior of British Columbia was still basically inaccessible to Reserve Commissioners or anyone but the Indians at that time, and was therefore very much bereft of the supposedly adequate land reserves. There were as yet no Reserves in northern BC. Trutch was a liar.

During these years there was plenty of correspondence between the British overlords and the BC colonials. The British were still, for whatever reasons, concerned with keeping an appearance of upholding their Constitutional directives from 1763 and 1867 respectively, which stated that the land is Reserved to the Indians as their Hunting Grounds, and that the lands belong to the provinces "subject to any Other interests." Section 109 of the *British North America Act*, 1867, says: "All Lands, Mines, Minerals and Royalties belonging to the several provinces of Canada, Nova Scotia and New Brunswick at the Union, and all such Lands, Mines, Minerals or Royalties, shall belong to the several provinces of Ontario, Quebec, Nova Scotia and New Brunswick in which the same are situate or arise, subject to any Trusts existing in respect thereof, and to any Interests other than that of the Province in the same." The Other Interest here is clearly that of the indigenous.

Official records of interactions between the indigenous and the Surveyors and Reserve Commissioners went like this:

They were then assured of protection, and that their tribes would not be disturbed in the possession of their homes, and their hunting and fishing grounds; and that the Dominion Government would provide them with the means of education, and assist them in their agricultural pursuits. The nature, also, of the Railway Survey was explained to them, and they were told that they need not apprehend any loss as the result of such survey.[6]

Letters to the newspapers of the day went like this:

Many of these reservations have been surveyed without their consent, and sometimes without having received notice of it, so that they could not expose their needs and their wishes. Their reservations have been repeatedly cut off smaller for the benefit of the whites, and the best and most useful part of them taken away till some tribes are corralled on a small piece of land, as at Canoe Creek or elsewhere, or even have not an inch of ground, as at Williams Lake. ... Besides their lands were valuable to the Indians for hunting, and now the game is receding far away before the whites.[7]

The Royal Commission on Indian Affairs' report, the Confidential Report of the Commissioners for McKenna-McBride, forty years later, noted:

The importance of securing, under the Provincial law, all requisite water rights for Indians cannot be over stated. In the dry belt water is an essential of the land. Without it the land is practically useless. It is evident that in the past systematic care was not taken to secure water rights in connection with the law. It seems to have been taken for granted that the allotment of water by the Commissioners who set apart Reserves was sufficient, though there is grave doubt as to whether the Commissioners had such power. And, from the evidence of Indians and enquiries made, it appears that there are numerous records of water for Reserves not noted in the Schedule of Reserves, and of which it may be the Department has no official record.

Fishing and the policy in operation thereanent *[sic]* give very grave concern to the Indians. ... At all meetings which the Commission held with Bands outside of the strictly agricultural and stock raising areas, expression was given to a sense of injustice consequent upon the operation of the fishery regulations as they bear directly upon the Indians.[8]

In April of 1873, the Superintendent of Indian Affairs in Victoria estimated there were 28,500 Indians in British Columbia. The Chief Commissioner of Lands and Works wrote back to him (in one of the later of a long series of letters back and forth with the Dominion Government asking for specifics and statistics, the province guaranteeing they had been sent—then later acknowledging they didn't exist) saying not eighty but six acres should be reserved per family, and a family should be six people. So in 1873, the province intended that less than 30,000 acres be Reserved for the Indians of British Columbia. In 1873, the non-native population of BC was less than 10,000 (although they had upped it—on paper—to 30,000 for the benefit of the per-capita transfer agreements under the Terms of Union with Canada in 1871). BC claims a land base of about 25 million acres. The Indian share of the land would be less than one eight hundredth; just more than one tenth of one percent.

One wonders what the Chief Commissioner thought the Indian people would do in the next generation, with one acre each.

Although the point of this writing is not to discuss the justness of the size of Indian Reserves, far from it, the following exchanges speak to the character and competence of British Columbia's early colonial leadership.

Report of a Committee of the Honorable the Privy Council
March 21, 1873
… Mr. Powell… accordingly suggests that each family be assigned a location of eighty acres of land of average quality, which shall remain permanently the property of the family for whose benefit it is allotted.

W. A. Himsworth, Clerk, PC

The Superintendent of Indian Affairs to the Lieutenant Governor of BC.
June 21, 1873
…in respect of the urgent necessity of adjusting existing Indian Reserves—extending them where required and of setting apart Indian lands for tribes not now provided for… I am informed at different places, just visited by me, that in some instances great injustice has been done to the Indians in not reserving sufficient land for their use… abundant discontent prevails among the Indians both on the Island and Mainland, and I regard it as a matter of urgent and paramount importance that … their complaints should be adjusted…

.   I. W. Powell

Note that the Dominion government now recommends that 400,000 acres be reserved; just over 1% of BC's land base. At this time, the single white male homesteader receives 160 acres as a pre-emption: his for two dollars, with the option to buy hundreds of acres more on promise-to-pay arrangements.

> *Report of a Committee of the Honourable the Executive Council, approved by His Excellency the Lieutenant-Governor of BC*
> July 25, 1873
> …The Committee remark that this quantity is greatly in excess of the grants considered sufficient by previous Governments of British Columbia, and recommend that throughout the Province Indian Reserves should not exceed a quantity of twenty acres of land for each head of a family of five persons.
>
> W J Armstrong, Clerk, EC

> *The Provincial Secretary to the Superintendent of Indian Affairs*
> July 28, 1873
> … all future reserves for Indians will be adjusted on the basis of twenty acres of land for each head of a family of five persons.
>
> John Ash

> *The Superintendent of Indian Affairs to the Provincial Secretary*
> July 29, 1873
> I am not aware that any restriction of the kind is customary in the other provinces of the Dominion, and, before communicating the same to the Department at Ottawa, may I beg of you to inform me as to whether it is intended to restrict the proposed grant of twenty acres of land to a family "of five persons" and, if so, the particular quantity of land which may be reserved for a family of two, three, four, six or more persons.
>
> I W Powell

> *The Provincial Secretary to the Superintendent of Indian Affairs*
> August 1, 1873
> …to each five persons there shall be allotted twenty acres of land.
>
> John Ash

> *The Superintendent of Indian Affairs to the Provincial Secretary*
>
> August 23, 1873
>
> ...I have the honour to state that I am authorized to accept the proposition of the Government to make the quantity of land to be hereafter reserved for each Indian family in the Province *twenty acres*. As the restriction of twenty acres to each family of *five* persons, besides being quite unusual in other Provinces of the Dominion, would tend much to complicate matters in connection with Indian lands, I am to express the hope that the Government will not insist upon the acreage referred to being confined to any specified number of persons in a family, and should be glad to have your earliest reply. [emphasis in the original]
>
> I W Powell

No response from the Provincial Secretary was recorded in this collection in "Papers Relating to the Indian Land Question, 1850-1875," published by the Queen's Printer for British Columbia.

What stands out is the total lack of procedure. As Amor de Cosmos pointed out in 1858, and to emphasize the aforesaid, "Our government—the guardian of our lives and liberties—must be systematized and receive a settled form." There was no reference to the 1763 Proclamation or the 1867 Constitution in those exchanges about Reserves. No legal resource was referred to in these letters and directions, merely the fact that it was indeed eighty acres per family that had formed the basis of treaty lands elsewhere in Canada. Apparently the whim of BC's new government carried the day. That whim was quickly modified, at least in the case of some places in Secwepemc, where the Provincial Secretary then begged the Superintendent for permission to grant forty acres per family in hopes of averting the course of war then popular among interior Chiefs.

> The tribes now dread the idea of being placed upon and confined to these reserves, as they have ascertained that the Indian Department intend, if possible, to carry out such a course. ...and intimate their intention of resisting such a step.[9]

A year later, in 1874, the Minister of the Interior characterized British Columbia's actions in response to the Indian Land Question "as little short of a mockery of the claims."[10] At the same time, the petition of 109 Chiefs written at Hope included an alternate way of looking at the same matter:

Our hearts have been wounded by the arbitrary way the
Local Government of British Columbia have dealt with us
in locating and dividing our Reserves.[11]

And yet, the Minister and any other authorities shirked their
responsibilities under the British North America Act, and even the 1871 Terms
of Union, which stated in Article 13:

> The charge of the Indians, and the trusteeship and
> management of the lands reserved for their use and benefit,
> shall be assumed by the Dominion Government and a
> policy as liberal as that hitherto pursued by the British
> Columbia Government shall be continued by the Dominion
> Government after the Union.
>
> To carry out such policy, tracts of land of such extent
> as it has hitherto been the practice of the British Columbia
> Government to appropriate for that purpose, shall from
> time to time be conveyed by the Local Government to the
> Dominion Government in trust for the use and benefit of
> the Indians on application of the Dominion Government;
> and in case of disagreement between the two Governments
> respecting the quantity of such tracts of land to be so granted,
> the matter shall be referred for the decision of the Secretary
> of State for the Colonies.

The Reserves would not have been big enough even for one generation
to grow up on them and start new families. Indians were not allowed to pre-empt
land as the settlers did: new arrivals simply selected a site they liked, drew a
map of it, and registered the drawing with a written description at a house of
government in Langley or Victoria. Indians could not individually own land and
register it under their name by any means—unless, hypothetically, with Special
Permission of the Governor—which was never given, although often sought.
The Indian Reserves were Crown lands owned by the Queen, and She would not
divide her holdings. Some individuals held Certificates of Possession recognizing
their priority right over other Indians at certain places within Reserves.

Some insisted that the presence of the whites could do nothing but
good for the wandering Indian, "bind him to the soil" by agricultural pursuits
and make him industrious and civilized. This was not consistent with what
was happening. The whites were going about making sure there would be
no more Indians, civilized or not – that they would be unable to provide for
themselves as Indians, and if they were civilized, they would no longer—by
government definition—be Indians.

The federal Indian Act would soon come to assist the province in 1876. Possibly as evidence of the solution this Act was meant to have provided, the "Papers Relating to the Indian Land Question" collection fails to include correspondence after 1875.

Thereafter the Joint Commission was appointed to survey the Indian Reserves, a collective approach between the province and the federal government. This Indian Reserve Commission, as it was also called, surveyed most of the Reserves in BC until its end came in 1910. It had not, however, resolved the disagreement between the governments which both claimed that they "owned" Indian Reserve land. The Province

> claimed the right to disallow any Reserve that the Indian Reserve Commission allotted and protested the amount of land that the Indian Reserve Commission set aside as Reserves.[12]

Many more dispatches regarding the Indian dissatisfaction were authored.

How the Reserves Were Fought

In 1886 provincial surveyors arrived for a second time in the Nass Valley to mark out Indian Reserves. The Nisga'a expelled them. Nisga'a and Tsimshian Chiefs went to Victoria, met Premier Smithe, refused to give in to his humiliating treatment, and succeeded in convincing him that the Haida, Tsimshian and Nisga'a all wanted a proper treaty. In 1887 the first Royal Commission, a joint federal and provincial endeavor, began hearing and documenting the debacle which was the fallout from Trutch's Reserve selection process—mostly in response to the Nisga'a.[13] David Mackay, Nisga'a, told the Commission:

> What we don't like about the Government is their saying this: 'We will give you this much of land.' How can they give it when it is our own? We cannot understand it. They have never bought it from us or our forefathers. They have never fought and conquered our people and taken the land in that way, and yet they say now that they will give us so much land—our own land.[14]

No one else liked the government's approach either. Judging by the following exchange, the Chiefs were quite conscious of enduring their adversary's exercise in "passing the buck," which left them constantly attempting to rectify "failed" communications between one level of government and another. The Surveyors, Commissioners and elected officers were in the habit of lying to the Chiefs' faces and blaming any resulting misunderstanding on the absent official. In 1887, at Fort Simpson, a series of meetings one after the other between Reserve Commissioners and Chiefs proved too intense for the strategy to work:

> A. Shakes (Tsimshian): No; we only tell you what belonged to our forefathers, and what we claimed is getting smaller all the time. You said yesterday "the Naas didn't belong to us," and we were surprised to hear it.
> Commissioner Cornwall: Who said that?
> A. Shakes: Mr. Cornwall.[15]

During those hearings, all the Chiefs within a two day journey of the meeting places at the Nass, Fort Simpson and Metlakatla insisted they did not want the *Indian Act*, they wanted recourse to the Queen's law. "... ...we Tsimpseans want to take charge of our own land; that is why we want power from the Queen to use her laws. Dr. Powell put laws into our hands, and those people made fun of them, so we know it is not strong."

In 1906, Cowichan Chiefs along with some leaders from the interior went to England to register their complaints.

In 1909, the British Columbia Indian Rights Association was formed. Representatives of twenty nations traveled to England to assert to King Edward VII that British Columbia's government was in need of check, and the Cowichan Petition went with them.

In February of 1910, James Teit wrote to Franz Boas,

> ... I have been busy traveling around, and speaking to the Indians so as to get them united in an effort to fight the BC Government in the Courts over the question of their lands.
>
> Owing to the stringency in the laws, increased settlement in the country, and general development of the Capitalist system, the Indians are being crushed, and made poor, and more & more restricted to their small, and inadequate reservations. The BC Government has appropriated all the lands of the country, and claims also to be sole protector of the Ind. Reserves. They refuse to acknowledge the Ind. title, and have taken possession of all without treaty with or consent of the Indians. Having taken the lands they claim complete ownership of everything in connection therewith such as water, timber, fish, game, etc.

They also subject the Indians completely to all the laws of BC without having made any agreement with them to that effect. The Indians demand that treaties be made with them regarding everything the same as has been made with the Indians of all the other provinces of Canada and in the US, that their reservations be enlarged so they have a chance to make a living as easily and as sufficient as among the Whites, and that all the lands not required by them and which they do not wish to retain for purposes of cultivation and grazing, and which are presently appropriated by the BC Government be paid for in cash. The Indians are all uniting and putting up money and have engaged lawyers in Toronto to fight for them, and have the case tried before the Privy Council in England.[16]

In 1910, "Friends of the Indians" was organized by white settlers, and they went to Victoria to interview the Premier on his plans to resolve the land title question. In March of 1910 another deputation of Indian leaders went to Victoria and was told by Premier McBride that it was his view that the Indians had no title to any lands whatsoever. He was to make that view quite clear in his consent to the 1912 Royal Commission bearing his name.

In August of 1910, some 80 Chiefs of the Interior authored the Memorial to Sir Wilfred Laurier, Prime Minister of Canada, as transcribed by Teit. Laurier had met with the leaders at Prince Rupert and at Kamloops during the summer. Officially submitted by the Secwepemc, Okanagan and Nlakapa'mux, the document was also signed by Chiefs from further nations as witnesses. It reads, in part,

After a time when they saw that our patience might get exhausted and that we might cause trouble if we thought all the land was to be occupied by whites they set aside many small reservations for us here and there over the country. This was their proposal not ours, and we never accepted these reservations as settlement for anything, nor did we sign any papers or make any treaties about same. They thought we would be satisfied with this, but we never have been satisfied and never will be until we get our rights. We thought the setting apart of these reservations was the commencement of some scheme they had evolved for our benefit, and that they would now continue until they had more than fulfilled their promises but although we have waited long we have been disappointed. We have always

felt the injustice done us, but we did not know how to obtain
redress. We knew it was useless to go to war. What could
we do? Even your government at Ottawa, into whose charge
we have been handed by the B.C. government, gave us no
enlightenment. We had no powerful friends. The Indian
agents and Indian office at Victoria appeared to neglect us.
Some offers of help in the way of agricultural implements,
schools, medical attendance, aid to the aged, etc., from the
Indian department were at first refused by many of our chiefs
or were never petitioned for, because for a time we thought
the Ottawa and Victoria governments were the same as one,
and these things would be charged against us and rated as
payment for our land, etc. Thus we got along the best way we
could and asked for nothing. For a time we did not feel the
stealing of our lands, etc., very heavily. As the country was
sparsely settled we still had considerable liberty in the way
of hunting, fishing, grazing, etc., over by far the most of it.
However, owing to increased settlement, etc., in late years
this has become changed, and we are being more and more
restricted to our reservations which in most places are unfit
or inadequate to maintain us. Except we can get fair play we
can see we will go to the wall, and most of us be reduced to
beggary or to continuous wage slavery. We have also learned
lately that the British Columbia government claims absolute
ownership of our reservations, which means that we are
practically landless. We only have loan of those reserves in
life rent, or at the option of the B.C. government. Thus we find
ourselves without any real home in this our own country.[17]

A year later, on May 10, 1911, the Memorial to Frank Oliver,
Minister of the Interior and Superintendent of Indian Affairs, followed it to
the unresponsive governments. In part:

Premier McBride, speaking for the BC Government, said
"We Indians had no right or title to the unsurrendered lands
of the province." We can not possibly have rights in any
surrendered lands, because in the first place they would not
be ours if we surrendered them, and, secondly we have never
surrendered any lands. This means that the BC Government
asserts that we have no claim or title to the lands of this
country. Our tribal territories which we have held from time
immemorial, often at cost of blood, are ours no longer if

Premier McBride is correct. We are all beggars, and landless in our own country. We told him through one of our chiefs we were of the opposite opinion from him, and claimed our countries as hitherto. We asked that the question between us be submitted for settlement to the highest courts, for how otherwise can it now be settled? His answer was: "there was no question to settle or submit to the courts." Now, how can this be. That there is a question is self-evident, for Premier McBride takes one side of it, and we take the other. If there was no question, there would have been nothing to talk about; and nothing to take sides on. We wish to tell you, Chief, this question is very real to us. It is a live issue.

Then we were promised full freedom to hunt, fish and travel over our country unrestricted by the regulations of the whites, until such time as our lands were purchased or at least until treaties were made with us. Another promise broken, and so on with all.[18]

Following from Sir Wilfred Laurier's promise in Prince Rupert of a judicial hearing of the tribes' complaints against BC, finally Duncan Campbell Scott, Superintendent General for Indian Affairs, prepared an Order in Council to allow their claim to go to the Privy Council. George Manuel, Secwepemc, described the proposal in his book *The Fourth World*:

But not directly to the Privy Council. The case would have to begin in the Exchequer Court of Canada, a court that mainly dealt with highly technical administrative questions and whose bench was traditionally filled with retired civil servants who are highly expert on obscure questions of tax law. But our fathers were told there was no other way to the Privy Council than through an appeal from a lower court.

This much could have been accepted.

But there were four other principle conditions:

1. The Chiefs had to agree in advance that if the court upheld our claim to title, we must surrender the title to the Crown for whatever compensation they might choose to give; and, the Chiefs would accept in advance the judgement of the McKenna-McBride Commission as the full allotment of reserve lands.

2. The province, by agreeing to this commission's report—which its own Premier had helped to write—would have satisfied all claims against it;

3. The Indians would be represented in court only by lawyers chosen by the Dominion government; and, the case could only go to court if the province agreed to be represented by lawyers it could choose for itself;

4. If the courts decided that we did not have title, the Dominion government would ever after be the sole authority to decide what was in our interest, without further protest.

The Indian Tribes walked away. It would not be until 1949 that the Supreme Court of Canada replaced the British Privy Council as the highest settler court in the land.

In late 1911, Laurier lost the federal election to Robert Borden, a Conservative. Laurier had taken considerable steps towards getting the BC question into a court room of the Judicial Committee. Borden went completely the other way and immediately struck a Reserve Commission in 1912. Robert McKenna was Canada's Special Commissioner of Indian Affairs, and Richard McBride was still Premier of BC. The two set out the terms for the Commission. Forty-eight Chiefs then protested the Commission by meeting in Spences Bridge on May 23, 1913—there was no Indian representation on the Commission. The Commission went ahead.

In the preamble to the Terms of the Royal Commission, it states: "it is desirable to settle all differences between the Governments of the Dominion and the Province respecting Indian lands and Indian affairs generally..." But the Commissioners did not attempt to do everything the preamble suggested. Specific reference to the land title question was not made in the eight paragraphs of agreement and instruction.

Opposition to the Reserve Commission had resulted in creation of the Allied Tribes of British Columbia, through much initiative by coastal Indians. The circumstances resulting are best, and most succinctly, reported in a statement from the British Columbia Indian Conference held at Vancouver, 20th to 23rd June, 1916. Issued by the Committee appointed by the Conference, and put into the hands of the Government of Canada and the Secretary of State for the Colonies, it was published in the press of Vancouver and was sent to each Indian Tribe:

The Indian Tribes of British Columbia have always claimed tribal ownership of the lands of the Province as the lands of their forefathers, and under Royal Proclamation, but since the days of Sir James Douglas the local Government has not admitted their claims.

All the Indians of the Province have for many years desired that this land question should be decided, and to that end in the year 1909 sent a petition to the late King Edward VII, and his Imperial Minister, the Secretary of State for the Colonies, asking that the Imperial Government refer the land question to the Judicial Committee of His Majesty's Privy Council.

When, by reason of refusal of British Columbia to agree to a reference, and the McKenna Agreement afterwards entered into by the Governments of Canada and British Columbia, it seemed that the door of the Judicial Committee had been closed against the Indians, the Nishga Tribe was advised that if one tribe presented a direct and independent petition to the King's Great Court, His Majesty's Privy Council, the door of the Judicial Committee might in that way be opened, not only for that one tribe, but for all other tribes. The Nishgas therefore decided to take the responsibility of presenting such a petition for the benefit of all the tribes.

With the approval of the Counsel for the Indian Rights Association, and after full consultation with the Government of Canada, the Petition of the Nishga Tribe was lodged in the Privy Council in May, 1913. That action was taken by the Nishgas with the earnest hope that the other tribes would unite in recognizing their petition as a test case relating to the claims of all the tribes.

After the Nishga Petition had been lodged, the London lawyers of the Nishga Tribe received from the Lord President of the Privy Council a letter stating as reason for not referring it to the Judicial Committee the supposed fact that the Royal Commission appointed under the McKenna Agreement was considering the aboriginal claims, which are the subject of the Petition. Soon afterwards the Nishgas presented to the Royal Commission a memorial in answer to which they were informed that the Commissioners were not considering, and had no power to consider these claims.

Subsequently the Nishga Petition was very fully considered at Ottawa, and as result in June, 1914, the Government passed an Order-in-Council asking that the Indian Tribes accept the findings of the Royal Commission, and agree to surrender their rights if the courts should decide that they have any, taking in place of them benefits to be granted by the Government of Canada.

The Nishga Tribe and the Interior Tribes allied with

them, were unwilling to accept these conditions, but made proposals of their own, suggesting that the matter of lands to be reserved be finally dealt with by the Secretary of State for the Colonies and that the matter of fixing compensation for lands to be surrendered be dealt with by the parliament of Canada.

These counter proposals the Government of Canada rejected by Order-in-Council passed in June, 1915, mainly upon the ground that the Government was precluded by the McKenna Agreement from accepting them.

The Nishga and Interior Tribes being still unwilling to accept the Government's terms, and believing that all or nearly all of the tribes of the Province would be unwilling to accept them, in April last sent delegations to Ottawa.

The delegates spent six weeks in Ottawa, and placed the case squarely before the Prime Minister of Canada, the Minister of the Interior, and the Deputy Superintendent-General of Indian Affairs. They also interviewed Sir Wilfred Laurier, who when Prime Minister promised that the land question would be brought before the Judicial Committee.

The delegates devoted much attention to the expected report of the Royal Commission, and asked that the report be not finally dealt with until the issues contained in the Nishga Petition should have been decided, or at least until the Indian tribes should have an opportunity of making representations regarding its findings.

Having failed to secure any definite answer from the Government, the delegates, before leaving Ottawa, in a statement placed in the hands of the Governor-General of Canada, the Prime Minister of Canada, and the Minister of the Interior, and sent to the Secretary of State for the Colonies, declared their determination to do all in their power by independent efforts to secure that the Nishga Petition shall be referred to the Judicial Committee.

After making some progress at Ottawa, the delegates sent to the Executive Committee of the Indian Rights Association an invitation to join them in a conference for the purpose of considering the interviews had with the Government of Canada, and the whole position reached in efforts being made for the Indian cause, with a view to securing the fullest possible harmony and co-operation. This invitation was accepted and the Conference opened in

Vancouver on Tuesday, June 20. At a number of meetings held from that day until the following Friday, outstanding features of the situation were discussed with some fullness. The members of the Conference also attended a gathering of natives held on Thursday, June 22nd, addressed by Mr. Duncan C. Scott, Deputy Superintendent-General, whose views then expressed were carefully considered at subsequent meetings of the Conference.

The main result of the Conference was that unanimously the following resolutions were adopted, the first on Tuesday, June 20th, and the second on Friday, June 23rd:

> 1. That this meeting of the Chiefs of the Indians of British Columbia with the Executive of the Indian Rights Association assembled, repudiate any suggestion that we are satisfied with the terms of the Order-in-Council passed in June, 1914, and Mr. Clark, K.C., of Toronto, quite misunderstood our instructions if he stated to Hon. Dr. Roche that the Indian Rights Association accepted the terms of such Order-in-Council.

> 2. That a committee be appointed to agree on a general plan of action for the Indians of British Columbia and report to all tribes the result of their deliberations, with power in meantime to take any necessary steps to preserve all rights and claims on the lines of co-operation with the Nishga Tribe.

…In connection with the land question, and all other matters considered at the Conference, the Committee thinks it important to point out that, while the Indians of this Province are subjects of His Majesty, and an obligation for their protection has been placed upon and accepted by Canada, they are neither wards of the Government nor citizens of the Dominion, and that to this day there is no real relation between the Indian tribe and the people of Canada, the tribe remaining a community not yet part of the Canadian people.[19]

The McKenna-McBride Commission continued apace, apart from Chairman Wetmore's resignation, November 29, 1913 at Victoria. He explained his leaving in an illuminating letter:

> While I found the work very monotonous and uninteresting I cannot say that so far it has been strenuous. The Commission

has visited and inspected the Indian Reserves in the Cowichan, Bella Coola, QCI [Queen Charlotte Islands, or Haida Gwaii], Okanagan and Kamloops Agencies, and a portion of the Reserves in the New Westminster and Lytton Agencies. ...we traveled by car and rail...

I have obtained information from the Agent of the Stewart Lake and Williams Lake Agencies, and those in the northern parts of the Province, the Babine, Stikine and Nass Agencies will have to be visited. I have obtained information from the Agent of the Stewart Lake Agency what the going through that Agency involves. Namely, a ninety mile ride on horse back and return, occupying eight days, another horse back ride occupying two days, and the rest of the travel (excepting possibly a short distance by the Grand Trunk Pacific, and that is very doubtful) will be partly in canoe and partly on Buck Boards. .... Now I am too old to go through what I have described; I will be seventy three years of age next March. Riding on horse back is entirely out of the question for me; I am also very obese and shorted winded [sic] and I cannot get into canoes and settle down in them without very great inconvenience and distress, and when I get in them I would suffer still greater distress in getting up and out of them. The matter of camping out is most objectionable to me; I have bodily infirmities that render it very desirable that I should have the facilities afforded by a bed-room, and to be without them I would undergo very great inconvenience and distress.

About the 3rd January I expect to leave for England, and my address there will be The Grand Hotel, Trafalgar Square, London, England.[20]

The chasm between Mr. Wetmore and the peoples whose lands he had been selected to preside over shaping defies overstatement. The Chairman was replaced in the form of N.W. White, no more suitable in terms of experience or worldliness in other cultures, and the Commission produced four boxes of transfers of Reserve land to the PGE Railway, now in the BC Archives in Victoria. Almost 40,000 acres of mostly good arable land, convenient land, was cut-off from Reserves while approximately 80,000 acres was added back in their place. The latter was characteristically steep or rocky terrain and valued altogether at about half what the cut-off lands were.[21]

On December 6, 1917, a meeting of the Tribes was held at Spence's Bridge to protest the results of the Royal Commission. They passed a resolution rejecting the entirety of the four years of Commission work. They also said,

> We are sure that the government and a considerable number of
> white men have for many years had in their minds a quite wrong
> idea of the claims which we make, and the settlement which we
> desire. We do not want anything extravagant, and we do not want
> anything hurtful to the real interests of the white people. We want
> that our actual rights be determined and recognized; we want
> a settlement based upon justice. We want a full opportunity of
> making a future for ourselves. We want all this done in such a
> way that in the future we shall be able to live and work with the
> white people as brothers and fellow-citizens.[22]

A comprehensive indigenous counter-proposal was offered in their "Statement of the Allied Indian Tribes of British Columbia for the Government of British Columbia," which rejected the Commission and its findings and was delivered at the end of 1919.

In 1920, the federal government passed Bill 13 to accept and implement the Reserve Commission's report, and attendance at Indian Residential Schools became mandatory for indigenous children, on pain of parental imprisonment for withholding a child from independent contractors hired to round them up each September.

Approval by the provincial and federal governments of the Reserve Commission, however, had to wait until 1923 and 1924 while adjustments were made by W.E. Ditchburn, the Federal appointee and a Department of Indian Affairs official, and Col. J.W. Clark from the Provincial Department of Lands and Works. They disallowed some of the new Reserve lands.

The Allied Tribes of British Columbia had worked since 1916 in pursuit of the land title answer. By 1919 they had attracted a larger membership, and appointed James Teit to the post of "Special Agent." They researched and organized, and raised funds to support their work, which resulted in a hearing in Parliament through the appointment of a Judicial Committee in 1926. The two men who presented to the Committee were Reverend Peter R. Kelly, Haida, who was leader of the Allied Tribes, and Andrew Paull, Cowichan, who was Secretary. The Committee was dismissive, derisive and often openly hostile to the material which the men presented. They concluded that there was no merit to the Indian land question in BC, and therefore a court hearing was not necessary.

In 1927 the Indian Act was amended to prohibit gatherings of more than three Indians whatsoever; gatherings to discuss the land question; the hiring of a lawyer by Indians; and activities meant to raise funds to pursue the land question. Written records fall silent over the next decades, except for the works of the Native Brotherhood of the coast.

After the Second World War, a new era was ushered in by veterans' organizations, churches, and citizen groups across Canada who called for a Royal Commission to investigate the administration of Indian Affairs, and the conditions prevailing on Indian Reserves. No doubt the veterans had fresh and deep-running sympathies for the native sharp-shooters and front-line sacrifices that had made their safe return from war possible. But all wanted a complete revision to the *Indian Act* and an end to discrimination against the Indian.

No Royal Commission was appointed, but a Parliamentary Joint Committee of both the Senate and House was created in 1946 to study and make proposals on Canada's Indian Administration, and the revision of the *Indian Act*. After two years of hearings, the Joint Committee recommended:

a) The complete revision or repeal of every section in the Indian Act.

b) That Canada's Indian Act be designed to make possible the gradual transition of the Indian from a position of wardship to citizenship. To achieve this goal the act should provide:
   i. Indian women be given a political voice in band affairs.
   ii. Bands should be allowed more self-government.
   iii. Bands should be given more financial assistance.
   iv. Indians should be treated the same as non-Indians in the matter of intoxicants.
   v. Indian Affairs officials were to have their duties and responsibilities designed so as to assist the Indians attain the full rights of citizenship and to serve the responsibilities of self-government.
   vi. Allow bands to incorporate as municipalities.

c) The guidelines for future policy were to be:
   i. The easing of enfranchisement procedures.
   ii. Indians should be given the vote.
   iii. When possible cooperate with the provinces in delivering services to the Indian people.
   iv. Indian education should be geared for assimilation; therefore it should take place with non-Indian students.[23]

In 1949, Indians in BC could vote in provincial elections. In 1951, the *Indian Act* was amended and possession of alcohol was decriminalized. In 1960, Indians could vote in federal elections. The prohibition on hiring lawyers to pursue land claims was lifted.

The North American Indian Brotherhood had closely pursued the Joint Committee's work, holding meetings across Canada and especially in BC where it was clear that the first concern was the land question. A BC Chapter of the NAIB formed. They were, a century after the land dispute had started, gripped with determination and conviction that they would get justice. One of their memos on the subject of Indian rights in BC included the following:

> 8. Canada has already agreed that the Indians have title to British Columbia, otherwise the Indians would not be receiving $100, 000 per year by way of the BC Special in lieu of Treaty monies.
> 9. The difference is that at least theoretically the Indians in other parts of Canada agreed to their treaty money by having treaties signed by the Indians.
> 10. But BC Indians never signed treaties ...[24]

The "BC Special" was apparently the Allied Tribes' reward for attending the Joint Committee in 1926, where Peter Kelly and Alex Paull had brought the land question case to be considered for a Privy Council hearing. It is not what they sought, but the allocation of funds "in lieu of" treaty payments provides some recognition that the treaties' absence demands some remedy."

The BC chapter sent a Brief to their colleagues concerning employment, saying they couldn't get any in BC so most had to travel to Washington State for work, and concerning the recent Senate and Parliamentary Committee recommendation regarding the formation of an Indian Claims Commission. The Brief, dated November 19, 1963, made elaborate points about who should populate such a Commission: a senior American anthropologist, a Canadian lawyer specializing in international and British constitutional law, and a Chairman selected by the Secretary General of the United Nations. The BC Chapter of NAIB claimed, by way of an introduction to this document, that its membership could be characterized as,

> ...mainly an interior of British Columbia organization with token representation on the coast of this province. The Interior comprises approximately 15,000 natives, Chief Richard Malloway of the Fraser Valley and Chief Edward Thevarge, hereditary Chieftain of the 2,000 member Lillooet tribe were picked as delegates for these submissions.
> Clarence Joe, Senior Counsellor of the Sechelt Band, represents four different Indian Bands on the Southern Coast of British Columbia and Ross Modeste appears as a selected spokesman for approximately 7,000 Indians living on the West Coast and the southern portion of Vancouver Island.[25]

Thevarge, Malloway and Joe, along with their lawyer Henry Castillou, had just returned from a trip to New York and Ottawa where they were recruiting support for their position and giving television and radio interviews. During the trip they attended a luncheon in the Green Room of Parliament, they met with 23 Members of Parliament on the question of the Indian Claims Commission and Indian Affairs, and they had separate meetings with a number of Ministers and Indian Affairs officials. They also visited the Brantford Indian Reserve and the Mohawk community of Kahnewake.

The Liberal Party of Canada had issued a pamphlet before their election stating that, in 1963, the Liberals promised as follows:

> 1. Liberal policy now is to appoint as soon as possible an Indian Claims Commission, an independent, unbiased unprejudiced body with broad terms of reference, to review all matters pertaining to this issue.
> 2. With the objectives of achieving a fair and just settlement of all outstanding claims, it is Liberal policy that the Commission will include qualified authorities on British Constitutional law as it affects aboriginal hereditary and usufructuary rights.
> 3. To assure the objectivity which Indians of Canada have the right to expect after years of procrastination, Commissioners may be appointed from other parts of the Commonwealth such as New Zealand, where achievements in this field are regarded as outstanding. It is Liberal policy that the Commission will be unbiased and independent.
> 4. Appointment of the Indian Claims Commission, as described, is based on the fundamental Liberal policy that Canada's Native Indians must now achieve full equality without loss of aboriginal, hereditary and usufructuary rights. Canada, at this time in our history and today's war of ideologies, must erase the blot of second and third-class citizenship.

The Liberal promise of 1963 was adopted by the Federal Liberal Party under then Prime Minister Lester Pearson. It was no secret, it was much anticipated, as MLA Frank Calder indicated in comments after the *White and Bob* case had won recognition of hunting rights. Calder said, "In view of the forthcoming establishment of the federal Indian claims commission, the Nanaimo court decision is evidence in favour of the Indians land and aboriginal claims."[26]

Pierre Trudeau became the new Liberal leader and this second promise of a Commission disappeared. In 1969 Trudeau attempted to disappear Indians altogether.

Agents in Right of Canada

> *"Many of us have been led to believe that our aboriginal rights have been curtailed, restricted or taken away. This belief exists because foreign powers, meaning Canadian federal and provincial governments, have assumed authority over our lives, resources and our lands. The key word is ASSUME because that is how it was done. The problem that exists now is that many of our people have also assumed that the foreign powers had the right to control and manage our affairs."*
>
> **—Aboriginal Rights Position Paper—Resource Kit, Indian Government Portfolio, Union of B.C. Indian Chiefs, October 15, 1979. Part II, "Our Aboriginal Right to Govern Through Our Unique Forms of Indian Governments"**

In 1968, indigenous leaders from across Canada were engaged by the Department of Indian Affairs in a series of nineteen discussion meetings around revising the Indian Act. The delegates insisted that a commission of investigation into their claimed lands was prerequisite to any discussion of the Indian Act.[27]

Instead of doing that, Canada attempted to write Indians off the books with a white paper the following year.[28] A sea-to-sea wave of indigenous confidence and conviction followed the failure of Trudeau's white paper of 1969, which would have eliminated Indian Status without resolving the land question. The Red Paper Policy written by Alberta Chiefs to contradict it had been a huge success. As a result, a new era of Indian Agent began in British Columbia. That is, the existing Indian Agents were retired and the Band Councils took over the Agents' administrative duties. The elected Chief would perform the function of the Indian Agent directly. This represents a stage of colonialism that has never been reached by any other British colony, all of which were lost to new "national" independence movements while still at the point of delegated area control provided by the District Administrator.

Now people elected their own Indian Agent, or Chief as he or she would be called, in another game of appropriation, and that Indian Agent / Chief would administer the federally sponsored poverty, rather than the white, usually retired army officer, Indian Agent. This system continues today. The elected Chief was imposed in 1925—that person would deal with the Indian Agent. Hereditary chiefs, Elders' Councils, the family head system—or traditional governance—was denied its existence: its practice was criminalized.[29] The original Indian Agent, a federal delegate, had come about on request of the BC government in the 1880s, and the elected Chief later became his local informant and source of authority.

Prior to the reformation of the 1970s, Indian Band Chiefs just signed blank Band Council Resolutions which the Indian Agent took back to their offices and filled in as necessary, legitimizing infringement of water rights, concessions to Reserve land cut-offs, or acquiescence to housing money schedules. In spite of our academics' assertions about the importance of residential schools, many Chiefs couldn't read.

Forty years later, in 2012, the elected Chief and Council system has become entrenched; the hereditary lineages are powerless and certainly the socio-economic and political structures that had allowed them to function are no more. Whole tribal nations now repose all their confidence in their DIA Chief—a man or woman who is on payroll with Indian and Northern Affairs Canada, and whose reporting accountability goes up to the federal government; never around to the community. Indeed, any Band employee is entitled to receive the same benefits that any other federal government employee receives.

It should be understood, but it is not, that elected Chiefs and Councils on Reserves are not representing the indigenous title position, or indigenous rights of any kind, when they are representing their Reserve in undertaking *Indian Act* business. An elected Band Council and its Chief are sometimes, and their administrative staff are always, salaried by the Canadian government. When the on-Reserve Chief was made mandatory, the introduction of elections was purportedly meant to dispel the implied inequality under the previously held traditional systems.[30] It is safe to assume that the imposition of a single Chief on polities which functioned in the use of several Chiefs was meant more precisely to disrupt the cohesion of those peoples as much as possible. These were systems of familial autonomy, each family having a representative, lands, titles and other assets. For the first part of the elected Chief era, the family heads chose him together, at least they did so in many communities, just as they had made decisions previously.

However, what eventually happened in the elected system, once the family head system was fully bankrupted by displacement of the economy and viciously stripped of social power, was that any individual contender with the most voting family members would automatically attain the Chieftainship. This situation is obviously a DIA construct, though it is often and popularly remarked on as a flaw unique to indigenous cultures. While no majority group within an individual indigenous community or nation could have ever held sway under the traditional system, which involved family heads of equal decision making power, the government of Canada insisted on having a single individual to deal with in each Reserve, to which the indigenous communities were confined at the point at which this development occurred.

The elected Chief is, correspondingly, a servant of Canada. His or her role is to administer the Indian Act on his or her Reserve. That is the extent of his powers. This may mean he or she must strike up a housing committee, a social welfare department, a department of lands and resources, and so on. And he or she may receive an annuity, or a salary if the community so wishes, but certainly honoraria are awarded by government for attending meetings with the government. Given the imposition of this titular position in the community, the one that Canadian agents will deal with, the elected Chief was originally, naturally, one who could speak English. This prerequisite did not necessarily select the one who was most capable of articulating the community's political or legal position, or indeed, most committed to it. More recently, Chiefs with a western education were favoured, and now, lately, those with western business experience.

Off Reserve

When indigenous refugees from other colonies in the world arrive in Vancouver, it takes them on average three days to return to their social support worker with questions about why are there so many native people on the streets, and why are there native people here at all? They never knew there were indigenous people here. And why are they not at home, and why do their people from back home not come and get them? Are they outcasts?

They are not outcasts. They are driven out of their proper homes by the creation of adverse economic circumstances, by pain, and by conflict made insoluble by the imposition of a single Chieftain for each village. The poorest postal code in Canada is in the downtown east side of Vancouver, where the single dominant population is indigenous to BC. This does not distinguish Vancouver among other BC cities like Prince George, Kelowna, Kamloops, Victoria or Fort St. John, just in Canada. The situation of indigenous individuals forming the majority of the inhabitants on Skid Row also does not distinguish Vancouver from Winnipeg, Toronto, Montreal, Calgary, or Saskatoon; it's just that Vancouver is the very poorest.

The Reserve policy has successfully depopulated native villages. Urban aboriginals, as they are called, can be an important pawn in the politicking in Victoria, Ottawa and back On Reserve. "This Agreement will benefit our members living off-Reserve," states a Chief in regard to his latest capitulation agreement, in spite of the fact that there are no supporting plans in place to justify the argument, in order to gain those mail-in votes that will prove critical to the ratification of the Agreement.[31] The *Corbiere* decision in Canada's Supreme Court[32] made it necessary for Indian Bands to provide their members living off-Reserve with a vote on matters going to a referendum On Reserve. Interestingly, it did not change funding policies to support such expansion or the impact on Band decisions.

The Aboriginal Peoples' Congress is a Canada-wide lobby agency for urban aboriginal people. It plays an important role which is not well understood by Canadians who don't understand the different motives of indigenous people who live on or off Reserves. Perhaps 50% of native people in Canada have moved away from their ancestral communities, since they were snared within insufficient boundaries as described above. Organizations like the Council of Canadians publish reports on the well-being and needs of those natives displaced to cities while the title issue, the reason so many leave, is ignored. The title issue is ignored at every level of investigation into the indigenous condition: a provincial Missing Women Commission of Inquiry looked into the activities of serial murderer Robert Pickton, of British Columbia, and attempted to find the causative factors which led so many indigenous women to prostitution and to be so vulnerable in that trade as to fall victim to the killer. They decided the reason was poverty.

The BC Association for Non-Status Indians formed at exactly the same time as the Union of BC Indian Chiefs in 1969, and there was great sympathy between them—they nearly merged at one time.[33] Not everybody was at home when the Indian Agents or other state agents came by for enumerations and to assign Indian Status to the unwitting recipients, record their names and replace them with the serial numbers that were all the statistics department would need. This event is what originally separated Status from Non-Status Indians.

Poverty on the Reserves forces young people to leave them.[34] Away from home, it will become very difficult for future generations to prove the "continuing use and occupation," upon which aboriginal rights are contingent in Canadian courts. It makes retaining culture and language very difficult, to say nothing of their transmission to future generations.

Professor Hawthorn of UBC produced two reports in response to his commission from the Minister of Citizenship and Immigration, in 1964, to conduct "A Survey of the Contemporary Indians of Canada." Among his recommendations, "Special facilities will be needed to ease the process of social adjustment as the tempo of off-reserve movement increases." He acknowledged, "Integration or assimilation are not objectives which anyone can properly hold for the Indian," and suggested the department focus "on a series of middle range objectives, such as increasing the educational attainments of the Indian people, increasing their real income, and adding to their life expectancy."[35] The Professor was dealing in foregone conclusions that the supreme objective of federal policy was disintegration of the traditional communities, and he was merely making observations as to how the assimilation objectives might be accomplished—such as having provincial agencies replace the federal government in increasing provincial services not equally enjoyed by native people.

In some ways it is easy to mark government inaction against any kinds of political statements it may make or commission. It was not until 1999 that people who lived off-Reserve could participate in their Band's elections. This includes people living in the white towns that share a seam with the Reserves, people who lived just down the road, as well as people who crossed provincial borders to work in slaughter houses and mining camps to remit the achingly absent cash to their families at home—similar to the displaced worldwide. The *Corbiere* decision did what individual Bands couldn't do, or wouldn't do, given there was no funding earmarked for the procedure: it is now mandatory for each Band to provide a means for its members living away to vote in Band elections.

It was recommended by some now bleary figure in an earlier era of extinguishment that if the government set the blood quantum at one quarter, all it would have to do was wait until native people inter-married themselves out of existence. In 1985, Sharon McIvor had that fixed. A Penticton Band member, McIvor lost her Indian Status when she married a non-native man. So had every other native woman who "married out," and her later children too, even if their father was a Status Indian. McIvor sued The Registrar and won. It is the only aboriginal rights case to ever cause legislation, and in 1985 Bill C-31 was introduced, reinstating women who married out and their children. It also gave Status to those people whose great/ grand/ parents weren't home on enumeration day, almost a hundred years before, if they could prove their family history.

This move was not welcomed by every Band. Suddenly the enrolment numbers leaped, in some cases by 500%, but no implementation funding accompanied that human increase other than the usual per-capita amounts. It was not an exercise in self-determination. Suddenly claims on housing and services increased, a demand few Bands could dream of meeting since the housing crisis has been a hallmark of Reserve life since the 1950s. Before that, and after, it was more of an infrastructure crisis.

In 2007, McIvor did it again.[36] Her grandchildren would not be Status Indians, while a Status man's grandchildren would be—until the new ruling in her case. The resulting changes to Status, rolling out since 2008, will dramatically expand the Status population again, and again with no financial assistance to the Bands to cope with that. The population will be poised to crash back towards previous numbers in the next generation. The earthquakes in community administration may level out in a couple of decades, but the inequality in registration is still present—great grandchildren's status will depend on whether they are eligible for it because of a man or a woman; their status will be decided by the federal government unless things change..

The Indian Reserves have proven to be a temporary, rather than a final, solution for British Columbia. Those historical Reserve Surveys are now only so much evidence in the human rights case against the colonial government. Today, the government means to involve the indigenous in the Reserve Commission, and to have the result seen as consensual, final and certain.

Chapter 6

EXTINGUISHMENT ... WITH CONSENT

"Yeah, yeah yeah, we know the courts say they have aboriginal title and rights, and that's why we do these negotiations."
**—Mike Harcourt, Former BC Premier
and former Chief Commissioner of the BC Treaty Commission**

"Once you give consent, you're fucked."
—Hereditary Chief Qwatsinas, Nuxalk

BC knows now that it can't unilaterally extinguish aboriginal title and rights. After one hundred and thirty-four years of attempting to do that, British Columbia agreed to participate in tri-partite negotiations. "Political" negotiations, which would "*not* be modeled on rights-based litigation where the parties engage in debates about the nature, scope and limitations of Aboriginal rights and title for a particular First Nation,"[1] is how the BC treaty process was described by the Minister of Indian and Northern Affairs Canada.

In 1911, Prime Minister Laurier had brought BC Indians' concerns to the brink of a formal federal inquiry. British Columbia managed to secure a condition to that investigation: that the indigenous would release their titles beforehand and accept whatever rights Canada was willing to recognize after the inquiry. Canada accepted that prerequisite, but the indigenous did not – so they refused to press the case and that avenue was temporarily abandoned. In 1916 the first report of the Royal Commission on Aboriginal People in British Columbia was delivered to the governments; the indigenous followed it up, rejecting that process at the time, and producing an elaborate counter-petition, *Claims of the Allied Tribes,* three years later. That effort to have bilateral negotiations take the place of the arbitrary Reserve system failed. In 1926, further development of that counter-petition brought the matter closer to a Privy Council hearing – the highest court in Canada was in England. But first the government, notably Duncan Campbell Scott, insisted the matter go to a Judicial Committee for approval before the complaint progressed. At that stage, the issue was thrown away with undisguised contempt by the collection of bureaucrats and politicians who formed the ad-hoc and unprecedented Committee.

In 1969 the Prime Minister attempted unilaterally to obliterate the recognition of Indian Status and, along with any other reference to it, any land entitlement associated with indigenous communities and nations. In 1990, federal justice ministers and Cabinet ministers had refused four years of campaigning to have the Supreme Court of Canada hear the question: is there still aboriginal title to lands in BC?[2]

In 1992, the BC Treaty Commission was established: negotiations concerned the price of abandoning the Indian Land Question, since extinguishment was the end goal. The modern BC treaty process is premised on the First Nations, the individual communities, releasing all their land to Canada in exchange for rights which Canada will agree to recognize. The differences between this approach and the approach taken by governments in 1911 is that today the transaction is being labeled a treaty and indigenous communities are sponsored to take part in protracted negotiations over which rights will be recognized *before* the community releases all their claims and indemnifies Canada for all past harms. This time the Commission also has enormous and voluble support from the overwhelming majority of lecturers in the new field of First Nations Studies, as well as from an entrenched form of imposed administration— the elected Band Chief and Council system— with whom to arrange negotiations.

The BC Treaty Commission: Negotiating Extinguishment

The Premier's Council on Native Affairs was set up in 1989 and it recommended that British Columbia move to establish a process for negotiating First Nations land claims. In 1990, BC joined the federal government and the Nisga'a, who had been negotiating under the Comprehensive Claims Policy since 1976. Then the British Columbia Claims Task Force was established. This government initiative replaced the presentation to Indian Affairs Minister Tom Siddon of a Comprehensive Framework Treaty written by the Union of BC Indian Chiefs. The Task Force included indigenous representatives, notably Miles Richardson, Haida, who had been a vocal participant in logging blockades in his homeland just a few years prior. It also included equally staunch advocates of assimilation and extinguishment, like provincial Member of the Legislative Assembly (MLA) Mike deJong, non-native. The First Nations Summit was formed in 1992, per one of the recommendations of the BC Task Force. This body was then endowed with the position of representative of First Nations in BC interested in entering into treaty negotiations in the new Commission. The Summit endorsed the Task Force's Recommendations and was appointed the third party to the negotiations. BC, Canada and the Summit created the British Columbia Treaty Commission. BC produced the *BC Treaty Commission Act,* and money started flowing through the Commission to interested First Nation Parties to begin negotiations under its Terms of Reference. Those Terms were the 19 Recommendations of the BC Task Force.[3] Key to the recommendations was establishment of "a New Relationship based on mutual trust, respect and understanding through political negotiations."[4]

The scope of this negotiation process was immediately conspicuous in its lack of recognition of aboriginal title at the outset. It is in fact unnecessary to provide any kind of evidence of aboriginal title in order to enter negotiations to extinguish that title. Knowing that, Chief Clarence Louie of Osoyoos entered his community into the treaty process with a Statement of Claim which mapped the area his First Nation identified as their territory... in the shape of a perfect rectangle. This was not a sensitive reflection of the actual lands owned and used by the community, but it was an indication of the pre-condition that the old borders would be rubbed out anyway by ratifying a Final Agreement in which the people give up title of anything they thought was theirs to Canada and BC. Why go into painstaking detail to define the territories that were actually involved? The straight-edged map was perhaps a dare, to see if BC or Canada would object to his outing the insincerity of the process. There was no objection – the BC treaty process has nothing to do with recognizing indigenous title, only extinguishing it "wherever it might have been," as they say in the Final Agreements. No titles, no rights to share revenue from future resource development on those traditional lands, and no claim for past or future damages will survive ratification of the Final Agreement.[5] The federal Comprehensive Claims Policy does not allow for untidy results from negotiated settlements, and that is the forty year old policy which underlines the Commission. This policy is naturally underlined by the 150 year old policy – but that one wasn't written down explicitly.

Three years after the BC Treaty Commission's establishment, sovereigntists in Secwepemc would challenge the idea that they had to play by these rules of capitulate or languish. They put the governments' stated New Relationship, named in the Task Force recommendations, to the test and it failed fabulously. At Gustafsen Lake, the Secwepemc people and their comrades attempted to use their lands and were almost murdered for it. Professor Anthony Hall testified to the gridlock in British Columbia which made such confrontations inevitable, that is, the immovable position of the governments to refuse to engage at a nation-to-nation level or to discuss continuing indigenous titles and only to admit land conflicts to the BC Treaty Commission or Specific Claims process. He prepared his evidence at the Request of Mr. Paul Papak, Assistant Federal Public Defender in Portland, Oregon, to prevent the extradition of "OJ" James Pitawanakwat charged in connection with events at Gustafsen Lake in the summer of 1995.

Having studied the matter it is my expert opinion that the charges and convictions placed on Mr. Pitawanakwat were manifestly of a political character. Indeed, the inter-related standoffs at Ipperwash and Gustafsen Lake became extremely charged political events, where the police, the military and many of the media reporters covering the event became ensnared in a complex web of inter-connected political agendas.

These agendas involved efforts of officialdom, both Native and non-Native, to manipulate public perceptions to safeguard a fragile status quo in about 50 treaty negotiations then and now underway in British Columbia involving fundamental readjustments in the relationship between Aboriginal and Crown land title over the largest mass of this resource-rich province. These negotiations are very political exercises, whose very existence serves to illustrate that the Aboriginal land title in British Columbia is an extremely charged subject of political controversy, where the future disposition and rights to almost unimaginable natural-resource wealth hangs in the balance.[6]

Two years after Gustafsen Lake, a Supreme Court of Canada ruling in *Delgamuukw v. The Queen*,[7] on appeal from BC, decided that nothing British Columbia had done to date had extinguished aboriginal title. This was a profound new development and reasonably should have changed the game in crown-aboriginal negotiations. But the government only had enthusiasm to extinguish that title which it had never admitted to exist. Aboriginal Affairs Minister John Cashore told reporters: "It puts treaty-making in a stronger position, I look on it as a vindication for the treaty process... I don't think it is indicative of a fundamental change in the way we're approaching it."[8] The Supreme Court decision did not change anything in the BC treaty process.

Soon Robert Nault replaced Cashore. His contempt for the court's findings were more flagrant: "Why should we compromise the BC Treaty Commission, our flagship process, just because of a court ruling?" He was then responding to letters from the Delgamuukw Implementation Steering Committee—a group of notable indigenous leaders intent on implementing that court decision on aboriginal title.[9]

The top Canadian court had admitted that none of British Columbia's declarations of ownership or arguments of racial superiority or references to god-given rights conferred on them by their founding monarch had effectively dispossessed the indigenous of their lands without their consent. The rejection of all those arguments, arguments which underlie BC's present-day claim to the land, should have been a pivotal moment in British Columbian culture. It was not. The "flagship" process of extinguishment continued along the base lines of the 1974 and 1986 Comprehensive Claims Policy, despite the revelation that the colours it was flying were clearly piratical. Nor did the Canadian government intrude to protect the integrity of the federal courts and the rule of law.

The demand that indigenous peoples give up themselves and their lands as a sort of evolutionary inevitability, the "flagship," has been sailing for a very long time. After Prime Minister Trudeau failed in 1969 to make Indians disappear from Canadian governance, his Deputy Minister of the DIA noted the following:

> The policy in respect to Indian rights and the handling of claims arising from treaties or unsatisfied aboriginal interests is obviously a bone in the throat to many Indians. Nevertheless I believe it would be impossible for the Government to change its position on these matters now...[10]

From the expert advice of Trudeau's Ministers flowed the newly created Comprehensive Claims Policy of 1974 – immediately after the *Calder* decision. That Policy, which spells out that extinguishment is the pre-requisite for negotiations over Indian land in Canada, informs negotiations in the BC treaty process.

Many of the 19 Recommendations forming the basis of negotiations in the BC treaty process were instantly in conflict with the governments' longtime underlying objectives and limiting provisions in the original 1974 Comprehensive Claims Policy (CCP), the National Committee, and previous attempts to corral indigenous nations in court events where they were required to release any claim to their title and rights before court findings were made on the subject. A First Nation would engage in negotiations to seek the return of, reparation or at least compensation for lands and jurisdictions assumed by the crown. To complete CCP negotiations, the governments inflexibly require that the First Nation will cede, release and surrender to British Columbia and Canada the entire lands they laid claim to in their Statement of Intent to negotiate.

A good grassroots explanation of this situation is given out freely by Arthur Manuel of Neskonlith, Secwepemc:

> The Canadian Constitution 1982 requires the federal and provincial governments to recognize and affirm our existing Aboriginal Rights and the Supreme Court of Canada judicially recognizes our Aboriginal Rights. It is the federal and provincial governments that are acting inconsistently with having our Aboriginal Title and Rights recognized on

the ground. Instead both levels of government carry on a business as usual approach in our Aboriginal Title and Rights territory. This is very frustrating to Indigenous Peoples who are dependent on their Aboriginal Title and Rights to put food on their table.

The existing federal Comprehensive Land Claims Policy is the political decision of the Canadian government. The primary purpose of the federal Comprehensive Claims Policy is to extinguish our Aboriginal Title and Rights under the "modified and non-assertion models". This means that our Aboriginal Title and Rights will either be modified to provisions contained in a Final Agreement or that our Aboriginal Title and Rights will not be asserted except within the provisions of the Final Agreement. These two models will basically extinguish Aboriginal Title without using the internationally rejected terms of "cede, surrender and release".[11]

An explanation of the Comprehensive Claims is also available from the Auditor-General of Canada, who is equally specific about the policy's intent to extinguish Aboriginal rights and title in exchange for…whatever can then be negotiated:

> In 1973, the Supreme Court of Canada ruled, in the *Calder* case, that the Nisga'a held Aboriginal title before the British established sovereignty, but the court split evenly on whether this title had been "extinguished" when B.C. joined Canada. In 1973, in the wake of this landmark ruling, the federal government established its policy on comprehensive land claims. This policy was revised in 1981 and again in 1986 to become the Comprehensive Land Claims Policy. Under the policy, the federal government negotiates with First Nations a package of clearly defined rights and benefits in exchange for their claims to Aboriginal rights and title.[12]

The Union of BC Indian Chiefs has added, at least as recently as 2007, "It is fair to say that 100% of First Nations in British Columbia unequivocally have rejected Canada's Comprehensive Claims Policy and called for changes to it…"[13]

Rejections of government policy and calls for change, however, are some of the only domestic currency any indigenous community has. The positive result of any aboriginal title court case is never a court-ordered settlement or a court-ordered proceeding to some third party independent and impartial tribunal, but the direction that the governments and the indigenous should "negotiate" a political solution between themselves. That is what the judges said at the end of their reasons in *Delgamuukw*. Essentially the courts are condemning the aboriginal plaintiffs to extinguishment by negotiations with government; negotiations and outcomes which have been prescribed in a thoroughly circumspect manner by the same government.

When the extinguishment condition in the BC treaty process was brought to the attention of the United Nations Committee for the Elimination of all forms of Racial Discrimination, the Committee objected to it. When the treaty process adopted the alternative language that "all rights and title would be modified to be the rights and title included in this Agreement," the Committee remarked on Canada's good behavior including: "the assurance given by the government that Canada would no longer require a reference to extinguishment of surrendered land and resources rights in any land claim agreements."[14] The reality is that "modified rights" refers to rights which have been conferred by Canada in exchange for release of aboriginal title and rights, or, extinguishment. The modern rights are not acknowledged to stem from true, existing rights which have as their fount the nationhood of the rights holders. They seem to be legitimized by the state's recognition of them – the state which has never achieved legitimacy.

Eventually, in response to further more detailed submissions by indigenous parties, including the Indigenous Network on Economies and Trade, UN CERD acknowledged that the change of language had not actually changed the intent and intended result of the negotiated agreements, and the Commission should not proceed thusly.

Only the indigenous themselves can extinguish their rights. The governments' treaty negotiators understand this clearly. Tim Koepke, a provincial negotiator, explained it this way:

> I can't imagine what legislation Canada or BC could introduce that could override a Section 35 aboriginal right. You can't bring in legislation that overrides the Constitution. In treaty they are choosing to replace existing and undefined Section 35 aboriginal rights with defined treaty rights... an agreement negotiated by the three parties can be brought into effect by the three governments to the extent their rights are modified.[15]

Earlier versions of the BC Treaty Commission's website were very helpful in making sense of the new vocabulary. The website used to contain a glossary:

certainty provisions: treaty provisions designed to clearly
define the authorities, rights and responsibilities for all
parties to the treaty. See also extinguishment.

extinguishment: term used to describe the cessation or
surrender of aboriginal rights to lands and resources in
exchange for rights granted in a treaty. To date, Canada has
required full or partial extinguishment to conclude treaties.[16]

The glossary has been removed from the site.

So, at least since 1992, "negotiating" in BC actually means: *accepting
certain baseline positions of the federal and provincial governments which
render the stated objectives for self-government laid out at entry to the treaty
process as unachievable*. In BC, "negotiating" defies any existing definition.
As well as that, the 19 Recommendations which are supposed to guide these
"negotiations" are a far cry from the nation-to-nation agreements which are
required to address the issues. While treaty First Nations in BC claim that
they are practicing self-government since ratifying their treaty, this phrase is
not a good description of what they are actually doing. They have promised,
in the Final Agreement, to govern themselves according to a model which is
nearly indistinguishable from that provided for in the BC *Municipalities Act.*
When Tsawwassen Chief Kim Baird spoke of her treaty First Nation's "self-
government" at the UN Permanent Forum on Indigenous Issues in New York,[17]
she was merely using new vocabulary which the entire BC Treaty Commission
and all associated politicians, negotiators and contracted promoters have
decided on to mask the unpalatable truth that these agreements are in fact the
opposite of self-government. The treaty First Nation's every act, every process,
every option is prescribed in the Final Agreement. Baird didn't, incidentally,
remark on her First Nation's landmark achievement since treaty – which was
celebrated in BC press – of acquiring a Metro Vancouver bus stop on the
Reserve (now the Treaty Settlement Lands).

How can this be, that indigenous people would extinguish themselves
as peoples; would agree to conditions that switched off their powers of self-
determination after all these long years of seeking justice?

The government's long awaited outcome of poverty, discrimination
and education by bullying, if not straight out physical torture in Indian
Residential Schools, has arrived. The era of "negotiating" extinguishment has
been made possible by individuals who have accepted the job of representing
the indigenous side while destroying the indigenous side. Handsome salaries,
privileges and perks unknown are reliably rumoured to have been accepted to
carry out these "negotiations" on behalf of victims of the conditions calculated
to bring about the destruction of a people. Over the last twenty years many
aboriginal people have made a career in this new form of "negotiating." In

fact, a new generation, indigenous and non-native, has grown up without the ability to discern "negotiations" from "capitulation," "extinguishment" and "surrender." The results of the process are not treaties, as they are called, but rather nearly unconditional surrenders.

Native politicians, men and women now in their 40s and 50s, began in the 1990s to make bold and unprecedented statements of condemnation against those of their people who continued to fight, literally, for their land, rights and people. They also engaged in awesome double-dealing to sell out their lands, territories and people. They did this for their own personal gain certainly, but it is possible that they also believed their people would never win against the establishment. It's possible, given their western education in economics, that they couldn't foresee how their nations could be sustainable going forward, if not embedded in the Canadian economy. As then Chief Commissioner of the BC Treaty Commission, Steven Point, put it: "Not only is Treaty the best way to go, it's the only way to go."[18] Assuredly, it was the only way on offer. Perhaps they simply believed their non-native lawyers had their highest aspirations at heart when they considered rulings such as *Delgamuukw* and suggested they could live with it; as if what the lawyers could get along with was equivalent to what the indigenous nations should be satisfied with.

A journalist described his experience of watching the native treaty negotiators:

> These young men, the finest minds of their generation, got hooked on airline reservations, hotel food, cellular telephones, Jack Daniels, air-conditioning and $50 hookers and meetings, meetings and more meetings. And at the end of the day, every day, week in and week out, they would return to whatever solace they could find in the fetid and smoke-filled bar at the Chatcau Granville Hotel.[19]

This is perhaps an impoverished and less than holistic view, but somehow the negotiators had to find a way to continue. The native politicians and deal brokers in the treaties have been trying to please two very different interested parties: government – which pays them and keeps the process going, and their community – those who elect or appoint them to the negotiations to represent their people. The Chair of the First Nations Summit, Grand Chief Edward John, always explained that the BC Treaty Commission "has no teeth." But the courts, by their failure to effectively intercede, have indicated political negotiations are the way to go, presumably in full awareness of the imbalance in power between the parties seated at the table. Eventually, when Ottawa replied to the BC court decision in *Tsilhqot'in,* 2007, that it would not change its position on negotiations either, as quoted at the top of this chapter,

Chief John professes to have caught on. "So now, all these first nations who have been involved... find out that the Crown is at the table in complete and utter bad faith."[20]

Chief John might have noticed earlier: there was the First Nations Unity Protocol in 2006 – where all Chief Negotiators made a unified statement of protest on exactly that point; the comments from government after the *Delgamuukw* decision in 1997; the BC referendum seeking a caged negotiating mandate in 2002; the parameters of the Comprehensive Claims Policy of 1986; the result in the Nisga'a Final Agreement of 2000; the experience of entrapment which so many indigenous individuals sucked into the treaty process wrote letters about, starting in at least 1999; the warnings of any number of indigenous analysts. Instead John continued, "The Chiefs were involved, and the task force were providing drafts to the chiefs on a monthly basis. Not one chief in British Columbia said, 'Yes, we will have a non-rights based treaty negotiations process.' Not one."

And he's telling the truth: the chiefs never said they would have such a thing. But that's what they had. They participated in it and he participated in it – in spite of no recognition of aboriginal title in the negotiations—for fifteen years by the time that statement of shock was made in 2007. He might have noticed that in 1997, when there was no change even after *The Vancouver Sun* showed him on the front page, pointing at himself, with the caption: "'It's a new day': Chief Edward John says Thursday's Supreme Court ruling will force the government to renegotiate native land claims."[21] He might have noticed that his organization, the Summit, issued a response to the *Delgamuukw* decision in the form of a demand for better negotiating terms in February of 1998, and never got them.

The Nisga'a completed a deal that had no bearing on their rights:

> ...the provincial government refused to adopt a system of "interim measures" to halt the logging. This "talk and log" reality became what the Nisga'a call a "chainsaw-massacre" of the Nass forests and resulted in clear-cuts as large as 6,000 hectares. One internal Nisga'a study estimated that each year during the twenty-three years of the negotiations, 30,000 truckloads, worth $60 million, were harvested from Nass forests. ...a Price Waterhouse study conducted in the 1980s estimated that this logging represented $2 billion of lost economic opportunity for the Nisga'a.[22]

The Nisga'a settled for a capital transfer that was one tenth of that single lost opportunity—twenty years later.

That is another story. When James Gosnell died—James Gosnell of the Nisga'a who said "We own this country lock, stock and barrel"—the

Nisga'a negotiations changed dramatically. His younger brother had taken over to replace him in his illness. And somehow the position of the Nisga'a and other negotiators migrated from "But Matthias and Gosnell said they would never agree to extinguish aboriginal rights – rights to underlying title of the land, as well as the right to use it in the way their ancestors did – in exchange for treaties."[23] What the Nisga'a eventually ratified extinguished everything they had and gave them back some rights as Canadian citizens living in a Nisga'a municipality. In 1980, they had printed a pamphlet called *Citizens Plus, The Nishga People of the Naas River Valley in Northwestern British Columbia; Nishga Land Is Not For Sale.* It included the *Nishga Declaration*, which says at the end:

> Undergirding the whole of the above is the demand that, as the inhabitants since time immemoriam of the Naas Valley, all plans for resource extraction and 'development' must cease until aboriginal title is accepted by the Provincial Government. Also, we, the Nishga People, believe that both the Government of BC and the Government of Canada must be prepared to negotiate with the Nishgas on the basis that we, as Nishgas, are inseparable from our land; that it cannot be bought or sold in exchange for "extinguishing of title."

Why they let those beliefs go is a mystery. Aboriginal title was not accepted by the provincial government.

The treaty process is not a court-ordered mandate to make treaties to fulfill Canada's Constitutional obligations to the indigenous nations with whom Canada has not treated. BC judges have declared that they can see nothing which forces the governments to treat with First Nations; at least, they generously included this explanation when determining that *if* the governments elect to negotiate treaty, they really ought to do so in good faith.[24] The treaty process is not the result of a Royal Commission, monitored and implemented under third-party scrutiny. It is an elective opportunity, and the results will be seen as consensual. As one Wet'suwet'n involved in the *Delgamuukw* trials, Herb George, put it, "Delgamuukw doesn't impose a duty on the crown to negotiate with us. Our job is to compel you to negotiate with us."[25] He was the BC Regional Vice-Chief of the Assembly of First Nations at the time, and he was speaking to a non-native audience at a conference. George apparently accepted the job of assistant sales clerk, trying to convince the BC public that indigenous peoples are worth negotiating with. Any native individual with some entrepreneurial spirit can see what this opportunity might mean for them. Some Chief Negotiator salaries have six figures.

Some Elders maintained a different sort of logic against the cooperators: "They can have their treaty, but they can't use any of our land."[26]

The old-timers' hard line is ill-understood by younger generations who are offered employment by treaty groups in such areas as Land and Resource Management, Governance, and Education, but financed by repayable negotiating loans. The young peoples' participation in treaty-financed operations seems to be less than informed by the facts that they are receiving borrowed money loaned to and to be paid back by their own communities from funds yet to be won at the negotiating table, and running up bills which put their communities in a position from which they will find it difficult to escape. If they quit negotiations and the loans come due, how will they pay? The Canadian government, which runs First Nations' finances, will recognize the immediate debit of $35,000 per month—or more—in loan repayment as an indication of the need for third party remedial management. The harder (longer) they negotiate, the more costly it becomes... Punishment for exacting negotiations or withdrawal from the process has been built into the process.

"It's better to do something than nothing," declared an Elder defending the BC treaty process. With this sincere and sensible logic, many became involved. Why not? Confident in what they have, confident that everyone must realize BC needs their participation, and with a Supreme Court decision at their back, 120 of the 203 First Nations in BC became involved within ten years of the advent of the Treaty Commission.[27]

In that span of time, the Nisga'a Agreement had not been completed. Once it was, the others began to see the shape of their own Final Agreements as blue-printed by the Nisga'a. There would be no aboriginal title. There would be no avoiding taxation. There would be no more Indian Reserve—it would be replaced with fee-simple title holdings, with BC having the underlying title. The presently underlying aboriginal title would be extinguished and the lands registered to British Columbia. There would be nothing left to the benefits of Indian Status but the name "Status Indian." There would be no recourse: "*X* First Nation releases BC, Canada and anyone else from any and all claims..."[28] There would be no promise to conserve the fisheries, only a promise of compensation should they fail.[29] Fisheries, the "lifeblood" of indigenous peoples in the interior and on the coast, would, today, have to be protected as a matter of fiduciary obligations to an indigenous nation. Without lifeblood, land or recourse, what would an indigenous nation be?

Even Canadian reports recommend against the BCTC approach. *Treaty Making in the Spirit of Co-existence: An Alternative to Extinguishment*, a production of the Royal Commission on Aboriginal Peoples in 1995, stated: "The Report expresses the view that a policy that recognises and affirms Aboriginal rights and emphasises co-existence, mutual recognition, and shared ownership and jurisdiction is to be preferred over current federal extinguishment policy."[30]

What an admission! Politicians, however, disagree with the Commissioners. As a member of the Aboriginal Standing Committee, and

a former member of the BC Task Force, MLA Mike deJong carried on the
discussion around extinguishment in the Everyman vernacular, in this case in
response to a participant representing the dissenting Quaker view in one of a
series of public forums about the Nisga'a Final Agreement under construction:

> Thank you, Ms. Chandler. Let me try a proposition out on
> you with respect to the part of your submission dealing
> with extinguishment, because we've heard from people
> who are adamant that as a condition of signing a treaty,
> language containing the word "extinguishment" should be
> included. We've heard from others, most notably aboriginal
> representatives, who are as adamantly opposed to the
> inclusion of extinguishment language in a treaty. We tend
> to talk about it in very general terms, but here's what many
> people say to me on the practical side. If we are going to
> invest vast sums of money and human resources in reaching
> treaty settlements that contain in many cases, as in the
> Nisga'a AIP, provision for the transfer of lands, they don't
> want the same aboriginal group that is a party to that treaty
> to come back ten, 20 or 30 years from now and say: "Well,
> we have discovered that we have a heretofore unknown claim
> to additional lands." Now, that is a gross oversimplification
> of the issue. But what people want to know or what many
> people—not all, but many people—say to me is: the deal
> must be the deal. We don't want to be a signatory to that deal
> and then discover that in the case of land, for example, an
> aboriginal group comes back and claims additional land. I
> must confess that this expectation as it is expressed in those
> terms does not strike me as unreasonable. How does that fit
> within your understanding of the concept of extinguishment?

Mr. deJong is describing a final surrender, not a nation-to-nation
treaty crafted for the purposes of mutually recognizing one another in their
capacities as holding continuing ownership and jurisdiction.
The lady responded,

> I would not be willing for anyone to extinguish my rights. I
> expect that you would feel the same. ...Our concern is that
> the principle of extinguishment might be carried forward
> under a different name. We hope that it will not happen and
> that if there is a change in terminology, that will reflect a
> true change in policy.[31]

The "Modified Rights" language satisfies the linguistic preferences desired but, true to Ms Chandler and the Quakers' fears, changes little else, and certainly not the extinguishment outcome, in the end result. It looks like this example from the Tsawwassen Final Agreement, 2007. "Despite the common law, as a result of this Agreement and the Settlement Legislation, the aboriginal rights, including the aboriginal title, of Tsawwassen First Nation, as they existed anywhere in Canada before the Effective Date, including their attributes and geographic extent, are modified, and continue as modified, as set out in this Agreement."[32]

This treaty process pursues the municipalization of indigenous nations, the exact objective of the 1969 Trudeau white paper. Final Agreements, or "modern day treaties," in British Columbia have "Self-Governance Agreements" nearly identical to the BC Municipalities Act.[33] The people will have the power to call themselves whatever they like: a First Nation, a Tribal Council; as Premier Ujjal Dossanjh stated in a legislative debate about the Nisga'a: "This is not really a nation. All I care is what limitations, restrictions, restraints upon their rights are! The Nisga'a Nation would have attributes in this treaty, no more; no less. This is all they get, this is all the rights they have [smiling]. I don't care if they call themselves Tribal Council or Nation."[34]

Upon becoming nothing more than a municipality, indigenous nations will be entirely absorbed in the administrative prerogative of British Columbia and Canada. They will become tax-paying Canadian corporations. Treaty First Nations would pay 50% of revenues they generate post Treaty; businesses run by the First Nations would have a low ceiling on tax-free income, and after that they would contribute half to the province. They would pay property tax revenues to the federal government—actually creating a further layer of taxation of First Nation citizens and corporations that must pass on a portion of their profits to the First Nation government as well as to Canada and BC.[35]

It took three decades to produce an example of this type of First Nation Treaty municipality. The Nisga'a agreement was one of Canada's experiments in post-1969 White Paper Policy: Comprehensive Claims Policy. Other Comprehensive Claims tests included the James Bay Cree, the entire Yukon Territory Settlement Agreement, and the creation of the Nunavut Territory. In each of those cases the nations relinquished their aboriginal title in exchange for rights guaranteed in the agreements. They bartered their self-determination for delegated powers on the level of those held by School Boards, and for low level courts operating within Canadian legal parameters.

If this Comprehensive plan continues successfully, there would be no possibility for reconciliation—just municipalities with variations on the standard powers. There would not be indigenous nations, just Canadian citizens with protected rights to hunt and pick berries in accordance with BC-approved Land Use Plans, as stipulated in their Final Agreement.

This is clearly a method which Canadians and British Columbians accept as addressing their role in the futures of indigenous nations. There is no end to the history books, learned papers and publications of every type which end in some version of the lines, 'and now those land question problems are in the past, since we are moving forward with meaningful settlements negotiated under the BC Treaty Commission.' Almost anything on the subject since 1989 concludes the same way. Professor Hamar Foster gave a lecture to that effect for the BC Treaty Commission in 2002: "The reality, I think, is that negotiated settlements are, in the end, the only solution."[36] The concept of international oversight or third party mediation does not exist in the BC academics' world.

What may have been a bold or striking statement for the likes of Paul Tennant in 1989—the suggestion that the era of denial around land claims was about to end with the new treaty process—was wearing thin by 2002 and is simply inexplicable for John Lutz in 2008. In the intervening years there has been the Gustafsen Lake standoff, which was effectively an indigenous condemnation of the treaty process. In 2006 the First Nations Unity Protocol Agreement issued press statements explaining their demands for a common table to address the more outstanding insincerities in the process. There is the Halkomelem Treaty Group's petition admitted by the Organization of American States which thereby recognized the Group's contention that they have exhausted the domestic remedies to their land problem in Canada—which includes their participation in the BC Treaty process. There is the fact that the Gitxsan and Wet'suwet'n were in court for recognition of their title and rights when they were persuaded to instead join the treaty process to negotiate their progress so far with government, which they did in the summer of 1994. The province walked away from their table early in 1996, citing "fundamental differences," the Chiefs resumed the legal action, and they got the *Delgamuukw* ruling which left them – and arguably all aboriginal people in Canada—in a better position than has been afforded by anything that has happened since through the BC Treaty Commission.

The BC treaty process has, by 2012, been deserted by all but a handful of communities. There have been publicized statements by the Interior Alliance, a modern revival of the Allied Tribes of 1910: "To those who have suggested that we work inside the B.C. Treaty Process, we point out that it is just these types of treaties, both historic and modern, which call on us to extinguish our Aboriginal title to the land and its resources, that have left us in a state of poverty and dependence."[37] And there are a number of Nisga'a citizens ready to speak out, like Elder Rose Doolan.

> We lost our aboriginal title. Kincolith lost 100% of their ancestral lands. 8% was given back in fee simple title. Our Status is gone. It's taken quite a bit of our dental coverage.

Whenever we asked questions about it, they would shut us up. They would tell us to sit down. One person would answer the question and say, "He'll answer the question." Then that one would say, "Oh, someone is going to answer that." Then another one would say, "Oh, that person can answer that question." We came out of those meetings more confused than when we went in.

They paid the Elders $350 a day to sit in those meetings and keep quiet. After the treaty was signed, and they paid them the $15,000 that was promised, they dumped them. We have been sitting in on our Elders' meetings, and they're not doing too well.

They're preparing for 2012 when they're going to start taxing us. I don't know how they're going to do that, because the majority of people here are not working. They have $185 a month. It's like that in all four villages. There's only a few that aren't like that, and they work for the Lisims Government. Some of them that work there now were against the treaty, but then they get these huge cheques, they've got jobs, and they say, 'I'm getting $4,000 a month,' and they say, 'this is OK.' I know they're going to run out of money before time.

They have started selling off rights to the land. They are forging Elders' signatures to sell ancestral lands. They were handing out certificates to our Elders for 1,500 shares. It's the Nass Valley Gateway Project, and Mineral Hill Industries. That's going to come to nothing, $300 or less after the broker's fees. Men were here about a month ago, handing out shares. My husband just turned 65 years old. A lady from New Aiyansh brought my husband's 1500 shares and his certificate and the packages and said, "Don't worry about signing these, we already signed them for you." They're mining in Chief James Mountain's homelands, and others have interests there.

Last year all our young men left to go to Alberta for work. With this treaty we were supposed to become self-sufficient.

Our Chief Councilor has stated in public that the government would not tax poverty. So I wasn't sure if this is the vision they have for us? To keep us in poverty?

In 2012 they will start the house tax. They didn't explain that to the people, they just flashed around how much the

Elders were going to get and how well-off we were all going to be.

When they gave the books to the people, for the Final Agreement, the people couldn't understand most of the words in there. Some people didn't receive theirs until two weeks before the assembly. We didn't get ours until we got there.

A lot of the people who voted for it, they thought it was going to be a real good treaty. They're just finding out now that they're losing their identity as Status Indians. They're just finding out now that they'll have to pay taxes on their own houses.

One of our friends who works for the Lisims Government felt threatened just to be with us when we went to the court case (James Mountain's hearing in Vancouver). You have to make a sworn statement that you're not going to speak against the treaty, that's for all who work at the Lisims Government. This is what our people are facing. The people who have jobs, they can't say anything. We tell them, 'Speak out! Say something!' but they can't, they'll lose their job.[38]

Mrs. Doolan's experience is as the Final Agreement intended it to be. As Haida Elder Thowgwelth, Lavina White, put it, "The purpose of the BC treaty process is to legitimize the theft of our lands." And in the words of the government, which substantiate that view:

Jack Weisgerber:"What does it mean, "aboriginal title," that you are so eager to embrace? Not to my surprise, aboriginal title is not defined, yet a statement is included... it certainly isn't a constitutional right."
Ujjal Dossanjh: "The rights outlined in this treaty are the final rights of Nisga'a - we're not interested in defining title for other aboriginal groups to come at us with, and that's the end of it—no debate."
Weisgerber: "This is less than forthright."
Dossanjh:"To enshrine this would hinder us. We don't need that definition to deal with rights we've agreed upon."
Geoff Plant:"On the question of inherent versus delegated rights, we don't need to answer because everything is taken care of in this treaty? Now title, same question, same answer -"no debate," because the intent is to put all those questions to rest?"

> Dossanjh:"Thank you. The intention and purpose of
> negotiating treaties is to exhaustively codify rights... to
> exhaustively define and limit rights as modified by Nisga'a
> (treaty). To make sure our treatment exhaustively sets them
> down and then we put the law on it for certainty."[39]

Meanwhile others are formally leaving the treaty process, at least
those who can afford to. The loans that were extended to them in order to
pursue the negotiating process have instead taken on the appearance of an
entrapment. Valued in the millions of dollars, these loans must be repaid by the
indigenous nations if Final Agreements with Canada are achieved or not, or if
they wish to withdraw from the process. The longer the negotiations carry on,
the deeper the debt suffered by the indigenous nations—but often no escape
from the negotiation process is possible, as the loans would then have to be
repaid—an impossibility for most deeply impoverished indigenous nations.
When the Nisga'a finally settled, their negotiating loan was over $20 million.
Rather than confront this reality, many of the negotiating tables are simply
listed as "inactive" in the Treaty Commission's annual reports.

In keeping with the appearance of entrapment, entry requirements to
negotiate a treaty under the BC Treaty Commission are remarkably low. Aside
from needing no evidence of aboriginal title, a duly publicized community
meeting to inform the membership that a proposal is being put forward to enter
the process does not seem to be required either. Very occasionally this provides
an exit door—but getting out is harder than getting in. The N'Quátqua First
Nation at Anderson Lake reviewed its participation in the process quite early
on. As the Chief recalled,

> We did the findings on it, and previous Chief and Council
> had done an economic development study in the community.
> I guess that's where it evolved from—they took it and ran
> with it. There was only five or six members who showed
> up at the meeting for the show of hands to get involved,
> and that was the concern with the members. We did the
> referendum and the results showed it: 80% were opposed
> to the treaty process.
>
> We got into the treaty process illegally. Our legal
> counsel looked into it and we had never had a proper
> referendum to enter the process. We refused to pay anything
> back, it was an illegal situation. They would call me up
> looking for (loan) money and I would say, 'talk to my legal
> counsel,' and they would just hang up on me.[40]

But something happened in 2002 that should have sprung the loan trap on governments—and let the indigenous out safely. At least two First Nations took the opening provided, but their departure was not celebrated or even discussed because, as one of the Chiefs put it, "I've lost enough friends over this already."[41]

In 2002, the new BC government held a referendum in which it sought a public mandate to abandon the platform for negotiations under the BC Treaty Commission and its 19 guiding recommendations. They succeeded, and they rely on it. Their negotiators defer to that referendum mandate and not the mandate they set out with: "Each of the parties be at liberty to introduce any issue at the negotiation table which it views as significant to the new relationship." The introduction of issues such as Indian Status, continuing aboriginal title post-treaty, and taxation are not welcome at the table, and that is discussed in Chapter Ten. This change of government horses midway through the treaty process should have triggered a serious reevaluation of the status of negotiating loans—the purpose of which had just been altered. The First Nations Summit might have taken it up seriously, rather than just writing disappointed letters to the federal government. The First Nations Summit is supposed to be equally one of the Principals of the BC Treaty Commission.

Sechelt and Westbank made the announcement of "100% community support to leave the treaty process" on November 25, 2009 at the start of a three-day First Nations Summit meeting in North Vancouver. Sechelt Chief Garry Feschuk and Westbank Chief Robert Louie indicated they would both be initiating legal action to seek recognition of their aboriginal title.[42]

The Carrier Sekani Tribal Council's President, Chief David Luggi, wrote to all First Nations involved with the BC Treaty Commission on June 5, 2007, after thirteen years in negotiations and $18,227,929 accrued in loans. "My people have decided that the British Columbia Treaty Process is a dead-end for our Nation. ... The BC Treaty Process is corrupting, dividing and destroying our people; the White Man is using this process to bankrupt us, to deny our rights, and to insult our ancestors."

The Office of the Wet'suwet'en published a media release on December 18, 2009:

> Treaty negotiations have put Wet'suwet'en in debt to the Crown for almost $13 million over the course of these negotiations. Throughout negotiations Crown agencies have continued to alienate lands, impact water quality, and permit the development of resources. In October 2009, Wet'suwet'en attending an All Clans meeting clearly stated their frustration with Treaty negotiations, and recommended the Chiefs step away from the Treaty process.

We are seeking a distinctly Wet'suwet'en Treaty," stated Debbie Pierre, Executive Director-Office of the Wet'suwet'en, "It is time the Crown agrees to negotiate, in good faith, an agreement recognizing Wet'suwet'en title, and respects our right to determine land use and resource development within our territories."

Unfortunately, both the Federal and Provincial government have refused to engage in negotiations outside of their 5% land selection model. In effect, this model promotes a settlement package of existing Indian reserves, Crown lands, and willing sellers of private lands.

As a result of the inequities of the Treaty Process, the Wet'suwet'en have not signed any treaty related agreements with the Crown(s).

Others are finding it very difficult to leave, or even to get the matter into a Band meeting. The plaintiffs in *Spookw v. Gitxsan Treaty Society et al.,* 2011, which included six hereditary chiefs and four Gitxsan bands, commenced an action against the Gitxsan Treaty Society, which is the organization responsible for the negotiations for the Gitxsan, the Governments of Canada and British Columbia and the British Columbia Treaty Commission in relation to the funding of treaty negotiations. They contended that the Society did not have a mandate from the Gitxsan people to accept treaty negotiating loans. The Court held that the imposition of such a duty of care on the Commission would amount to indeterminate liability as there are 60 negotiations ongoing with 110 Bands currently involved in the treaty process and that this process covers some 200,000 First Nations individuals. The Court seems to feel the balance of convenience rests on the Treaty Commission's side, that its foray into indeterminate liability should be underwritten by the impoverished Bands.

Those who proceed to Stage 6, Ratification, have some very sophisticated soft technology to grease the Final Agreement's passage, as well as campaign literature that comes from a Canadian mint. Handbooks on how to achieve ratification are produced by and for each treaty group. Maa-nulth made a checklist for their ratification team, where number fifteen advises them to "Ensure a wide range of Ha'wiih (Elders), Chief and Council and influential members who endorse the Treaty are interviewed for the videos being produced by BC."[43] The province is a fanatical supporter of this stage, offering hundreds of thousands of dollars to "public relations crisis management" companies weeks before votes.

In the case of the Tsawwassen Final Agreement, last-minute funding to the treaty team included a "treaty communication budget" of $430,000.[44] With this they hired Counterpoint Communications, self-described PR crisis managers, to produce a document distantly related to the Tsawwassen Final

Agreement and yet attractive and confidence-inspiring. It was titled, *Survival Guide to the Tsawwassen First Nation Final Agreement 2007*. It showed disconnected and unexplained pie charts and bar graphs: that if they did not vote for the treaty and things remained the same, they would have an annual budget of $2 million – but within fifteen years of the treaty they would have an annual budget of $18.1 million. Unfortunately, now five years after the vote to ratify, Tsawwassen's fiscal progress is not on track as per the pamphlet forecast.

At the time of the vote, Aboriginal Relations Minister Mike deJong declared to interested media, "The government wants this vote to succeed and we don't apologize for holding that view." Bertha Williams, a Tsawwassen member, went to great lengths to oppose the treaty, including presenting her case to a United Nations Urgent Action human rights committee. She also asked Prime Minister Harper and Premier Gordon Campbell, in an open letter, "Do you see the Tsawwassen Treaty as so flawed and so against the interests of Tsawwassen residents that you must send in your own election consultants with bags of money to manipulate the votes and win the July 25th referendum on the treaty?"

There is no end to enthusiasm for weirder ways to convince aboriginal people to sell their title for absurdly small amounts of money, and relinquish any claims they may have to self-governance that exceed municipal status. Arguments range from sickly sweet BC Treaty Commission style propaganda —their website features several very expensive looking short videos, to the exact other end of the spectrum—the university supported esoteric. Efforts to find another way to word "legitimizing land theft" through negotiations abound:

> The neutral framework is developed by integrating concepts and approaches from anthropology, geomatics engineering and soft systems engineering. The neutral framework entails first using the comparative design criteria of worldviews, values, concepts, goals and institutions of members of a community. This allows the Aboriginal land tenure systems to be described and analysed from the cultural perspective of the subject Aboriginal group. The comparisons are then evaluated to identify reforms to be made to the existing land tenure systems that are systemically desirable and culturally feasible for the subject community.[45]

This oxymoron, recommending a neutral approach where one side of what needs to be reconciled is "subject" to the other, comes from an eastern Canadian university paper that finds positively for the outcomes of the Nisga'a treaty. One of the things which is not up for negotiation in the modern day BC treaty process is the role which First Nations must continue in: subjects of BC and Canada.

Many will continue to put their voices up against the heavily subsidized infrastructure of capitulation. David Dennis, a citizen of Huu-ay-aht, wrote to his community about the impending vote for or against a modern Final Agreement as part of the Maa-nulth Treaty Society:

> I would like you to take some time to consider what I am saying.
> 1) all of the material is biased towards a "yes" vote;
> 2) all of the public sessions have biased towards a "yes" vote;
> 3) there has been no opportunity, aside from attending the "yes" sessions, to produce any dissenting information to the membership;
> ...In other words, we have only heard from sources that want you to vote "yes" on the "treaty", NOT try to produce a clear understanding of what the treaty means.
> You should understand that through this Agreement, the non-native governments are achieving their goals of "finality" and "certainty", meaning that our laws are finished and their laws will apply and prevail over the land and over us. This is all designed to trump any future challenge to the authority and power of the non-native governments over our communities.[46]

Failures to break through the "yes" pressure have not been slow in wreaking heartbreak. Dennis Nyce, nephew to Nisga'a Treaty negotiator Joseph Gosnell, wrote on Monday, June 9th, 2008:

> To Whom it may concern,
> I, Dennis Nyce, as a protest against the misleading Nisga'a Treaty Promises, And the recent taking the meaningless Land Entitlement Document given to our people and disregard for our Ayuukhl, with regards to Traditional ownership to lands, and the families to whom they once belonged, will be starting a HUNGER STRIKE, to show the INJUSTICE to our people who entrusted this government with their LIVES. Since Time IMMEMORIAL we have supported the Chiefs in our Battle with the British and their Laws. After 113 years Our own people are our own worst Enemies. This Government has done to our people what we as citizens would call a ROBINHOOD attitude. Although you support the Village Officials, you turn your backs on the people

who ENTRUSTED their lives in this N(isga'a).L(isims). G(overnment).

I will TAKE this to the fullest extent, even if it means the taking, or giving up my LIFE for the cause of our people.

We were promised that we would never lose our TRADITIONAL PLACES OF RESIDENCE.

Unfortunately this was a farce. Without a place to turn I am Living on the street.

To the people of the NASS RIVER, I apologize for any embarrassment and Shame. To the Chiefs OF the valley, I honour you all, with no place to turn I Leave my life in the hands of this TREATY and the people who GOVERN us.

With REGRETS, DISAPPOINTMENT, and SHAME FOR THIS TREATY

> DENNIS NYCE,
> GITWINKSIHLKW B.C

Mr. Nyce originally supported the treaty, but changed his mind since implementation. Not long before this letter was written he had been evicted from his home in Nisga'a.

Chapter 7

ASSIMILATION OR CRIMINALIZATION

"Over in Ottawa, they call that policy "Indian Advancement."
Over in Washington, they call it "Assimilation." We who would be the
helpless victims say it is tyranny.
Your governments have lately resorted to new practices in their
Indian policies. In the old days, they often bribed our chiefs to sign
treaties to get our lands. Now they know that our remaining territory can
easily be gotten from us by first taking our political rights away in forcing
us into your citizenship, so they give jobs in their Indian offices to the
bright young people among us who will take them and who, to earn their
pay, say that our people wish to become citizens with you and that we are
ready to do it. But that is not true."
—Speaker of the Six Nations Council, Deskaheh (Levi General)
March 10, 1925, Rochester, Canada

Savages in a Christian Empire

For the crime of not being Christian societies, indigenous peoples of the Americas have paid dearly for over 500 years: over a quarter of the duration of the imperial Christian empire. The conversion to Christianity of every human being in the world became the legitimizing mandate for European conquest as soon as Europe itself had been converted. That particular mandate of a spiritual imperialism was more a case of justifying why the barn door was left open, once the horse is long gone. The men who set out from England to sack China, India, Africa, the kingdoms of islanders in the Atlantic and Pacific, and finally the Americas were seeking riches. They were expected to return to their patrons with evidence of precious raw materials, and of that priority purpose there can be no argument. The return of precious cargo and diagrams of military fortifications to defend the procurement of more was the effect of their voyages; not tallies of Christian souls.

The right of domination was pinned on the doctrine of Christianity. During Europe's race to the New World, European adventurers marked any population without its own Christian prince "savage," and therefore inhuman and therefore without human rights. Spain's "Catholic Monarchs" were granted the Americas by Pope Alexander, once Columbus "found" them after following up a lead he got in Guinea – where African sailors already knew the route.[1] On May 4, 1493, the Papal Bull named *Inter Caetera* summed up Alexander's interpretation of God's approval of decimating any peoples found to be in the way of his Holy Roman Empire's enrichment—should it be discovered they had no knowledge of the Bible. A Papal Bull was, and arguably still is—insofar as it governs those states who draw their legal lineage from the Vatican, the equivalent of a holy commandment. *Inter Caetera* read, in part:

> Among other works well pleasing to the Divine Majesty and cherished of our heart, this assuredly ranks highest, that in our times especially the Catholic faith and the Christian religion be exalted and be everywhere increased and spread, that the health of souls be cared for and that barbarous nations be overthrown and brought to the faith itself.
>
> We have indeed learned that you [the Catholic Monarchs of Spain: Isabella and Ferdinand], who for a long time had intended to seek out and discover certain islands and mainlands remote and unknown and not hitherto discovered by others, to the end that you might bring to the worship of our Redeemer and the profession of the Catholic faith their residents and inhabitants, ... chose our beloved son, Christopher Columbus, a man assuredly worthy and of the highest recommendations and fitted for so great an undertaking, whom you furnished with ships and men equipped for like designs, not without the greatest hardships, dangers, and expenses, to make diligent quest for these remote and unknown mainlands and islands through the sea, where hitherto no one had sailed; and they at length, with divine aid and with the utmost diligence sailing in the ocean sea, discovered certain very remote islands and even mainlands that hitherto had not been discovered by others; wherein dwell very many peoples living in peace, and, as reported, going unclothed, and not eating flesh. Moreover, as your aforesaid envoys are of opinion, these very peoples living in the said islands and countries believe in

one God, the Creator in heaven, and seem sufficiently disposed to embrace the Catholic faith and be trained in good morals. And it is hoped that, were they instructed, the name of the Savior, our Lord Jesus Christ, would easily be introduced into the said countries and islands. … you have purposed with the favor of divine clemency to bring under your sway the said mainlands and islands with their residents and inhabitants and to bring them to the Catholic faith. Hence, heartily commending in the Lord this your holy and praiseworthy purpose, and desirous that it be duly accomplished, and that the name of our Savior be carried into those regions, we exhort you very earnestly …(to) enjoin strictly, that inasmuch as with eager zeal for the true faith you design to equip and despatch this expedition, you purpose also, as is your duty, to lead the peoples dwelling in those islands and countries to embrace the Christian religion; nor at any time let dangers or hardships deter you therefrom…

And, in order that you may enter upon so great an undertaking with greater readiness and heartiness endowed with the benefit of our apostolic favor, we, of our own accord, not at your instance nor the request of anyone else in your regard, but of our own sole largess and certain knowledge and out of the fullness of our apostolic power, by the authority of Almighty God conferred upon us in blessed Peter and of the vicarship of Jesus Christ, which we hold on earth, do by tenor of these presents, should any of said islands have been found by your envoys and captains, give, grant, and assign to you and your heirs and successors, kings of Castile and Leon, forever, together with all their dominions, cities, camps, places, and villages, and all rights, jurisdictions, and appurtenances, all islands and mainlands found and to be found, discovered and to be discovered towards the west and south, by drawing and establishing a line from the Arctic pole, namely the north, to the Antarctic pole, namely the south, no matter whether the said mainlands and islands are found and to be found in the direction of India or towards any other quarter, the said line to be distant one hundred leagues towards the west and south from any of the islands commonly known as the Azores and Cape Verde. With this proviso however that none of the islands and mainlands, found and to be found, discovered and to be discovered, beyond that said line towards the west and south, be in the actual possession of any Christian king or prince up to the birthday of our Lord Jesus Christ just past from which the present year one thousand four hundred and ninety-three begins.

Furthermore, under penalty of excommunication *late sententie* to be incurred *ipso facto*, should anyone thus contravene, we strictly forbid all persons of whatsoever rank, even imperial and royal, or of whatsoever estate, degree, order, or condition, to dare, without your special permit or that of your aforesaid heirs and successors, to go for the purpose of trade or any other reason to the islands or mainlands, found and to be found, discovered and to be discovered, towards the west and south, by drawing and establishing a line from the Arctic pole to the Antarctic pole... We trust in Him from whom empires and governments and all good things proceed, that, should you, with the Lord's guidance, pursue this holy and praiseworthy undertaking, in a short while your hardships and endeavors will attain the most felicitous result, to the happiness and glory of all Christendom.

Let no one, therefore, infringe, or with rash boldness contravene, this our recommendation, exhortation, requisition, gift, grant, assignment, constitution, deputation, decree, mandate, prohibition, and will. Should anyone presume to attempt this, be it known to him that he will incur the wrath of Almighty God and of the blessed apostles Peter and Paul.

In this way, the Pope gave every people without a Christian prince, and their lands, "in the direction of India or toward any other quarter," to Isabella and Ferdinand, the Catholic monarchs of what is today Spain. He said that this transfer was provided to ensure the "health of souls," not the health of the Catholic monarchy's treasury. But it is surely only the latter which benefitted. Isabella and Ferdinand and their heirs were never reprimanded for their failure to uphold the conditions of their ownership to the western hemisphere: kill or Christianize everyone. They certainly tried.

The Vatican had remained the fount and informant of post-Roman-Empire British law. It was not until the sixteenth century that King Henry the Eighth nudged the Pope out of most areas of British business. Still, the volatile politics of Europe would not have permitted Henry to cut the Biblical strings He admitted to as part of His explanation of His appointment by God to the head of a Christian monarchy. Latin, the Pope's language, was the lingua franca of European courts into the eighteenth century. British exploration of America was, as explained above, not in the Pope's gift, but Spain obviously failed to convince the rest of Europe that He was capable of giving it exclusively to Spain. The weight of this Papal Bull which authorized destruction of non-Christians can hardly have failed to capture the imaginations of England, France, Portugal, and Germany. Spain led a vigorous example of how to maximize the papal license and the others did not deviate from it.

Half a century after *Inter Caetera,* Pope Paul III wrote his Papal Bull, *Sublimus Dei.* It is dated May 29, 1537, and reads, in part:

> To all faithful Christians to whom this writing may come, health in Christ our Lord and the apostolic benediction.
>
> We, who, though unworthy, exercise on earth the power of our Lord and seek with all our might to bring those sheep of His flock who are outside into the fold committed to our charge, consider, however, that the Indians are truly men and that they are not only capable of understanding the Catholic Faith but, according to our information, they desire exceedingly to receive it. Desiring to provide ample remedy for these evils, We define and declare by these Our letters, or by any translation thereof signed by any notary public and sealed with the seal of any ecclesiastical dignitary, to which the same credit shall be given as to the originals, that, notwithstanding whatever may have been or may be said to the contrary, the said Indians and all other people who may later be discovered by Christians, are by no means to be deprived of their liberty or the possession of their property, even though they be outside the faith of Jesus Christ; and that they may and should, freely and legitimately, enjoy their liberty and the possession of their property; nor should they be in any way enslaved; should the contrary happen, it shall be null and have no effect.

Though neither Bull was ever revoked, and the norm that more recent Decrees are meant to replace those ahead of them, the earlier Papal Bull continues to be relied on by many a scholar, anthropologist, and government lawyer; it suits their arguments asserting dominion. According to the Shawnee legal historian Steven Newcomb, the human/savage split described by *Inter Caetera* is embedded in the present day laws of Canada and the United States.[2]

A savage was convenient to deal with. He was not worth the effort of understanding: a savage had no rights and the newcomer therefore had no responsibility to him. The use of God to justify continuing acts of genocide against peoples from the Arctic to the Antarctic pole who have consistently demonstrated the highest Christian virtues and even the willingness to embrace

Christianity literally, if in other languages, is an aberration of the human condition.

By 1850, the definition of savagery was freshly established by would-be British Columbians in their new chapter of Holy work. According to Gilbert Malcolm Sproat, one of the first Surveyors working for the Colony of British Columbia in the 1860's, savagery was indicated by the practice of using medicine men to undo evil curses.[3] Interestingly, the Roman Catholic Church was never dubbed savage, even while they did trade in priestly exorcisms. Savagery, Sproat and his like opined, was inherent in the idea that a person could buy penance by appeasing a medicine man with gifts – ironically a practice reminiscent of many Christian denominations' economies in heavenly pardons, which would be written out in calligraphy and effective on purchase.

Indigenous peoples' gods were considered inferior to the Christian god. The people were, therefore, savages. It was still necessary in 1995 to clarify in BC Supreme Court that a native man is a human being, and has human rights. The BC courts tend to overlook this fact when they apply laws made by their state to indigenous individuals they have apprehended; laws which have assumed the subservience of the indigenous man and woman to the newcomer's laws. A human being has many rights, however, and the rights to a language, a homeland, an identity and a government all flow from being a human. Former BC lawyer Lyn Crompton recalls a case where a Hereditary Chief was making an appeal to international courts over violations of his human rights,

> I went to court one day with Laurence Pootlass (Hereditary Chief Nuximlayc of Nuxalk), and I helped him to ask the judge to take notice of the fact that he was a human being. And to put it on record that he took judicial notice of the fact that Laurence was a human being, because all rights come from being human. And the judge got very annoyed. The judge was trying to stop Laurence from speaking, and Laurence said, "I want Lyn Crompton to speak." I happened to be in the court room, but I had already quit law in protest. The prosecutor jumped up immediately and said, "I don't want Lyn Crompton to speak." The judge finally said, "you may speak to the limited extent to explain why you should be allowed to speak." Anyway, we got past that and all I asked him really was that Laurence was asking him to take judicial notice of the fact that he was a human being. The judge harrumphed and was very annoyed, so I said, "if you are unprepared, my lord, to do so, perhaps we'll call medical evidence."[4]

The judge in that case managed to sidestep the point Nuximlayc was making about his possession of human rights. But to the European conqueror, conveniently enough, a human being was not merely the sum of his physical parts: he was inhuman without Christ. And though indigenous peoples all have stories of prophets to rival anything the spirits and gods shared with peoples on the other side of the globe, their gods are not recognized as the gods of human beings. The people were reverent, spiritual, ceremonial, and they certainly had their own spiritual beings looking out for their survival, but those gods supposedly did not make a man with rights.

The argument about the importance of Christianity has worn thin over time. No amount of Christianization of Indians has stemmed the original attempts at genocide – which were justified by the newcomer's appraisal of them as incapable of worshipping the God of the Bible.

The converts did embrace the opportunity to pray in a new way, as if their sense of adventure and exchange included a truly entrepreneurial *spirit*. It was, in fact, the Indians who built the first churches in those early days of British Columbia. From many accounts, the Anglicans, Roman Catholics and Oblates impressed the people by claiming to be ministers of God, and the people promptly built houses for them–churches to share with their settler congregations.[5] James Teit authored a brief paper on the subject of Nlaka'pamux observation of Christian routine, and noted majority acceptance. Certainly most continued to pray in their own way. They did not abandon their spiritual lives for Christianity, but modern inventories of "Christian inhabitants" might well be revised while reconsidering *Terra Nullius*.

In the absence of any Christian mercy or protection, the indigenous spiritualists were criminalized in earliest BC for practicing their ceremonies. Among North West Pacific Coast people, the mark of a leader was in what he or she would give away to the rest of the community. In that ceremony, a potlatch, called by the family of a Chief, a deceased, or a bride or groom, wealth would be redistributed among the people. The practice was versatile and adaptable to all kinds of social, spiritual and economic requirements – sometimes even the giving away of everything in one's possession, which had better be considerable, for a titled position.

The Indian Act amendments to Section 3 in 1880 read,

> Every Indian or other person who engages in or assists in celebrating the Indian festival known as the "Potlatch" or in the Indian dance known as the "Tamanawas" is guilty of a misdemeanor, and shall be liable to imprisonment for a term of not more than six and not less than two months in any gaol [jail] or other place of confinement; and any Indian or other person who encourages, directly or indirectly, an

Indian or Indians to get up such a festival or dance, or to celebrate the same, or who shall assist in the celebration of the same is guilty of a like offence, and shall be liable to the same punishment.

The 1927 Indian Act, in section 140, tightened things further to prohibit any kind of Indian dancing or singing off-Reserve without special permission from the Superintendent General of Indian Affairs.

In 1895, the Nass River Indians presented a petition to BC leaders regarding the

> ... contradictory state of affairs adorning your civilization. Churches are numerous; the theatres are located in the various sections of the town; and saloons multiply in numbers; all of which are in conformity with your laws, consequently we wish to know whether the ministers of the gospel have annihilated the rights of white men in these pleasures leading to heaven and hell exactly in different directions...
>
> We see in your graveyards the white marble and granite monuments which cost money in testimony of your grief for your dead. When our people die we erect a large pole, call our people together, distribute our personal property with them in payment for their sympathy and condolence; comfort to us in the sad hours of our affliction. This is what is called a potlatch—the privilege is denied us. It is a chimera that under the British flag slavery does not exist.

The Nootka Chief Maquinna published an article in the Victoria *Daily Colonist* on April 1, 1896, complaining of the ban on potlatching and comparing the potlatch to a banking system:

> They say it is the will of the Queen. The Queen knows nothing about our potlatch feasts. She must have been put up to make a law by people who know us... The potlatch is not a pagan rite; the first Christians used to have their goods in common, as a consequence must have given "potlatches," and now I am astonished that Christians persecute us and put us in jail for doing as the first Christians.[6]

In 1923, *An Appeal by the Indians of Vancouver Island* was addressed to the Indian Department of Canada. The Nimkish appointed a Committee to plead for the repeal of the potlatch ban. The writers briefly detailed the critical aspects of the ancient evolution of their work and economy, and advised the Government, which had long since been sworn as their fiduciary protector, as follows:

> We now come to the part that affects us most in this custom, and not only us, but all the other tribes. ...When the young couple are married the father of the daughter would give to his daughter's husband (many things), and a *copper*. This is... what has been passed on until today. ...The copper is the main holder of our customs because the value of them is rising, and as they are passed on to others they increase in value. The copper forms a chief strength of a man who intends giving a feast and he sells the copper and what he gets for it he uses to make a feast. All the other things that we would have would be quite useless to us if the copper was thrown out of our custom. It is used in marriages in order to get the things to make a feast. If a father would die and leave the copper to his son, no other man could get the copper except the son who would hold it until he felt it was time to sell it, he will figure out what it will bring. When he is finished figuring, he will call all the people together and will dance for them and give what it is worth and afterward whatever is given away if any of the other chiefs return it to him as it will be of use to him for many years. These coppers are sold for a large sum of money, and no one will force a person who sells it to give it all away, so that he always has considerable left for his own use. When a man buys a copper he pays a deposit on it and a next man may buy from him and pay deposit on an increased valuation and so on, it may be through the hands of four or five, and still payment not be completed. If our custom is done away with these coppers will be useless, and will entail a big loss as all those who have an interest in them will lose all they have put in. ... When the white man came and we could earn wages in cash for our labour, we invested our savings in coppers and used them the same as a white man would do with a bank and would always expect more back than we had put in. We are giving you a list of the coppers belonging to the Nimkish tribe and their values, other tribes have their own coppers so that you will see great financial loss entailed on us if our custom is suppressed.

> We do not want to fight the Government nor do we expect the Government to repay us for the price of our coppers but we do ask to be let alone and left free to follow our men and our old ways, and these coppers represent the chief thing in our custom. … If it suits us and does not interfere with or hurt anyone else, why should we be stopped?
>
> We would ask you therefore to take the matters into consideration and remove from the statute books that part of section 149 relating to our giving away and our feasts and festivals.[7]

The outlawing of this practice, a rite which had the material effect of ensuring general well-being as a function of social mobility, was oddly followed by compulsory attendance at so-called Christian schools for the reform of the indigenous child. Ironically, any student of Christianity will readily find that giving away every material thing in return for respect, peace and equality was indeed a Christ-like deed, practiced most conspicuously by Christ himself.

The indigenous practice of giveaway has nevertheless survived and is today followed by individual families to ensure their continuity and legitimacy. Families seeking traditional authorization and acknowledgment of their young people, or to stand up and recognize members of their family as their leader, or to transfer names and places, give gifts to the people in payment for their acknowledgment and respect. They give salmon, jars of berries, T-shirts and blankets, and money. The tradition lives on, but in much more humble times. There are exceptions, such as one recent potlatch in Ahousat rumored to be worth a quarter million dollars, given by the family which produced Shawn Atleo, the current National Chief of the Assembly of First Nations. Without the coppers, however, the national "bank" and its ledgers are empty.

As for the modern papacy, Pope John Paul II visited the North West Territories and conducted Mass clad in deerskin robes in 1987. He prayed that Canada become "a model for the world in upholding the dignity of aboriginal people."[8]

Resistance: Criminalization

> *"I do not believe, Your Worship, that this Court, in inflicting penalties on me for the crimes for which I am convicted, should be moved by the belief that penalties deter men from the course that they believe is right. History shows that penalties do not deter men when their conscience is aroused, nor will they deter my people…*
> *I am prepared to pay the penalty even though I know how*

*bitter and desperate is the situation of an African in the prisons of
this country. I have been in these prisons and I know how gross is the
discrimination, even behind the prison walls, against Africans, how
much worse is the treatment meted out to the African prisoners than
is accorded the whites. Nevertheless, these considerations do not
sway me from the path that I have taken, nor will they sway others
like me. For to men, freedom in their own land is
the pinnacle of their ambitions, from which nothing can turn
men of conviction aside."*
**—Nelson Mandela, in his defense against charges of
inciting people to strike illegally, and leaving the country
without a passport, in his 1962 trial.[9]**

*"You are aware that I have had considerable trouble with
the Indians about my land. Yesterday was appointed for the trial of
one for trespass; he disregarded the summons and a warrant was
issued for his arrest. The constable, however, could not take him. The
Indian defied him with a bayonet on a pole, surrounded by a lot of
his friends. A number of men from the road party were called, and
also neighbours, but they could not arrest him."*
**—Mr. Dods to the Chief Commissioner of Lands and Works
at Cowichan, November 5th, 1874[10]**

"The only other way we're coming out of here is in body bags."
**—Wolverine, August 1995, explaining the Sundancers'
commitment to stay inside the Sundance camp at Gustafsen
Lake until their demand for a third party independent tribunal
to hear the land question is met.**

If a savage wanted to own land, he would have to become a Christian.
He would then disinherit himself, become a citizen of Canada; and then own
some of his people's land in the civilized way—as controlled, awarded and
registered by the new government—or not at all.[11] 'We don't know what it
means, a savage owning land,' say the Canadian colonials; 'we would have
to invent a whole new legal construct for that, call the idea "aboriginal title,"
and then decide what that title should include.' This is because a "savage,"
or aboriginal person—according to leading legal academics in Canada—has
never heard of land ownership. That is of course completely untrue, but it is
a modern position for the colonials in Canada to take: as aboriginal title land
cannot be registered, it is worthless as such: in order for aboriginal "groups"
to own land, they must do so in the manner prescribed by such processes as
the BC Treaty Commission. That is, they must first relinquish the land to BC

and Canada and then apply to have some of it under the provincial Torrens land title registry.

In the long run, it is not building a church that enables a person to own land, but tearing down one's indigenous identity and loyalty to the country it comes from. It is to the latter act that every indigenous nation in British Columbia has steadfastly objected, and it is for that they are excluded from progress and protection.

The point must be made that at no time since contact, until the year 2000 and the first modern day BC treaty, did any indigenous nation in BC ever capitulate to the newcomers. Joseph Gosnell, the Nisga'a leader who completed the Nisga'a Final Agreement with Canada and BC, was, by profession, a lay minister.

The tribal nations have exhausted themselves – their resources, young people and families – to save themselves from the measures intended to bring about their destruction. At all times, colonial governments have insisted that the mere presence of the British and their intention to dominate was sufficient to extinguish any claim the indigenous nations may have had on their homelands.[12] This is, as we have seen, neither constitutionally nor internationally legitimate.

A brief history of resistance to the assumption of indigenous lands may be helpful here, since there are few other places where it can be found, and this exclusion and inaccessibility leads to the problem with which this volume is concerned: ignorance.[13] The history of resistance itself is by no means brief. Resistance has, in fact, occupied the attention and energy of every single nation claimed by BC since its colonizing inception. From Ah-Chee-Wun's attempts on every white life that set foot on the Gulf Islands[14] to roadblocks of game wardens; from underground community meetings when it was illegal to pursue land claims to legal campaigns that took leaders around the world; from BC-wide publications, conferences and movements to the family struggles with incarceration and apprehension of children—precious little capitulation, surrender, cession or release has occurred here.[15]

People of the coast first found themselves in a dire position of defense when Russian mariners discovered the riches they possessed. Otter-rich sea waters in the 18th century were a modern day oilfield. The Aleut defended themselves, even though some of their people were enslaved by Russians to harvest the otter.[16] Then Spanish and British boats came up from the south, and they traded. Juan Perez and Captain Cook found the coastal people completely in control of their territories and traded on their terms. Competition among the British, Americans and unlicensed captains did not, ultimately, create a seller's market for the indigenous and as one-sided bargains began to mark trade characterized by a few nails for a pelt, disagreements, massacres and war ensued. British naval gunboats took to patrolling the coast to subdue and indeed decimate any insubordinate village they could get in range of their cannons, and the coastal people retaliated enthusiastically.[17]

In the summer of 1808, Simon Fraser, the North West Company trader and explorer, was escorted down the river that now bears his name by indigenous canoe pilots, interpreters and Chiefs. Though his journey may have been rigorous, as he describes in his journal, it would have been impossible without the labours of many local people, as is also described inadvertently in his record. The Musqueam, living where that river meets the sea, were perhaps more familiar with white ways of business and were not so accommodating. They turned Fraser and his guides back upriver simply by appearing to them, with such dread had their neighbours anticipated the Musqueam reaction to their mixed presence.

When early settlers and explorers describe the new people they met as "indolent, thievish vagabonds," as Simon Fraser did in his journal and so many others did similarly, perhaps that needs to be considered in a more critical light. It doesn't sound as though Fraser commanded their respect. Alternatively, he demanded it and, in so doing, clearly did not win it. What, in the circumstances, might have made a stranger seem thievish and indolent? A rag tag red faced guy, starving, lost, and without a hope of surviving, showing up and acting all uppity? No wonder the less powerful people of the community might have eyed Fraser as a bit of carrion with breath still in him. But for some reason, and clearly to their lasting credit rather than to Fraser's, the interior leaders insisted he be humoured. "There were some Indians there who wanted to go after these white men and steal all their possessions, but their leader told them, 'Don't bother them; they might be able to help us one day!'"[18]

If indigenous leaders had not decided to allow the whites passage in the first place, never mind actually assisting them, making their business enterprises profitable and saving their lives over and over again from starvation and illness, the colonization of "Canada" might have had to wait until the intervention of the helicopter with the infrared scanners, the airborne bombers and tanks. Although a 70 year old indigenous man did disable an Armoured Personnel Carrier with a .22 hunting rifle during the siege of the Sundancers at Gustafsen Lake in 1995 . . .

British Columbia is no Great Plains. The British and Canadians had been able to exterminate the buffalo and starve plains people towards relying on the forts for regular sustenance; they had split the prairies with the Red River Settlement and a competitive fur trade; and there, their horses and supply wagons could cover ground in straight lines, in keeping with the style of European warfare. The Redcoats were eventually able to oversee the signing of Treaties 4 and 6. Not so in the mountain ranges of the coast, the benches and plateaus of the interior, the Fraser watershed and the peaks which taper westward from the Rocky Mountains. Most of the numbered treaties in Canada were made after British Columbia became a colony. If British soldiers could have marched and captured the 30 indigenous nations in BC, they would have extracted treaties from the imprisoned ranks. But they could not have hoped to. It took a year to get five Tsilhqot'in Chiefs into what they said was a peace talk, after Waddington's road builders were slaughtered in 1864, and that was only accomplished by convincing Chief Alexis to convince them in turn. The result was not a peace talk! It was the assassination, in custody, of more than half the Chiefs of that nation, most of whom were understood to be innocent of the crime of killing the road making crew. The example that was made of them is an indication of the colonials' appreciation of their limitations in being able to offer the Indians anything they did not already have, and of the fact that the colonials were well aware that force would not be a decisive method against the remaining dozens of capable nations. Intimidation and coercion were to remain the only tools of negotiation possessed by the newcomer.

Indigenous capacity for resistance to the soldiers was substantial. Their resistance to disease, on the other hand, was minimal. A measles epidemic swept the province in the last decades of the 19th century. It was closely followed by the flu at the turn of the century, which spread among the peoples of the south and the interior largely at the salmon canneries. Tuberculosis lingered for decades, claiming unknown numbers of people living in Reserves. When the Spanish Flu followed soldiers home from World War I, that too exacted a high cost in native life. The diseases did not stop, nor were they mitigated by non-native doctors. Critical preventive measures were never the subject of meetings between Indian Agents and their charges, between western doctors and traditional healers, nor between teacher and student. A photo of young Ernest Willie at the Alert Bay Indian Day School in 1955 shows him and his winning entry in the province-wide education poster contest. His poster proclaimed in large block letters: "T.B. THRIVES ON SUPERSTITION."[19] It was well known at that time that tuberculosis is indifferent to superstition. The infectious respiratory disease thrives in close living conditions which are damp and cold and have dirt floors—the precise conditions in which Indians were left on their little Reserves. Apparently the education system for Indian children in British Columbia was satisfied to use the human crisis of unmitigated outbreaks of preventable disease across Indian communities to emphasize the inferiority of "superstitious" savages against the healthy, Christian whites. Indigenous doctors were being criminalized for practicing their effective medical treatments.[20]

The British would have liked to starve the Indians out. By the turn of the 20th century, people at the headwaters of Fraser River tributaries had to fight for their salmon weirs. In three decades of exploitation since 1871, the commercial canneries on the coast had made a dramatic impact on the sockeye and Chinook runs of the Fraser—the largest single salmon producing watershed in the world. Business people and the sparsely located Fisheries officials were content to blame the crash on traditional fisheries upriver. The salmon weirs used by interior peoples to harvest fish selectively were eventually smashed by the settlers in spite of serious native opposition. In at least one case, the Tachie Barricade Agreement of 1909, the people negotiated compensation for the weirs: seed, agricultural implements and schools. It was probably not the Tachie people's expectation that they would be dumped with barley seed, which would not grow there, or that the "school" they would eventually have benefit of would be the Lejac Indian Residential School,[21] some hundred miles away.

Engagements with Game Wardens could be dangerous and debilitating, and were interminable – lasting at least until the 1970s. From the armed Secwepemc blockade of a Warden visit in 1885 to Frank Gott's murder of a Game Warden in Lillooet in 1932,[22] through decades of harassment across the province, so many hunters were deprived of their kill and jailed. In a few cases, charges under the Wildlife Act were dropped when Chiefs attended the trial and defended their hunters simply by challenging the judge to cite any grounds for imposing his law on their people. Later, judges agreed there was no explanation for limiting the native hunt when whites were strategically decimating the wild herds.[23]

Resistance took different forms depending on the type of offensive. Indigenous diplomats, Christian moderators and violent opponents of encroachment took turns defending their peoples, but most efforts had culminated in the political arena by the 1880s. Petitions were written, great meetings held, trips to Victoria were made and then trips to England. Declarations asserting their title were made by the indigenous nations at the end of the first decade of the twentieth century. The Cowichan in 1906 sent a petition to England; in 1910 the Tahltan, and then in 1911 the Lillooet Tribe, declared themselves the only rightful owners of their territories. The Nisga'a had long since established their Land Committee to guard their borders against diminishment. The Indian Rights Association pooled international resources against the common threat.

In 1931 a meeting between Haida and Tsimshian people founded the Native Brotherhood of BC. In 1940 the Kwakiutl Pacific Coast Native Fishermen joined under the umbrella of the Brotherhood. Although meetings to pursue the land question were outlawed under the Indian Act, these people held their strategic meetings under the guise of commercial fishing business. They started the magazine, *The Native Voice*.

In 1945 Andy Paull left the Native Brotherhood to establish the North American Indian Brotherhood. This group pursued issues such as securing voting rights without losing Indian Status rights. They advocated change to liquor laws prohibiting native indulgence which, at the time and for some time, supported whole settler villages on the fines collected for violations. Their presentation to the Parliamentary Committee in 1948 resulted in changes to the Indian Act in 1951; the Potlatch Law and the ban on Indian organizing were repealed, and the legal definition used in Canadian legislation, "a person is any other individual than an Indian," was altered to allow for Indians to be persons.

Late in the 1950s the Indian Homemakers Association of BC was formed by women who raised funds for church maintenance. They turned their attention to the lack of running water in their communities, the absence of sanitary infrastructure, the shocking state of their children who were in government care or in residential schools, and the matter of title and rights. They organized the Moccasin Walk of 100 Miles, from Vancouver to Hope, to raise funds for themselves and the formation of the Union of BC Indian Chiefs. In 1958 the Aboriginal Native Rights Committee of the Interior Tribes of British Columbia was formed.

In 1968 the National Indian Brotherhood was established with the Federation of Saskatchewan Indians and the BC Brotherhood at the lead. They hammered Ottawa for recognition of aboriginal title and rights and overdue compensation for the overuse of lands and resources critical to Indian survival.

In 1969, the Union of BC Indian Chiefs was organized, in part as a response to Canada's *White Paper Policy* which sought to assimilate the indigenous by the book. George Manuel, the Chief of Neskonlith, was the first President. His cry for Indian Government reverberated through the province. The Union organized around education at the grass roots level. They published *Nesika,* a monthly magazine full of Indian news. The BC Association of Non-Status Indians formed at the same time, organizing and advocating for the care of those numerous individuals whose mothers "married out," or who were not at home when Commissioners assigned Indian Status numbers.

One of the first acts of the Union was to reject an offer of provincial funding. In 1970, at the moment of flooding out the Kwadacha, Tsay Keh Dene and Athabasca Chipewyan people to create the reservoir behind Premier WAC Bennett's dam on the Peace River, the province created the First Citizens' Fund. A $25 million trust administered by the provincial Cabinet would pay out the interest to fund proposals submitted by Indian Bands and organizations. The fund committee granted the union $53,000. The Union, representing 167 of the 188 Indian bands in B.C., stated:

> In the hope of receiving what in most cases is much needed finances, various Indian organizations have applied for grants. We feel that these applications have been handled in a manner that plays off one organization against the other and thereby perpetuates the divide and rule principle used so effectively in the past.
>
> We are rejecting the grant we received from the fund.[24]

Beginning in 1971, UBCIC President George Manuel started

traveling internationally. Over the next few years, he met with representatives of indigenous peoples in Sweden, Kenya, Tanzania, Australia, New Zealand, Bolivia, Mexico, and Guatemala. He also met with representatives of the International Labour Organization and the World Council of Churches.

In 1973, a delegation of 150 members of the Native Youth Association occupied the Ottawa Indian Affairs building for twenty-four hours. Led by Manuel's son Arthur, the group's statement called for a halt to James Bay hydroelectric development, and serious government engagement in addressing the BC land question – and the land question that was emerging from the dust of broken treaties across the rest of Canada.

In 1974, the first armed road blockade by indigenous people in many decades took place around Cache Creek. It was staged because an Elder's house had burned down, and there was no way for the community to rebuild it. They were not allowed to cut down trees and plank them and build another house, and the federal government would do nothing. Once surrounded by police, the road blockers manufactured scarecrows which they placed around the night campfire. These fooled the cops while they escaped through the dark.[25]

That event did not end in a trial, but the year marked the amendment of jury selection guidelines to include on-Reserve voter lists. Previously the white courts would not suffer native opinions on the institutionalized criminalization tactics against them.

Throughout the *Indian Act* prohibitions against meetings, potlatches and cultural practices like sweatlodges, little old ladies and their followers found ways to carry on under the nose of the Indian Agents and RCMP. Lookouts hired by the Agents often functioned as spies in the other direction, providing cover for meetings and informing their neighbours of Agent movements. When children were home from residential school, their grandmothers would sneak them out across the back river to the sweatlodge.[26]

In 1975, the Union of BC Indian Chiefs organized a Rejection of Funds campaign to wrench themselves from *Indian Act* controls. All the Band Councils in British Columbia refused monies from Ottawa: everything—including payments for welfare and housing.

The founding conference of the World Council of Indigenous Peoples was held in Sechelt, on the Reserve, in October, 1975.

The Central Interior Indian Tribal Council, which included Secwepemc, St'át'imc, Nlaka'pamux, Okanagan and Tsilhqot'in leaders, grouped together in the 1970s. They supported each other politically and sent crack delegations to Ottawa armed with film and stacks of paper documentation of British Columbia's decimation of the Fraser River fisheries through pollution, unmitigated diversions, and commercial over fishing. When St'át'imc fishermen defied DFO closures, and the skirmish at the river led to charges and Bradley Bob's trial in 1978, the proceedings had to be moved from the little courthouse to a community hall to allow for attendance of many hundreds of community representatives from up and down the Fraser.

In September of 1976, some 80 Lil'wat people were arrested in a confrontation over access to traditional fisheries.

On November 17, 1977, the Gitxsan-Carrier Declaration was released. It starts out, "Since time immemorial, we, the Gitksan and Carrier [Wet'suwet'en] People of Kitwanga, Kitseguecla, Gitanmaax, Sikadoak, Kispiox, Hagwilget and Moricetwon, have exercised Sovereignty over our land."

In November of 1981, the UBCIC launched the Constitution Express - a delegation from BC by rail to Ottawa, to ensure that aboriginal rights would not be struck from Canada's new Constitution. They carried on to the UN in New York, to the House of Lords in England, and they succeeded.

On January 17, 1983, the Declaration of Secwepemc Sovereignty was signed by Chiefs of the seventeen Shuswap Bands. The last line read: "We declare our support in the struggle for self-determination and independence of indigenous and third world nations."

The World Council of Indigenous Peoples (WCIP) had been set in motion—due in part to George Manuel's extensive traveling and discussions with indigenous leaders in Africa, South America and Australia, and their agreement about the source of their problems as peoples being colonized. In Panama the WCIP issued its first Declaration of Principles, after meeting from September 23-30, 1984. It started out, after affirming the humanity of indigenous peoples in Article One, by stating:

> 2. All indigenous peoples have the right to self-determination.
> By virtue of this right they can freely determine their political,
> economic, social, religious and cultural development, in
> agreement with the principles stated in this declaration.
>
> 3. Every nation-state within which indigenous peoples live
> shall recognize the population, territory and institutions
> belonging to said peoples.

On October 23, 1984, 48 hereditary chiefs from Gitxsan and Wet'suwet'n sued the BC government for recognition of ownership of 57,000 square kilometers of land, the right to self-government, and compensation for losses. This would be the first step toward the 1997 *Delgamuukw* ruling in the Supreme Court of Canada.

In 1985 the Haida people blockaded a part of their lands called Lyell Island, effectively shutting down logging operations.

By 1989 a fishing alliance between every Band on the Fraser and Columbia Rivers—about 90 Bands, had formed into the Inter-Tribal Fishing

Treaty. The Treaty formed a determined organizational block which required unprecedented concessions from Ottawa to crack. Provisions under the Aboriginal Fisheries Strategy (AFS), the federal response to the Treaty *and* the Supreme Court decision in *Sparrow,* arising from another set of fishing charges against an Indian in BC, made for predictable access to fisheries and even community allocations in the Harvest Management Plan. But it took a little something more to ice the Fishing Treaty. Federal Fisheries agents showed up uninvited to an ITFT meeting and invited any participant who passed their base of operations, in the lobby of the conference center, to partake of a healthy pot of funding: these AFS funds were only available to Bands who were not part of that fishing treaty.

In 1989 the Tsilhqot'in issued a Declaration of their sovereignty over their traditional territories.

The BC Association of Non-Status Indians survived an attempted and failed merger with the Union of BC Indian Chiefs, to become the United Native Nations. This group continued with such works as the creation of BC Native Housing. In order to build those housing units, they broke through barriers like provincial requirements that any such housing be 80 kilometers from a town or city. The UNN was performing tasks required to keep off-Reserve individuals' bodies and souls together, forming working relationships with interested non-native organizations, and contributing to conferences like "Towards a Dialogue: a Conference on Native Issues," held in Vancouver in January of 1991 with the Affiliation of Multicultural Societies and Service Agencies of B.C. No federal organization had attempted to fill the divide between natives and non-natives which deepened after the 1990 Oka standoff.

In 1990, the Oka crisis in Quebec was echoed by demonstrations and at least one roadblock in BC. That year saw blockades for several reasons, including blockades against logging at the Brittany Triangle in Tsilhqot'in. There was also a prolonged blockade of a logging road in Líl'wat territory, where 63 people, representing all the Líl'wat families, were arrested (brutally), charged with contempt of court, and most spent at least five weeks in jail because they would not give the court an English name. The ensuing five months of trial, in which their defense pertaining to the court's lack of jurisdiction on unceded lands was not allowed to be argued, proved so illuminating that it formed the substance of "Prisoners of Democracy: The Líl'wat right to an impartial tribunal,"[27] a thesis submitted to fulfill the requirements of a Master of Laws Degree at the University of British Columbia in 2006. *Prisoners of Democracy* exhaustively documents the BC court's partiality and has not been published.

In 1995, the Gustafsen Lake standoff saw thirty-one days of shooting leading to four injured – three of them RCMP. The stand, the refusal to leave the Sundance grounds, was backed up by promises to retaliate by Chiefs across Canada, including Chief Richard Hill of the Kahnewake Mohawk. At the same time, Nuxalk Hereditary Chiefs blocked logging operations at their sacred island of Ista.

In early 1998, the Native Youth Movement occupied the BC Treaty Commission office in downtown Vancouver for a long weekend. Under the leadership of David Dennis, the occupation lasted five days. In that time many long-distance calls for solidarity were made, and many documents photocopied—including records of accounts which showed treaty-making Chiefs' horses and dogs on the payroll.[28] There were fourteen arrests—not of the Chiefs benefitting from fraud, but of the youth who attempted to expose them.

In late 1998, on the one year anniversary of the Supreme Court of Canada *Delgammukw* decision, fires were lit next to highways across British Columbia where indigenous people sang and spoke about bringing the court's decision to bear on the unresolved land question.

Beginning in 2004, Secwepemc people attempted to occupy their lands at a place where one Sun Peaks ski resort had developed a sizable business. Peacefully, they rallied, built homes, distributed information, and then defended themselves in court. At about the same time Tahltan Elders were roadblocking mining developments. The following year they would occupy the Band office for nine months.

The full extent of indigenous roadblocking and resistance to logging, hydroelectric development, road building, mining, water diversion, and cattle-ranging, to say nothing of opposition to human rights violations, attempted Constitutional coups and the unchecked apprehension of children, has never been exhaustively written, nor even attempted. The *Warrior Publications* chronology of just a few decades gives some indication of the innumerable blockades and court proceedings that indigenous peoples have mounted, just to hold their ground from the 1980s to 2006.[29]

The resistance has led to a present-day indigenous generation stepping up to confront the ever expanding industrial machine of resource development and genocide, now in movements like the Indigenous Assembly Against Mining, the Walk 4 Justice and Valentines Day marches for the memory of missing women, migrations of people walking and canoeing against salmon farms on the coast, conferences on sustaining languages, petitions to the regional branch of the United Nations (the Organization of American States) by treaty groups and individuals standing up for their right to self-determination as indigenous nations and not as a Band council, logging road blockades—especially in watersheds and reservoirs for Reserves like at Brown's Creek, opposition to new pipelines and oil tanker traffic on the coast, and the ongoing roadblocking of ski resort development and expansion in the last pristine watersheds.

The indigenous do not have access to any court or legal mechanism where their just demands are recognized. Their issues are not heard, and sometimes are refused hearing. Instead the expressions of frustration, the endless requests for meetings to resolve the obvious and outstanding problems, are simply transformed into criminal acts by the state, with the police and military defending the "private property" of the colonizer.

Capitulation: Assimilation

> *"I said to my wife: "I wonder where all my contemporaries went from the 1960s? Where are they today? Where are the champions of social justice; where are the radicals that we knew?" She said, "I have a theory. I think they have all gone off to join one cult or another. You know, those groups where everybody talks the same, walks the same, dresses the same, and thinks the same." I said, "Give me an example." And she said, "You know, the Royal Bank of Canada, MacMillan-Bloedel, and perhaps the political parties."*
> **—Ernie Crey, Sto:lo; Vice President of United Native Nations addressing "Towards a Dialogue," January 25, 1991**[30]

The interminable gap between native sovereigntists and the colonial governments has created a wide scope for native opportunists to gamble in. Any time a roadblock goes up or a court action is launched, someone else pops up and agrees to negotiate concessions to the traditionalists' demands. These negotiators are not representative of the traditional people who are raising the stakes and pushing the issues of their nation's survival; they are not representative of the people's aspirations to have their indigenous nation survive. They are like actors promoting the American Dream – showing off the lush pampering afforded a few, while an ongoing nightmare continues just out of televised sight. It is anyone's right to choose where and how to live, but trying to convince one's own people to assimilate to a foreign culture – while being on the foreign culture's payroll and expediting a foreign goal which does not feature the well-being of the people in question, is not to be swept under the rug.

Today, there are many successful native politicians in Canada. In that collection, where success means a paying job as a government policy parrot, characters are limited to approved stereotypes: the Patrick Brazeau variety—a native man convicted in the media of being an alcoholic woman abuser, based in a big city with a pro-urban native organization – the Congress of Aboriginal Peoples, is made a Senator. Or the Ed John variety: a trustworthy advocate of Canada's methods to solve the "Indian Problem" by extinguishment, as the first and continuing Chair of the First Nations Summit – a twenty year position by 2012. Magically, he rose to higher service as the North American member of the United Nations' Permanent Forum on Indigenous Issues (PFII) over several terms, while continuing to lead the Summit's shepherding of native nations toward subjugation through colonial policy, and was elected Chair of the Permanent Forum in May of 2012. Canada's governmental delegate to the UN PFII 10th session, May 2011, said to the assembled: "We are proud of Ed."

A film maker at the United Nations General Assembly caught a picture of Ed John sharing a laugh with the Canadian delegate, immediately after Canada voted "no" to the United Nations Declaration on the Rights of Indigenous Peoples on September 13, 2007.[31] This moment of camaraderie reflects the reality of who Ed John's boss is, and who his friends are. It's not the traditional indigenous—it is the lucrative and growing multinational gyre that makes indigenous societies disappear cleanly. Mr. John, a BC lawyer, gives addresses to North American delegates at workshops on using the United Nation's Committee for the Elimination of All Forms of Racial Discrimination to protect inherent indigenous rights and treaty rights. The same body, CERD, has repeatedly reported criticisms of Canada and British Columbia's treaty process because it requires the surrender of aboriginal title. In his role as Chair of the First Nations Summit, Ed John promotes and facilitates First Nations participation in that extinguishment process. The December 2011 CERD workshop in Ottawa was financed by the First Nations Summit and the Assembly of First Nations, among others. What appears truly ironic may be a revelation: that the Summit would pursue CERD when the Committee is critical of the BC treaty process is an indication that CERD's mandate is discrimination and its highest award is special measures, the equivalent of affirmative action.[32]

The National Chief of the Assembly of First Nations, Shawn Atleo, was elected shortly after neighbours of his home community of Ahousat, the Maa-nulth, ratified an extinguishment treaty. Atleo has always supported them in that process. Jody Wilson-Raybould, Kwagiulth, is a BC lawyer who emigrated through the Crown Counsel realm, prosecuting poor people in Vancouver's Downtown East Side, to emerge as a BC Treaty Commissioner and then Regional Chief of BC's Assembly of First Nations. Wilson-Raybould's community is also in negotiations.

Government and industry have created, usually jointly, many high visibility positions especially for pro-business indigenous leaders. Usually the appointment to such a position comes after some less-than-visible influences.

Chief Clarence Louie of Osoyoos is the first and continuing Chair of the National Aboriginal Economic Development Board. There was a fairly audible silence when the Osoyoos Indian Band's book keeper opened the big red binder on the podium at the St'át'imc Cultural Center gala fund raising dinner in Lillooet, in 2007. She and Chief Louie had been invited to explain how they created the Band's own cultural center and winery. The book keeper read from the binder: then the federal government gave them tens of millions; then the provincial government gave them more tens of millions. Her statements, unexpected and shocking as they were, somewhat undermined the Chief's own speech, given just before hers, where he gave the distinct impression that the business successes were theirs alone, accomplished by hard work and a selfless embrace of the dominant economy. He had spoken at length about how some people are still trying to ride around on a hundred year old horse—meaning they still believe the Declarations and sacrifices of their grandparents are worth upholding and actually confirm significant legal protection against the extortionist colonial regime today.

Chief Clarence Louie has made a name for himself by delivering speeches to corporate conferences where he begins by saying, "People often say to me, 'How you doin'?' Geez—I'm working with Indians—what do you *think*?"[33] Did this fluency in denouncing native people, and the curious appeal of his being native himself, make him able to attract unprecedented government investments to his entrepreneurial visions? British Columbia needed a way to finish the sentence, "you should just work hard and be more like…," while admonishing First Nations for their (manufactured) dependence on federal welfare. But until Louie, there wasn't such an example—there was no way to finish that sentence.

The Canadian Aboriginal Minerals Association is chaired by Jerry Asp, former Chief of the Tahltan at Telegraph Creek. He was run out of the community by Elders who occupied the Band office for nine months in protest of his self-serving business sense. They were opposed to his indiscriminate and certainly unauthorized guarantees of the Band's consent to such mining companies as Shell and Petro Canada in areas sacred to the Tahltan.

Calvin Helin is a BC lawyer whose indigenous family is from the coast. Helin wrote a book, *Dances With Dependency,* which has been celebrated by anti-indigenous politicians, journalists and leaders of opinion. The book's central theme is that First Nations across Canada must roll up their sleeves and go to work: their young people represent the demographic which is going to power Canada's economy with their labour, and since the average Canadian worker is nearing retirement, they had better get to work without delay. Helin made an unconvincing argument that engaging in big industry could be accomplished by First Nations without compromising their traditional values. The book neglected to mention the pertinent details of his success story examples, such as those of the Innu of Labrador whose financial momentum came out of an agreement with the Canadian military to dot their territories with microwave communications towers. The impact of that sort of development on wildlife is not positive, nor would partnering with Haliburton appear consistent with traditional north pacific coast philosophies, but these are the unnamed powerhouses behind the two most substantial examples of Helin's new plan.

Calvin Helin visited China in 2008, where a Memorandum of Understanding was signed between Shaanxi Provincial Bureau of Economic and Technical Cooperation and Helin's Native Invest and Trade Association (NITA) and RCI Capital Group to "work together to explore mutually beneficial cooperation and investment opportunities of bettering the living standards of their respective populations and for the purpose of increasing economic cooperation, cultural understanding, mutual respect and friendships between the parties, their respective peoples and communities on various levels." Helin was reported in Chinese news circulation as "Great Chief of Canada indigenous people."[34] Helin told his new business partners, according to the Chinese news, "At the same time as a lawyer Herring [Helin?] has always attached importance to the economic development of the indigenous people, he said meaningfully, in fact scientists have confirmed through DNA, Canada and the indigenous people of East Asia have Chinese blood, probably in about 10,000 years ago, to move to North America. Canadian aboriginal communities in many ways, retains the same with the Chinese tradition, such as respect for the old, and so on." The Ministers of BC who followed up his visit didn't try to correct the mistaken identity, instead moving on to try to seal deals initiated by the Great Chief under the auspices of his blessing. The Chinese Business Development Association had issued statements before that, that continuing political and economic instability caused by unresolved Native land claims issues is compromising investment potential in BC. They recommended swift resolution of land claims issues. Helin fills a desperate want for "certainty" in Canada's foreign trade and investment ambitions. He told the Globe and Mail newspaper, "We have a new generation of leadership now and so the leaders are looking for capital to develop our natural resources."

This leader of that "new generation" says, "A lot of our people think that we are owed something because of all of the bad things that have happened." The value of a person like Calvin Helin to Canadian opinion makers is in his ability to take that unremarkable statement and use it to assuage the Canadian conscience, to turn that simple, accurate and sensible concept on its head. He assigns the following interpretation to the widespread indigenous expectation of compensation, further blaming the victims for having asked for it: "Basically what you are saying is that it is okay to sell your dignity and your control over your life for a few welfare crumbs. It's not ... It is simply not acceptable that we be taking our women and children and ... throwing them to the sharks. That's what we are doing right now. We've got to do something that is different."[35] Although he has written two books on the subject, it is unclear what grand things Helin wants aboriginal people to do other than forget the past, go into whatever kind of business they can get and work hard. Needless to say, Helin's books have received much notice.

Chief Kim Baird is celebrated as the foremost influential aboriginal woman in BC and indeed in Canada. She was recognized as one of the 150 most important British Columbians, as was Chief Louie, in 2008; she has been included among Canada's Most Powerful Women Top 100; and received the National Aboriginal Women in Leadership Distinction Award.

Baird delivered the first modern day treaty negotiated through the BC Treaty Commission. In this she accomplished the rather bizarre feat of selling aboriginal title to ~~4,000~~ *thousands of* hectares of the most prized real estate and coastal waters in the province for about $22 each, while actual market value in the area is a few thousand dollars per square foot.[36] The Tsawwassen First Nation is now integrated with Metro Vancouver and the GVRD, and the revenue-generating ferry terminal, deep sea port and waterways all belong to BC. The previous gem of traditional Tsawwassen lands, a huge migratory sea bird sanctuary called Burns Bog, is now under development for an eight lane freight highway from the terminal. Baird spoke about "moving forward" at a side event of the 10th Session of the UN PFII in New York, promoting municipal status and self-government, a Canadian slang term which people in other countries still believe means 'self-determination,' in front of the curious uninitiated South American participants.

The incredible Canadian legal achievement of the Tsawwassen Final Agreement was not even understood by the public of British Columbia. On the night of the successful ratification vote, Tsawwassen got about sixteen seconds on local TV news service. Perhaps some victories cannot be celebrated publicly. Chief Kim Baird, recently out-campaigned by a twenty-year-old boy for the Chieftainship, nonetheless has a career for life. As Tsawwassen member Bertha Williams put it at a recent Gathering of the Clans Conference in Vancouver, "The federal and provincial governments were sending Kim Baird all over the place: up to the Yukon, back to Ottawa. She was even invited to Venezuela last week to teach the governments how to screw the indigenous people down there. She's been asked to go to India and China."[37]

Many of the most quoted native leaders in BC appear to be working out of the governments' collective briefcase. The First Nations Leadership Council has become a sort of hydra capable of saying anything the Premier wants it to. The Council is a union of the executive of the Union of BC Indian Chiefs (longtime staunch hardliner on Indian government and maintaining title); the First Nations Summit (a principal of the BC Treaty Commission and facilitator of extinguishing title for municipal status as a Treaty First Nation); and the Assembly of First Nations BC Region (the governments perceive all First Nations to be part of the AFN by virtue of being First Nations, but the AFN has had little weight in British Columbia since it changed from being the National Indian Brotherhood in 1982). These leaders signed an agreement to work together in 2004, the Tsawwassen Accord, after the death of a baby indigenous girl, young Sherry Charlie, who had been poorly cared for by the BC Ministry of Children and Families which took her from her mother. Shortly after creating itself, the Leadership Council participated in media events with Premier Campbell and the Liberal government to endorse The New Relationship. The only thing new about the Relationship was the fact that the Leadership Council, representing almost the entire indigenous population through one of the three organizations, was consensually involved in it. Grassroots indigenous people throughout British Columbia thought the apocalypse had arrived.

In 2006, the BC government passed the *New Relationship Trust Act*, creating a corporation outside government that transferred $100 million to a provincial fund that would purportedly meet the needs and priorities of First Nations, not unlike the First Citizens Fund of 1970. The Leadership Council facilitated a series of consultations across the province with First Nations and urban native groups, where a clear consensus emerged that 80% of the money should be spent on immediate, urgent needs like language recording and curriculum, traditional health and healing centers, and a good portion of it on business that would start generating income. The Council decided instead to reinvest $80 million in publicly traded companies working in the provincial economy. The remaining $20 million went, in the first year, to administration and then began trickling out towards the 203 Bands and the dozens of urban organizations for summer youth employment schemes and small grants to health, Elder and business concerns. The Trust Fund's administration would not release details of which companies the New Relationship was investing in.[38]

The Trust Fund was the financial midwife at the birth of an unprecedented creature. The first indigenous propaganda corporation emerged to authenticate the reversal of roles – where now indigenous leaders themselves would manufacture consent for government initiatives. Coppermoon Communications produced the beautiful pamphlets, websites and banners that signaled what a great thing the New Relationship Trust truly was, and which disappeared any appearance of contradiction between what communities wanted and what the Trust Fund administrators were doing. This company has continued successfully, and gainfully, to promote lose-lose deals to First Nations in British Columbia using social and all forms of media. Their recent contracted campaign to produce a "yes" vote where eleven First Nations would surrender all the land and water BC Hydro wanted in their territories, a campaign which left few tactics unused and delivered the very economical result desired by the province, was written up and forwarded as an urgent action submission to the United Nations Special Rapporteur on Indigenous Peoples in 2011.[39]

Grand Chief Doug Kelly, Sto:lo, worked closely with the Leadership Council and has long promoted his people's surrender in the BC treaty process, but he appeared genuinely surprised by the province's failure to keep on dishing out cash when the Leadership Council couldn't deliver First Nations approval of provincial legislation to close the question of who's boss of BC.

> B.C. First Nations want some action to back up the new relationship promise made by Premier Gordon Campbell, or they're going to take some direct action of their own," says Sto:lo Grand Chief Doug Kelly. "If the premier doesn't move this new relationship forward in a pro-active way, it's going to result in increased direct action and increased litigation," Kelly said last week. "When I talk amongst my colleagues at the Sto:lo Tribal Council and other First Nations leaders from other parts of B.C., they don't see any cause for celebration, …We're looking at opportunities to crash a few parties.[40]

The First Nations Leadership Council hired NATIONAL Communications Group to answer the phone during its campaign for the provincial Recognition and Reconciliation Act, 2009. NATIONAL is a new partner company to Burston-Marstellar, the infamous corporate spin doctor.[41] The fact that the First Nations Leadership Council required – and could afford – that caliber of assistance with its "communications" should give pause. If First Nations in BC had been coerced – probably by faith in the Leadership Council – to let that legislation pass, or even support it as the Leadership Council suggested they do, it would have been a vote of support for provincial power to answer the question of how to deal with aboriginal title in the province.

The media in BC does not report the betrayal of the indigenous cause by opportunists because it does not report the indigenous cause in the first place. Without direct contacts in indigenous communities, and several of them, a non-native person would have no concept of the depth and prevalence of government influence among "successful" First Nations individuals, or the truth of their work to undermine traditionalists and stamp out the drives for self-determination which go unannounced.

Bill Lightbown and Lavina White, a married couple from Haida, had been working with lawyer Bruce Clark for some time, even launching several actions together. They were, therefore, very involved in the communications and then the court proceedings flowing from the Gustafsen Lake crisis of 1995. Several Chiefs and persons of non-descript origins appeared at 100 Mile House while the police contained the Sundancers at their camp. They came and presented themselves as representatives of some or other indigenous nation, and repeated the mantra that violence was not the answer and that the Ts'epeten Defenders did not represent the majority aboriginal view. Thick in the scrum between the one-eared media reporters, police, various handlers and desperate families outside the Gustafsen Lake camp boundaries, Lightbown recalls discovering that a few of these spokespeople were paid a $1,500 *per diem* for their help providing RCMP-friendly sound bytes—and then perhaps as an offset to their costs as crown witnesses later.[42] Those individuals friendly to the crown at that time have done well.

Sophie Pierre, a longtime Kootenai Chief, and involved in the BC treaty process with her community, eventually made her way to the Chair of the BC Treaty Commission. She was used as a media tool to convince British Columbians that land claims settlements in BC would be worth more to them than the 2010 Winter Olympics. The exact nature of her pitch was to explain the value to the public economy of getting "certainty" on aboriginal title lands. This instance of a native woman taking a job to convince British Columbians of the urgency of extinguishing her people's titles and rights is a painful but unexceptional example of the kinds of opportunities the assimilationist orientation provides to a few. Vancouver's Downtown East Side is rife with instances of what it provides to the many.

Allegiance to financial success instead of one's people is a new opportunity for indigenous individuals, statistically part of the most marginalized, most dispossessed demographic in the hemisphere. Where at one time the entire population of a nation would go to court together on the same ticket, like in the *Calder* case,[43] or representatives traveling to Buckingham Palace really did represent their entire people and all wanted the same thing—their land—today there are acrimonious court actions between individuals and Band Councils or by Councils against individuals, and since Frank Calder there is only one single instance of a community with a consensus position on their priorities going forward and how to realize them. The Tsilhqot'in people were all represented in the *Tsilhqot'in* case which resulted in Justice Vickers' BC Supreme Court opinion that they had proved in his court ownership of much of their territory. That 2007 *obiter dicta,* non-binding judicial opinion, has resulted in over five years of government refusal to enter negotiations with the Tsilhqot'in. Both sides have appealed the decision and the court's wheels spin on government counsel's procedural delay expertise.

Indigenous architects of community dispossession play obvious roles in relation to their communities, but some of them drift into the elite mist of manufacturing public opinion in general. Unfortunately, many artists have also accepted the invitation to the warped mirror where parts are pinched off.

Kevin Loring, of Nlaka'pamux heritage, became a Governor General's Award winner for Drama in 2008. *Where the Blood Mixes*, his second and winning script, is the story of a few residential school survivors in Lytton and their ongoing healing. It was certainly timely, and the high endorsement from BC and Canada arts foundations signal that Canada is whole-heartedly behind the Indian Residential School Survivors' Settlement and can admit with maturity the wrongs of the past. The play was re-staged in Kamloops in 2012 – the closest city to the site of the play, launching on the closing date for Indian Residential School Survivors' claims of sexual and physical abuse to the IRS Settlement Agreement. Daryl Cloran, the Artistic Director of Western Canada Theatre Company (WCTC) at the time, gives us, in the program:

> In 2007 we received a major grant from *Arts Partners in Creative Development* to develop this script through a tour of a workshop production. Produced with the Vancouver Playhouse, in conjunction with the Savage Society, the tour started in Kamloops and played as a staged reading in local communities, including Kevin's hometown of Lytton, BC. … WCT was very involved in developing the script and presenting the workshop tour… We are so proud to bring it to you now.

Loring's initial playwriting effort, in Langara College, was titled, "The Little Red Warrior and His Lawyer."

Much like the adult-child in the *Blood Mixes* story, Lytton was not Loring's hometown although it is in part his ancestral home: due to larger forces which are not contemplated in the script. The WCTC General Manager adds, in the programme, "The day *Where the Blood Mixes* opened at the Magnetic North Theatre Festival in Vancouver in May 2008 is the day the Federal Government issued an apology for its part in the residential school system and the resulting damage." The coincidence of the date of the launch of his play and the announcement of an apology to Residential School Survivors was more than opportune for government. Government grants had ensured the play would be ready. The similar coincidence that the play was staged at the close of the Residential School Settlement Agreement compensation programs ties a knot between the end of an era of liability and public willingness to recognize the atrocities which produced the liabilities, the message being: this issue has now been fully addressed, and it's over.

Where the Blood Mixes is a paralyzing specter which revives the ghosts that haunt most any indigenous audience member. The cathartic value for them is doubtful, so one might wonder: why this play, why now, and for whom? The play made not a single move to situate those characters and that legacy in a highly charged present day political reality where indigenous communities, so deeply injured by the loss of their children over at least two generations, still limp along in the struggle for their land and recognition.

On the gusts of his 2008 success, Loring performed at Spences Bridge, his ancestral home, on the 100th anniversary celebration of the Memorial to

Sir Wilfred Laurier; in 2010. He had been asked to dramatize the Memorial, which he consequently decided was literary and dramatic enough to be good theatre, but then merely employed a few other actors to read it aloud. He told the assembled, "This is the first time I have ever read this Declaration."

Acceptance by the colonized of whatever features the colonizer cares to endow him with is par for the colonial course. These personal attributes are necessarily ungenerous and generally humiliating. The Governor General's Award winner moved on to portray the projected colonized attributes on daytime television. Loring took an acting job playing a native anomaly—a professional hockey player—who has been put out of the game by injury. Other than that, the character's alcoholism, pot smoking practice, and dead-beat-dad status bring viewers back to the typical negative stereotype, with lines like, "When do people who work work until?"[44]

Young and authentic native influences in BC culture are hard to spot—but not because they aren't there. The Talking Stick festival in Vancouver was developed by the indigenous dancer Margo Kane. At the 2010 festival, a dozen new native writers were crammed into a café that seats about 20 people—the organizers didn't think anyone was going to show up.

Even when the whole world shows up and watches native talent, it doesn't attract the BC public's attention. When four Líl'wat, four Squamish, four Tsleil-Waututh and four Musqueam people took the stage at the opening ceremonies of the 2010 Winter Olympics in Whistler, they did a great job making BC look good. They made BC look like the ultimate fusion of traditional and progressive peoples. But there was not a single aboriginal athlete in those Games. Not one of the indigenous individuals in the Opening Ceremonies, not even the young man who spoke for the Four Host First Nations and welcomed the world into his territory, was interviewed by mainstream, province-wide media in BC. Instead, the more formal and more cultivated indigenous media spokesperson, the Chairman of the Four Host First Nations Society, Tewannee Joseph, appeared in every journal, magazine, newspaper, and TV news hour. His stock refrain to characterize his participation in the Olympics was that he wanted to show the world he is "not a dime store Indian." He doesn't look old enough to have ever seen a dime store. Joseph has gone on to speak at business seminars on the topic of getting First Nations on board with industrial development. His other repetitive statement to February 2010 visiting media was that First Nations make good business partners. An investment guide to BC, produced by the news journal *Business in Vancouver* to coincide with the Games, featured a full-page ad for gold mining: a picture of an open-pit mine.

Someone who had seen a dime store, George Manuel, was nominated for the Nobel Peace Prize in 1977, 1978 and 1979; he was offered an electorate to run in from three different political parties in BC but declined them all, and he was made an officer of the Order of Canada. He is now unknown among

"BC's most influential people." Instead, the likes of Clarence Louie and Kim Baird are ubiquitous.

Aboriginal politicians who wish to succeed in the "broader society" must travel the path laid down by their non-native mentors. It was not until 1949 that a native person was elected to the House of the Legislature. That was Frank Calder, in the first provincial election that native people could vote in, and he won the Skeena-Bulkley riding. That electoral district includes a lot of Nisga'a voters. He is the only man ever elected on a platform that related to indigenous title. The second and only other native person to be elected to office in the history of British Columbia's government was Leonard Marchand, in Kamloops, who ran with Pierre Trudeau in 1968. He was the first Status Indian to become a Member of Parliament.

Joseph Gosnell was the final Chief Negotiator of the Nisga'a Final Agreement. During his leadership of the negotiations, raids of intimidation on the Nisga'a community of Kincolith were carried out, specifically targeting opponents of the treaty. Kincolith had overwhelmingly opted out of the treaty process in a community vote, but somehow failed to extricate themselves.[45] Gosnell did not accommodate the village's dissent but pushed the settlement forward over them. While people in Nisga'a Treaty Settlement Lands now watch their young men and women leaving home one after another to find employment elsewhere, they say Gosnell owns hotels in Hawaii and Tokyo.

Steven Point was an outspoken Chief of a Sto:lo Band at one time. He agreed with the rejection of Indian Act funds that the Union of BC Indian Chiefs effected in 1975. A lawyer, he was eventually transferred to the Bench. After many years as a BC judge, Point became the Chief Commissioner of the BC Treaty Commission. He spent his time lying to otherwise destitute First Nations about the wonderful benefits of signing a BC treaty.[46] Unfortunately, he was lobbying in areas where unprecedented corporate sharing had already occurred directly with Indian Bands – in the blue gold rush of run-of-river power projects and in a cooling investment climate the government can't seem to warm by itself—without the treaty he was saying could be the only accelerator of such revenues.[47]

Point was, soon after ratification of the Tsawwassen and Maa-nulth treaties, appointed Lieutenant Governor of BC. As Chief Commissioner of the BC Treaty Process, Point oversaw the development and finalization of those Final Agreements. The Lieutenant Governor is responsible for signing ratified treaties, or Final Agreements, into law for BC. His next official acts were to go to Bands whose activities in the treaty process had stalled, or were meeting internal opposition, and support their renewed participation in the process.

The decision to represent the Queen to his own people is a perplexing one for those indigenous people who believe, with every shred of evidence required, that they are not citizens of Canada. It is reminiscent of the choice some indigenous men made during HBC times to allow themselves to be decorated in uniforms, hats or medals to indicate their loyalty to the greater, just powers the fur traders purported to represent. Their allegiance was most bitterly unrewarded,[48] and so is Point's as he is made to do things which humiliate the subjugated nations from which he came. The LG inexplicably played host to the likes of Norwegian salmon farmers, come to inspect the farms of Atlantic salmon on the Pacific coast of BC. The farms, internationally recognized as bio-hazards responsible for the decline of wild salmon populations around the world, are a subject of outrage among indigenous nations in BC. Point was their foreign owners' gracious host.

Indigenous Academics

It's a curious contrast that in British colonies such as India, Nigeria and Kenya, the missionary schools were gripped with the ambition to send their successful pupils off to study in England, and very often did so. In British Columbia, the main goal seems to have been *not to produce* successful pupils. The earliest missionary boarding school, St Mary's at Mission, had started in 1862. Fourteen more followed, at Alert Bay, Chemainus, Cranbrook, Fraser Lake, Kamloops, Lower Post, Lytton, Metlakatla, North Vancouver, Port Alberni, Sardis, Sechelt, Tofino and Williams Lake.[49] The last one to close was the first to open: Mission, in 1984. These schools produced few successful graduates.

In 1949, there were sixteen Status Indians enrolled in Grade 12 in public British Columbia high schools. And those were the first. Indian Residential Schools graduated their students to the work force at Grade 8 at that time and Indians had only just been accepted in a few public schools, so the survey of the public schools is an accurate census of the number of native graduates of Grade 12. Enrolment of indigenous children in public schools, upon the closure of the residential schools, did not produce much success either. In 1985, five hundred Status Indians who lived on a Reserve in British Columbia were enrolled in Grade 12.[50] That was by no means a good representation of the overall numbers of indigenous students. In 1991, a survey showed that 95% of native children enrolled in public schools would drop out before Grade 12.[51]

The first native students entered BC universities in the 1950s—precious few of them, a hundred years after the first Indian schools. Judge Alfred Scow, Kwicksutaineuk, was the first indigenous person in BC to graduate from law school. He was called to the bar in 1962. In 1971 he was made a judge, the first indigenous person from BC to enter that part of BC society, and one of only two to date.

The written and oral accounts by Indian residential school survivors explain their "education" as largely manual labour—farming, field work, sewing, cooking, irrigation, collecting firewood, taking care of farm animals. None of these efforts returned to them in the form of well-heated dormitories or a diet that could be considered much better than starvation.[52] Teenage girls often worried when their menstrual cycle had stopped: but it was because they weren't eating enough that their bodies could afford to keep it going. The cold of the dormitories in winter is almost universally recalled. These cannot be considered conditions conducive to study. They certainly were not intended to be. The boys were given four options upon completing Grade 8: carpenter, minister, plumber or electrician.

Some extremely determined individuals have beaten those odds. Indigenous teachers of First Nations studies today are taking the allowed curriculum materials to the limit and adding their own exercises and reading selections. This is happening mostly in tiny classrooms sponsored by tribal councils. From large institutions, such reports as the following come: "When I first started teaching at York (University) in 1999, I was surrounded by white Indian Experts and I was just getting in their way." A lecturing professor seeking tenure at UBC spoke these words shortly after he pulled his tenure file from the institution's cold storage. He is indigenous to one of the nations here swamped by British Columbia.

The marginalized indigenous academic voice, a voice which is blacked out by the media and publishers and universities of all kinds, is hard to hear. It is even hard for young native people to hear. It's not that the books aren't written: George Manuel, Secwepemc, wrote *The Fourth World* in 1974 for instance; *The 500 years of Resistance Comic Book* was written by Gord Hill, Kwakwakawak. These BC books don't exactly make the best-seller list. They don't even get reviewed in mainstream journals and papers.

The book by the late Chief George Manuel and Michael Posluns, *The Fourth World*, summed up the situation in British Columbia and Canada succinctly and brilliantly. Manuel explained his theory of the Fourth World and this was released in *From the Heart,* a film by his daughter, Doreen, in 2001. "I have said many times that while we identify in many respects with the third world community, we are not a third world. We are of the fourth world, the forgotten world, the world of aboriginal peoples: locked into independent states but without an adequate voice or say in the decisions that affect our lives." So few copies of his book were printed that the only ones now remaining fetch prices north of $500 in online bookstores. It is out of print.

Ruby Helen Sakiskanip, a Clinical Counselor with a Master's Degree, wrote and published her book, *The Headman's Granddaughter.* It is a gripping tale that spins out a most timelessly popular human theme—self discovery of a hidden identity. Possibly the only unpopular or unsuitable aspect in her case is that she describes a journey that leads to the present day state of her indigenous identity, overcoming sheer obstacles and achieving ultimate personal success consistent with her grandfather's traditional mores. It's clearly not fit for publication in this time and place; at least, she was so sure of that that she did not even try to seek out a publisher.

Rising intellectuals somehow disappear. Just before Ethan Baptiste, a radical and brilliant young man from a long line of an Okanagan family that resisted colonialism, was about to begin his first year teaching at UBC in First Nations Studies, he died in a horrible car accident. When Neskie Manual, another part of an important family in Secwepemc politics, the grandson of George Manuel, was about to become involved in his father's anti-BC treaty newspaper, and on the eve of an appointment to meet with people organizing resistance to a big deal with BC Hydro in a neighbouring territory, he went missing. He was found 35 days later, the cause of death being pronounced "unknown."

Most indigenous academics and intellectuals have been focusing their present-day efforts on educating their own people. Native learners have experienced, over many generations now, a caustic school environment designed to scrub them of any identification with their own people. This, say the native academics, Elders and leaders, must be remedied. There is a lot to show for it at this point, with immersion schools emerging and more programs to accredit teachers along criteria that come from the native nation they live and wish to work in.

When Lorna Williams, Líl'wat, Canada's First Nations Academic Chair, was working for the Ministry of Education in BC, she commissioned a few studies. She then traveled the province, using roadmaps indicated by the studies, to see for herself. She was interested in what innovative language teaching materials and curricula had been developed by indigenous teachers. After visiting every immersion and cultural school, every public school aboriginal program, including language programs, the instructional materials and texts did not fill one small cardboard box. This was in 2009. Those pieces she did get, including language class texts, were almost entirely hand-made by the teachers themselves.[53]

Indigenous teachers in the public schools don't tend to push the issue of their under-funded efforts, their lack of curriculum resources or financing to develop them, or the way their colleagues make time for extra events, like school photos or assemblies, during their language classes. Native teachers in BC public schools are disproportionately accosted by internet hate, rude graffiti across cultural icons outside their schools, and even the traditional content of their lunches "tastes like shit" according to their colleagues in the staff rooms.[54] So prevalent are these attacks, apparently, that when one native teacher went to the local RCMP with evidence of obscene internet hate and then refused to have the event buried in the unceremonious manner recommended by her Administrative Officers in the high school, the BC Teachers' Federation advocate encouraged her to pursue the matter. Rarely do the teachers formally object to such treatment.

Displays of power are too meaningful: in the course of the events above, two boys posted violent sexual descriptions of the school's native language teacher and what she did with her fish down at the river, on a website featuring an interview with her about traditional fishing. The local RCMP station that had received her evidence issued a false press release to the media describing closure of the matter in a non-existent reconciliation process.[55]

After a graffiti event at a Fraser Valley school where two totem carvings outside the front doors were disgustingly augmented with paint, the school's leadership simply had the graffiti removed over the weekend and never raised the matter with the staff or student body.

Efforts to incorporate local native participation in the school planning and curriculum delivery tend to be relegated to the high-profile type of engagement. The high-minded words of inclusivity do not trickle down to teachers, principals or indigenous students in the form of action. A Social Planning and Research Council of BC program to study ways of implementing St'át'imc culture in School District #74, the Power of Place project, conducted extensive surveys, interviews, and consultation sessions and presentations. The end product, a list of feasible activities and willing and able Elders and cultural resource people, has laid dormant ever since. Aboriginal Enhancement Agreements, in effect in most School Districts, have the stated aim of improving aboriginal academic achievement, not enhancing culturally relevant aboriginal learning.

The additional funds BC schools receive from Ottawa for each aboriginal head enrolled have long been a curiosity. "Indian Money" was used to buy volleyball uniforms while the native elder who volunteered her time to teach the local language was denied her request for fifteen dollars a week in consideration of the cost of gas, since she had to drive twenty kilometers to the school and back, three times a week.[56] The "Indian Money" was $800 a head per year at that time. It's $1,100 now, and the Aboriginal Support Workers it is spent on retaining reportedly spend their time as photocopiers and go-fers for the teachers. Their job title is another interesting play on words. Do they work to support aboriginal students, or are they support workers for the school who happen to be aboriginal? These workers keep a log book to record a description of each interaction with a native student over the course of the day; this is accountability to the mandate.

The indigenous children have not failed to notice the way their languages and cultures are ignored and the way that successful native people speak English and work for non-native people. Two young schoolboys were overheard during a Xit'ólacw Community School field trip in 2008, discussing their recent transfer from the Pemberton public school:

"Do you like this school better, or the one in town?"
"This one."
"Yeah, they don't beat you up so much in this one."

The political situation is not lost on the children. They may not be able to articulate the situation, may be very unaware of how the larger environment affects their experience where sometimes being aboriginal is okay and sometimes it's not, but the children know enough not to talk about it.

Sticks and stones have broken bones, particularly in inter-racial fights in the public schools, and names have clearly hurt many. A number of Indians, by the 1950s at least, preferred not to register as Status Indians, not to live on a Reserve, not to send their kids to residential schools, not to be fenced in, and not to be subjected to the *Indian Act*. They did not require the benefit of residential schooling, as so many university published authors insist, to carry on with lives on the run. Many moved across the US border to reinvent themselves and come back later.

If they had delayed their return to the present date, their children would still not be equal students in BC schools.

When a fourth grade student in Lillooet explained to her mother that she needed to bring news of some current event to class for discussion, the mother suggested the situation of the new bridges being built in the Duffy Lake corridor. The St'át'imc Chiefs Council had formally opposed the sudden start of bridge construction since a Government-to-Government protocol meant to facilitate agreement on such developments was still in progress. Although progress was worryingly sparse and slowing, when the bridge project began the government had simply replied that the St'át'imc had already been consulted. The mother kept trying to complete the thought but was interrupted each time by an increasingly voluble cry of, "Mom!" So she asked, "What is it?" The child explained: "Normal people don't talk about St'át'imc stuff!!"[57] That was in 2010.

Chapter 8

IMMIGRATION
OR ESCAPEMENT

"There are plenty of bad eggs making a go of it in Canada."
—U.D. - fur traders' journal

*"Nevertheless, the brave little creature did so fix her heart on
her brother's rescue, ...she pinched and scraped enough together to ship
him for Canada. When he was tired of nothing to do and disposed in its
turn to cut even that, he graciously consented to go to Canada."*
— *Little Dorritt*, by Charles Dickens

Who Were We Then?

What was happening in Europe when people were leaving there to come
to Canada? Who were these "civilized" and "superior" people when they were at
home?

When Europeans colonized North America, they were slave traders. They
were burning women and children in Spain for "witchcraft." The English were
starving Catholics in Ireland; schooling their elite boys on Welsh girl children; and
freeing serfs from the land to a new level of peasantdom that would see generations
of families registered in the census as "In Service"—1.4 million by 1914—and
with no address of their own. Disembowelling and burning alive were still on the
statute books. They were collecting taxes in France to an extent that would have
left rural farming families with a block of cheese and a loaf of bread less than
they needed to pay what they owed for the privilege of working. When BC was
being colonized, Britain was on its second wave of opium-fueled war with China;
the masses across castes in India had mutinied under British extortion and been

massacred by the British East India Company – forcing a shift in administration from Company to Empire.

They were warring across Europe and treatying at such a frantic pace that a person's nationality was in some places a fairly hypothetical notion. In some cases they were just warring—for a hundred years at a time—as in the case of Britain and France. They were hewing their nations from the human wreckage of the tribal whites that Celts and then Holy Roman soldiers and then expansive Kings and Emperors had left behind. The massive conglomerates of state power that were being forged in the wake of Crusades and Inquisitions and industry were beginning to appear in their present forms of Spain, Portugal, Germany, England, France, Italy, Turkey and so on. Many people were displaced, and war was expensive.

As the Industrial Revolution moved a stream of gradually more desperate rural people into the cities for work which did not exist, centers like London found themselves with a truly disposable labour force. Occupied territories like Ireland found themselves with too many hungry peasants on their hands, as landowners exported food up the chain of power and off the island.

The boats that rolled into Eastern Canada from Ireland were overfull with people who lived and breathed, if they could, for a fair chance at life. Those ships are known today as Coffin Ships, since the number of passengers who could live and breathe by the end of the voyage was substantially less than when it set out. People from Wales, deprived of nationhood; people from Scotland, war-weary, landless, persecuted, or in Domestic Service in England—they all left home by boats and very few ever returned. Very few of the children, or their children, ever returned. It wasn't home, but Canada was a place where anyone from Europe could get 160 acres if they wanted it.

People from Ukraine sold their miserable plots and everything they owned for the price of sea-passage and arrived on the prairies to collect title to hundreds of acres of forest. People from China, where they could not have hoped to profit in a lifetime the way they might in one day on a moderately successful BC gold field, left in whatever numbers their families could afford. People from Denmark, Italy, India, Poland, France, Hungary, Russia and Czechoslovakia came here because they believed in the chance that Imperial Britain offered along with the sacrament of citizenship. The devil they knew was clearly not better than the devil they didn't.

Perhaps an illustration of the demon they knew, from mid-19th century England, is illuminating. Describing people who came to aid their friends or relatives, or clientele, at the Marshalsee debtors' prison in London, Charles Dickens wrote in *Little Dorritt*, in 1865:

> The shabbiness of these attendants upon shabbiness, the poverty
> of these insolvent waiters upon insolvency, was a sight to see.
> Such threadbare coats and trousers, such fusty gowns and shawls,

such squashed hats and bonnets, such boots and shoes, such umbrellas and walking sticks, never were seen in Rag Fair. All of them wore the cast-off clothes of other men and women, were made up of patches and pieces of other people's individuality, and had no sartorial existence of their own proper. Their walk was the walk of a race apart. They had a peculiar way of doggedly slinking round the corner, as if they were eternally going to the pawnbroker's. When they coughed, they coughed like people accustomed to being forgotten on doorsteps and in draughty passages, waiting for answers to letters in faded ink, which gave the recipients of those manuscripts great mental disturbance and no satisfaction. As they eyed the stranger in passing, they eyed him with borrowing eyes—hungry, sharp, speculative as to his softness if they were accredited to him, and the likelihood of his standing something handsome. Mendacity on commission stooped in their high shoulders, shambled in their unsteady legs, buttoned and pinned and darned and dragged their clothes, frayed their button-holes, leaked out of their figures in dirty little ends of tape, and issued from their mouths in alcoholic breathings.

By contrast, a priest on board with Juan Perez remarked in 1774 of the Nootka,

These people are very fat, of good appearance, red and white in colour, with long hair… They are not at all noisy, and seemed to us mild and good-tempered.[1]

Maybe Europeans and the original North Americans could have traded, even inter-married and become allies along an honourable route that would make Little Dorritt's neighbours fat and healthy too.

That evolutionary branch was pruned. The new growth nurtured by Britain was endless, genocidal war. The soldier she chose to fight it was none other than little Dorritt's brother.

There is a profound misunderstanding in the modern day colonial. The colonies were not meant to be societies in their own right, nor were they formed as a social experiment in bettering humanity. They did not enjoy the support of the sheltering British navy to pursue such ends as democracy or liberty, fraternity and equality – that firepower was afforded them for a less altruistic purpose. Colonies were formed to secure access to resources. There was Greater Portugal, Greater Spain, Greater Holland, Greater Russia, Greater Britain – all exacted from indigenous nations. Whether a colony then became a worthwhile society with a culture edifying to the human race was entirely up to them, and we have seen their early limitations. Those new cultures' meanest habits, such as genocide against the original peoples, were not rebuked by the parent societies: they were encouraged by fiscal rewards for the appropriated bounty. Whoever it was that returned the goods to Europe, and by whatever means, was not a point of concern.

The British advocate for free trade with America, John Bright, had suggested the wholesale abandonment of British North America to the USA to secure uninterrupted trade with the United States. That was shortly before 1867, when a course which would lead to the *British North America Act* was instead pursued – at the urging of those in the Canadas, New Brunswick, New Found Land, and Nova Scotia. The cession had been acceptable to Gladstone, the British Prime Minister. In considering the sacrifice of British North America for the purpose of easing trade relations, Bright made no mention of a grand plan for the colonial; there was no divine duty with which he had been sent forth. It is established that the spread of Christianity was just a ruse; humanity's hopes for a heroic attempt to improve society on a British satellite apparently paled into insignificance next to the prospect of improving trade. Colonists had not been selected for moral fiber or any special potential: they were meant to be disposable, they were going to die building a road into the heart of resource-rich territories. These were territories, we might well consider today, which the peoples had conserved and protected and enlivened to the point where, in the year 2013, the natural endowments are so rich as to be traded in the public markets as carbon credits.

The disposability of people involved in the founding of colonies is framed spectacularly by a summary explanation of England's war of extermination against the Maori of New Zealand:

> It was all about war for us. The Brits fought a war of attrition—they could just keep fighting forever, with Irish, Scottish, landless peasants. We slaughtered them by the thousands, but they just kept coming. They had this inexhaustible supply of people who would just come to our country and die. We slaughtered them in the thousands. But we could never win.[2]

The majority of immigrants didn't have any appreciation for laws when they came to British Columbia. They were fleeing laws. As it was well stated, somewhat apologetically, at the beginning of *Tales of Conflict*, an account of the war HBC gunboats waged against coastal villages: "The European trader, having only a hazy idea of the multitudinous laws of his kind was equally ignorant of the customs of the native, but assumed that he was a superior being and consequently held the red man in contempt."[3]

Europeans who came to British Columbia were, for the most part, fleeing laws which did not serve them but had preserved their poverty and criminalized them for it. The first sets of colonists in what is now eastern Canada came straight from the French prison cells in 1598, and promptly were abandoned and died.[4] Almost three centuries and several successful settler grafts later, "Colonists in Canada, however, for the most part were illiterate, and didn't understand the workings of assemblies. Voting in a free election was completely new to them."[5]

Questions arise in considering native / newcomer relations from the spiritual and therefore legal perspective. At that time, only a human being had human rights, and only a Christian was a human. But what was a heathen, savage red man to an illiterate heretical white man? Just because Dickens eyed the impoverished and indeed the jailed with a jaundiced eye does not mean that there were not honourable people among them, and indeed Christians. But they were certainly Protestants. Among the numberless heretics, Protestants, who fled to Canada for their lives, who among them could distinguish himself from a heathen? If one agreed that any of the Kings or Queens could have power independent of Rome, was that not heresy? According to the Pope, it was. And the Pope was one of the more forceful purveyors of Christianization.

But the settlers were not concerned with god—they wanted land to live on and were indifferent to the fate of any they might need to remove from it in order to do so. For the men and women who sought a place to live, the church was meant not to be an obstacle – as it had been back home. If killing heathens made life easier, then god, any god, was welcome in condemning them. And perhaps heresy was not the issue, because of the simple fact that the one who could kill us for being a traitor to the King was much closer by than the one who could kill us for heresy and lived far away.

The "superior men," and they were only men,[6] who colonized British Columbia occasionally contemplated themselves, grappling with the contradictions. In the chapter, "Right of Savages to the Soil," in Gilbert Malcolm Sproat's fabulous timepiece called *Scenes and Studies of Savage Life*, he claims:

> For instance, we might justify our occupation of Vancouver Island by the fact of all the land lying waste without prospect of improvement, and our conquest of a people and cultivated country like Oude [South Africa] by some such consideration as this—that the State was delinquent before the world, and by its corruption put the welfare of neighbouring and progressive English territories in danger. It would be necessary in all cases to remember that, though the right of the intruders might be justified by some of

these considerations, the intruders would be bound to act always with such justice, humanity, and moderation as should vindicate fully those superior pretensions which were the ground of the right of occupying. Any extreme act, such as a general confiscation of cultivated land, or systematic personal ill-treatment of the dispossessed people, would be quite unjustifiable. Probably, no other circumstance than a continued wanton quarrelling with their fate, after the occupation of the country by a superior race, ought to be held as sufficient cause for depriving savage aboriginal inhabitants of their title to a limited and sufficient property, enjoyable under certain conditions. So much they could claim as our fellow-men, and they would also have other obvious claims on the consideration of a Christian nation.

It is important to recall that Christianity was the source of the explorers' and colonizers' "superiority," and was said to be the cause of the need to colonize the new heathen world. The doctrine of *Terra Nullius* allowed the Christian European to pronounce any territories he arrived in as empty if the people there were not Christian or did not have a Christian prince.

Once this extension of the British god had taken hold in the land of the west and, as Governor Richard Blanshard described its purpose, had worked to "repress and over-awe the natives," all manner of humanity felt free to carry on all manner of activity under its shelter.

The people that came to places like BC under the guises Sproat described, however, were hardly Christian, nor superior, nor civilized. They were destitute and desperate and had none of the qualities that the elite used to characterize the virtues of their race. Most Europeans who arrived in early British Columbia came via California and had long since disassociated themselves from virtues cherished by Europeans. They were merely protected by an umbrella identity that was required by the imperial colonizer to continue to control the lands for itself. They were merely meant to form the imperial presence, clear the land and ship the goods back to Europe.

The Hudson's Bay Company carried the god-given right to carry out acts of justice, or juridical sovereignty, since they had received the King's Charter in 1670. Instead they did not hold the trials they were warranted to, but carried out extrajudicial murders. The Hudson's Bay Company held their first trial in 1853. James Douglas, then Governor of Vancouver Island, took the HMS *Thetis* and 130 officers to the mouth of the Cowichan River and Nanaimo, where two native fellows were produced by their villages—both having acted in the murder of an HBC employee. They were convicted and hung.

Britain reserved to itself the ability to be peaceful, god-abiding and just.

By and large, the newcomer in his unenlightened state brought no appreciation of the idea of god-given rights, justice, rights of property—because he had never really had any before.

Americans who had run out of gold in California went north to BC. Much of the eastern seaboard was developed by "criminals" working off the terms and conditions of "Transportation" from Newgate prison on the Thames of London. Much of California was populated and mined and built by them and the descendants of those people in 1849, the California gold rush, and thereafter. Many of them left for the Fraser gold rush in 1858, and then for the Cariboo and Yukon gold rushes.

> I'm dead broke, I'm dead broke, so I've nothing to lose;
> I've the wide world before me to live where I choose.
> I'm at home in the wild woods wherever I be;
> Tho' dead broke, tho' dead broke, the skedaddler is free.
>
> Tho' creditors curse, me I care not a straw,
> I heed not old Begbie, I laugh at his law.
> There is game in the mountains, the rivers yield fish,
> And for gold I can prospect wherever I wish.
>
> Where I fancy a spot, I my blankets unfold
> And remain a time there to prospect for gold.
> And ne'er as a debtor shall I go to the quod
> While my keep I can make with my gun and my rod.

Folk songs were written down later, at least those that survived the ungodly campfires of the day. The one above is called, "The Skedaddler," a tune from the 1860s, from the Shuswap area of Cariboo.[7] This was sung by the men that Surveyor after Indian Agent after Parliamentarian would defend as "superior" to the "savage," and therefore having rights to the land. A description of the men of the Yukon gold rush is available from a Chief in northeastern BC:

> Thousands of miners flooded into northern British Columbia on their way to the gold fields. They were a rowdy drunken bunch who disrupted the lifestyle of my ancestors by killing the scarce game, breaking their traps and stealing their horses. They liked to fight a lot—if not with each other then with the native people.[8]

The elite now explain to colonials that European systems of land ownership, the implosion of the British Commons and the Magna Carta, the democracy of the French revolution, the amalgamation of German princes, are the distinguishing superior achievements of the Caucasian race. At the time of their escape to America, these lofty concepts were immaterial to the vast majority of those who traveled. If those great pillars of civilization had been helpful, perhaps they would not have needed or wanted to leave?

The newcomers to Vancouver Island were, according to businessman Alfred Waddington,

> ...an indescribable array of Polish Jews, Italian fishermen, French cooks, jobbers, speculators of every kind... To the above lists may be added a fair seasoning of gamblers, swindlers, thieves, drunkards, and jail birds let loose by the Governor of California for the benefit of mankind, besides the halt, lame, blind and mad.[9]

It seems that what the immigrants really needed was to replace themselves at the bottom of the barrel in order to rise. They also needed land. Britain performed this miracle in a stroke of what is today called British Liberalism – that anyone willing to pay taxes on that land to Britain could be a British Citizen. And any British Citizen could take possession of land in BC. Except indigenous people, who could do neither. "British Liberalism," in one of the phrase's several usages, refers to the wake of "democratic" societies which the British would leave behind in their civilizing mission: as soon as a man's uncivilized, pastoralist, heathen or egalitarian society was dominated by the British, it would be transformed into a modern and "liberal" democracy. The heathens of what was named British Columbia were apparently not yet ready for this leap in early days of contact – as no conquered peoples were until they had proven over time they would maintain themselves that way.

Before British Liberalism could come into effect in the colony, England provided orders which effectively had Hudson's Bay Company men living in a military regime in their forts. The pioneering masses who followed answered to no such leadership. The BC homesteader was the original outlaw, the ultimate rebel: no church, no school, no community, no parents, no brothers or sisters...

What was the article most in demand in the new colony of God's superior children? After food, it was not bibles or books or ink and fountain pens, but whiskey and prostitutes.

> It would take almost a line of packet ships, running regular between here and San Francisco, to supply this Island with grog, so great a thirst prevails among its inhabitants.[10]

Refugees from bankruptcy, disgrace, or family strife, suffered in some other part of the world, are to be met with in Victoria every few yards. ...Society in the interior is very depraved. ...little trace of Sunday is at present visible... Out of the five thousand souls in Victoria, a few may be found who respect the ordinances of religion. Up to the present there have been but two places of worship in Cariboo... Profane language is almost universal, and is employed with diabolical ingenuity. The names of "Jesus Christ" and the "Almighty" are introduced in most blasphemous connections. Going to church is known among many as "the religious dodge"... [11]

Victoria was described as "...a city which has more drinking places and opium dens than any place of its size in the Dominion," on June 5, 1886 in the *Vancouver Daily Advertiser.*[12] Fort Yale in the Fraser gold rush was "a modern Sodom." One of Yale's gold rush entrepreneurs ran down his contemporaries as follows:

A worse set of cut-throats and all-time scoundrels than those who flocked to Yale from all parts of the world never assembled anywhere... Decent people feared to go out after dark. Night assaults and robberies, varied by an occasional cold-blooded murder or a daylight theft, were common occurrences.[13]

BC was the hideout of the most scandalous sort of American criminal, from William Clarke Quantrill—involved in his gang's raid of Lawrence, Kansas, where some 150 men, women and children were slaughtered, to Billy Miner, the "gentleman" bandit.[14]

That is to say nothing of the ilk that was entrained in BC. Donald McLean arrived from Scotland at the age of 20 and started in HBC employ. He was made Chief Factor of a trading post shortly after shooting an entire native family to death to settle a score over an assault by one of their relatives.[15] According to R. C. Lundin Brown, in his book *Klatsassin,* McLean had personally killed nineteen native people in his career. He was picked off in turn by Chilcotin sharpshooters in 1864 while guiding a hunting party pursuing the men suspected of murdering Alfred Waddington's road building crew in Bute Inlet. McLean's grandson carried on his cause, writing two books about how his grandfather and uncles had played a vital role in opening up the west and describing sympathetically the trials and the obstacles presented to them by "ignorant Indians" and "greedy old chiefs."[16]

It was 1863 before a free school opened in Esquimalt—the first in BC. The European population of Vancouver Island was 774 in 1855—half of them children. It was 1890 before authorization for the first university came through to I.W. Powell. It was 1930 before a man born in BC became the Premier of it—S.F. Tolmie—some 120 years after white men began to live here; 72 years after the colony was founded and 59 years after it became a province.[17] Access to a recognized education, i.e., one that was taken in England, was not something that many colonizers had.

By 1858, however, indigenous communities had been building churches, some of them after the Gothic fashion in France, with hand-planed lumber on foundations of river rock.[18] In some cases it was Indian men and Indian money that built churches for the small settler populations, as in the Cowichan valley, on Comiaken Hill, in 1863.[19] Many of the churches, some stone and some cedar, are still standing today.

Their pains were not rewarded. The native fishermen twenty years later, working in the competitive field of supplying salmon to the canneries along the coast, were outpaced by Japanese who would not observe the Lord's day of rest on Sundays.[20] While the Christian people of Neskonlith filed to church on Sunday mornings, the ranchers and proprietors of the log sorts and booms across the river would laugh at them as they worked the dollar-yielding waterway. George Manuel, a foreman on the log boom, wrote of how disconcerting this was to him, week after week, in the 1930s.[21] After all, it was the white people who had convinced his people of the importance of putting down their work and other traditions to satisfy the god of the church building.

The superior people laughed at the church goers. The superior people, at the same time, were according themselves privileges on account of having brought that very god with them: the god they laughed at the natives for honouring.

Christianization of the indigenous was not an early obstacle. They were already very pious people. It was the new population of the Monarch's frontier, from the old world, that Christendom never really had hold of. Even those who insisted on practicing their traditional and religious communal life, like the Doukhobors of Siberia – who came to British Columbia to escape Imperial Russia's use of them—even they had no difficulty building a new place for themselves on top of someone else's village sites, trails and bread baskets.[22]

It has been said by the more self-satisfied anthropologists that indigenous societies represent the childhood of humanity. This thinking seems to recommend that there is something more mature about using the capacity to cross oceans to wipe out other societies; that there is something humanly improved in outgrowing the fear of god. Perhaps it is merely a fatalistic approach, deriving from the fact that most indigenous societies in the world are quickly wiped out by the military organization of industrialized or oligarchic societies. It was certainly the military organization of the oncoming peoples which was categorically superior; not the people themselves. Or more in keeping with the beliefs of the "adult" representatives of humanity: that children, like the indigenous, should be seen and not heard; they should obey; that youth is wasted on the young and that the indigenous are too freedom-loving.

The promise of betterment in the "New World" and the notable exclusion of Haudenoshonee, MikMak, Cree, Salishan, Innu and all the existing nations from that promise is conspicuous. People who left Europe starving, defeated and wretched, still held the belief that they were superior to "savages," and did in turn to the newfound "children" that which their own "fathers" had done to them. And they defied every rule that Imperial Britain wrote for them.

Our Loving Subjects

Who? The ones in the Americas who would revolt ten years later?

A sort of conciliatory love letter was written at the end of the Seven Years War by King George III of England to the colonists of North America. It was particular to the protection of the Indian Nations. "Our Loving Subjects," he wrote in 1763, in all of several existing and different renditions of the original Royal Proclamation, "should be informed of our Paternal care, for the security of the Liberties and Properties of those who are and shall become Inhabitants thereof... ."

As we know, most of those Loving Subjects departed from all reciprocally loving pursuits shortly afterwards, in the American Revolution, won in 1783. That is to say, they decided to keep for themselves that which they were stealing fairly and squarely rather than have George interrupt them with his restrictions and taxes.

The facts that Tecumseh guaranteed the success of that Revolution against the Crown, and that Pontiac was the reason for the British defeat of the French in Lower Canada are not illuminated moments in either Canadian or American history. Once France had been defeated in Canada, and England immediately failed to fulfill its promises to Pontiac and his allied warriors, Pontiac launched a campaign against the British forts in Upper and Lower Canada. He was fighting for favourable terms from England, for the upkeep of George's promises to him. His effort precipitated and largely necessitated the Proclamation of 1763 which then caused the Americans to revolt.

Of the promises Britain made to Pontiac to bring him to their side of the war, some are recorded in the *Articles of Capitulation of Montreal*, 1760. Article 40 reads:

The Savage or Indian Allies of his Most Christian Majesty
shall be maintained in the lands they occupy if they wish

to remain there; they shall not be disturbed on any pretext whatever for having taken arms and served his Most Holy Majesty.

Having been dependent on the Indian General and his soldiers for their defeat of the French, the British – later to become Canadian – government also adopted and indeed enshrined their obligation to the people that had secured their territories against their longtime European foe. The resulting fiduciary obligation is one that literally requires that the stronger nation protect the weaker nation with whom it was allied – not annex or assimilate the weaker nation, as has been Canada's aspiration ever since. The international implications of such legal documents as the *Articles of Montreal*, protecting the indigenous peoples, or "Tribal Nations," as King George III put it, are substantial.

This excerpt is from the Royal Proclamation of October 7, 1763, which remains part of the Canadian Constitution, Section 25:

> And whereas it is just and reasonable, and essential to Our Interest and the Security of Our Colonies, that the several Nations or Tribes of Indians, with whom We are connected, and who live under Our Protection, should not be molested or disturbed in the Possession of such Parts of Our Dominions and Territories as, not having been ceded to, or purchased by Us, are reserved to them, or any of them, as their Hunting Grounds; We do therefore, with the Advice of Our Privy Council, declare it to be Our Royal Will and Pleasure, that no Governor or Commander in Chief in any of Our Colonies of Quebec, East Florida, or West Florida, do presume, upon any Pretence whatever, to grant Warrants of Survey, or pass any Patents for Lands beyond the Bounds of their respective Governments, as described in their Commissions; as also, that no Governor or Commander in Chief in any of Our other Colonies or Plantations in America, do presume, for the present, and until Our further Pleasure be known, to grant Warrants of Survey, or pass Patents for any Lands beyond the Heads or Sources of any of the Rivers which fall into the Atlantick Ocean from the West and North-West, or upon any Lands whatever, which, not having been ceded to, or purchased by Us as aforesaid, are reserved to the said Indians, or any of them.
>
> And We do further declare it to be Our Royal Will and Pleasure, for the present as aforesaid, to reserve under

Our Sovereignty, Protection, and Dominion, for the Use of the said Indians, all the Lands and Territories not included within the Limits of Our said Three New Governments, or within the Limits of the Territory granted to the Hudson's Bay Company, as also all the Lands and Territories lying to the Westward of the Sources of the Rivers which fall into the Sea from the West and North West, as aforesaid; and We do hereby strictly forbid, on Pain of Our Displeasure, all Our loving Subjects from making any Purchases or Settlements whatever, or taking Possession of any of the Lands above reserved, without Our especial Leave and Licence for that Purpose first obtained.

And We do further strictly enjoin and require all Persons whatever, who have either wilfully or inadvertently seated themselves upon any Lands within the Countries above described, or upon any other Lands, which, not having been ceded to, or purchased by Us, are still reserved to the said Indians as aforesaid, forthwith to remove themselves from such Settlements.

And whereas great Frauds and Abuses have been committed in the purchasing Lands of the Indians, to the great Prejudice of Our Interests, and to the great Dissatisfaction of the said Indians; in order therefore to prevent such Irregularities for the future, and to the End that the Indians may be convinced of Our Justice, and determined Resolution to remove all reasonable Cause of Discontent, We do, with the Advice of Our Privy Council, strictly enjoin and require, that no private Person do presume to make any Purchase from the said Indians of any Lands reserved to the said Indians, within those Parts of Our Colonies where We have thought proper to allow Settlement; but that if, at any Time, any of the said Indians should be inclined to dispose of the said Lands, that same shall be purchased only for Us, in Our Name, at some publick Meeting or Assembly of the said Indians to be held for that Purpose by the Governor or Commander in Chief of Our Colonies respectively, within which they shall lie: and in case they shall lie within the Limits of any Proprietary Government, they shall be purchased only for the Use and in the Name of such Proprietaries, conformable to such Directions and Instructions as We or they shall think proper to give for that Purpose: And We do, by the Advice of Our Privy Council, declare and enjoin, that the Trade with the said Indians shall be free and open to all our Subjects whatever; provided that every Person, who may incline to trade with the said Indians, do take out a Licence for carrying on such Trade from the Governor or Commander in Chief of any of Our Colonies respectively, where such Person shall reside; and also give Security to observe such Regulations as We shall at any Time think fit, by Ourselves or by Our Commissaries to be appointed for this Purpose, to direct and appoint for the Benefit of the said Trade; And We do hereby authorize, enjoin, and require the Governors and Commanders in Chief of all Our Colonies respectively, as well Those under Our immediate Government as those under the Government and Direction of Proprietaries, to grant such Licences without Fee or Reward, taking especial Care to insert therein a Condition, that such Licence shall be void, and the Security forfeited, in Case the Person, to whom the same is granted, shall refuse or neglect to observe such Regulations as We shall think proper to prescribe as aforesaid.

And We do further expressly enjoin and require all Officers whatever, as well Military as those employed in the Management and Direction of Indian Affairs within the Territories reserved as aforesaid for the Use of the said Indians, to seize and apprehend all Persons whatever, who, standing charged with Treasons, Misprisions of Treason, Murders, or other Felonies or Misdemeanours, shall fly from Justice, and take Refuge in the said Territory, and to send them under a proper Guard to the Colony where the Crime was committed of which they stand accused, in order to take their Tryal for the same.[23]

The above is cited in such length because it has been regarded as a foundational legal obligation undertaken by the British in relation to the indigenous nations. It used to be cited, as in *Calder*, as the source of indigenous rights. In truth, it is the most substantial law upon which present day Canadians can stand and demand that the previous and present Prime Ministers, judges and other descended "governors" be brought to justice against their only set of relevant laws.

The Canadas and the French population living in them were "given" to England in the peace terms of 1760. But France did not own the land that was transferred at that particular Treaty of Paris any more than they owned the territories described in the Louisiana Purchase which Napoleon sold to the United States to finance his war; nor any more than the Hudson's Bay Company owned Rupert's Land—which it sold to the government of Canada. The Proclamation had the desired effect, however, of assuring Pontiac and the tribal nations of their lands and of peace with Great Britain as their ally.

The King's decree fueled the opposite sentiment among the seven colonies south of Canada. In 1775, the war that would forge the United States of America began.

Fifty years after the United States won their independence, the question of whether King George's Proclamation still applied to America came to court in a very literal way. In 1832, Chief Justice Marshall ruled in favour of Indians' undisturbed presence on their own unceded lands. His decision in *Worcester v. Georgia* was not well received. President Jackson responded, according to most accounts, "John Marshall has made his decision; now let him enforce it!"[24] It was a rhetorical suggestion, as the Chief Justice is meant to write orders, not execute them. Enforcement of the law is the job of police. The same attitude of political defiance of legal principles has prevailed in Canada.

The Royal Proclamation of 1763 was posted by Nisga'a leaders in the Nass Valley once they began to recognize the signs of even more trouble ahead with the Colony of British Columbia. This document has taken on a magnitude that it can be reasonably assumed was never intended in a contest that was probably never imagined. Some BC lawyers have the notion that the existence of Rupert's Land made BC immune from the directions given in the Royal Proclamation of 1763, because Rupert's Land was in some way an exception to those directions, and that Rupert's Land included BC—which it did not. In 1869, England miraculously "bought" Rupert's Land from the HBC for Canada though the HBC did not own the land, just the trading rights—which England itself had bestowed on the Company. When it was bought, it became Manitoba. Not Saskatchewan or Alberta, and certainly not British Columbia. Rupert's Land included the watersheds that drained into Hudson's Bay. Judges have opined that the Royal Proclamation, an Executive Order, does not apply to BC because at the time the place was *terra incognita.* Clearly none of the lands "to the west" had ever been seen before—not by Englishmen.

Although it was more ignored than not, some settlers understood that the British fathers had described a mechanism by which they would be free of unwanted Indians on newly pre-empted lands, and they asked, "Why is not the Indian title to Cowitchen extinguished at once… We want farmers, and the best way to get them is to open the lands of Cowitchen to actual settlers by extinguishing the Indian title."[25] The settlers at least understood that some procedure was required to get the Indian land. In July, 1864, settlers there took an alternative position and actually petitioned Governor Kennedy to save them from molestation by the Indians:[26] the exact reverse of the Proclamation's words.

Contraventions of the Proclamation should have been brought to justice. The Privy Council of England was the court of appeal and the highest court for every British colony. It was the highest court in Canada until 1949, in spite of the creation of the Supreme Court of Canada in 1875. By the time British Columbia was a colony, peoples in India, Nigeria, Australia, New Zealand, South Africa and others had attempted to have the Judicial Committee of the Privy Council hear their complaints against the colonizers. These were all complaints about actions that Britain had already forbidden its settlers, generals, soldiers and governors to commit, but which its colonial Governors had failed to resolve. Unfortunately, access to this Committee was outmaneuvered by Canada when lawyer Edward O'Meare came within a breath of bringing the Claims of the Allied Tribes before it in 1919. The Prime Minister and Chief Justice of Canada were members of the Privy Council.

In 1884 at the Conference of Berlin, it had been further determined between the colonizing European states that colonial powers could not hear cases involving indigenous against settler which arose in their own satellite spheres of delegated influence.

The fact that the newcomers were not following their Great Father's instructions was known to the indigenous of British Columbia. The fact that they could not get justice from the newcomers who were committing the injustices against them was no mystery. At least as early as 1906, trips to visit that Great Father were seen as necessary by the otherwise beleaguered Indian nations in British Columbia. The Cowichan Chiefs traveled to England in that year, and they were accompanied by others whose trip has been less well documented. James Williams of the Carrier Sekani, deep in the interior of British Columbia, recalled:

> You heard Wilf talk about our Chiefs going to Ottawa in 1906. One of them was my grandfather Jack Williams. It took him three months each way. You heard about the gold. In one of their meetings while they were in England, they went into a private room and they were shoveling around the gold and offering it to them. He said, 'no,' he was there for the land, for the hunting and fishing rights. He did right not to take that gold.[27]

At least going to England allowed the Chiefs to discover where the newcomers had learned how to behave.

The indigenous leaders then attempted to follow the letter of the British law when the newcomers were clearly contravening it. This led them to the Privy Council. Their indigenous territories were not British soil, but they believed, as per the European code as they understood it, that because Great

Britain had either "discovered" or won from other "discoverers" by inter-European war, exclusive rights to make treaties in North America, they would be sure to do so. They felt England and its colony would have to be made to abide by the terms of discovery, and consummate "possession" with purchase.

The Supreme Court of the United States considered the doctrine of discovery, basically the simple assertion of the Christian European nations that they could do as they pleased with non-Christian peoples in lands they arrived at before other Christian European nations, in *Worcester*. Chief Justice Marshal gave his opinion of the meaning of "Discovery":

> The great maritime powers of Europe discovered and visited different parts of this continent at nearly the same time. The object was too immense for any of them to grasp the whole; and the claimants too powerful to submit to the exclusive or unreasonable pretensions of any single potentate. To avoid bloody conflicts, which might terminate disastrously for all, it was necessary for the nations of Europe to establish some principle which all would acknowledge, and which should decide their respective rights as between themselves. This principle, suggested by the actual state of things, was, "that discovery gave title to the government by whose subjects or by whose authority it was made, against all other European governments, which title might be consummated by possession." (*Johnson vs. McIntosh*, 8 Wheaton's Rep., 543.)

Dr. Bruce Clark interpreted those paragraphs in a recent turn of the century submission from within Canada to an international court, attempting to show ecocide and ethnocide:

> This principle, acknowledged by all Europeans, because it was in the interest of all to acknowledge it, gave to the nation making the discovery, as its inevitable consequence, the sole *right of acquiring the soil and of making settlements on it. It was an exclusive principle which shut out the right of competition among those who had agreed to it; not one that could annul the previous rights of those who had not agreed to it. It regulated the right given by discovery among the European discoverers, but could not affect the rights of those already in possession, either as aboriginal occupants, or occupants by virtue of a discovery made before the memory of man. It gave the exclusive right to purchase, but did not found that right on a denial of the right of the possessor to sell*. [Emphasis added.]

The relation between the Europeans and the natives was determined in each case by the particular government which asserted and could maintain this preemptive privilege in the particular place.[28]

The doctrine of discovery only came into existence in hindsight, often attributed to Marshall, and refers to the Europeans' gentlemanly understanding that they would avoid warring each other for newfound lands. It is sometimes made out to seem as though the colonial directive was simply to exterminate or dominate – but that is to blur the fine line between state and church objectives. Certainly the Papal Bulls recommended "dominion,"[29] but agreements between states were more legalistic, at least in Dr. Clark's opinion:

> The doctrine of discovery gave the "discovering" nation particular rights under international law as against other European or colonizing nations, namely the exclusive right to acquire land and resources from the Native or indigenous nations. The "doctrine of discovery" gave the "discovering" nation no legal right as against the Native nations or peoples.[30]

The trips to the Privy Council mentioned above were ineffective. The letter of the law meant very little to the colonists next to the tallies in the Fort Clerk's ledgers; the Captain's trade logs. They certainly meant nothing to the individual explorers, pioneers or politicians.

John Marshal wrote, in, *Worcester v. Georgia*, 1832:[31]

> Soon after Great Britain determined upon planting colonies in America, the king granted charters to companies of his subjects who associated for the purpose of carrying the views of the crown into effect, and of enriching themselves. The first of these charters was made before possession was taken of any part of the country. They purport, generally, to convey the soil, from the Atlantic to the South Sea. This soil was occupied by numerous and warlike nations, equally willing and able to defend their possessions. The extravagant and absurd idea, that the feeble settlements made on the sea coast, or the companies under whom they were made, acquired legitimate power by them to govern the people or occupy the lands from sea to sea, did not enter the mind of any man. They were well understood to convey the title which, according to the common law of European sovereigns respecting America, they might rightfully convey,

and no more. This was the right of purchasing such lands as the natives were willing to sell. *The crown could not be understood to grant what the crown did not affect claim; nor was it so understood.*

Certainly it is, that our history furnishes no example, from the first settlement of our country, of any attempt on the part of the crown to interfere with the internal affairs of the Indians, farther than to keep out the agents of foreign powers, who, as traders or otherwise, might seduce them into foreign alliances. *The king purchased their lands when they were willing to sell, at a price they were willing to take; but never coerced a surrender of them.* He also purchased their alliance and dependence by subsidies; but never intruded into the interior of their affairs, or interfered with their self government, so far as respected themselves only.'

Though speaking more particularly of Indian lands and territories, yet the opinion of the Court as to the maintenance of the laws of the Aborigines, is manifest throughout. The principles laid down in this judgment, (and Mr. Justice Story as a Member of the Court concurred in this decision), admit of no doubt. [Emphasis added.]

If this was all true at the time of writing, it certainly hasn't been true since then. And in fact, there must have been much revisionist history in the popularization of the understanding of the Doctrine of Discovery, which as it currently surfaces is widely understood to confer right of title.[32] Royal control of "territories lying to the west...," and the attendant requirements made on any entering of same, became something of a multi-level-marketing technique in early times. Middle men in the "undiscovered" countries brokered their own arrangements based on might and means available at the moment.

A 1670 Royal Charter like the ones described by Justice Marshall had established Rupert's Land, and the Hudson's Bay Company, and the Hudson's Bay Company's exclusive right to trade there.[33] This Charter should have prevented other traders from conducting business there. The document alone was clearly unable to do so.

Serious competition between the HBC and the North West Company, a rival fur trader, eventually reached a head – within the lands which were supposedly the exclusive trading domain of the Bay Company. Rupert's Land, as per their Royal Charter, was authorized for international trade only under the banner of the HBC. The challenge to this monopoly came from Montreal, from the XYZ Co, then to become the North West Company, which grew from business ties and fur trading practices between Canadien and Scottish traders. Their man, Alexander Mackenzie, reached the Pacific Ocean first in 1793—the first European by an overland route. Then Simon Fraser, also theirs, followed the course and found the head of the river that now bears his name in the interior of British Columbia. David Thomson went next, charting maps through the Columbia River in the Oregon Territory, and he also has a river named after him. All of them were trading with the indigenous—else they would have died very quickly—and making crude but essential gestures of more business to follow wherever they went. Fraser built forts for his company.

These fellows were out of bounds delineated by the British. Yet they were knighted for their work. There is no explanation for the presence of competing traders within the boundaries of a King's Charter – except that rules and regulations authored in Britain never did survive the sea voyage to North America. Ultimately, they were unenforceable.

When the HBC tired of the competition, and well after NWCo. men had done a lot of dangerous fort-building and map-making work, they built an instant settlement of re-located Scottish people, perhaps from Lord Selkirk's own estates in the Scottish Highlands, in the middle of the Red River Valley. They then went about cutting off critical NWCo. lines of supply with the Métis, in what is now Manitoba. Ultimately fights ensued, a shoot-out occurred, several were jailed, and Great Britain took the matter into its own hands. The North West Co. was absorbed into the Chartered HBC in 1821.

Whatever their status, as outlaws or friendly competitors, the most famous Nor'westers are accepted by British Columbians as founding fathers.

From Henry Hudson's Bay to Simon Fraser's River

"I hate the place and the Indians."
**—Simon Fraser, in a letter from what is now British Columbia
to John Stuart, September 29, 1806**

"...Fraser River takes its name from my father, now an aged man of 86 years. ...his exertions and enterprise in all probability secured to the British Crown what promises to be a Province surpassing in every element of natural greatness even our own Canada, the "brightest jewel" in the British Crown."
**—John A. Fraser, Simon Fraser's son
to the Editor of the *Hastings Chronicle*, February 10, 1862**

A prominent BC university is of course named after this "explorer," while the expression of his above mentioned hatred and contempt is evident and appalling throughout his journals and letters. Fraser is revered as a sort of hero. His journals are by no means thorough, but they do cover the extent to which he and his men were packed, portaged and piloted down the interior river to the sea by indigenous men. They also show that, "Among these Indians we observed a variety of tools, pieces of iron and of brass, a bunch of brass keys which were from the crew of a ship that the Indians of the sea had destroyed several years before."[34] Fraser seemed to feel he could compete with such booty, and documented the fact that he "…gave also a few trinkets to an Indian of a different nation in order that he might show them to his friends."

Fraser needed to make himself indispensable to the peoples of the interior, but they were already enjoying the fruit of sea-going trade. The Grease Trail included several points of entry from the coast and crossed the Rocky Mountains, but neither Fraser nor any other white man knew that. They were too busy "exploring" to communicate with the local people as to what thriving businesses were already in play. The best they could do, when they had established forts in the interior, was to bring rum into the territories and "harass" and "intimidate" the hunters and trappers to sell pelts, according to Father A.G. Morice.[35]

George Simpson took over operation of the forts Fraser had built directly from North West Company control in 1821, commanding the post of "Governor" of that district of the Hudson's Bay Company.

It is told, by those who recall what was told to them, that Simpson agreed to a treaty with the Chiefs he met. That discussion is known today by a very small circle as the 40/40/20 agreement. Of any "improvements" on the lands, perhaps roads or dedicated gardens or forts, or sales from which, the "King George Men" colonists and the HBC would receive 40%; the Indians 40%, and the monarch of Great Britain 20%.[36] In some seven meters of stacked written record that Governor Simpson produced in his official time and which is archived by the Company in an office in Manitoba, this otherwise exceedingly important record, if it is there, is neglected by our published researchers.

Simpson did a great deal more international footwork in his time. In about 1827, when it became clear that Fort Vancouver would be on the south side of the divide between British interests and those of the USA through what they called the Oregon territory – now British Columbia, Washington State and Oregon, he established Fort Langley. Fort Victoria was then built as a coastal military outpost in 1843.

Great Britain turned its Chartered west coast trading sphere into a colony in 1849. It turned its fur trading Company into the government. James Douglas had succeeded Simpson as Governor of the HBC, and so became the Governor of the colony of Vancouver's Island—after Governor Richard Blanshard had resigned in 1851, apparently after two years of ceaseless complaint and in a morphine-induced fog.[37] Vancouver's Island was made a colony to check any American ideas about expanding north. It's interesting to think that at the time that Great Britain was announcing a new settlement presence in the west, its colonial subjects in the east were in a crisis of relations between America and Britain and between French and English that nearly defies articulation; suffice it to say that effigies of embroiled politicians were marched, burning, down the streets of Montreal.[38]

Douglas, while head of HBC and after the colony had been created, had been directed to get treaties with the people on Vancouver's Island. He made a list of family heads and enumerated village populations and assigned each person some HBC store credits, to be taken in blankets, in exchange for the lands of the southern tip of Vancouver Island. The Chiefs appear not to have performed the somewhat inadequate gesture of making an X mark on the transactional documents. The letter was then sent overseas for double-checking, and whatever was returned is what we have now as the "Douglas Treaties," to which there were fourteen native "signatures."[39]

By this the Governor claimed to have secured all the area around Victoria, paid for those lands as well as coal-promising areas at Nanaimo and Fort Rupert, and demarcated lands to be saved for the Chemainus and the Cowichan. Empire is a convenient marriage of business and politics—much of the payment was given in HBC credits.

The Hudson's Bay Company, whose Charter by now provided for access to the Oregon Territory (the mainland from California to Alaska), complied with sharing its fur-trader governor with the Crown as governor for the new colony of British Columbia in 1858. A separate Governor for the colony of British Columbia was appointed in 1864.

The first Governor for BC was Frederick Seymour. He called upon Chiefs from the Interior to meet him at New Westminster and celebrate the Queen's birthday shortly after he was made the first Governor of the mainland colony. He gave out 100 silver topped canes "of an inexpensive kind," pipes, and 100 "small and cheap" flags.[40] Seymour helped author the flag emblems of the new colony by confirming Simpson's treaty with his indigenous counterparts, reportedly including Nlaka'pamux, Secwepemc, Tsilhqot'in, Carrier, Babine, Nisga'a, Sto:lo and Okanagan leaders: *As long as the sun shall shine, the three rivers flow, and the grass grow, this nation shall belong to both of us equally, as brothers.* Hence the original BC flag, with the rivers demarcated by three blue wavy stripes, the sun at the top, the green grass somewhere stripy in the middle, and the Union Jack and Crown below. It is not hard to imagine that a compact was required by the indigenous nations who had by now experienced the fall-out of two gold rushes, but the provincial record of it cannot be found.

The expansion of the "Confederation League" began in 1868 in British Columbia. July 1st of that year celebrated the first anniversary of the creation of the Dominion of Canada. July 4th was at the time a more popular celebration, as most of the non-native population of British Columbia was actually American.

In 1867 Great Britain had issued the *British North America Act*, marker of the Dominion of Canada. British Columbia reluctantly joined four years later. The major reason for that was the promise of a railroad which would connect west to east. Also there was a generous per-capita payment to the colonial government, and the rest of Canada didn't scrutinize the new province's estimate of its population. That estimate was inflated by three times the actual. Both parties agreed to the *Terms of Union,* 1871, and BC became the fourth province to join the Dominion of Canada.

Within a decade, as the promised railway failed to materialize, BC threatened secession. There was some concern that the Indian lands had not been tied up tightly enough. In 1874 the BC legislature passed *An Act to amend and consolidate the Laws affecting Crown Lands in British Columbia.* This *Lands Act* would make the whole place belong to the province by an act of the Legislature. This Act flapped so wildly in the face of everything Constitutional and associated with legally plausible assertions of sovereignty and ownership of the lands that Ottawa disallowed it. The *Lands Act* blatantly and without precedent assumed control, in fee simple, of all the lands of BC – which were all untreated—by the province: hardly federalism.

Almost certainly as a measure to reassure the Pacific province of immunity to Section 109 of the Constitution, the section which stipulated the provinces could only claim that which was not more clearly another's Interest, like the land base, the Indian Act was born in 1876. Two years from the Duty of Disallowance which scrapped BC's *Lands Act,* the indigenous peoples were criminalized in the use of their international treaties, Tamanawas—or potlatch— for example, and, from time to time, more and more specific Indian Act prohibitions on their activities would defend BC from any aspersions on its ownership claims on and use of indigenous lands. Indians, the Indian Act provided, could not own land. The crucial aspects of indigenous economies were effectively outlawed: their thriving fishing industries, their right to amass wealth and sturdy relations through marriages, their previously uncontestable right to charge passage on anyone travelling through their territory, the exclusivity of hunting grounds, and, equally importantly, their practice of securing such things in common with bordering nations whose mutuality could be assured by sharing.

After that, the trans-continental railway surveys and planning were begun in earnest, and construction started in 1880. None of those plans, none of the land registries started by Judge Begbie's offices, observed the Crown precondition that the land had to be bought from the indigenous owners first. The Crown let it go. Trutch, the BC Commissioner of Lands and Works, was knighted and so was Governor Douglas; and still were other BC Premiers knighted, to the present day, as have spat in the faces of the Chiefs who traveled to see them in Victoria.

The pioneers of British Columbia certainly saw no contradiction in the expansion of their world. Some have been gloriously vindicated by their heirs.

Leon Ladner's father and his brother arrived in BC in the summer of 1858, just before it became BC. He wrote a book stressing his family's independence and hard work and their success without subsidy. He writes, "In those days, no benevolent government gave any assistance or even encouragement to immigrants." In "...the land of the individual, no government helped him other than with a certain broad intimation that it was intolerant of robbery and killings to the extent it could would [sic] punish those who were too careless with other people's property or lives."[41]

Mr. Ladner certainly was not including indigenous people in his use of the words "people's property and their lives." His father and uncle, among those who left England, crossed America and entered BC via the empty California goldfields, are the subjects of his book, *The Ladners of Ladner: By Covered Wagon to the Welfare State.* The first foreign entrepreneurs to BC, he lectures, enjoyed no such government welfare as can be witnessed today in the form of subsidized childcare, hospitals, schools, and even disability pensions.

Quite at the furthest end of the book from these opening claims of "achieving destiny" independently, Ladner gives us the numbers. The Ladners were the very much subsidized recipients of 2,000 acres at the site which is now named for them in the Fraser Valley. The two brothers pre-empted most of that, meaning they paid not more than ten shillings an acre for it after a two year period working the land to raise those funds. The remaining acres they bought at four shillings and two pence each or, as Ladner wrote in 1972, a dollar. They had a great pre-emption near Tsawwassen also. Asssuredly all of these were subsidized by government policy towards the Indians: the Tsawwassen location "was a matter of some consequence as some of the help that the Ladners used on the farms and in the salmon canneries were Indians from that area."[42]

His book will be very helpful to anyone wishing to read more tales of how these early travelers shot, burned and hung people in the way of their travel from California to the Fraser "El Dorado," and to anyone who does not understand the early and continuing demographics of the elected BC governments and opposition representatives. BC has always been governed, in the vast majority, by those men who had the most holdings in the lands and resources. The government has been represented by law firms of the same lineage, including Ladner, Downs, now Borden Ladner Gervais – Mr. Leon Ladner's company. Their court cases were judged by Honourable recruits from the same society. Ladner mentions many of those family friends, some of whom were also, like him, "a dedicated friend and servant of The University of British Columbia," according to the institution's memorial tribute page.

The Colony as a Province

> *"From my first arrival in Canada I have been very much pre-occupied with the condition of the Indian population in the Province. You must remember that the Indian population are not represented in Parliament and consequently that the Governor-General is bound to watch over their welfare with special solicitude. Now we must all admit that the condition of the Indian question in British Columbia is not satisfactory. Most unfortunately as I think there has been an initial error, ever since Sir James Douglas quitted office in the Government of British Columbia neglecting to recognize what is known as the Indian title. In Canada this has always been done: no Government whether Provincial or central has failed to acknowledge that the original title to the land existed in the Indian tribes and communities that hunted or wandered over them. Before we touch an acre we make a treaty with the Chiefs representing the bands we are dealing with, and having agreed upon and paid our stipulated price often times arrived at after a great deal of haggling and difficulty we enter into possession but not until then do we consider that we are entitled to deal with an acre. The result has been that in Canada our Indians are contented well affected to the white men and amenable to the laws and Government. The title of your Petitioners has been wrongfully repudiated and ignored by the Government of British Columbia."*
> **—Lord Dufferin, Governor-General of Canada**
> **to the Legislative Assembly of British Columbia**
> **made on the 20th day of September, 1876;**
> **as included in the Cowichan petition, March 1909**

Lord Dufferin had accurately spotted the pivotal flaw in Canada's use of the Indian Act as a substitute for purchasing land from Indians. His words here represent the most substantial support for the dispossessed of British Columbia ever to come from the mouth of a politician associated with the power to assist them. What he may have underestimated were the geopolitics of the day.

In 1926 Canada was signed into the League of Nations along with Australia, South Africa, India and New Zealand – under the hand of the "British Empire."[43] It was not by any means unusual that the British Empire did not blink at destroying those indigenous nations whose land they preferred. The reality was an old one by the time Churchill needed backing for his second world war:

Canada is the linchpin of the English-speaking world.
Canada, with those relations of friendly, affectionate

intimacy with the United States on the one hand and with her unswerving fidelity to the British Commonwealth and the Motherland on the other, is the link which joins together these great branches of the human family, a link which, spanning the oceans, brings the continents into their true relation and will prevent in future generations any growth of division between the proud and the happy nations of Europe and the great countries which have come into existence in the New World.[44]

Both British Columbia and the Dominion were formed by England, and England gave them the greater part of the law which they now follow—or not— as their own. God didn't make Canada, as it apparently did England, so Canada's law-making methods vary from those of England where the monarchy still condescends to augment Parliament with divine right. In England, anything Parliament does becomes Constitutional. Any Act or Measure is immediately accorded the status of a Constitutional instrument by virtue of the British tradition of common law. Not so in Canada. The Constitution was originally something of a gift, albeit to men who had influenced its design extensively, and it brought with it certain limitations. In order to amend the Constitution, all the provinces must agree. Canadians will remember how they did not agree at Meech Lake in 1990.

Since 1871 Canada has been totally complicit with ignoring the treaties, its own constitutional law, and the lamentable circumstances foisted upon the indigenous nations. What has Canada's role in British Columbia's business been since Confederation? "A policy as liberal as hitherto pursued by the British Columbia Government... ", as Article 13 of the 1871 *Terms of Union* decrees. This is to use the word "liberal" in its most flexible incarnation. Cooperation between the province and federal government in pursuit of destructive policies towards the Indians has already been demonstrated.

Canada has never weighed in on the side of applying truth to these affairs—not in Royal Commissions, not in implementing Reserve Commission recommendations. Speeches from the Throne have never made more than passing and careless reference to the situation, and only on a few occasions. This is in some contrast to the result of investigations made by government agencies themselves. The denial of aboriginal title impacts every aspect of indigenous people's lives, and the federal government is completely, insidiously aware of those aspects because they do carry out the first part of their obligations to indigenous peoples—studying their condition. Next steps, such as acting on those findings with a view to remedying the problem, are not taken.

There once was a Prime Minister who promised results to the hundred or so Chiefs who traveled from all over the province to meet him. The Memorial to Sir Wilfred Laurier records the content of that address. Letters record his insistence that these issues should be properly heard. When he was succeeded by Robert Borden at the critical juncture, his promises turned to the ashes which can be found in the 1912 Royal Commission on Indian Affairs for the Province of British Columbia.

In a new, and only, series of biographies of Canadian Prime Ministers, nothing west of Saskatchewan is referred to for Laurier's part. Nothing north of it either, save the Alaska pan-handle.[45]

British Columbia's role in Canada is considered unremarkable, aside from occupying geography of strategic military and trade importance. An exploration of the making of Canada and its Constitution, *The Journey to Canada*,[46] does not even include the words "British Columbia." Canada was made well before BC latched onto it. "The West," in Canadian history, refers to what's west of Ontario, not what's west of the Rocky Mountains. When British Columbia historian Jean Barman went to write about the west coast province, she called it *The West Beyond the West*.

No percentage of the vote in BC has ever affected a federal election. Neither before nor after 1949, when the indigenous were enfranchised to the provincial vote, or after 1960, when aboriginal people were enfranchised to the federal vote. In a majority democracy, aboriginal peoples are hopelessly marginalized. In Canada, so are British Columbians – being only four million of 37 million voters, and the last to the polls. The Prime Minister is elected before British Columbians have finished voting

When native people were in number of voting consequence in BC, they were denied the vote. Approximations vary, but one mid-line source suggests that in 1870 indigenous people were 70% of a population of 36,247. In 1881, they were half the population of BC, the total being 49,459; in 1891 only 36% of 98,173; and by 1911 only 5% of the people in British Columbia were indigenous, out of a total 392,480.[47] Natives did not have a vote until 1949, when they were 3% of 817,000. Aboriginal people have been in the minority in BC as a whole, but still have been in the majority in some rural areas. There they elected Frank Calder, Nisga'a, and Leonard Marchand, Secwepemc.

The time has come when BC's Governors' promises are meaningfully forgotten by the colonists and the elevation of the crown has been arbitrarily made. In 1960 – over one hundred years since the original promissory agreement, and many tens of thousands of lifetimes of anguish later, the BC flag was simply inverted. Simpson's 40/40/20 agreement now meant nothing, and it was being disappeared. This gesture didn't go unnoticed by indigenous people, and the story of it is important enough to have been included in a 2008 submission at the United Nations Permanent Forum on Indigenous Issues:

...The Great Seal is the agreement of the parties, 1811, King George III "For as long as the sun shines and the three rivers flow, we will live together, the sovereign Bear clan (Kusk'kalxw—Salish Peoples) and the Crown as represented by the United Kingdom of Great Britain as trustees of Her Majesty's subjects. Secured and sealed by Her Majesty Queen Victoria's 60/40 agreement of 1837 reaffirmed by King Edward VII in Coat of Arms 1906 and symbolized by the flag that flies.[48]

The settlers' records are not so detailed. In a book published by the Canadian Broadcasting Corporation, *BC Almanac*, we learn this of the BC Coat of Arms:

The Union Jack symbolizes BC's colonial origins. The wavy blue and silver bars and the setting sun represent BC's geography, settled between the Pacific Ocean and the Rocky Mountains. BC's flag was adopted in 1960, and duplicates the design of the coat of arms.[49]

The tokens distributed by Seymour in 1864 live on in the locked boxes of descended hereditary Chiefs, along with ceremonial rifles that were silenced by selective colonial memory. The promise illustrated in the flag, however, is absolutely dead. Any modern reinvention would be removed from that promise by centuries. The gesture of physically turning the visual symbol of the old compact upside down is an accurate reflection of the colonial attitude, and the narrative of modern invention, as sampled from the national media, is the second most used tool in digging the graveyard of BC history.

Chapter 9

THE ROLE OF LAW

"Political participation by the marginalized cannot make sense when the rules of engagement are determined by the powerful."
—Oby Obyerodhyambo, Luo, Kenya

In British Columbia, the rule of law is held captive by political forces. Since Great Britain colonized what is now British Columbia without regard to its own laws, and then allowed the colony to carry on without regard for or application of the British North America Act; and since BC and Canada succeeded in derailing the aspirations for reconciliation and justice pursued by indigenous nations to the Privy Council, the United Nations, or any third party impartial and independent tribunal (including Queen Anne's Standing Committee of 1704[1]), judges and courts have subsequently made up whatever reasons suited them when tossing native people in jail for attempting to assert their sovereignty over their lands by way of activities that disrupted resource development or challenged settler control.

A judge can decide a case the way he wishes to, provided he can be creative with legal principles. For instance,

> …the accused were guilty. They were unable to show any treaty, statute or agreement having statutory effect conferring upon them the right, or any aboriginal right, to fish as they saw fit in contravention of the Regulations made under the Fisheries Act. Although in former times there may have been a policy allowing considerable freedom of action that does not create legal rights which can be relied upon when the authorities decide different policy considerations must be applied because of a change in the situation.[2]

This *Regina v. Jack* ruling was made after *White and Bob,* where two native men had just shown that Governor Douglas' promises that they could fish and hunt "as formerly" were treaties, and the judge had referred to the Royal Proclamation of 1763 as evidence that the province could not disturb the indigenous in their own pursuits on unsold lands. Two years prior to the decision above regarding the guilty fishermen, Justice Hall in the Supreme Court of Canada had given the minority opinion in *Calder,* 1973:

> ...that the appellants' [the Nishga tribe's] right to possession of the lands delineated... and their right to enjoy the fruits of the soil of the forest, and of the rivers and streams within the boundaries of said lands have not been extinguished by the Province of British Columbia or by its predecessor, the Colony of British Columbia, or by the Governor of that Colony.[3]

Given that the *Calder* ruling left the issue of aboriginal title undecided at the Supreme Court of Canada level, an individual judge could subsequently rely on the three arguments against or the three in favour of aboriginal title in the split decision. A judge was also at liberty to choose whether the lack of ruling at the top court meant he was left with abiding by the BC Court of Appeal ruling. Deciding a case of whether provincial laws should affect aboriginal hunters who did not have treaty rights, BC Provincial Court Judge O'Connor's decision in 1974 was summed up as follows:

> Indians hunting for food on their traditional hunting grounds on unoccupied Crown land have always had an aboriginal or native interest or title to do so, and such rights have not apparently been, in general, extinguished. Whatever else the aboriginal title may encompass, the right to hunt for food is certain. Therefore where, in respect of such activities, an Indian is charged with unlawfully hunting wildlife contrary to a provincial statute, the Wildlife Act, ... he must be acquitted, since provincial legislation cannot extinguish or restrict such a right.[4]

Previously, BC judges had interpreted a change to the *Indian Act* in 1951, Section 88, to mean that provincial laws of general application are applicable to Indians whenever those laws don't directly contradict treaty rights, specific federal legislation, or provisions of the Indian Act. In the ruling above, O'Connor went the other way by deciding that since *Calder* was undecided at the Supreme Court of Canada level, then so was the BC Court of Appeal decision in regard to that case.

Judges can be critical of their fellow judges' decisions when they are influenced too much by economics rather than law. See Justice Locke in 1989, considering the case of Westar Timber Co. against the Gitxsan Wet'suwet'n Tribal Council:

> I do not subscribe to the view that the ad hoc decisions of the courts of this province from time to time constitute the correct legal response to applications such as this. … I think the matter should be solved on principle, and not upon the varying views of judges who, from time to time, will have to hear evidence and give their views on matters essentially economic as to whether a particular application constitutes such a danger to the public interest it should not be granted. That depends upon fluctuating commercial factors, even new political administrations, and not upon legal principles.[5]

Or, conversely, Chief Justice Antonio Lamer in the *Delgamuukw* decision of 1997:

> In my opinion, the development of agriculture, forestry, mining and hydroelectric power; the general economic development of the interior of British Columbia, protection of the environment or endangered species, the building of infrastructure and the settlement of foreign populations to support those aims, are the kinds of objectives that are consistent with this purpose and, in principle, can justify the infringement of aboriginal title.[6]

The judges' highly personal and often economics-based rulings continue to shift legal ground under the indigenous march for justice. But slowly, one painfully by one, such rights as selling six fish were indeed understood to be rights that were nothing if not traditional and aboriginal in nature, as in the 1996 case of Mrs. Van derPeet of the Sto:lo.

In *Van derPeet,* the Supreme Court of Canada ruled on the existence of aboriginal rights, some fourteen years after they were enshrined in the Constitution Act in 1982. Here, the judges said,

> The doctrine of aboriginal rights exists, and is recognized and affirmed, because when Europeans arrived in North America, aboriginal peoples were already here, living in communities on the land and participating in distinctive cultures as they had done for centuries. Therefore, a declaration of substantive rights must be directed towards the reconciliation of the pre-existence of aboriginal societies with the sovereignty of the Crown.[7]

That statement, apparently based on Justice Judson's remarks in *Calder* in 1973 when he decided that Nisga'a title had been displaced by British assertion of sovereignty, is not the whole story of why the doctrine of aboriginal rights exists. What the judges neglected to add is that the British King embedded deference to aboriginal title and rights in His conditions on settler activity in the colonies, including settler governments. Aboriginal rights exist and are largely undefined by Canada not because Canada hasn't gotten around to defining them, but because there are no treaties with the aboriginal nations which could otherwise establish the relinquishment or codification of those rights in a way that made Canada an equal participant in defining them. Those missing treaties are long overdue because only they would legally permit the development of the "Indian lands," as they are known in the relevant Constitutional instruments. Canada is not in a position to unilaterally make a declaration of "substantive" aboriginal rights. Canada is a party to international conventions which protect the indigenous nations' self determination and political, economic, social and cultural rights. Canada continues to illegally pursue unilateral decisions.

Every time an aboriginal person, community or nation takes their case into court, government lawyers trot the judges around the interminable, and growing, track of burdens of proof. Every time an aboriginal rights or title case gets a ruling, the precedents that are set increase the difficulty and complexity of proving such rights for the next person who might want to prove an aboriginal right.

There is not so much a need for a substantive unilateral declaration as there is for internationally acceptable treaties. The consistent theme, however, is that a judge will make a decision and few people can afford to appeal. Canada will continue to argue at international forums that the indigenous have not exhausted the domestic remedies available to them in Canadian courts. When Canada's right to jurisdiction over indigenous nations is questioned in an international forum such as the Inter-American Commission on Human Rights, as occurred with the Líl'wat *Loni Edmonds v. Canada,* Petition 879-07, 2007, and is pressed repeatedly by the IACHR, the Canada Responses simply repeatedly ignore the issue.

Canada acts as if the rights of people who have never sold their lands or relinquished their jurisdiction are its own invention. Indeed, scholars like John Borrows become quite poetic: "…the development of Canadian law, the body of case law dealing with Aboriginal issues is, in the end, "indigenous" to Canada."[8] More accurately, the laws have been developed here to the exclusion of every international instrument, every Constitutional law and Executive Order provided by England, and every precedent in the world which might have influenced Canadian law to respect the indigenous nations' existing laws and jurisdiction, as well as respecting Canada's own legal limitations. It has ignored the most fundamental human rights of possession, ownership, and self-determination, making "aboriginal law" necessary to control entrapped and oppressed nations.

British Columbians and the whole rash of settler champions—leading academics, lawyers, judges and media—rely on instance after instance of judge-made law as if it was equal to Constitutional law. It is not. What is required is clear: Canada's Constitution says that no one can proceed on untreated Indian lands: Section 25 of the 1982 Constitution Act affirms the Royal Proclamation, the Executive Order, of 1763. The British North America Act of 1867, Section 109, also part of Canada's modern Constitution, provides that the provinces have rights to all lands and resources subject to "Other Interests" in those lands and resources – meaning the indigenous interests. In lieu of law, the governments push negotiations to resolve the issues, negotiations which insist on the extinguishment of aboriginal title and the modification of aboriginal rights.

Unfortunately, the contemporary society continues to flout the constitutional law. *Canadian society depends* on suppression of the relevant law. The judges ignore constitutional law and refuse to admit it on those few occasions that a person brings it before them, just as they ignore the individual precedent-setting cases. It has been remarked that, in England historically, law was behind social developments by some fifteen years. That is, improvements in the way society conducted itself came about before laws existed to enforce such improvements. After awhile, the new customs would be defined legislatively – for example, where a dismissed secretary's employers were ordered to give her severance pay because other employers were doing so. In Canada, society is about 249 years behind the law. In Canada it is just the reverse: the existing and constitutional law is centuries ahead of the willingness of the settler population to comply with it, and nearly the whole of their political, judicial, media and academic apparatus are unwilling to face up to that.

In the meantime, the function of the courts in British Columbia is transparent. The political objectives and economic outcomes are quite clear and consistent. When law is bad for business, say for example collecting fines from forestry companies who have logged over streams in salmon habitat, it is ignored or never enforced.[9] The judges themselves defer to "socio-economic mores" in their reasons for justifying the infringement of aboriginal title.[10] When indigenous court defense arguments include aboriginal title, the title aspect is simply removed from the indigenous defense at the discretion of the judge, as in cases like *Wilson* in BC. Specifically, the judges only consider the socio-economic mores and needs of the settler population, or, in the modern era, those of large corporations.

Since 2006, courts of international law have come to the conclusion that when a state's judges refuse to abide by their own laws, with the result of genocide, other governments can choose to hear the case in question.[11] Perhaps Canada and British Columbia are waiting for another state to dare to do so.[12]

Chicanery Today

Immediately after the *Delgamuukw* decision, which ruled that if the Indians hadn't ceded, sold or otherwise released their territories to the crown, then those territories were aboriginal title lands, most First Nations in BC came up with ways to test that theory. The Tsilhqot'in, for one, with an active court case to defend their forests at the Brittany Triangle, went out on the roadblock to ensure discussions would be had before logging proceeded as usual. The Forests Minister of BC declared, "the natives must understand the existing industry is not going to move aside because of the court ruling."[13] And it did not.

In 1999, Chief Ron Derrickson of the Westbank First Nation sent some of his men out logging. They were quickly issued a stop-work order, but a judge in Vancouver heard their lawyer's point that the court should first consider whether the Band already has the right to log on land which is part of its aboriginal territory. The constitutional challenge was understood, and the Westbank stopped logging with the proviso that the province would not license any more forestry operations in its territory. At least not without meaningful discussion and agreement. Then Chief Dan Wilson of the Okanagan Indian Band started logging, and so did other Okanagan Bands. They were all issued stop-work orders, and it was Wilson's initiative that ended up as the test case.

Wilson insisted that the Forestry Act infringes upon aboriginal rights. The Supreme Court of Canada thought it was a worthwhile question and awarded costs in advance to continue the suit. The indigenous position was, *we are logging on our own territory which belongs to us and we therefore do not need a license from BC.* The actions were aimed at getting this case, as a test, into court. Almost ten years later, a BC Court of Appeal justice's ruling did them one better: she disallowed the title aspect of their argument, confirming a lower court judgment and making the Okanagan position insensible. The province had, in the interim, acted on a case arising in New Brunswick, on the Atlantic coast of Canada, and declared that aboriginal people can log for domestic purposes on crown lands, subject to justifiable regulation. By 2008, this case, which had been considered important enough to the public to be awarded costs in advance, became obsolete because the aboriginal loggers' defense and their larger question of title to the land was disallowed. Two of three judges ruled that the Okanagans' 1999 question had been made irrelevant by provincial changes in the *Haida* and *Taku* cases. The question of whether logging by aboriginal people on aboriginal title land can be infringed by Canadian legislation was no longer important to BC.

The provincial government not only has no plans to uphold the law as it respects unceded indigenous territories: it advertises that fact to industry. It is typical to read in the closing lines of news articles about conflicts over mining projects, logging operations, the transfer of contentious parcels of land from one corporation to another, a comment from an "anonymous government spokesperson" noting that his Ministry hopes the company will re-open talks with the First Nations.

Since the *Haida* ruling in 2004, it's actually the government that is responsible to consult and accommodate aboriginal people, not a corporation, when "…a crown actor has knowledge, real or constructive, of the potential existence of aboriginal right or title and contemplates action that might adversely affect it." That is, they can't issue licenses for development that might result in such damages.[14]

In the *Haida* ruling quoted above, the province lost at the Supreme Court of Canada when it was shown that BC had transferred Tree Farm License 39, from a company to a private individual, without consulting the Haida and over their objections. Logging that area in particular, the Haida argued, would result in irreparable harm to their way of life and cultural identity. An unfortunate qualification was placed on the trigger for consultation. The process was now to be fashioned "proportionate to a preliminary assessment of the strength of the case supporting the right or title, and to the seriousness of the potential adverse effect upon the right or title claimed." Many government workers in resource licensing offices are expert at *not knowing* these strengths and adverse effects. So any corporation can be licensed to do anything that impacts aboriginal title lands, as long as the licensing officer *did not know* of those impacts. This leaves the First Nation in the position of launching a court action for compensation, which is usually all that is available by the time their case gets through court—the contentious activity proceeding all the while. They are tasked to prove that a specific right specific to their culture, which they practiced "before contact" and still practice today, has been impacted. It is difficult for small, cash-poor communities to run a complex legal case and a campaign to protect land at the same time.

The government's response to the *Haida* ruling was the immediate implementation of Forest and Range Agreements, or FRA. This scheme was little more than a waiver which First Nations would sign, agreeing that their economic and aboriginal interests had been met in regard to any planned logging in their traditional territory for the next five years. In exchange, they received a payment determined by their population and unrelated to the value of logging in their area.[15] The Musqueam, therefore, surrounded by Metro Vancouver, would receive proportionately the same amount of money for their Agreement as, say, the Huu-ay-aht on the mid coast of Vancouver Island—rich in cedar and fir. The government asserted that it had fulfilled its obligations to consult and accommodate in this economical and unobtrusive way.

In 2005, *Huu-ay-aht v. British Columbia* emerged from BC Supreme Court. Madam Justice Dillon reasoned, "The fact that some First Nations have accepted the FRA offer indicates only that those groups made a business decision to accept the offer in a practical sense. It is not reflective of the sufficiency either of the consultation process or of the accommodation offered."[16] Consultation was specified in the FRA policy, but the Huu-ay-aht First Nation sued because it was not happening. In their area, they learned outside of FRA discussions, a million cubic meters of wood was slated for removal every year for the next five years—more than the total Annual Allowable Cut for the entire forest district. The judge awarded declaratory damages and observed, "In this case, the government did not misconceive the seriousness of the claim or impact of the infringement. It failed to consider them at all."[17]

What is marvelous is that the Supreme Court of Canada had scolded the province for "sharp dealing" in *Haida.* We are not sure which government would be more smug at these high jinks: the federal government and the judiciary has no more intention to bring BC into line than BC has to correct its work. It has been engineering government programs, along with the feds, to sidestep court advances since there have been any. The "Forest and Range Opportunities" program followed *Huu-Ay-Aht* – a revised FRA, without challenge to date, and without significant improvement. Government changed the name and some key wording to avoid similar litigation to the Huu-ay-aht's.

The governments fight indigenous legal advances every step of the way through court, and take a damage-control managerial attitude to any human rights that are proved there. Madam Justice Satanove pointed out in 2008 that there is no aboriginal right which has not been defined by the Supreme Court of Canada.[18] And once it has been defined by Canada, it will be licensed and regulated by Canada.

In 1984, Ronald Sparrow of Musqueam went fishing at the mouth of the Fraser River. He was using a sixty foot long gill net, over regulation size, and got charged for it under the Fisheries Act. In 1990 the Supreme Court of Canada gave out its ruling on the matter, which had by then shifted from whether the fisherman was libel for using restricted gear to whether the Fisheries Act could reasonably apply to him without infringement of his aboriginal rights. The case was ordered to be re-tried to see if indeed his aboriginal rights had been infringed, but that hearing never happened. What was adopted by the courts, however, was that there are some times when infringement of aboriginal rights by the state is justifiable.[19]

The case also provided the articulation of "Aboriginal Food, Social and Ceremonial fisheries," which are to be given priority over commercial and recreational fisheries, but not conservation. Government employees do not know what that means, either. Twenty years after *Sparrow*, Fisheries officers specializing in Aboriginal relations cannot, in court and under oath, define what exactly the "Social" part of that right is.[20]

Government again put great energy into manufacturing a program to get around the legal obligation to satisfy aboriginal fishing needs with minimum inconvenience to settler preferences for the salmon fisheries. The Aboriginal Fisheries Strategy (AFS) was then invented to prevent the successful aboriginal court advances from being further pursued. The AFS captured, in its rather over-legal-size mesh, the aspirations of fishing communities and their members. In exchange for annual funding to a new Band-run fisheries program, the Band would agree to receive notifications of fishery openings and closures, they would fish in agreed areas and they would accept Communal Fishing Licenses in recognition of the Department of Fisheries and Oceans as the manager of the fishery resource.

These sorts of arrangements between Bands and government usually are hedged by the words "without prejudice," meaning that neither party admitted to the contents as affecting their position about aboriginal title. However, the sheer number of these piecemeal agreements is beginning to take on the appearance of Common Law and makes the disclaimer hard to believe in. First Nations have little viable alternative to signing them.

In case after case since *Sparrow* and *Van derPeet*, *Delgamuukw* and *Haida*, government has aimed at closing every exercise or defense of aboriginal title and rights. Legal trilogies of despair such as *Halfway River*, 1999, *Douglas*, 2007, and *Taku River Tlingit*, 2005, all BC Supreme and BC Court of Appeal rulings, have led to an impoverished definition of acceptable aboriginal consultation and accommodation. If a government ministry representative calls a Band office inviting them to a meeting, but he just leaves a message on the answering machine because no one answered, they have had their chance at consultation although they could not attend the meeting for various pressing reasons (*Douglas, 2007*). If they do take the meeting and engage in advising the corporate consultants, they have certainly been accommodated—whether that advice is taken or not—since they participated in the planning process (*Halfway River*, 1999). If they are unsatisfied, they are pointed back to that same planning process *(Taku River Tlinget, 2004)*.[21]

In *Halfway*, the people of that community in north-eastern BC discovered that the courts commanded them to participate in the consultation process offered, stating that they had no right to refuse to meet (their only way to forestall), and that the Crown has the privilege, according to their historically numbered Treaty 8,[22] to expropriate any part of the treaty land for development. The BC Court of Appeal judge further imposed that the Halfway River people had no right to frustrate economic development by making "unreasonable" (environmentally sensitive) demands in the process. As a result, First Nations have no choice but to engage with consultations on resource development. In *Taku*, where the people did willingly and fully participate in the consultation process concerning the development of a mine and the road to reach it, they were informed that they had exhausted their right to make their recommendations, and were considered "consulted." Contrary to their recommendations, the road would go directly through their remaining hunting area. They could, according to the decision, continue to engage in further consultations. In *Douglas*, where a fateful phone message was left, the community discovered that they had no recourse or input in recreational fishery openings once they had declined that single offer to meet. Since the issue has been made to hinge on consultation rather than on consent, any purported protection of indigenous rights thereby has been rendered meaningless.

Aboriginal title presumably affords the indigenous nations substantially more power over their lands than these cases dictate – but aboriginal title has never, to date, been declared by a judge to have been proved in a particular place in British Columbia. Since proof of "exclusive and continuing occupation" is a Supreme Court of Canada standard for the finding of aboriginal title to a place, and since the people have been confined to Indian Reserves and criminalized for practicing their traditional economies and ways of life outside of those small boundaries, aboriginal title has become prohibitively difficult to prove. One must first prove an aboriginal right in court in order to then make a case for that right having been infringed. Section 35 of the *Constitution Act* may affirm the proper indigenous titles, but every aspect of their title faces challenges *ad nauseum* by government lawyers. No one has yet met the challenge and won a declaration of title.

Proof of aboriginal title was recognized in a non-binding opinion in British Columbia Supreme Court in the *Tsilhqot'in* case, 2007. It took almost twenty years in court to get it. Like John Marshall a hundred and fifty years before, Justice Vickers of the BC Supreme Court gave an opinion that it would be inappropriate for the government to legislate over indigenous people on their homelands. Vickers' reasons in *Tsilhqot'in* were 500 pages long and some 80% of that was *obiter dicta,* or judicial opinion. The Canadian government did not make such a statement as President Jackson, but its response, or lack of which, was effectively the same as Jackson's advice to Marshall: "enforce it yourself."

However Justice Vickers did not make a Declaration of the Tsilhqot'in aboriginal title, which he said had been proved in his court, because of a deficiency in the pleadings. The indigenous plaintiffs, the entire Tsilhqot'in people represented by Roger William of Xeni Gwetin, had not asked that the judge make a finding of aboriginal title to parts of the claim area, but only the whole area – which he decided he could not do.[23] Immediately after his extensive opinion was delivered, the Tsilhqot'in, British Columbia and Canada embarked on a one-year agreement to discuss how the opinion might change their relationship – all promising not to launch any new court action during that period. Immediately the province busied itself with awarding forestry and mining licenses in exactly the same area, without so much as a phone call to the Tsilhqot'in title holders. The intended gold and copper mine at Fish Lake, or Teztan Biny, is within their eastern trap line; within the exact area that Judge

Vickers had indicated is aboriginal title land. Even after a year-long federal Environmental Assessment Review rejected the project—only the second of two mines to ever be rejected in BC—the province still granted road building and exploration permits to the same company upon their resubmitting the proposal.

Most Indian Bands do not have another 20 years of knowing and claiming their lands, and certainly not of using them, to meet the criteria set in *Tsilhqotin.* The speed of development is break neck and all-reducing on those lands. The legal criteria Canada and BC have established for claims of Indian title to meet is basically unattainable. It is certain that Elders who possess the required evidence will not last long enough to present it in courts pandering to the eternal delays of the crown's prerogative. Certainly not at the cost and time involved. So the legal criteria have created an unattainable level of evidence which will necessitate the decline of those remaining indigenous peoples unable to meet it. And the legal criteria continue to develop in an increasingly narrow and exclusionary direction. No one alive today, for instance, can prove they hunted elk in a place where those animals are now extinct; or to have fished in streams that were flooded for hydroelectric production fifty years ago.

These are the uses to which "law" is put by the colony.

Terra Incognita

Where is aboriginal title land? No one using BC courts knows. There isn't any aboriginal title land in BC that we know of, just unextinguished aboriginal title to the land.

One case has underpinned recent faith in legal developments: *Delgamuukw*, the Supreme Court of Canada decision in 1997. The Supreme Court decided that aboriginal title could not have been extinguished by any act of the provincial government. In other words, aboriginal title still exists, unextinguished. Not only is it unextinguished, but it *cannot be extinguished by BC unilaterally.* The provincial government had tried everything by 1997, and if none of that worked, nothing will. Nothing but consent from the indigenous peoples, that is, or a Constitutional amendment removing the stipulation to buy the Indian lands before proceeding or assuming jurisdiction and title. Such an amendment would not withstand international scrutiny.

The Supreme Court found that aboriginal title lands must exist, but they did not address a loophole sewn earlier into the the *Delgamuukw case.* A 1987 ruling in the case declared that aboriginal lands cannot be registered in the Torrens system in British Columbia, where land ownership is transferred through registration of title instead of using deeds.[24] And this is the point of re-entry for the interminable chase of the tail end of indigenous title while everyone pretends the Constitution of Canada is irrelevant to the BC question.

In 1987 the British Columbia Court of Appeal ruled in *Delgamuukw* that aboriginal title land is inalienable and therefore not marketable, so it cannot be registered with the land titles because it lacks the element of marketability necessary to establish a "good safe holding and marketable title" as required under the Land Title Act. The Supreme Court of Canada refused the *lis pendens* issue raised by the Gitxsan by denying leave to appeal. It is "inalienable" because only the crown can buy Indian land; that's what it says in the Royal Proclamation of 1763, which is part of Canada's constitution today.

The question of registering aboriginal title land was pressed by the Skeetchestn Indian Band in 2000, when they attempted to lodge a caveat and register a Certificate of Pending Litigation claiming aboriginal title to lands registered in the Kamloops Land Title Office.[25] They were declined, but at that time the courts officially announced that indeed whatever aboriginal title lands may be found, they have no value since they can't be registered and are therefore not marketable. It was a test of *Delgamuukw*—that the aboriginal title to the land would give the title holders the right to use it and choose what to do with it and benefit from it economically. So they tried to register it, or at least their claim to it. But just as aboriginal title land cannot be registered, neither can registered land be aboriginal title land—because clearly that land was not continuously used and occupied by the claimants in question, as per the title test established in the Supreme Court of Canada. Some indigenous people have investigated the fact that present day land titles registered in the province do not have a "good root."

The BC Court of Appeal ruling in *Delgamuukw*, in *Westar v. Ryan*: "The legal rights of the Crown are known. The aboriginal claims of the applicants, while the subject of the action yet to come to trial, are prospective and unknown…."[26] But how can that be? If there are two parties to a dispute over ownership of, say, a piece of cake, how can the judge know the rights of one if there is a question of the rights of another which he claims not to know, unless he has already decided that the other is subject to whatever is left over from and defined by the rights of the first? Perhaps if the judge and jury are parties to the dispute? This is of course the fundamental fact of the matter: the government unilaterally created and asserted the rights of the province of British Columbia so of course they are known and codified as law: and the judges swear to uphold that domestic law which does not recognize aboriginal title. It has never done so yet.

When the Queen of Hearts tried Alice, in a Wonderland court, She did not have the benefit of such precedents. Perhaps Alice would not have escaped.

Judge Locke stated in his reasons in *Westar*: "…claims of aboriginal rights in respect of land cannot be assisted by the land title laws of this province as being claims unknown to and not recognized by such laws…" Simply put, the laws are the product of generations of happenstance based upon an illegal assumption of jurisdiction that denied aboriginal rights in respect of land. It wasn't that the judiciary *didn't know* these rights, it *flatly refused to recognize* them; and now the courts are completely incapable of applying the truth of affairs to the cases that come before them. Particularly because the courts, the judiciary, are implicated in those affairs.

The colonial courts have always aided and abetted the contravention of justice in British Columbia. The statement made by Governor James Douglas on February 14, 1859, was false. He claimed the lands, minerals and soil generally for the Colony,[27] but he had no right to. The laws that followed to back up Douglas' assertion are truly, as Locke put it—of no assistance.

When judges say that the lands of what is now British Columbia were *terra incognita*—unknown lands—at the time of the Royal Proclamation, the Executive Order, of 1763, they were probably right: unknown to them. Then they say that because they were unknown, they can't possibly be covered by the Proclamation. But the unknown lands still fit the description of being west of the Rockies. The fact that no Englishman had ever seen Rupert's Land certainly didn't stop the Hudson's Bay Company from accepting the King's Charter for a trading monopoly in the region described in relation to other known landmarks. But perhaps the aboriginal title lands of today better fit the description of *terra incognita* than they did three hundred years ago. Now, after Supreme Court of Canada definitions of what aboriginal title lands are, no one in the 21st century has ever seen them.

The Frozen Right

> Applying the principles of *R. v. Van der Peet* and *Mitchell v. M.N.R.* to the allegations in the Amended Statement of Claim, the plaintiffs must prove that before contact with the Europeans:
>
> A. the Coast Tsimshian were members of an organized society;
> B. from which the plaintiffs have descended;
> C. who used and occupied the Claimed Territories;
> D. from which they harvested Fish Resources and Products as an integral part of their distinctive culture;
> E. traded them on a scale akin to commercial as an integral part of their distinctive culture; and
> F. have continued to do so in a contemporary fashion.[28]
> —Madame Justice Satanove in her reasons in
> Lax Kwalaams, 2008

It is from the title to the soil that aboriginal rights flow. One of the legal capers to preclude indigenous economies is the invention of the "frozen right." Canada and British Columbia argue that only economic practices that existed before Britain asserted that it was sovereign over the place can now be claimed as aboriginal rights. The aspects above must be exhaustively proved by experts of financially exhausting stature. While the Supreme Court of Canada in *Delgamuukw* instructed its peers that nothing the colony or province have ever done has extinguished aboriginal title, the province and the federal government maintain an assumption of control and jurisdiction over the people, their land, and everything they do on it.

This neat disposal of the indigenous right to evolve economically—to develop— was first introduced by the Indian Act and its earlier drafts even before 1876, when Indians were forbidden to own or pre-empt land.[29]

British Columbia affords some world-class examples of this repression, a kind of paralytic that Canadians and British Columbians more often associate with British East Africa or Tibet.

Canada and BC appealed the 2009 BC Supreme Court decision that the Nuu-chah-nulth have a right to fish commercially, at least within 9 miles of their coastline. Canada's counsel in the BC court room spluttered and stuttered and paused throughout her argument, but one of the judges in the Court of Appeal helped her out a few times. The main gist of her argument against Nuu-Chah-nulth people having any recognizable or defensible right to fish commercially was that there was no evidence they had ever done so in the past—specifically, before 1842: the magical date after which any activities by aboriginal people ceased to have the protection afforded by an "aboriginal right" to do it. Her main sources of information were the diaries of Perez and Cook, sailors who had recorded incidents of meeting the people. She didn't have any of the Russian sailors' notebooks, although they might have visited the people even earlier. With Cook's diary in hand, what she clearly ignored was Cook's observation of the "Nootka," where he wrote, "I have no where met with Indians who had such high notions of every thing the Country produced being their exclusive property."[30]

The Nuu-chah-nulth right to commerce is frozen in time at a date set by the Supreme Court of Canada—past which they should not augment their economy with technology more recent than what was available in 1842. In order to continue practicing their right in their homelands—now occupied by Canada – they must do so as they did nearly two centuries ago. Better, as they "have continued to do in a contemporary fashion." They cannot do anything other than what they did 180 years ago, unless they have continued the practice all this time. Activities which meet the criteria Justice Satanove lists above can then be defended as an Aboriginal right in Canada. The obvious difficulty for the Nuu-chah-nulth and all other indigenous peoples in Canada is that Canada itself prevented them from practicing those activities!

It is of course nonsense that Canada protects aboriginal rights, even when they are found, proved and practiced today, or at least attempted. Canada denies, questions and attacks the exercise of aboriginal rights at every vulnerable point—including perpetrating the decimation of the lands or waters in which key rights are practiced.

The key point for Canada in denying the Nuu-chah-nulth was, they said, that there is no evidence that these people ever traded in fish. The fact is, however, that the Nuu-chah-nulth are a coastal people who, at the time of contact, used elaborate trading routes into the interior. Canada's argument ran that they never traded in fish because all their indigenous trading partners would have had enough for themselves anyway, so the first time they ever carried out this type of trade was with hungry ocean-going explorers. This is a spectacular display of obstinacy and deliberate ignorance. The trade route aforementioned is known as the "Grease Trail" because it was the conduit of the extremely desirable eulachon and whale oil prepared and packaged so expertly by the coastal peoples. The diverse places the Grease Trail visited enriched its users with products unique to the environment where they were made: no more could coastal people process wind-dried salmon than could people of the Interior Plateau preserve whale oil. A fourth grade student could compare Canada's argument to her very superficial school textbook:

> In order to obtain metals from the sailors, the Nuu-chah-nulth
> brought items to trade. One of the sailors described them:
> Trading began between us and both sides behaved with great
> honesty. Their trade goods included dried fish...[31]

Presumably the men packing trade goods between regions would have at least had to restock lightweight high-protein food for their return inland. Presumably the book is being written in Nuu-chah-nulth which documents the variability of fishing years; how interior people occasionally escaped disaster by trading for fish from more abundant areas. The fourth grade textbook goes on to describe how sailors were charged a levy for cutting grass onshore to feed the ship's goats and sheep. Would Nuu-chah-nulth people today have a right to sell hay?

The Nuu-chah-nulth case cost them their participation in the BC treaty process. The BC Treaty Commission does not allow for negotiating tables to also engage in litigation. Their migration from the treaty table to the court also caused the Tribal Council they belonged to, and with whom they were negotiating the Final Agreement with BC and Canada, to re-form a new Treaty Society, a move which will have repercussions for their people.

Twenty years earlier, in the *Gladstone* case, Canada made substantial out of court promises to a nation just north of Nuu-chah-nulth in recognition of Canada and British Columbia's disruption to their traditional sea-based economy. The reasons included that:

> Despite the large quantities of herring spawn on kelp traditionally traded, the evidence does not indicate that the trade of herring spawn on kelp provided for the Heiltsuk anything more than basic sustenance. There is no evidence in this case that the Heiltsuk accumulated wealth which would exceed a sustenance lifestyle from the herring spawn on kelp fishery. It follows that the aboriginal right to trade in herring spawn on kelp from the Bella Bella region is limited to such trade as secures the modern equivalent of sustenance: the basics of food, clothing and housing, supplemented by a few amenities.[32]

Canada committed to economic assistance and restoration of a sustainable Heltsiuk economy, or perhaps "basic sustenance," at the end of the hearing. The question in court had been, ultimately, whether the Heltsiuk man, William Gladstone, was entitled to make a living from his own nation's resources or not. The precedent set in *Gladstone* of no entitlement to anything more than "sustenance" to be made from trade in ocean resources is kept on the books. It was referred to in *Ahousat Indian Band and Nation* (the Nuu-chah-nulth case), and informed the court's decisions on how much fishing constitutes an aboriginal rights commercial fishery. Apparently not very much at all.

"Basic sustenance," or "subsistence," – as it was called in *R. v. Smokehouse*, another case against selling fish, is what the courts have decided that Indians can earn from their traditional economies. This is another outstanding example of the outrageous behavior of newcomers. That a Canadian judge should be so ignorant of the wealth and abundance, of the flourishing art and culture of the coastal people, is a statistical improbability. "Subsistence" is not a good description of the traditional northwest Pacific coast economies.

But the economies on west coast Indian Reserves over the last hundred years have been made so desperate that they make mere "subsistence" look like great success. Twenty years after his out-of-court settlement, Mr. Gladstone and his Heltsiuk community felt compelled to issue press releases and attend province-wide meetings to advise of the complete failure of Canada or the Province to keep any of their promises to inject the Heltsiuk economy with life, and listed the extensive social pains they experience as a result.[33] The press releases were not picked up by media.

Indigenous poverty is manufactured by modern Canadian legislative instruments, positions like "the frozen right," and by institutionalized and often violent racial discrimination. It is manufactured by the denial of Canadian Constitutional law, which upholds the title of "the Indian Nations, with whom we are aligned," without ambiguity.

Indigenous poverty was manufactured by the Indian Act. The Indian Act is a piece of legislation which guards the economic gates; criminalizes the traditional economy and rations welfare payments as meanly as if they were a non-renewable resource. There is a freeze on the Indian bank account: no access to the land. In the camps where people are confined, the Indian Reserves, it is not possible to own property. Canada maintains that land is owned by the Queen, and now the federal government, or crown as it is also called. If an Indian moves off the Reserve, she is no longer entitled to make a living without paying taxes, and she is often then too far removed to access other programs or funding subsidized by and available on Reserve. Tax-free Indian Status was one of the early forms of recognition by the governments that indigenous people living in their own homelands were not Canadian subjects. How could they be? Their people had never surrendered. The Indian Act was of course applied selectively and also schizophrenically—native people were subject to the opinions of circuit courts, surveyors' arbitrary land restrictions, jails, and the criminal code, but were not availed of the benefits of the Canadian Charter of Rights and Freedoms wherever those provisions contradicted the Indian Act. Indians were not persons until very recently. The Indian Act remains one of the grandest vestiges of legislative Imperial domination in the world.

Indigenous people can't go logging on their traditional territory, or even cut a few trees to build a house. They can't sell any amount of herring roe on kelp, whale oil, or dried salmon beyond what a judge would call subsistence, and Fisheries officers are inclined to act as if that amounts to none.[34] Business plans that might see the back-of-the-truck variety of berry picking move to something more lucrative are hampered because no one on Reserve owns anything that can be borrowed against.

The Indian Bands are isolated in tiny communities from the rest of their nation, isolated from the richness of the land by the Reserve boundary, and entirely dependent on the federal government. Dependent on month-to-month fully earmarked transfer payments for operations, which can be withheld at a moment's notice for any accounting questions the Department may have. First Nations are hamstrung.

The number of cases of infringement of aboriginal title, impacts to aboriginal rights, failures to apply ready information to resource extraction licensing processes, and general racially motivated obstruction altogether would clog the courts for further decades—if the suffering individuals and small communities had the money to pursue their grievances.

A Haida man and wife launched a fashion outlet in Prince Rupert. It was an instant success, but they did not realize that all the stores in that town were owned by a handful of people. Several other business managers coerced them out of their rented space and into another, just as its lease expired, right before Christmas. They were finished. When a lawyer followed up on their behalf, he returned with paperwork that constituted a slam-dunk case of conspiracy involving the business owners in Prince Rupert. What the couple lacked was the funds to pursue it.[35] The right to recourse is not accessible to people who cannot afford to push back against discrimination and who can't muster support from their community – when the community itself has been rounded up into a camp. The right to participate in a legal system has been suspended since the potlatch, the gathering, the possession of anything worth having a law about, were cut off.

Local politicians don't find much currency in advancing this sort of on-the-ground truthing. The fact that indigenous people can't participate fairly in business or hold on to some ground in their struggle to rebuild their own communities is not the subject of town hall meetings or electoral platforms. There are many an old rusty can in many a cupboard in many a rural household in British Columbia which contain arrow heads, flakes, stone tools, stone carvings. The owner will coyly display them to an unwary guest: "This is the kind of thing that gets us in trouble."[36] The items are evidence of aboriginal title. Somehow that kind of hard evidence never does show up where it was found, or at the table when discussions about the land are under way. Even when the stone artifacts are still part of a massive overhanging boulder on a trail through a densely wooded valley – they will go missing and no one can recall ever having seen them. At least no one who is non-native. With the right kind of funding, a case of conspiracy might involve more of British Columbia than a few shop owners in Rupert.

It's not as if rogue racist cops or judges on the take have been operating in a separate sphere to aggravate the fate of indigenous nations and people. As has been observed by at least one of academia's investigators in BC, perhaps more delicately,[37] all along it has been *the people of British Columbia themselves* who demand to be above the law and to have indigenous peoples sacrificed for their progress. They have friends, their friends have friends, in high places.

Royal Commissions

A Commission of Inquiry is a court hearing—sometimes a protracted series of hearings, and sometimes incorporating public forums. A judge leads the Inquiry and uses his knowledge of the law to elicit the relevant testimony, usually with the advice of special counsel to the Commission. It is struck by government when there is marked dissatisfaction by the public over its government's actions, often in cases where a breach of duty is implicated or alleged.[38] Commissions can also function, however, as a strategy to give government two or three years of suspended sentencing on serious human rights violations. They issue a set of recommendations that cannot be enforced by anyone but the governments who caused the problems in need of remedy. The discretion as to whether to implement the recommendations are in the hands of that same government which must have been a party to the problem and which commissioned the investigation.

In 1912 a Royal Commission was struck to look into the size of Reserves in BC, or to determine whether BC had any stake in Reserve lands, or to secure more land for the PGE rail, or to forestall the approach people were making to the Privy Council—depending on your perspective.

There wasn't anything particularly Royal about it: BC and Canada were continuing their juggling act over responsibilities to the Indian welfare, as well as trying to get out of promises Sir Wilfred Laurier had made the BC Indian leaders to hear their complaints, so they struck up this Commission, supposedly with at least Royal Assent. The Privy Council then responded to the appropriately placed Nisga'a petition for formal inquiry into the question of their lands and advised no such petition could be heard until the Royal Commission of Inquiry into the Indian Land Question in BC had been completed. It was not until later that the Allied Tribes discovered that making inquiries into the land question was specifically excluded from the mandate of the Commission. It was a Commission into Reserve boundaries, which ended in cutting a lot of them shorter than they already inadequately were.

One need only glance through the four boxes of reporting, now a hundred years old, that was made during the three year enquiry to find that the real work of the 1912 Commission was to secure lands for the Pacific Great Eastern Railway Company, lands that were part of Indian Reserves. The so called "Interim Reports" are all land sales between the federal government, the province, and the PGE. That is to say, almost the entire content of the Royal BC Museum Archives' records of the official Minutes of that Commission are transfers of Reserve lands to the rail company between the Parties. For instance, by May 4, 1914, 32 "interim reports" had been made and every single one of them was an application for land for the PGE.[39]

Although clearly designated and acknowledged as understood to be outside their mandate, the five Commissioners did release a Confidential Report on June 30th of 1916, on such issues as they encountered regarding education, fishing, water rights, liquor laws, hunting, trapping, nursing and medical care, and agricultural and horticultural development.

The Commissioners would have Canada fund Indian schools itself, ensuring that lack of funding did not contribute to lack of learning and that graduates of Indian schools would pass exams in general practice in the Province. They wanted the liquor laws relaxed, so that the Indian need not pay $5.00, as compared to the white man's $2.00, for being found in public in an intoxicated state—or $25.00 for being in possession of any amount of alcohol, an offence no white man could actually commit. They recommended that girl students demonstrating an aptitude in the sciences should be assisted to training as nurses, and then returned to their communities with the resources to manage dispensaries and basic medical care. They said "fur-preserves" must be recognized as vital to the protection of the animals from indiscriminate white trappers, and as a crucial supplement to the cash economy of the Indian who was not in a proximity to succeed with fishing or agriculture. They complained that hunting opportunities were unfairly and dangerously limited. They recommended the placement of expert scientific agricultural teachers and horticulturists in circuits to assist the development of that industry in likely places.

In 2006 it was considered, in one remote community in BC, novel and revolutionary that a girl was pursuing education with the intent of returning home to be a nurse.[40] Liquor laws, the infringement of which furnished many a white town's mayor and priest with substantial Indian revenues,[41] were not fully repealed until 1958. Horticultural and agrarian schemes were executed at various times, and many of them were later casualties of the province's expanding network of highways. There is no present-day support for farmers on Reserve, although many native families originally took to farming successfully, even ferrying cattle and pigs and chickens across lakes and rivers where necessary to access the Reserve lands that were fit for grazing.[42] The decisive moment occurred when the critical labour to run those farms, the youth, were all removed to residential schools.

No limits to deleterious trapping practices—practices by white trappers, as the Commission noted—were ever placed. The collaring, or radio-chipping, for study of the last remaining vestiges of fur bearing animals in the province today is evidence enough of the result. The racist exclusion of Indian fishermen from the commercial fishcries, except as wage labour or as attached to canneries, played out meaningfully in the Fraser watershed while coastal nations were invited to participate in the industry that slowly but surely resulted in the sockeye, Chinook and Coho collapses of the present day.

Finally, the 1916 Commissioners suggested that it might be well to actually provide copies of the now 40 year old Indian Act to the Indians themselves. The evidence suggests that this did not happen either.

That Reserve Commission, as it is called today, was supposed to have been struck to address the complaint that the Reserves were too small for the 1910 indigenous populations. The main effect of the Commission was to further delimit those boundaries, while in some cases replacing the good land that was cut-off for the benefit of settler farmers with alternatively rocky hillsides for the Indians. Those Reserve boundaries, considered inadequate and entirely rejected by the people meant to live within them in 1916, have never been expanded or revisited since then, except in a review by Ditchburn and Clark in 1920. They altered little. Every recommendation made by Commissioners reporting to the crowns in Canada, the fount of the claimed law of the settler, was loudly ignored.

The most recent Royal Commission specific to aboriginal peoples in Canada reported in 1996. Those of the 440 recommendations which government adopted were presented to the public in *Gathering Strength - Canada's Aboriginal Action Plan*, 1998. Investigations into the state of aboriginal peoples in Canada are always "Royal" events, even after the Constitution of 1982. This last one, while denouncing the conditions found on Indian Reserves, merely recommended "reconciliation," as in the act of "making up" between two estranged partners. It did not discover a need for a third party tribunal to hear the land questions but allowed its confidence to rest with the government. It is said that the reason for this Commission had been the armed confrontation between Mohawk people and the Sûreté Québec, and then the Canadian Armed Forces, at Oka in 1990.[43] Others hold that this Commission was brought on by the Líl'wat and their blockade of the Lillooet Lake Road, and their defense in court which—although it was never allowed to be argued before the court_was that the courts have no jurisdiction on unceded lands.

The Commissioners recommended a declaration of recognition of the aboriginal peoples and an apology to the indigenous from the crown for past harms. On January 7, 1998, the Minister of Indian Affairs, Jane Stewart, read out *Statement of Reconciliation: Learning From The Past,* on Parliament Hill. Instead of embarking on some of those new decisions, like recognizing the indigenous peoples and their rights, she said Canada wants to, "…find ways to deal with the negative impacts that certain historical decisions continue to have in our society today." Rather than apologizing for attempting genocide against them, she said that "The Government of Canada today formally expresses to all Aboriginal people in Canada our profound regret for past actions of the federal government which have contributed to these difficult pages in the history of our relationship together." She did specifically apologize to victims of physical and sexual abuse in Indian residential Schools, and announced the Aboriginal Healing Fund.[4]

The initial report took an encompassing view of the situation in Canada. They estimated a cost of $7.5 billion to the federal government for maintenance of the unhealthy aboriginal population, and that this figure would be $11 billion in 2016, before inflation. They indicated an alternative plan: "The agenda … calls for minor increases in spending on aboriginals during the next five years but then a surge of as much as $2-billion to be sustained for at least 15 years… toward building new health centres, stimulating the aboriginal economy, upgrading sewers and housing and building new community institutions."[45] The

Commissioners recommended training for 10,000 aboriginal health workers, social service agents and managers, and a ten year training program to prepare the natives for self-government. Formal self-government agreements were to be phased in after schooling aboriginal candidates for the job.

The failure of the various schemes produced by *Gathering Strength* are documented in Reports of the Auditor General for Canada and British Columbia, and in statistics from the census and other surveys. The overall plan detailed by Commissioners—to promote health, business and empowerment among the aboriginal peoples and then enter a phase of self-government agreements coupled with substantial treaty payments—was not implemented. The federal government explained it would be too costly, and that they were already having great success with aboriginal people in existing programs.

In 2009, a federal Commission was finally struck to consider the lifeblood of coastal and interior peoples in BC. From reef nets in the ocean to weirs across streams in the Fraser, Columbia, Skeena, Nass and Taku watersheds, indigenous peoples here draw their staple food: salmon. In 2009, the Federal Inquiry Into the Collapse of Fraser River Sockeye, the Cohen Commission, was mandated. The Commission crammed eighteen indigenous witnesses into three days of hearings under the section heading, "Aboriginal Worldview." As one of the Chiefs put it on the stand,[46] his time and the money spent on the Commission, upwards of $25 million, could have been put to better use—for the salmon, that is. But that Commission has bought the government of Canada, and its wet aspect, the Department of Fisheries and Oceans, fully three fishing years of indecision and delay.

At the time, vaguely conscious statements like, "hopefully the stars will align with the Cohen Commission," were made then by Minister of Indian and Northern Affairs Chuck Strahl, MP for Chillwack/Fraser.[47] His riding contains in its boundaries the largest piece of the Fraser River of all, as well as three distinct indigenous nations whose people rely heavily on the salmon. Whatever those stars are, the government has some conspicuous actors in charge of revealing them. Appearing for the province were Clifton Prowse, Q.C., and Boris Tyzuk, Q.C. In 1990, both these men had represented the province in seeking the criminalization of Líl'wat protesters, a group of 63 who insisted the court did not have jurisdiction to reach a verdict on their behavior at events which occurred on their unceded Líl'wat lands.

Twenty-one parties were granted standing at the Cohen Commission, eight of them representing First Nations. Not one of their counselors pointed to the fact that Canada had never successfully treated with their indigenous clients for the right to license, harvest and export Fraser sockeye. The First Nations Coalition, an unlikely group of over 50 Bands, was represented by a lawyer from the firm Mandell-Pinder, specialists in admitting Canadian jurisdiction over unceded territories and then expecting good will and scraps in exchange. The Coalition's lead counsel already had an impressive resume of encouraging settlements and agreements between Bands and the provincial government which allow resource sector business to carry on as usual. The fact that all those First Nation leaders consented to proceed in these circumstances rates a diagnosis of post traumatic stress disorder. An empty chill drifted over First Nations communities in the absence of salmon in the summers of 2008 and 2009. It settled into the people's hearts as they must have believed the end was nigh, and that emptiness settled in the stomachs of many as well. There is no substitute for salmon.

And the lawyers were not about to rock the boat. Tim Dickson was one of the lawyers for Cheam, a Sto:lo Band on the lower Fraser whose members fish with determination and with contempt for the DFO. He asked, during the sessions on recreational fisheries on sockeye in the Fraser, whether there might be some consideration for First Nations economies in the opportunity presented by thousands of men out on the river. They needed outhouses and places to stop for water or possibly emergency supplies, and couldn't the First Nations take advantage of those chances for commerce? The recreational fishery itself, in reality, or an increased absence of the quarter-million participants in it, would be more pertinent to the sustainability of the sockeye.

Provincial Inquiries into matters concerning indigenous peoples and their lands are so rife with the conflict of interest that they are not exercises in justice but opportunities for the dominant society to justify itself. If BC is the fox left guarding the chicken house and the indigenous are the chickens discovered absent in the morning, a provincial inquiry regarding aboriginal people is a eulogy—composed by the fox while eating the chickens and their feed in the warm glow of their heat lamp—which closes with the lines: "I will do it again whenever I have the chance." Several such compositions scar the human condition.

The first, the Metlakatla Inquiry of 1884, was an attempt to smoke out the Missionaries who had introduced Nisga'a and Tsimshian leaders to the text of the Royal Proclamation of 1763. The Commission was delicately charging the churchmen with making Indians recalcitrant, encouraging their refusal of an Indian Agent and exciting their objections to Reserves. The Anglicans defended themselves, and the province would try another route to subduing the coastal peoples four years later.

There was a "Commission of Enquiry Concerning the genuineness of an alleged transfer, dated the 23rd day of June, 1884, from certain Indians to one J. M. M. Spinks." The stamp of the independent Commissioner, none other than Matthew Bailie Begbie, affirmed that the transfer to the railway interest was legitimate.

Papers related to the 1888 joint federal and provincial Commission to enquire into the state and condition of the Indians of the North-West Coast of

British Columbia record the statements made at formal hearings between the Indians of Haida, Nass and Tsimshian. The three days of hearings are variations on a theme: the Indians say "how can you allocate small parts of our land for us? It's our land," and the Commissioners say, "The Indian Act will provide all you need—you don't seem to realize that."

There is a dearth of Commission reports, provincial or federal, pertaining to aboriginal people between 1916 and 1996.

Since the 1990s, women have been marching for justice for the missing and murdered aboriginal women whose police files have been closed, "unsolved," without investigation. The government of British Columbia created the Missing Women Commission of Inquiry in 2010. Less organized indigenous outcries have been audible since the 1970s.

By contrast, after the 2010 Winter Olympics some unfortunate had the grizzly duty of shooting a hundred sled dogs that were no longer required for big tourist events in Whistler. Perhaps twenty-four hours after the revelation of this slaughter, a provincial enquiry was announced.

Wally Oppal was appointed Commissioner for the questions about missing women: were police investigations into missing and murdered women in Vancouver done properly? And was it right for the B.C. Prosecution Services, the Criminal Justice Branch of the B.C. Ministry of Justice, to have stayed charges in 1998 that had been brought against the serial rapist and killer Robert Pickton for attempted murder?

To give some idea of the federal sincerity involved, the lawyer for Canada remarked at the outset of the hearings on the question of the delayed or denied response by police to the literally thousands of reports and complaints. He suggested that these women, the victims—and most were aboriginal—were clearly hopeless cases anyway and any earlier investigation or report would have done nothing to save them from themselves. One of the RCMP officers working to provide police disclosure to the Commission received some media attention while engaged with the Commission. He had just posted to the internet a series of photos of himself: first stalking a woman down Hastings Street in Vancouver, site of the start of many of the crimes being investigated by the Commission, then capturing her and removing her to a location where she was caged, and the picture story culminated in images of himself with nothing on but his police-issue boots and hat, torturing the caged woman with a butcher knife, and on the point of ejaculation.[48] There was some debate among lawyers for the Parties to the Commission: police and government lawyers did not see how this event should disqualify the cop from further participation.

Robyn Gervais, the only indigenous lawyer who represented parties as counsel at the Commission, had left by that time. She explained at court her decision to quit the Inquiry:

> The delay in calling aboriginal witnesses, the failure to provide adequate hearing time, the ongoing lack of support from the aboriginal community and the disproportionate focus on police evidence have led me to conclude that aboriginal interests have not and will not be adequately represented in these proceedings… I regret that I could not find a way to bring the voices of the missing and murdered aboriginal women into this room. While I recognize that it is necessary to hear from police, I became increasingly concerned that you would not hear from aboriginal witnesses

At that point, the inquiry had been sitting for 53 days, on 39 days of which police gave evidence. Minimal evidence from the aboriginal community was afforded. Commissioner Oppal said to Gervais, "You lent a very credible voice to the inquiry," and urged her to reconsider her decision. "I wanted you to stay to represent aboriginal interests."[49] Gervais later told reporters, "Initially, I thought it was better to have some aboriginal voices at the table, but, as the process unfolded, with most of the evidence coming from police officers and little from the aboriginal community, I saw I couldn't do my job and staying would lend credibility to the process."[50]

A parallel report critical of the process in this Commission has borrowed for its title a popular police expression of contempt towards missing aboriginal women, an expression documented in the hearings: "Wouldn't piss on them if they were on fire."

This is the mechanism that law provides in British Columbia: a theatre for the grotesque. The acting extra-legal policies, performed and personified by the characters described above, play the supporting role in a society that is about much more, or perhaps less, than superior civilizations.

Chapter 10

THE RULE OF IGNORANCE

"This reminds me of the time I went to the bank rep to see about buying a home. After about a half hour of filling out papers and questions, she said, usually native people don't talk like you. I said, what does that mean? She said, natives usually only care about their next welfare check and where they're going to get their next drink of liquor from. I said that's a pretty racist attitude. She said, but I thought every native gets their own free house, education, tax free (and this is my FAVORITE part) I thought all Native people received a monthly check in the mail for food, clothing and shelter.
Since I had been meditating all morning I smiled and said, you're right to have that perception because this is how the government taught you to view me. You've been told we are not the same as you, not worthy of the same things as you, but here I am, in front of you, proof that those are lies and you have been mis-educated. She completely agreed and said she will never look at a native that way again. Whether she is telling the truth or not, you can bet I didn't leave until she knew what it really meant to be a strong Indian woman and gave her a thorough history of how she was indeed sitting on unsurrendered indigenous land."
—Alaina Tom, St'át'imc, facebook posting, December 2011

Ignorance of BC history and therefore of current affairs among British Columbians is staggering. It is, in fact, uniformly staggering. The BC public has not been the beneficiary of an investigative, keen and edgy journalist tradition bent on ethics and social mores, but rather of an industry-backed monopoly of denial and myth-making on its most deep-running social, political and legal reality. That is to say, its ongoing condition of being seated on unsurrendered indigenous lands that international credit agencies know it doesn't own, and of continuing to create circumstances calculated to bring about the destruction of the peoples who do own them.

The Corporate News Disservice

There is a very simple cycle to explain the bias in reporting that so reliably corrupts popular understanding. A newspaper starts up. Completely aside from the fact that it is likely started to promote a political view and is likely backed by money from same view, this newspaper must turn a profit. Actual newspaper sales account for a very miserable percentage of available revenues—except insofar as a large circulation attracts advertisers. Radio and television rely entirely on the same economic driver that newspapers and magazines do: advertisement. So the media wants to sell ads. To whom will they sell them? To businesses. Businesses in BC are resource extraction companies. Will Tolko Forest Products, General Electric, Plutonic Power Corp, RealTek or Prosperity Mines place an ad in a journal which reports thoroughly and without bias on such matters as the Indian land question? No. Will service providers who would like to have those industrial titans in their accounts advertise in that sort of responsible media? No.

These are businesses. They may have editors, but the real power of discretion lies with the advertisers. Corporations that appear to dictate the incessant, toothless content of the media are not interested in criticism. The indoctrinated public is not really capable of giving it to them. And few workers in British Columbia are not associated with those corporations. As patrons of the media, businesses dependent on the subsidized access to lands and resources—for example logging, mining, commercial fisheries and charters for recreational fishing— they too do not support journalism that researches the true cost of their activities. The costs would certainly be newsworthy. Costs associated with deforestation, environmental pollution, the extinction of species, the eradication of potable water in natural settings may make survival difficult for future generations in this area of the world. Costs which may be exacted by local, national and international forces—costs like infringement of aboriginal title, denial of aboriginal rights, and enforcement of conditions calculated to bring about genocide—these costs will prove high.

This is the scenario which effects the media blackout of aboriginal title issues.

In Canada, much of that blackout is achieved by a very few sources. The poverty of diversity in Canadian media has been well noted, but never with a particular view as to how it affects indigenous peoples. Senator Laurier LaPierre, speaking to a 2003 journalism class, noted the concentration of media ownership, which "limits the possibility of a marketplace of ideas," and added, "in the marketplace of ideas the citizen must have access to the means of production." LaPierre pointed to the statistics. "Seventy-four per cent of people in B.C. receive their information from CanWest," he said, "this is unconscionable." LaPierre was a Liberal appointed to Senate by Jean Chrétien. Anyone who doesn't receive their information from CanWest gets it from Black Press, as in, Lord Conrad Black who went to jail in the United States for fraud. These two controlled, almost exclusively, the English print press in BC.

The media blackout of the aboriginal title issue is no accident. It's a corporate agenda. Many journalists are unabashedly promoting their sponsors' cause, and receiving promotion as a result. Rafe Mair is a BC lawyer turned politician then journalist. He worked in radio, reportedly drawing more listeners than any other program on the station, and his attitude towards indigenous peoples was consistently one of hostile dismissal. He wrote a book about why native nations should have none of the Constitutional protections that were "affirmed" in 1982: *Canada: is anyone listening?* He wrote a forward to his friend Melvin Smith's self-published trial of Indians in absentia, *Our Home OR Native Land?*, in 1995. Mair, who opined frothily and often at the cost of implementing or operationalizing indigenous rights and self-determination, was not a good journalist. He was an activist. He purveyed a kind of hysteria-mongering among a Canadian population that he knew very well was, and is, completely ignorant of the cost-benefit analysis of successfully paying out indigenous peoples for their lands and suffering. "Tiny communities are given enormous tracts of land… Incredible sums of money are spent – worse, even larger amounts are committed to be paid by future generations."[1] These and the rest of his foundational arguments are so far from the truth that their popularity with the non-native audience is a grim testament to the status quo. His claims of daylight robbery are never, ever, contrasted with what indigenous peoples have lost, nor the value of resources gained, nor situated in the context of a Constitution which requires purchase before settlement.

Mair received the 2003 Bruce Hutchison Lifetime Achievement Award for Journalism. When he offered up his memoir in 2004,[2] well after the Nisga'a agreement of 1998, he didn't mention Indian "land claims," or any pride in having stampeded rank public racism towards the provincial referendum of 2002 where the provincial government sought to eliminate most of the nineteen recommendations of the BC Task Force from their treaty negotiating mandate. He did include a chapter about the death of his favourite dog.

There have been many career-minded and locally celebrated journalists at work in British Columbia. An American by the name of Margaret Lally headed to Vancouver when she decided she would rather die than become another Kansas farm wife. She found work as a secretary in spite of very little education, and later married her boss, George Murray, a budding Liberal politician and a newspaper man. The duo was dynamic and founded several newspapers, not least the *Bridge River – Lillooet News*. Murray was a mediocre politician and doubtless did benefit from his wife's tireless work promoting his politics through the thin veil provided by the regular publications. The newspapers from Vancouver to Prince George simply promoted development and George's election campaigns. "Ma" Murray, as she would become known, was interviewed by a big Canadian magazine and highlighted for her spectacularly unpolished but diamond-hard manners. Today, awards in journalism in British Columbia are named for her and usually announced in ceremony at a Richmond casino. It's a crapshoot, and, as "Ma" would so often say, *that's fer dam shur.*

Some BC journalists today have been writing for three decades and have proved resilient to the events in which native people have been defamed, denied, dehumanized, deprived and detested. They have remained true to their purpose: writing prejudice to persuade.

Newspapers in BC very often run stories about aboriginal people. They just never run accurate, informed, relevant, timely, thorough, well researched or unbiased stories about aboriginal people.

We have arrived at a place where the first drafts of history, the newspapers, have for lifetimes reported such warped portraits of the indigenous that the non-native population of BC cannot understand why there are still Indian land claims in a treaty process *after all we've done for them,* much less why these peace offerings and pocket change are not being gobbled up.

Freedoms of the Press

In British Columbia the noble aspiration of "freedom of the press" has become something more along the lines of "a law unto themselves," illustrating Mark Twain's truism that the freedom is really only available to someone who *owns* a press.

In the late 1960s, a retired, silver-haired man reflected on his life as a reporter at the Legislature for British Columbia newspapers. Once in a few hundred pages of dear-diary quality material, Russell Walker named the magnetic center of his autobiographical record: "I hated *details* to get in the way of my little empire."[3] What Walker describes is his ability, as a regular contributor to the dailies, to broker the content of news pieces, editorials, advertisements, and to give advice on campaign promises and election speeches from his vantage point at the feedback loop of the public pulse, and his direct line to doctor all of these. According to his memoirs, he traded with politicians in promises of discretion, access to people and information, perquisites and posterity, and steady work. Walker's focus was on the politicians of early BC and the reflected light gives a clear outline of what position the media was in during the relevant events.

The BC media coverage of indigenous news went up a steep curve in the 1990s. Coming from a place where all it did was interview local ranchers or loggers or frustrated tourist shops whenever there was a roadblock, as it continued to do in 1990 with the blockade of the Lillooet Lake Road at Mount Currie, media in the new era of reporting on Indians was confronted by a Mohawk army at Oka. Although "land claims" was part of the issue, reporters and editors were still able to treat the thing as a law enforcement issue, if a colourful one.

The Royal Commission on Aboriginal Peoples which followed allowed for some very polite discourse and passive aggressive remark over four years.

Soon the BC Treaty Commission would challenge the studied but indifferent approach, and the criminalize-first, investigate-later tactics because it brought forward the land claim issue without any balaclavas, criminal records or police. What would the papers say now? Writers from the Fraser Institute, the opposition Liberal party, and activists like Rafe Mair provided a lot of column inches. At this time, proponents of feel-good logic around letting Indians get into the dominant society entered the public record, read Steven Hume and Terry Glavin. Somehow, someone somewhere finally realized that if Canada could put an end to the Indian land question in the Yukon and at James Bay, which they did using the Comprehensive Claims Policy of 1974, BC could do it too. All they needed was a rational public that could read, do math and recognize an extinguishment procedure when they saw one. And tolerate the contrived displays of native button-blanket-wearing Premiers which might fool the grassroots indigenous back home into thinking BC was sincere about leaving them some space to live.

This was a leap that British Columbians would not make in one bound. The public met with the idea of treaties like vinegar meets baking soda. A century and a half of brutally denying the indigenous in courts, hospitals, schools, in fact in every settler institution, had not prepared the non-natives for a more subtle game. The most reactionary and racist elements of society took charge of the press, announcing that private property would be plundered as a result of treaties, the cost would bankrupt the province, and that Chief Justice Alan McEachern was right when he dismissed the Gitxsan and Wet'suwet'n case in 1992: pre-contact native life was "nasty, brutish and short," and the province of British Columbia had generously heaped improvements upon them that they were too stupid to even recognize.

As already mentioned, in 1995, the largest ground assault by Canadian Forces since the Korean War (1950-53) was launched just outside 100 Mile House in British Columbia, against twelve Sundancers and some associated campers. The Sundancers had taken a petition to London England with the demand for a third party, independent and impartial tribunal to hear their outstanding grievances against the colonizers of British Columbia. Back at the Sundance camp, the RCMP fired a few shots and waited to receive the media, which came running. The RCMP invited all the journalists into a room and closed the door. They then told them what to report. The media emerged and declared the Sundancers were terrorists. Communications in and out of the camp were shut down by the 400 officers and six armoured personnel carriers surrounding it. The media printed what the RCMP told them to.

RCMP Staff Sergeant Peter Montague was captured in footage of "Camp Zulu"—the name of their central operational base at Gustafsen Lake—outlining his diverse strategies to deal with the occupants of the camp and their issue. He ordered his media men to target the Sundancers' lawyer, Bruce Clark, who had written that petition to the Queen. Montague said, "Kill this Clark. Smear the prick and everyone else with him." He said, "Smear campaigns are our specialty." This quote emerged in an RCMP training video produced during the event, part of two hundred hours of video recording that was entered as evidence in the Sundancers' trial.

Clark was assaulted in the media, repetitively. He was "dreaded," and "William Kunstler with a lobotomy."[4] He was, at best, renegade, radical and controversial. Bruce Clark was defending the Sundancers' right to be a sovereign people in their homelands – not wards of the state or subject to Canada's Indian Act. He was, according to the largest Indian Act organization, the Assembly of First Nations, Chief Ovide Mercredi and Gitxsan leader Don Ryan, the biggest obstacle to a peaceful resolution of the conflict. Ryan called him "an extremely dangerous man with eccentric legal views no one supports. He's financed very well by the extreme right wing. He's exploiting aboriginal people for his own gain."[5]

The Globe and Mail's article, "Militancy: Beat the Drum Loudly," covered fully two pages of comment about the lawyer, none of which was supported by an attempt to convey the legal position he was bringing forward. The writers' remarks about Clark's indigenous clients were positioned next to the point that Dudley George had been shot in Ipperwash, creating the appearance that the Ipperwash protesters were also Clark's clients, which they were not. The article presented disassociated quotations from a meeting, a ceremonial meeting with many cultural references, which came across badly. The writers also quoted a number of Indian people who have felt rejected and "condemned" by Clark because they disagreed with him: notably, individuals with a career in the Indian Act system which Clark had shown is nothing but a vehicle easily controlled by the state. The newspaper's report merely ploughed on with the collection of disaffected comments and failed to locate any of them within the political context of the various speakers' realities.[6]

Premier Mike Harcourt called the Sundancers "fanatics" seized by a "cult mentality."[7] Reporters did not question him on that. The Attorney General, Ujjal Dosanjh, called them terrorists. Dosanjh publicly rejected calls for political action to engage with the Sundancers; he rejected his own sworn duty to receive from them and forward their notice of a plea to the Queen, the

Head of State of Canada, to the Governor General; he rejected the suggestion of the intervention of international observers and United Nations peacekeepers; and he largely rejected the notion that a peaceful resolution was possible.

The media called the people in the surrounded camp thugs, rebels, and renegades, and took pains to justify the names.[8]

After 77,000 rounds of ammunition were fired into the camp, one woman was shot in the arm, three police were injured, communications and supply were cut off and the media was pumped with the criminal records of those in the Sundance camp and spoon-fed incendiary conjecture. With a straight face, Ujjal Dosanjh told media, "I'm wonderfully delighted that we haven't had to use force."[9] The Attorney General, just appointed weeks before the first shots were fired in the siege, had spent all his first days in office providing media with an extensive rationale for the free rein he had given the RCMP to shoot to kill the protesters.

Only one objection to the way media was cut-off from actual events at Gustafsen, and pressed into service by the RCMP as a communications branch to prepare the civilians for massacre, was printed in a BC newspaper:

> There is a common denominator in this conflicting perception of what actually happened: The absence of the media. During the Gustafsen lake stand-off, reporters capable of verifying the official version of events and comparing it with the unofficial version were kept isolated and at a far remove from what was happening. They were therefore compelled to write about shots they had never heard and events they had never witnessed.
>
> If Gustafsen lake is a harbinger of the future, it should bring a chill of foreboding to everyone concerned about democracy and the right of every citizen to be as fully informed as is reasonably possible.[10]

Kenneth Price, editor of *The Verdict,* a trial-lawyers journal, reported on the situation from a legal point of view:

> ... the tactics of the RCMP in manipulating the media to inflame public opinion against the group of Native and non Native activists.
>
> It was evident right from the beginning of the standoff that the RCMP were intent on marshalling the media, and, thus, public opinion, into making certain bald assumptions about the background and motives of the protestors, so as to justify all methods used by police in the standoff. From

the outset, the RCMP were clearly intent on managing the politics of the situation so as to leave the impression that the armed campers were terrorists... The [RCMP's] news conferences at 100 Mile House [led by Staff Sergeant Montague] took place in the atmosphere of a military strategy briefing. What purpose did these news conferences serve? Clearly they had no impact whatsoever in dealing with the problems of reducing tension and ending the stand-off. To the contrary, the news conferences were obviously designed to inflame public opinion against the protesters, and to disseminate propaganda designed to give political justification to the actions of police.

Obviously, information regarding criminal records of the protesters was released with similar intent. The media were never allowed to go into the camp and interview the protesters. The police took special care to ensure this would not happen. Obviously, for the RCMP, one side of the story was better than two... The same thing happened in the Gulf War.[11]

Nisga'a Chief Negotiator Joseph Gosnell explained clearly to media that events at Gustafsen Lake had greatly accelerated progress for his treaty. "'It must have played a major part,' Gosnell said yesterday after the provincial and federal governments agreed on a 50/50 cost-sharing formula so Nisga'a land-claim talks can resume."[12] In 1996 the Nisga'a Agreement in Principle was signed. "This treaty will haunt Canadians for generations to come," said John Duncan,[13] then a Reform Party MP and their aboriginal affairs critic – now a Conservative MP and the Minister of Indian Affairs. *The Vancouver Sun* printed vast extracts from the Nisga'a Agreement in Principle, but also ran frothing indictments of the process from the point of view of people who are not accustomed to having to share anything whatsoever with the peoples whose lands they have settled on.

When the *Delgamuukw* ruling was given by the Supreme Court of Canada in 1997, BC newspapers wrote about it a lot. Kind of do-it-yourself handbooks were published: "How to know aboriginal title and rights when you see 'em,"[14] for instance, giving quotations from the ruling. Not everyone was supportive, and instead of envisioning a province where aboriginal title was acknowledged and respected and brought into a role with substance—a role that would succor the aboriginal peoples, headlines pointed down. "By ruling that aboriginal title to land has never been extinguished, the Supreme Court casts a thick cloud of uncertainty over the future of British Columbia's logging and mining industries."[15] Referring to the way the Supreme Court had relied on oral history in evidence, the ever-present Fraser Institute reactionary, Owen Lippert, added a headline or two: *Are BC's treasury, economy in peril of going for a song?*[16] He opined, "In the end, no one, including aboriginal people, will benefit from hobbling the economy with a torturous redistribution of land and tax dollars." That idea is impossible for the informed observer to believe, but such things make the content of the BC media.

The province's true colours were vivid. Morley, also a professor at the University of Victoria, BC, left little to the imagination: "The SCC decision on the Gitxsan case... shows a reckless disregard for public opinion and popular sovereignty."[17] He continued at length:

> If aboriginal title is a right to the land itself then it is also an entitlement to what the economists affectionately call the "rents" from the land and the resources attached to the land.
>
> If the revenues from crown land, combined with compensation from infringed land, are disproportionately awarded to aboriginal peoples, then British Columbia will someday become a "have-not" province unable by itself to sustain national standards of health, education and social services.
>
> In the interim ... it will be extremely difficult, if not impossible, for the provincial government to obtain new investments in BC.
>
> The premier, who has some considerable experience in making demands on Ottawa, should insist that the federal government commit itself to fixing the effects of this imprudent decision.
>
> ...As for the distant court cocooned in Ottawa, its members should reflect on the hard reality that in a free society the law is not, as some of them fondly believe, what the judges say it is. The law is also the rules that the people, through forms of democratic expression, consent to obey.

The professor's worries that BC will be a "have-not" society if it reconciles outstanding grievances with indigenous nations is a sad outlook, probably reflecting colonial greed better than any indigenous influence.

When the Nisga'a ratified their Final Agreement in 1998, *The Vancouver Sun* gave Liberal opposition leader Gordon Campbell a series of full-page editorials on the subject of why the treaty was objectionable, and how pressing it was to have a province-wide referendum to let the BC public decide whether the Nisga'a should have a treaty with them. Rafe Mair wrote letters to the paper and called the projected Treaty First Nations "Bantustans."[18]

Campbell eventually got his referendum, but not exactly as he posed it then. Once his party was elected in 2001, he became a great advocate for the BC treaty process and approved in parliament three more Final Agreements. He appointed Steven Point, formerly Chief of the BC Treaty Commission, to the post of Lieutenant Governor, where he would sign the Agreements into law for the province. He made his colleague Geoff Plant the Minister Responsible for Treaty Negotiations and established that new Ministry. It's unlikely that anyone would be elected in BC on a platform of support for the treaty process, for reconciliation; but Campbell was fully aware of the value of extinguishing aboriginal title in that process and he carried on with it once he won the office of the Premier.

Since that previous decade, perhaps since the Liberals came to power in the province in 2001, the lid has been re-adjusted on indigenous media content. Coverage has deteriorated further still.

Tahltan Elders occupied their Band office for nine months in 2005. They stayed, slept and ate there to protest the elected Chief's exchanges with oil drilling and mining companies—notably Shell. Before that, they had already blocked a mining exploration access road and gone to jail for it. They were eventually tricked into leaving the office when RCMP officers promised them they would have an election for a new Chief. "Then they said if we leave the building, the Chief will have no more power, and lose his authority, and they said what was going on with the developments had nothing to do with him. But we didn't get it in writing. We decided to leave the Band Office, and then nothing changed. He carried out his two year term as Chief—he was elected in 2000, and then he was in business with the mining and oil drilling contracts."[19]

There was little media coverage. A 150-word article which appeared in the *Vancouver Sun* made the protesters' position out to be uninformed, even illiterate and irrelevant, as well as opposed to economic growth in general, and the reporter avoided mentioning the title question.[20] He certainly did not quote from the Elders' press release of January 31 that year, which stated: "The Tahltan elders are demanding the resignation of the Indian Act Chief Jerry Asp. In their words they have fired the past Chief. We are united on this stand. One elder says, 'He has done enough harm to our People, and puts us in danger of losing everything.'"[21] More recent reporting on Asp's work as the Chair of the Canadian Aboriginal Minerals Association does not mention that particular assessment.

Neither do BC records document the uprisings of grass roots native people who do something for themselves, something inarguably positive, safe and inspiring to help themselves in healing. Not if it isn't brought to their attention by some sanitized, government-affiliated agent.

In 2007, over six hundred former residential school students gathered for three days in Lytton. They were attracted to an information summit on the

Indian Residential Schools Survivors Settlement Agreement. The volunteer organization Empowered Residential School Survivors organized the event with funds they raised themselves. They were doing this because they noticed that the Assembly of First Nations was not doing a very good job of providing information and discussion around the Settlement Agreement, in spite of being heavily subsidized to do so. The Lytton event was reported by a single media outlet in BC: *The St'át'imc Runner*, a monthly journal published by the Lillooet Tribal Council.[22] Although the First Nations Edition of *BC Media Monitor*, an expensive news clipping service, maintained a subscription to *The Runner*, it did not clip and note this event either.

The court-ordered settlement, jumped up by the AFN in concert with the state, which apparently provided the ready complaint for them (the class-action suit which Canada accepted within twelve months of the AFN's announcing the idea—an impossibly short time to represent the estimated 80,000 Survivors), precluded some 3,330 existing court cases involving alleged abuse; hundreds of years worth of court hearings; and projections of multiple billions of dollars in damages to individual claims.

The destruction of whole communities due to seizure of their children was dealt with by means of a "common experience payment" averaging about $28,000 per adult survivor. Only survivors alive in 2005 would be eligible for these payments. No one was compensated for the thousands of children dead in the schools, and those who died at home immediately after being released from a school on account of fatal illness. No one was compensated for the loss of language, except by the Common Experience Payment. No one questioned the obvious cost of the First Nations' ensuing incapacity to pursue their land rights, never mind being able to keep up their gardens, once the communities were reeling from the loss of the children.

The Settlement Agreement was foisted on the Survivors as an ultimatum: if too many people drop out, 500 or more, no one will be paid at all. The Agreement sought to close the door to court action against church or state by any affected person whomever by asserting that the matter had been lawfully concluded by the process of posting public notice of its intention to do so. The Assembly of First Nations made millions just in its 15% administration fee for (not) delivering the communications and services requisite to properly carrying out the consultative and consensual criteria. Well-paid delegates visited a few communities but left again without having imparted the real crux of the matters contained in the Settlement. This was certainly clear to the Empowered Residential School Survivors Society, who even created a DVD called "Prep for CEP," CEP meaning the Common Experience Payment that former students would receive as compensation for loss of language and loss of family life. The presentation was a collection of interviews with lawyers, accountants and clinical councilors who offered analysis of the Settlement and anticipated matters that would arise in participating.

But people left to rely on the AFN's bulletins did not understand the "alive in 2005" condition. Spouses of deceased former students did not know they should have their children formally withdraw from the Agreement or be bound by it, even when their loved one had not benefited by it. Most survivors knew they would never be able to sue for damages once the Settlement Agreement was passed unless they had opted out – but most did not know that in order to collect the compensation for gross physical abuses, associated with the Settlement's Individual Assessment Process, they would have to testify, to call witnesses, and to endure the same court procedures that had deterred them from pressing their cases independently. They were also not given a comparison estimate of the difference in value of an independent court award for the most serious abuses and an award under the Independent Assessment Process stipulated by the Agreement.

Under the Settlement Agreement, adults who pursued their grievances of sexual assault while in residential school were compensated according to a never before seen points-system model of assessment of harm. One rape, two rapes, 35 rapes; vaginal, oral, anal; one beating, five beatings, 60 beatings; all led to a sum of points which were then assessed at a uniform dollar value. The humiliation experienced by these adults at having to put forward their most painful personal losses in such hearings defies description. That is to say nothing of revival of old wounds, the sense of injury, the sense of further victimization at agreeing to settle so low. Victims of sexual assault were compensated in the order of possibly 10% of settlements awarded in similar cases arrived at in individual suits as early as 1997. Victims of physical and mental abuse fared worse comparatively. Loss of income and loss of employability worked in favour of those who had lived all their lives after as alcoholics—and then quickly drank themselves to death after receiving their payments—but it worked against those individuals who did have the strength or unknown combination of support and luck to carry on. Two women who suffered the exact same abuses were awarded compensations varying by $50,000, the rationale given to the one who received a $16,000 pay-out for her complaint of several rapes being that she had managed to carry on a comparatively normal life: to hold down a job, raise a child and maintain a relationship.[23]

Many Survivors finally succumbed during the Settlement process—by suicide carried out near in time to hearings of the past abuses; by overdose or intoxicated accident after compensation was received; and even by murder when events at the schools, long kept secret, came to light during the Settlement-induced chaos.[24]

Ignorance is the only explanation for the success of the Indian Residential Schools Survivors Settlement Agreement, IRSSSA, 2008.

Somehow the mainstream media managed to touch on a court-ordered class action settlement agreement that involved over 80,000 individuals over a period of 100 years without ever explaining enough about it to incite some kind of non-native response. That is, any response other than the usual hate-literature that flows from events concerning native people. The Indian Residential School system was mandatory for native children from 1920 into the 1950s. It removed all children from the communities for at least ten months of the year. In school the priests and nuns who were the teachers forbade children to speak their own languages, taught mainly Bible stories and industrial skills rather than academics, and collected money per-head from the government for their charges. The schools produced graduates at approximately a Grade 8 level – both in terms of age and schooling achievement—at a time when Indians were not allowed in public schools and therefore could not complete a high school education. The incidence of abuse of the children by the priests and nuns was so high, their habit of trying to wash the children clean of their brown skin and their most repeated lesson about how all Indians were savages and therefore evil and disgusting, that the Indian Residential School experience is one that no other Canadian could possibly relate to. The impacts in the nations have been catastrophic.

No Canadian media so much as referred to the statement, *An Historic Non-Apology, Completely and Utterly Not Accepted,* By Dr. Roland Chrisjohn, Professor Andrea Bear Nicholas, Karen Stote, Professor James Craven (Omahkohkiaayo i'poyi), Tanya Wasacase, Pierre Loiselle, and Andrea O. Smith. This excerpt is from that paper, released immediately after Prime Minister Steven Harper's national address of apology to residential school survivors in 2008.

> We also doubt that the Conservative party didn't have a team of lawyers, rhetoricians, and spin doctors, if not writing the statement, at least agonizing over every phrase, every word, every revelation in the evolving document, considering in detail every implication and weighing each possible consequence.
>
> No, what we saw was carefully considered, and when such a carefully prepared and comprehensively vetted document does some things (and not others) it is no accident.
>
> We had no trouble seeing through the Prime Minister's tortured prose because we're well aware of related issues that are no part of what the average Canadian is supposed to know and what government and church officials know all too well: the United Nations Genocide Convention and Canada's role in it...

Bringing genocide to the table would take the churches, but more centrally the government of Canada, into the exhaustive examination of additional regions of its policies and programs with respect to indigenous peoples, regions that, up until now, it has successfully avoided (or at least, as it is now trying to do with residential school, managed to isolate from other policies). And, what is perhaps even more important, establishing that Canada's policies toward indigenous peoples constitute an historic and ongoing genocide rules out Mr. Harper's statement as an apology, since such would violate the second feature of a genuine apology; someone who is still doing it can't be promising not to do it again.

Intended as in support of Harper's apology, Canada suggested compensation to individuals presided over by the federal government's compensation program and its Truth and Reconciliation Commission. These payments for personal damages did not address—indeed sought to bypass —the collective dimension of the crime: forced assimilation, ethnocide, and in effect thereby, genocide. In international legal terms, the commensurate remedy requires, inter alia, restitution and reparations to the indigenous nations concerned, not just to individuals. And indeed, to cease from continuing efforts, by other means, towards the same end.

As for the suspected team of lawyers and spin doctors behind the public apology, if they weren't there at that point they certainly were there when it came time to devise a system through which survivors of physical and sexual abuse would be compensated. A junior employee with the Department of Indian Affairs was offered a job description one day, and her supervisor explained that if she took it there would be an immediate promotion for her within the Department, followed by a second promotion within the year. The job description was not permitted to be removed from the supervisor's sight, much less from the office; she was not allowed to make a copy. The lucky candidate, a sharp woman fresh off the job of surveying and reporting on the state of native court services in Saskatchewan, chosen especially because she herself had Indian Status, had to read the job offer and return it immediately. She had been hand picked for the job of working in a team to find ways to minimize payments to the claimants. Chantal Perrault left the Department then and sought out organizations that were actually attempting to advocate for indigenous peoples.[25]

The IRSSSA cost Canada $2 billion, money budgeted for the settlement, and it included: the Individual Assessment Process: compensation for physical, sexual, emotional and psychological abuse; the Common Experience Payment: compensation for loss of family life, language and culture; and the Truth and Reconciliation Commission: documenting Survivors' stories (begun one year late of schedule, collapsing two years later and beginning again four years behind schedule).

British Columbia alone can make $2 billion in eight years from forestry licenses and stumpage rates in one Tribal Council area with seventeen First Nations.[26] There are 650 First Nations in Canada. This is revenue the colony would be unlikely to easily procure if two or three generations of children had not been removed from the communities there and raised in residential schools.

Ignorance of these matters is fostered, empowered, imposed, and reinforced by the media. Newspapers and online journals black out aboriginal title issues. They obscure them, misreport them or simply fail to report them. Instead they focus on natives who have successfully assimilated, or instances of abject failure about which they generalize. There is no connection made between the Indian Residential Schools and indigenous title matters in BC media. Or indeed genocide.

When young people returned home from Indian Residential Schools, they could not—or would not- speak their parents' language. Their parents certainly could not—or would not—speak English. With this disconnection, the disappearance of substantial indigenous culture and thinking must have resulted. There is so little memory of indigenous life before 1920, it makes Duncan Campbell Scott, the orchestrator of compulsory residential school attendance and the Superintendent of Indian Affairs for Canada, look like a genius. He was, in fact. Never before in the British colonies had the history of the colonized been so rudely or abruptly cut off. Elders today, who have earlier retreated to learn their own language properly, still have very little recollection of their parents and grandparents' stories. That's because most couldn't communicate with them. This loss has been pivotal to the ongoing crusade for indigenous assimilation.

Under the general silence about Indian Residential Schools, people are certainly titchy when matters like children's graves next to the schools come up. The public's champions don't fail them, though. Terry Glavin joined the somewhat inglorious fray that was the campaign against former United Church Reverend Kevin Annett, who has, with all the more brazen agents of controversy, loudly pointed to the seemingly fathomless church and government capabilities to deny the hideous extent of Indian Residential School atrocities. Glavin takes a position of denying this issue in his effort to publicly convict Kevin Annett of total insanity and to defend Grand Chief Edward John who was accused by Annett of various acts of complicity, particularly silence.[27]

Unfortunately, Glavin's black and white approach has the effect of erasing a few easily documented graveyards of the kind Annett has been shouting about. A former student from Mt Currie eventually answered his daughter's repeated questions about where her name came from? It was his sister's name—his sister whom he had buried, unwittingly, during the course of his assigned duties as grave digger for the St. Mary's Mission Residential School in Mission. In *Stolen From Our Embrace*, Suzanne Fournier and Ernie Crey document a statement issued by Commissioners who reported on an Inquiry conducted by Secwepemc of Alkali Lake into residential schools, 1997: "High government and church officials knew that Indian children were being neglected, abused and even killed."[28] In *The Circle Game*, by Haudenausaunee Professor Roland Chrisjohn, each and every claim that Annett ever made is amply documented, in its conservatively patient and plodding footnotes and references.[29] It seems that many thousands of children died in the schools.

Tales from the Sechelt school in BC were retold, maybe once or twice, by a wide-eyed former student who obviously still could not quite believe what he was recalling. His old friend, who lived and died drunk after returning from residential school, had an odd hole in his back—an indentation so complete that his small daughter could fit a fist into it. That mark was given him with a branding iron when as a child he was in the wrong place at the wrong time, and witnessed the murder of a fellow student.[30] The lasting hole, surely among others less tangible, was meant as a reminder for him to be sure not to tell what he had seen. There is no doubt that knowledge of these kinds of events has been almost impossible for most former students to live with, much less actually repeat and tell to someone else.

The invested media and its embedded journalists occasionally broadcast the gory details of ongoing assaults against indigenous nations. They show faces of people on hunger strikes, details of the deaths of small children while in extended family care, and mouldy houses. What they never do is turn the focus onto the instruments which inflict the wounds. News coverage of the amputated remains of aboriginal rights is usually sputtered over by newspaper editors more than it is researched by the journalists. The CBC radio broadcast more lively coverage of major daily editors explaining why indigenous opposition to Bill C-45, *Jobs and Growth Act 2012,* including hunger strikes, mass demonstrations and rallies, was *not* front page news than it did of investigations into the actual meaning of the events.[31] When court rulings on aboriginal rights, and the accompanying legislative scrambles, occur in British Columbia, the public is not assisted by mainstream media.

The attitude of the modern BC press can be summed up in an example. Early in 2008, in an especially sensitive moment of race relations between indigenous peoples and the genus *sports fisherman,* a daily reporter had botched, bungled and produced backward a story on a strategic session between First Nations and the DFO. When someone who actually had attended the meeting supplied him with corrective information, his response was, "What's your point?"[32] Media in BC does not delve into areas where details of the indigenous side of the story are available.

When the 2007 *Williams* decision was released concerning Tsilhqot'in title to half their traditional territory, the working journalists were unable, or not allowed, to make sense of it in the media. What the BC public learned was that some mysterious and worrying new precedent had been hatched in BC Supreme Court, and the case had cost them $30 million. Something about aboriginal title having been discovered and how urgent it was to put the hurry-up in the province's get-along in negotiations for Final Agreements: that political negotiation was desperately preferable to a legal remedy.

> Indeed, Vickers suggested British Columbia has been violating aboriginal title in an unconstitutional and illegal manner since it joined Confederation in 1871. ... A court proceeding is by definition confrontational, where one side wins and the other loses. A treaty negotiation aims to produce a win-win settlement that allows all parties to celebrate their achievement. ... But the courts cannot balance the needs and interests of a modern indigenous population with those of the broader society. ... In recognizing aboriginal title to land, the court has sent a clear message to Victoria to shift the treaty process into high gear or risk losing jurisdiction over the province it is supposed to govern.[33]

Aboriginal title, in Justice Vickers' opinion, meant the province's system of licensing logging and mining did not apply on aboriginal title lands. The reason for this was not addressed by reporters, just that this "presents serious challenge to B.C. forestry regime."[34] Reporters were not trying to find out, "what does this mean for the Tsilhqot'in people?" Even the straight reporting on the ruling in BC Supreme Court was given to invoking the spirit of logging blockades and advice on how to haggle downwards from the title position.[35] Sadly, like Justice Garçon of the Spanish Constitutional Court, who ruled that Spain had indeed responsibilities to the indigenous peoples of its colony in Guatemala, Vickers died shortly after giving his ruling and opinion.

The proposed Prosperity Mine, an open-pit gold mine that would turn a 113 hectare lake into a tailings pond, is in the title area of the Tsilhqot'in— would the mine go ahead? What would this mean for the economically depressed areas around Williams Lake? While news reports claimed that logging would be suspended in the title area, road building and exploration for Prosperity continued and became the subject of a roadblock by the Chief of Xeni Gwetin in late 2011 when she discovered it was happening.

If native people want something reported properly, they apparently have to write it themselves. In 2010 and 2011, coverage of the Gitxsan people was especially bizarre. Neil Sterritt, a Gitxsan, finally attempted to address some of the more clear points which had been bent out of shape on the anvil of the press.

> The Gitxsan Nation and people have been in the news a lot lately, mainly in relation to the proposed Northern Gateway oil pipeline. ...The chief negotiator and executive director of the Gitxsan Treaty Society claimed in December that the society had reached an agreement with Enbridge Inc., the proponent of the pipeline, on behalf of the Gitxsan Nation. It is doubtful that the society had the legal or moral authority to make such an agreement, and it has been a subject of considerable debate among the Gitxsan people.[36]

The papers will occasionally run such submissions—but never are there such simple, informative pieces by their own staff.

Sometimes the indigenous have to take out advertisements in order to be heard, messages such as: "The Gitxsan Hereditary Chiefs (GHC) want to be free to achieve economic self-sufficiency... Fighting the myriad issues that stem from problems such as substance abuse, unemployment and youth suicide, the GHC is breaking ground and stereotypes by asking the Canadian government to end their reliance on the Indian Act."[37] This is just the start of a two page advert in a monthly BC magazine. Another paid ad in *The Vancouver Sun*, September 16, 1999, called attention to the *Delgamuukw* ruling in a way that news reporters hadn't:

> *Notice:* To all shareholders of B.C. forestry companies and consumers of their products. The Interior Alliance, representing the five Nations of south-central British Columbia, is calling an international consumer boycott of companies who are destroying forest resources with destructive logging of Aboriginal title lands without our consent.
>
> First, aboriginal title encompasses the right to exclusive use and occupation of the land; second, aboriginal title encompasses the right to choose what uses the land can be put, subject to the ultimate limit that those uses cannot destroy the ability of the land to sustain future generations

of aboriginal peoples; and third, the lands held pursuant to aboriginal title have an inescapable economic component.

It was the first time that the salient details of the 1997 Supreme Court of Canada ruling had appeared intelligible in a BC daily.

Most of the pertinent information from indigenous peoples comes out in the form of press releases such as: "Negotiations have been ongoing since the Supreme Court of Canada recognized their commercial fishery 13 years ago. Yet, to date, the Federal Crown has yet to confirm a mandate to settle their claim for the losses the Heiltsuk have sustained as a result of the Crown's denial of their commercial right."[38] They're cheaper than advertisements – but they rarely receive so much as a return phone call from the news desks, unless they come out during direct actions.

Roadblocks usually attract media attention, but the years of events leading up to them do not. In the year 2000, several First Nations were trying to buy back a sacred site from the settler owners. Their unreported press release explained: "Adding insult to injury, the lawyers for the Smiths rebuffed an offer by the Okanagan Nation Alliance to pay $500,000 for the property that encompasses Spotted Lake. 'The offer we made was twice as high as the $250,000 estimated value of the property,' said Chief Moses Louie."[39]

Publications like *The Native Voice, The Indian Voice, Haada Laas, The St'át'imc Runner, The Secwepemc News,* all have attempted to present stories which cover the relevant details. More lucrative publications like *Western Native News* and *The First Nations Drum* reprint government press releases and sell the remaining 75% of the pages to industry and government in the form of ad copy, making sure that circulation liberally supplies Band offices and Indian gas stations throughout the province.

A National Broadcasting Corporation.

> *"Some principles, such as 'Parks and protected areas should be maintained for the use and benefit of all British Columbians,' are phrased so broadly and in such a "motherhood" way, so that 'yes' responses are virtually assured, the critics said."*
> —CBC News Online, July 02, 2004
> **discussing the BC government referendum on the BC treaty process.**

If the Canadian Broadcasting Corporation journalists are unprepared to square off with the assertion that there is something simple or unassailable in the referendum question about Park status in BC being superior to aboriginal title, and unprepared they clearly are, they are then reinforcing a lie by repeating it. That is to say nothing of the insult to mothers, whose job is rather more intricate than passing on unexamined rubbish to their children.

The CBC has been, without question, the single greatest purveyor of one-think and double-speak on the aboriginal title issue. They have established stereotypes of native people; they have reduced the scope of discussion around aboriginal title; and they have pigeon-holed that debate in an answers-before-questions approach with the authority only a state-run media can command. Terri John, who discovered how severe that treatment can be during a blockade of a logging road being built into Líl'wat burial grounds, told another reporter: "It's very one-sided media, especially the CBC... to the point where I'm losing the desire to even talk to them."[40] John was the spokesperson for the Líl'wat People's Movement at the time.

While reporting on the federal Conservative government platform on gun control and stiffer sentencing for petty crimes, ahead of the 2011 election, the CBC radio journalist interviewed a native woman in Prince George to get her perspective on what the new controls and stricter penalties would mean. The radio picked a lady in a poor neighbourhood and apparently conducted the interview over the fence in her backyard. They captured her sense of relief at increased controls, and then re-played the slobbering, slurring monosyllabic contributions of what were portrayed as her drunken neighbours, all with heavy native accents. Medical institutions have studied the coincidence of residential school internment, sexual abuse and poverty with alcoholism among native people.[41] Although they have once or twice allowed some of the findings to be broadcast on their station, the use of a drunken Indian in the background still suffices to make a point about the importance of gun control.

At the time of the Gustafsen Lake crisis, before he was incarcerated for contempt of court, Bruce Clark was interviewed by CBC radio on two occasions. Well, "interview" is not really the right word. Hal Wake had the lawyer on his show, and introduced him as failing to appear in court to face charges of contempt, indicating Clark was in a "scuffle," and described his clients as "rebels." Wake then invited Clark to explain why he had fled to Amsterdam rather than appear in a BC court, and engaged the lawyer about his legal career – until Clark steered the conversation from his reputation as a law-breaker to the reason why the judiciary was attempting to criminalize him. At that stage, the conversation went like this:

> Wake: You could be making the argument in court rather than... although I know you have... rather than... thank you.
> Clark: But that's the point. When I made the argument in court, I was cited for contempt.
> Wake: Thank you for taking our call.
> Clark: Thank you for cutting me off.[42]

Vicki Gabereau, host of *Gabereau*, a two-hour daily interview show on CBC Radio, did the same, adding the extra dimension of her verbose outrage at the idea that the Sundancers had something to complain about, and her equally lengthy ridicule for the idea that an external tribunal might be necessary in the matter. Gabereau took up more air time than her guest, and pieced the thing off by playing an unusually long promotion for other CBC shows in the middle of it.

CBC TV interviewed Clark on September 12, 1995, during the siege of Gustafsen Lake. While asking the lawyer to explain the legal situation, which he did very briefly, the interviewer stated, "I would suggest that a lot of people in this country, including our political leaders, the RCMP certainly at Gustafsen Lake, would argue about the genocide aspect and suggest to you, and the RCMP has said, that what we're dealing with are criminals with a criminal agenda."[43]

The state-sponsored media has had the advantage of being able to subsidize its messages about aboriginal people without the pressure of needing to sell subscriptions or advertising. Usually subject matter related to aboriginal issues does not sell, unless perhaps in the more pointed coverage like the column "Aboriginal Concerns," in *Business in Vancouver*, where advice on circumventing or minimizing corporate obligations to natives is peddled to the grateful business community.

A quick review of CBC's online archives reveals copious quantity of celebration over signing of Final Agreements of all descriptions, controversy over the Residential Schools Settlement, political banter between propped up puppets and their puppet masters as they discuss the Indian Act and benefits sharing deals well within the government's comfort zone, and very few pieces reviewing the most significant and dangerous confrontations, such as the one at Gustafsen Lake. There are even fewer, if any, which are addressed to a serious investigation of human rights and indigenous peoples. There is very little reference to that at all, while the majority of pieces focus on the dilemmas which result from the human rights abuses. Under the archive file tag "Racism," there were 33 entries. Two of them are about the indigenous. "What I was taught in school ... and from all the things I've seen and heard, Indians were treacherous, skulking, low; sort of savage..." says CBC's Percy Saltzman, revealing a common view of native history in the early 1960s in a broadcast titled "Savage or Chieftain? Six Nations Reclaims Its History.[44] This illustrates nicely the kind of back-handed abuse the radio can dole out, with the sound of a smile on the announcer's face. "Most nations consider the notion of land to be an important one. But to Canada's aboriginal people, it is also a strong cultural symbol. Native identity is drawn from the land: it has been a form of subsistence, and an integral part of creation myths. For this reason, it is only with recognition of treaty rights that Canada's native people can expect to survive culturally..."[45] But the larger implications remain unspoken: if Canada's native peoples do not survive "culturally," then effectively they will have ceased to exist as such, and all the ways in which Canada has created conditions leading to this disappearance will implicate it in this ethnocide—a more popular term for the stark reality of genocide.

An instance of adding words into mouths: "But the Haida are not against all forms of logging in the area. As chief Tom Green explains, 'We never ever said we would stop logging, we never once said that. We just want to control logging.'" The misquoting in that TV clip summary, which text introduces the archived TV footage, is interesting. Chief Green actually said, "We just wanted controlled logging."[46] There was no regulation of the clearcut logging of ancient cedars in practice at the time of their blockade.

The only writing by a native person in the CBC publication *The BC Almanac* was solicited. Grand Chief Edward John, founding Chair of the extinguishment-mandated First Nations Summit which co-created the BC Treaty Commission, told a story about what a great British Columbian Joe Matthias was because of his role in inventing the BC treaty process.[47]

The CBC has contributed to a vast number of publications which lay out the approved versions of history. In *Canada, A People's History,* released in 2001—it is a huge, beautifully illustrated book—there is little mention of British Columbia. It mentions the Mackenzie Valley Pipeline, the Metis episode and Louis Riel, Elijah Harper, Oka, George Erasmus. It never mentions the title question. The first chapter, "Taking the West," starts and ends east of the Rockies. British Columbia is never actually the subject of a single paragraph. While a few paragraphs about a Band-run school in Bluequill, Alberta, emerge from the context of Trudeau's 1969 white paper on eliminating Indian Status, there is no mention of the resulting Comprehensive Claims Policy or any of the continuing struggles against the exclusion of Indians from the 1982 Constitution Act. It winds up as a sort of "good news" story with pictures of school children.

Comments about the Oka crisis from John Ciaccia, Quebec's Minister of Indian Affairs, were provided to shore up the Canadian attitude towards roadblockers who pursue international ideas: "The Warriors wanted the army because then they could say they were fighting nation against nation, the Mohawk army against the Canadian army. ...They played it for all it was worth around the world." That's as close as the book gets to acknowledging the ongoing international debacle of denying the rights of indigenous peoples in Canada. Although it was printed in 2001, this book does not mention the Gustafsen Lake crisis of 1995 and their appeal to courts beyond Canada. Almost no "histories of Canada" reference Gustafsen Lake.

A 1993 documentary, a CBC Film Production, was actually titled *The War Against the Indians.* Director Harry Rasky's two and a half hour film is little more than a dismissal of those affairs. While other film makers have needed the whole bill to address the siege at Wounded Knee, or at Oka, or the decimation of the Huron, for instance, Rasky covers these and Custer, residential schools, Columbus, Spanish massacres, the demise of the buffalo, and "the great art and music of the First Nations people" in a little over two hours.

An exhaustive study of CBC's promotion of racism against indigenous people and their delivery of mixed messages—and if it can be deemed inadvertent—is truly overdue. Such a study might review what seems to be their careful editing and selection of actual messages being delivered in public by indigenous people; and the methodical black-out of the most profound aboriginal title news.

In May of 2011 an independent delegation from Líl'wat attended the Permanent Forum on Indigenous Issues in New York City. Pau Tuc La Sim told the 1,800 or so delegates from around the world that they do not recognize the Indian Act, that they have no treaty with Canada, and that the state continues to apprehend their children in spite of having no arrangements with them to so much as enter their territory. After careful orchestration of phone interviews from New York, and the recording of that interview by phone, the CBC morning news editor decided it was not worth airing. CBC did not attend a press-conference organized ahead of the delegation's departure, either. A list of critical happenings in the movement for aboriginal title in BC that were *not reported* on CBC would dwarf a similar list of actual news coverage—both in length and in magnitude of content.

The mainstream media of the globe demonstrated their mastery of the lesson in basic indifference to the issues of the indigenous when they visited Whistler and Vancouver in December of 2009; they largely ignored a special alternative media conference set up for them by an affiliation under the banner "No Olympics on Stolen Native Land." A press organizer from Reuters was hosted on a CBC radio show where he was given the opportunity to assure listeners that he thought the proponents of the indigenous perspective had "missed the point" of the Olympic Games.

The Fickle Nature of Stupidity

Today, the corporate or "free enterprise" governance of British Columbia relies very much on the ignorance that has been manufactured in the electorate. Should the BC treaty process continue? Thus wondered the newly elected Liberal government of 2001, to the tune of a $60 million general survey.

The 2002 referendum on the treaty process, where the Liberals were trying to get a public mandate to confirm their policy of not giving anything more than municipal status to Indian Bands in negotiations, has been interpreted in two mutually exclusive ways. Only about 30% of eligible opinions were registered in the poll, 80% of which supported the government's lead.

Chief Stewart Phillip, President of the Union of BC Indian Chiefs, says British Columbians boycotted the vote, showing they didn't care for Campbell's attempts at political manufacturing where legal rights should prevail. Premier Campbell said the results were overwhelmingly supportive of the government's motives and negotiating plan.

Coming directly after the effective date of the Nisga'a treaty, the referendum on the BC treaty process asked British Columbians to vote with their aggravated fear of losing private property, park status and exclusive domain over the province. Astonishingly, this event was marked by the first significant public demonstrations by non-natives supporting an indigenous campaign. But on further consideration: they came out defending the treaty process in its present form: based on extinguishment of aboriginal title.

These were positions favored by the labour federation and Business bureaus; they allowed their organizations' support to be construed as sympathetic to the native plight—as if simply supporting this treaty process (whatever its parameters and hidden—or not—end goals might be) is an indication of solidarity. However, as they stated exhaustively in any letters or statements to the effect of supporting the treaty process, their primary concern is certainty and investment in BC, which is hard to get when the land issue is as outstanding as it is now recognized to be. Their final word was to encourage people to participate in the referendum—it would certainly advance their hand for the government to get a "yes"—as this result would most support the Business Council's objectives of business as usual.

The referendum was an opportunity for British Columbians to state their opposition to any kind of concessions to indigenous nations—land, fiscal or political—through the BC Treaty Commission. The eight referendum questions were openly admitted by Attorney General Geoff Plant to be seeking "yes" answers.

In media discourse, the actual meat of the problem was thrown away and the opinion makers picked over the bones. They asked, ironically, is the referendum constitutional? Is the referendum intelligible, or is it crafted to produce only a yes? Media discussion was diverted to the referendum itself, not the merits of the BC treaty process or the greater meaning of BC's need to make treaties at this stage. Their answers to their own questions were not informed by a present-day fluency in the gravity of the matter at hand.

To have a debate over whether British Columbians support the treaty process or not is like asking, do you want the government to continue to seek extinguishment of the rights of indigenous peoples, or do you prefer the simple criminalization of people who practice or seek to exercise those rights? While the media may have misunderstood some of the subtle complexities involved, they certainly misrepresented the powerful ramifications of answering "yes" to a question like, "Should First Nations have municipal powers?" To answer yes to this question would be to deny indigenous nations self-determination, as called for in international law, and indeed, discourage its pursuit.

But then, all of the questions were designed to elicit a "yes" response. The remaining poll questions asked for "yes" or "no" to whether private property and park land should be removed from negotiations of treaty lands; whether tax-free Indian Status should be discontinued after a Final Agreement; whether existing leases and licenses on lands which may become treaty lands should be protected; whether hunting and fishing rights for "all British Columbians" should survive Agreements; whether provincial standards of environmental protection should continue on treaty lands; and whether treaty First Nation powers of government should be limited to what would be delegated by BC and Canada.

All of the questions were presented from the point of view of Canadian as opposed to indigenous interests. Even Stewart Phillip of the UBCIC was very publicly campaigning for a boycott of the referendum as a way to express opposition to the Liberals' thinly veiled attempt to cancel the government's earlier and preferable acceptance of the 19 Recommendations as the basis of negotiations (see footnote 3 in Chapter 6). The Union, however, has always officially rejected the BC treaty process and its extinguishment policy, and the membership of the Union can be contrasted with that of the First Nations Summit on that single point. Chief Phillip came out holding grand rallies to oppose the referendum, saying it threatened the BC treaty process.

That the loudest cries against the referendum came from native leaders themselves created the appearance that native leaders approved of the BC Treaty Commission and its mandate, as this was purported to represent the other side of the coin. Approval of the BCTC process could be construed as evidence of the capitulation of those leaders to an inevitable minority status: to the extinguishment of their national titles, enshrining the entrapment of their nations in municipal status. Either way, the referendum was set up as a win-win for the government and unsubsidized voices which might have spoken were not heard. They would not have been able to make their point in the usual space allotted for quotations in BC media. Final Agreements negotiated in the BCTC process read almost exactly like the BC Municipalities Act. But indigenous nations are not municipalities—they are nations with the right to self determination—and as municipalities with land ownership in fee simple title, their complete disintegration as a people would be made possible.

The debate of the referendum did not feature criticism of the outrageous inadequacies of the BC treaty process. The fact that aboriginal title is *not* the basis upon which negotiations should be undertaken in any BC treaty process is the first hurdle of competitive scrutiny that every media outlet failed to clear. There is no recognition of aboriginal title effected in these modern treaties, but that title is released.

Could the ignorance of the BC public be used as rationale for any government policy? Unless it gave rise to an initiative to curb that ignorance; something like an unprecedented historical literacy campaign ushered in by a brand new kind of government, the answer should be "no." Ignorance should clearly not be relied on to inform government action *vis a vis* steps required to reconcile the newcomers' claim to title with the existing indigenous title, especially when such reliable assistance as that provided by constitutional law is available.

The attempt to use miseducation to justify democratic action has been tried—and backfired as spectacularly as only that level of ignorance can allow. In 1998, the BC New Democratic Party was trying to make something of the only test case of Canada's Comprehensive Claims Policy within the province's borders—the Nisga'a Final Agreement. So the NDP spent $5 million in that election advertising the "gains" made by extinguishing Nisga'a title for the paltry sum of $200 million, trying to make it an election issue. Needless to say, the BC public, completely unaware that they might owe anything at all to the people who own the land under their feet, did not respond positively. The response learned by rote from that same media was immediate: pay Indians? For what? British Columbians regard the concept of their government and society having these legal and moral obligations as unthinkable. Perhaps to someone who has worked all their life to buy a house and pay off the mortgage, unthinkable is what it is. But it is a fact. The Nisga'a treaty did not become an election issue for the values the NDP was promoting – fairness, justice and reconciliation. The government that won was led by the man who sued the NDP for ratifying the Nisga'a treaty.

Public demonstrations appearing to generally support indigenous nations have increased to a very unpopular and marginal level at the end of the first decade of the 21st century. Indigenous-led movements on missing women, on opposing major increases in mining activity, oil and gas pipelines and Atlantic salmon farms in the Pacific Ocean have attracted non-native support. Public demonstration concerning indigenous peoples was, historically, entirely unsupportive.

In 1992 the federal government cobbled together the Aboriginal Fisheries Strategy out of various requirements of their exercise of control over aboriginal fisheries—seizing upon the regulation of completely unextinguished rights which were very defensible in court, and the subject of a three year old Inter Tribal Fishing Treaty at that moment. Instead of understanding the incredible coup their government had transacted, including the dissolution of the Fishing Treaty, British Columbians went on the march to oppose *any kind* of descriptive recognition of aboriginal rights to fish. They were not able to understand that the Strategy had the effect of exchanging a few thousand dollars worth of Band fisheries funding for agreement by the participating

Bands that they were operating under the Fisheries Act with rights that only existed because the federal government had provided them. Up until that moment, Bands and their members were fishing because they had every right to do so—none of which had been supplied by a government that did not have a treaty with them, much less any control over the unceded waters and rivers the fish swim through, or over the people who harvested them as they had done for millennia. The British Columbians no longer understood "progress."

FIRE—the Foundation for Individual Rights and Equality, was formed by angry British Columbians who got together in their frustration at being delayed by roadblocks at Douglas Lake, Adams Lake, and Apex ski resort in 1995. They described themselves as, "...not anti-native; our organization is opposed to government policy." They said, "The so-called land-claims settlements which these governments propose to negotiate exceed all legal entitlements and will destroy the livelihoods of many citizens and communities."[48]

Satisfied Confusion

There is a lingering haze of satisfied confusion among non-native people in British Columbia in the thought that "We don't know what they want." While that may be true, it is simply a mark of the so-sayers' ignorance—not for any lack of indigenous people communicating their wants. Since at least 1874, when a petition was drawn up and presented to the provincial and federal governments by 109 Chiefs, indigenous peoples have been clearly asserting and declaring their position.

In 2008, when the First Nations Unity Protocol blocked a Nanaimo ferry sailing, media was interested in how long ferry-goers had to wait and the resulting traffic flow problems, and whether it is reasonable or even necessary for natives to be taking such upsetting action.

A Victoria newspaper, the *Times Colonist,* opined that causing a 40 minute delay was the wrong thing to do in this day and age, since British Columbians understand the land claims process so well and support the Indians' position that the BC government should do more negotiating with them. (The *Times Colonist* was certainly first with the story on that one!) Just prior to that column, a survey indicated that 70% of British Columbians think, "all commercial fishers, regardless of whether they are members of First Nations... should be treated equally by the law." Only 31 per cent agreed that aboriginals "should have their own fishery because their rights are enshrined in agreements and treaties." Although the wording is a little problematic, as there are no such proper agreements or treaties in British Columbia, a minority of British Columbians do realize that there are possibly trampled rights at issue.

There is always a sort of vacancy behind the expression of one who is asked: why are modern day treaty efforts in BC not working? Well, the public would be hard pressed to answer this, because their media blacks out the answers which otherwise cooperative native politicians shout from canoes blocking ferry sailings.

So, instead of accurately, the public sentiment, generically, is 'Oh, they want too much;' or, 'We can't have them running their own governments;' or, 'Those people are not capable of doing what they want rights to do.' Or, 'They can't agree among themselves.' Or, 'It's ridiculous—natives claim 110% of BC'—an ever popular card, spectacularly misunderstood, played as if it were a trump. Unfortunately these are just further examples of the blind ignorance the colonials in general still manifest toward native societies—unaware that these often worked with sharing as a foundation of international understanding and featured border communities sometimes populated by both nationals to ensure the peace and protection of their children, hence the overlapping claims. Such diplomacy is out of memory for the war-forged capitalist settler.

Actually there are six very clear reasons why the BC treaty process is not producing results, even among those First Nations already willing to sell their entire claimed territories for $4 per hectare, such as Yale First Nation in the Fraser canyon above Chilliwack is presently doing. These reasons, never having seen the business side of a colonial printing press, are very straightforward.

The Chair of the First Nations Summit's Chief Negotiators' Table organized something of a following among those native nations involved under the BC Treaty Commission who were dissatisfied with the governments' refusal to negotiate some originally negotiable matters. At least, BC should have been negotiating those matters according to the nineteen recommendations of the BC Task Force. The group called itself the First Nations Unity Protocol, and it attempted to force the government to a Common Table with all Chief Negotiators to address the points of common concern to them. Every First Nation in negotiations, except one—perhaps refraining to win government-issue Brownie points—was involved. Robert Morales of the Hul'qumi'num *Treaty* Group, the main Unity Protocol organizer, sent out a press statement:

> The Unity Protocol, which was formed in October 2006, is intended to jointly engage Canada and British Columbia in the negotiation of principles or options that all parties can rely upon when negotiating individual treaties. Specifically this involves negotiations on six key issues, including: Certainty; Constitutional Status of Treaty Lands; Governance; Co-Management throughout traditional territories; Fiscal Relations and Taxation; and Fisheries.
>
> "The reality at many negotiating tables is that Canada and British Columbia have imposed rigid positions with pre-defined outcomes that are contrary to the sincere, good-faith

negotiations that are a requirement for this process to be a success. As the Auditor-General recently reported, since 1992, it is estimated that over $1 billion has been spent on negotiations. If we are to truly have resolution and certainty in our province, we simply cannot continue this way," said Morales.[49]

But these simple statements do not find their way, intact, into the media and into the public discussion.

The Hul'qumi'num *Treaty* Group has since taken BC and Canada to the Organization of American States' Inter-American Human Rights Commission. The OAS is a regional forum of the United Nations. The Commission agreed that the Hul'qumi'num had exhausted domestic remedies in their attempts to make Canada and BC negotiate the return of vast tracts of their territory which had been "awarded" to the H&G Rail Co. in the 1880s. They had the support of twenty indigenous organizations and First Nations, including *amicus curae* briefs and individual affidavits.

The BC Treaty Commission's website—the Commission that describes itself as the "independent and impartial facilitator of treaty making"— does not even refer to those six pivotal complaints. It does not post the strategically brief document prepared by the First Nations Unity Protocol to explain them.

No wonder the slightly more attentive BC rate payer will throw up his or her hands and regurgitate the polarity stressed in the news media: "They can't agree among themselves! One guy is out on the roadblock and refuses all development, and right next door another guy wants his share in the mine!" The tax payer does not appreciate that the latter advocate's position is likely fully subsidized by his own yearly tax payments, in the transmuted form of treaty incentives, seats on a board, or just direct cash payouts—possibly from a slush fund such as the BC Lotteries Commission, proven so versatile by former Premier Glen Clark. The sophistication of this political situation, where one indigenous person, holding fast to his authentic rights to self determination and his own native nation—and getting nothing for it but trouble, contradicts another—beholden to the income provided for over-loud assimilation, is too much for the average British Columbian to grapple with. Or, more probably, he is absolutely unaware of the possibility that his governing corporate bodies are discreetly paying out subsidies to such mouthpieces. And this sort of divide-and-rule tactic eludes his carefully engineered sense of the historical character of the place where he lives and the people who run it.

Almost no one in BC (except the indigenous people themselves) is aware of the relevance of the legal situation. The province has a line item in its financial statements to Standard and Poor's for its credit rating—'we are acquiring title to the land through the BC treaty process,' and there they list all the First Nations who ever became involved in that through the BC Treaty Commission,[50] the list adding up (fraudulently now, as many of those First Nations stopped participating a decade ago) to more than 50% of BC's claimed land base and over 60% of the native population in BC.

Sadly, the BC government's greatest strength in the combat for title to the land is the ignorance and racism of its settler citizens. The contest is not watched very closely and is entirely subsidized by taxpayers—and of course by revenues from licenses issued by the government over lands it cannot prove it owns. Even when modern day treaties are arrived at, the profound disinterest of the public is startling. In 2006 the Lheidli T'enneh were first to complete a Final Agreement since Nisga'a. The most thorough reporting amounted to a 500 word article.[51]

British Columbians are very pleased by the apparent absence of serious human rights problems emerging from their province; there are no formally acknowledged human rights issues in BC. *The Vancouver Sun* ran a Special Edition that was co-edited by His Holiness the Dalai Lama. The focus was on world peace. There was no mention whatsoever of the crisis going on in BC and Canada.

Perhaps there is no political will for ethical resolution, but that can only be because there is so little public will when it comes to upholding constitutional duties to indigenous nations, or abiding by international laws which protect them. The public good will which exists is often misinformed by the very interested corporate backers of government policy makers.

Keeping It Simple

Terry Glavin is a successful BC writer who specializes in reporting on salmon and native people. But more than anything, he prefers a good old fashioned yarn replete with popular morality and supporting stock characters. To his total discredit, he has chosen to make up these fables using real people and events as the backdrop. In his brutal massacre of real events, entitled "The Circus Comes to Gustafsen Lake,"[52] the 1995 siege is only identifiable through the archival equivalent of dental records. Glavin has rancher "Lyall" (Lyle) James and Secwepemc Sundance Chief Percy Rosette as country bumpkin types who "always got along fine." This premise is essential to his tale that relations between settlers and Secwepemc in the BC interior were "fine" before self-promoting and inflammatory characters with outside agendas descended on Rosette's Sundancing cause and turned it into an example of the outstanding legal and human rights issues which plague BC today. The premise flies in the face of armed roadblocks in the area since 1865.[53] The essay gives off the feel of a campfire interview with the two men, but the critical errors and omissions betray a contrived story.

Glavin has James giving a sigh of relief in 1994 when it seems the Sundance series is at an end, and he has patiently weathered it with the occasional grim-but-neighbourly smile in Rosette's direction. The truth is that James was involved with the police away ahead of the time. The rancher snubbed an invitation to a public forum from the spiritual leader in 1993 and sent details of an agreement between himself, the Minister of Indian Affairs and the RCMP in his place. The parties had worked out terms of access to the contested Sundance site, located within a cattle grazing permit held by James, without Rosette's input.[54]

A particular reporter is touted as the writer of the "straightest, cleanest most useful coverage of the debacle" which ensued, but that reporter stuck to the single-most misleading media line: that James owned the Sundance site property. James never did produce a deed in all the years this was asked of him, and instead made a claim that the land had been sold to him by the Department of Indian Affairs.[55] The land was actually the subject of a Ministry of Agriculture grazing lease held by the rancher. A grazing lease is not required for private lands, in fact in itself it is a proof of non-ownership. Even the conservative, outspokenly anti-Gustafsen leadership of Canoe Creek First Nation stated, in its press release at the end of the stand-off,[56] that the place is unceded land belonging to the Band. "The Circus" repeats the "ranch owner" lie just as every other media outlet did; it is the inaccurate foundation of the story. Ownership of the land at Gustafsen lake was every part a piece of the question.

Where Glavin invokes the BC treaty process as the cause of white paranoia amplifying the stand-off event, it is not referenced as one of the absolutely key causes for the stand-off in the first place. "White paranoia," was represented during the siege at Gustafsen by some hundred people marching the main street of 100 Mile House with signs reading, "We support the RCMP," and "End it now," but was strangely unrepresented in "The Circus." It would certainly have contradicted the theme that native and non-native people get along fine when they're left alone in the rural areas.

The Secwepemc had found themselves backed into the corner that BC's negotiated-extinguishment process created for them. Lawyer Bruce Clark had written up a Petition to the Queen on behalf of participants at the Sundance, dated January 3, 1995, complaining about the entrapment of Indian jurisdictional aspirations in such processes as the BC Treaty Commission, and it was to have that petition see the light of day that the Sundancers stayed in camp. This petition was even comparatively well reported on in BC papers.[57]

But Clark, in Glavin's fairy tale, had lost every case he launched where the lack of jurisdiction of BC courts in untreated Indian lands was a signal issue. The truth is of course that Clark had been *prevented from raising* that defense in every case he had tried to do so, which is very different than losing a legal argument. In order for Glavin's story to work, however, the lawyer is "bombastic," "notorious," "posturing" and "preposterous;" "from another planet," "weird," amid "all the other sad little midway freaks." The native participants—other than Rosette who is a good old boy drowned out by circumstance—are dubbed, "often violent," "paranoid," "eccentric," and "given to apocalyptic visions." It must be that Rosette was in some way kidnapped by the dangerous influences around him.

"June 13 changed everything" in the development of events at Gustafsen, says Glavin. This is to fundamentally misunderstand and utterly miscommunicate the Gustafsen Lake history. On that date, the rancher supposedly "obtained an eviction notice" ordering the removal of the Sundancers. What he actually did was drive into camp with four trucks and twelve men, desecrate the Sundance arbor by filming it, desecrate a sacred staff (Glavin calls it 'a "sacred" staff') by sticking the actual and only "eviction notice" onto it (which included the ultimatum for non-compliance: that he was going to "string up some red niggers"—not worthy of repetition in Glavin's version), and drive off again without ever exchanging words with Rosette – who was not there at the time. In Glavin's account, it was just the ranch hands who did this, understandably riled by the outrageous claims of unceded Secwepemc land title being made, and who were beyond James' control. But on that date, the ranch hands were able to accurately inform the camp that the RCMP was planning an invasion. If they were already planning to overwhelm the camp then—which indeed they were, since at least April, according to RCMP Superintendent Len Olfert's testimony during the ensuing trial – in what way did June 13 change everything? It did not change anything, it was just a moment on a much larger continuum, one which celebrated BC authors like Terry Glavin would have us believe is merely the figment of paranoid, often violent, apocalyptic imaginations.

The fairy tale ending of this "very exciting" but "not quite real" event is supposedly that after a disagreement that "got a bit out of hand," there will still be these two old cowboys living out in the bush, one native and one white, and that is the real, lasting and only important truth of it. The presence of the Canadian Armed Forces in 100 Mile House was very real, but that is not mentioned. The 77,000 rounds of ammunition that they and the RCMP (400 of them) discharged against the dozen or so people in camp were real, but they weren't mentioned. The Standing Committee to investigate crimes committed by colonists against their Royal masters' directions, struck in 1704 by Queen Anne and appealed to by the Sundancers in January of that year is quite real, but that was not mentioned.

The exciting thing about that summer was that the indigenous people were standing up for their rights and their land; that they successfully made the point that it would be as well for them to leave the camp in body bags as to carry on living without freedom or justice; and that they had the support of their community whether those people were interviewed in the press or not. Wolverine's $10,000 bail was posted by five different men from his community, all promising to ensure his good behaviour. He was the War Chief who led the people in holding their ground.

Glavin, however, in the true pioneering spirit of the historiomythologists, reduces the stand-off at Gustafsen Lake to an exercise in sin and "angry talk," which he seems to hope the people will forgive each other for.

Critics of this kind of literature might not be so forgiving: the readership would have had no way of knowing to what extent the story was made up. This fable rewards ignorance with conviction. It is a corner legend of the new mythology.

Chapter 11

TESTING THE NEW MYTHOLOGISTS

> *"We do not wish to sell our land nor our water;*
> *let your friends stay in their own country."*
> **—A Seshaht Chief to Surveyor Gilbert Malcolm Sproat, 1860.**[1]

A key concept in the elaborate story of why non-native people should control British Columbia is the assertion, albeit indefensible, that Indians are better off this way. Further, indigenous individuals will have more for themselves and more to offer the world if they assimilate among the new industrial capitalists. Never has the suggestion been considered that the presence of post-industrial capabilities and technologies could be used at the discretion of the indigenous nations for their own benefit and development within the exercise of self-determination in their homelands.

The result of an entire settler culture's unexamined acceptance of the myth of the benefits to Indians of crown sovereignty is the utter inability of the present majority population to hold an informed and sensible range of alternative opinions. Indigenous nations have the right to choose their own destiny; they are peoples; they are fighting for their collective right to continue to exist as such. However, with forest products, minerals, fish, and energy constituting 80% of its 2011 international exports – all coming from resource industries whose costs are effectively subsidized by the denial of aboriginal title, British Columbia is not open to a meaningful resolution of the indigenous land question. British Columbians have a different way of talking about the facts. It is so different that it might reasonably be called lying.

Improvement

> *"A great deal has been said about the improvements, government,*
> *and regulation of this village, and it seems to me that you do not fully*

understand that which you have talked to us about. You seem to me not to be aware that the "Indian Act" supplies most distinctly the remedies for the wants and difficulties which you have described."
—**Addressing Tsimshian Chiefs, The Honourable C.F. Cornwall, Commissioner for the Dominion government, Commission to enquire into the state and condition of the Indians of the North-West Coast of British Columbia, Fort Simpson, October 22nd, 1887[2]**

Every fur trader, explorer, settler and government official needed Indians to work for them, to move and pack for them. "Let your friends stay in their own country," the Chief of Seshaht said to Sproat. He had no need of them; he did not want their improvements. They came anyway without the invitation, and they said, with the mouth of Simon Fraser, and James Douglas, and Joseph Trutch: work for us. Europeans in Victoria lived quite well with native and Chinese domestic servants. With the mouths of the 1913-16 Reserve Commissioners, they said, "work for us"—in canneries, fisheries and agriculture.[3] With the mouth of Pierre Trudeau in 1969, they said, "Work for us—forget about being an Indian, be like us and get to work and pay taxes."[4] They said it with the mouth of BC Minister of Aboriginal Affairs and Reconciliation Barry Penner in 2010, in Port Douglas, "There are more opportunities for employment and training, if your children are going to be employed the way we need them to be."[5]

Gilbert Malcolm Sproat wrote about his envisioned "improvements" to the west coast in 1864, and he listed the names of resource extraction industries and their potential activities. Perhaps it did take 150 years to understand that his concept of improvement was not a good one. At the time, he also wrote lovingly of the "marine nooks," and "gardens of zooplankton" there in the territory where he was stationed: "Such places, on a summer day, strike the imagination of a loiterer like the creations of a happy dream…"[6] There are few such happy dreams remaining in this province. They have largely been replaced by the barren or contaminated nightmare and the social cacophony of the "improvements."

The desire for such changes, however, has not succumbed to time, as BC Minister for Mines Rich Coleman showed in his reasoning out the benefits of turning Fish Lake into a mine tailings dump:

Some people desire to roll the clock back a century or two. Things were not better back then than they are now … they were just different with a totally unique set of things that could cause problems for mankind.

Would we trade going back to the way things were 100 years ago, 200 years ago.

I don't need to explain all of the things we would no longer have if we rolled the clocks back … Prosperity Mine should go ahead—it means NOT just the well-being of the province, it means good well-paying jobs for everyone in the region, including First Nations people.[7]

Junior Minister for Mines Randy Hawes chimed in: "I don't understand why they [the Tsilhqot'in] would put [Fish Lake] ahead of their future for their kids." And: "As the mayor of Williams Lake said, if this mine doesn't go, there are going to be some very severe racial problems because a lot of the people, who are counting on this mine and are looking at it for hope, are going to blame the aboriginal community."[8] Hawes carried on blithely into the realm of the uninitiated *faux pas,* stating on record one of the more carefully unspoken mythical pillars: "Some First Nations reject mining for a more traditional lifestyle—those ways are linked to lower birth weights, higher birth rate deaths and lower life spans. Improving those outcomes requires sharing the wealth and jobs that come from mining."[9] The reality is that life spans of traditional aboriginal people before contact were often double the present day average, confirmed by the newcomers' sacrilegious practice of exhuming, withholding and testing ancestral remains. Evidence of the alleged high rates of infant mortality among the traditional societies is all but nonexistent for pre-contact times. Traditional knowledge of safe birthing practices was passed on successfully to midwives of the generation that brought today's Elders into the world. The things that killed their siblings, aunts and uncles and parents were not related to childbirth but to the flu, tuberculosis, smallpox, measles and residential schools. Incidentally, one of the safeguards practiced by pregnant native women is drinking nettle tea: it ensures a small, healthy baby, and therefore a safer birth.

The well-subsidized aboriginal voices of agreement are on file with the media for all the obligatory sound bytes. "I believe that economic development is the single most important factor to promote Aboriginal self-reliance, as well as address poverty and quality of life issues among Aboriginal peoples. A decent job that provides real opportunity is the best social program." So says Chief Clarence Louie of Osoyoos, the first and continuing Chairperson of the National Aboriginal Economic Development Board. Former Hupacasath Chief Judith Sayers was made entrepreneur-in-residence with University of Victoria Business and an adjunct professor with University of Victoria Law. After an 18-year career in law, one of her special fields has been promoting extinguishment under the BC Treaty Commission while simultaneously a Chief Negotiator and elected Chief. "We're extremely delighted to tap into Ms. Sayers' expertise," said Dean of Business Dr. Ali Dastmalchian.[10]

Separating Business and Politics

The new settlers wanted Indians to assimilate successfully into their new economy and "values." Lately some Bands have become engaged in resource extraction businesses. Usually this amounts to a stipend in exchange for becoming a consensual "partner," and thereby eliminating the risk of land claims unsettling the company's investors. They are criticized for this by armchair supporters, usually environmentalists. They are criticized for refusing such developments by the rest. They are encouraged to "separate business from politics," in speeches made by politicians, academics and business advice agencies who muddy the definitions of both. Specifically, they are asked to isolate the matter of Indian sovereignty from the potential for the short-term cash benefits of partnering with resource-liquidation schemes.

There can be no room for doubt about the effect of unresolved aboriginal title in BC on foreign investment. Jerry Lampert, when President of the BC Business Council, made many references to the importance of the BC Treaty Commission to economic certainty and investment in BC. The BC Treaty Commission itself advertises those benefits: "BC's treaties mean jobs, more business, community development and infrastructure for First Nations and all of us."[11] PricewaterhouseCoopers, an industry advisory agent, reported the value of certainty-by-extinguishment to BC in 2009.[12] News services headlined the report with its observation that concluding Final Agreements now underway would boost the BC economy by $10 billion over fifteen years. Lampert, previously Chief of Staff for two Premiers, was appointed a Commissioner in the BC Treaty Commission by Canada in 2007.

Because there are almost no treaties in BC, government and industry have done somersaults to accommodate First Nations as "partners" in developments, thereby masking the legal reality. One aspect of the legal reality, at least under Canadian law per the *Delgamuukw* ruling, is that lands subject to Aboriginal title cannot be put to uses that are "irreconcilable with the nature of the occupation of that land and the relationship that the particular group has had with the land which together have given rise to aboriginal title in the first place."[13] For example, aboriginal title land that was previously a hunting ground may not be used by the aboriginal people holding that title in such a way as to destroy its value for hunting. This is clearly a prohibition which forbids industrial development, and it means, therefore, that business partners do not seek designations of aboriginal title on lands they wish to exploit; they merely offer shares to the First Nation in closest proximity to the project.

But when a Band initiates a logging venture with a foreign partner, paying BC stumpage and export tax all the while, suddenly forestry takes on new moral and environmentalist meaning for British Columbians. "They're clearcutting!" "What hypocrites!" "How could they?" Development of Independent Power Projects is another major bone of contention for those settlers who know what's best for native communities. Many activists who had put themselves in front of logging equipment in 1992 to save Clayoquot Sound, a successful protest aligned with the indigenous there, were scandalized when the Tla-o-qui-aht First Nation later accepted an interim-treaty-initiative and began logging the place themselves.

The aboriginal economic reality occupies a place in British Columbians' collective blind spot. The things First Nations do to make money in that cold void of neglect are largely self-destructive. For instance, in spite of coastal salmon farms' international reputation as biohazards and "disease vectors," with reports showing that wild fish stocks decline by 75% everywhere farms have been introduced,[14] some coastal First Nations are business partners in salmon farms in their traditional territories. Several have accepted the invitations, the well-paid consultation meetings and a negotiated number of jobs for Band members, possibly even an annual stipend to the Band administration. One fellow campaigning for the position of Chief in Homalco, on the coast at Bute Inlet, was reported promoting salmon farms just before the election and using Canadian currency in place of campaign literature.[15] The recipient electors must have made a business decision that was not influenced by politics when they accepted the money for their vote. Salmon farms had been run out by the previous Chief, who was successful in a court action which won an injunction against their expansion.[16] Other examples of business over politics include First Nations taking their share of mining ventures, or at least a pitifully small share: $30 million over ten years from the Ruddock Creek gold and copper venture, anticipated to be worth several billion dollars; $100 million over fifty years for the McLeod Lake Band in the hotly contested Mt Milligan mine, projected to be worth even more billions.

How could a First Nation actually go about clear cutting, mining or damming creeks for electricity? How could they approve placement of alien salmon farms in their precious fishing grounds? The question really is: what else are they supposed to do? British Columbia has criminalized any traditional economy they might try to practice under their own auspices, for example, commercial fisheries or manufacture of medicines—they are not allowed on their own homelands which extend so much further than the postage stamp acreages to which they are stuck in Reserves. Where they would gather the essential materials and ingredients, the little marshes or hillsides or river shores are fenced and inaccessible: you can't pick mock orange on private property. Where they do have recognized rights, the new society has already committed ecocide: in the cities, in the clearcuts, along the highways and train tracks, under the power lines, in the massive free range cattle grazing permits, where streams are pulverized into muddy drains by the animals' innumerable feet. There are a handful of working exceptions to the industrial model of economic developments now taking place on Reserves, such as the Siska Saskatoon jam venture, which is conducted entirely on Reserve, and the same Band's fish processing venture.[17]

"Separating business and politics" has a double meaning: one for academics who study indigenous people, and one for the traditional indigenous people. The non-native Indian experts make use of the slogan as if it were an instrument of reform: they at once charge native people with being unable to refrain from nepotistic allocations of fees and positions. The business advisors insist that elected Band officials cannot be in positions of power over Band companies, and that day to day management of business should be performed by someone with a mandate separate from that of the elected leadership. This, they say, is the separation of politics from successful business management:

> The separation of business and politics is a hot topic in any discussion of First Nations economic development. .... Political imperatives are often at odds with business needs. For example, band-owned companies are often at risk of being under-capitalized because the directors, generally chief and council, are under enormous pressure to take any profits out of the business on an immediate and continuing basis. Band members tend to want to see immediate benefits in terms of improved public services or, in some cases, per capita distribution of cash.[18]

There are nearly countless examples of this mundane definition of "separating business and politics":

> Separation of politics from day to day business decisions: Political leaders should set direction and policies; they should not be involved in decisions dealing with hiring, purchasing, operating hours, remuneration issues etc. Otherwise the business won't survive.[19]

> The community needs to decide if they want their Chief and Council to be on boards of companies and societies or if they prefer to separate business from the government/politics. The practice differs from community to community. There is much research including from the Harvard Project that indicates First Nations businesses are more successful when they operate separate from politics.[20]

In a fourteen-page paper prepared for the American Leadership Institute by a chartered accounting firm, there are fourteen cautions to separate politics from specific aspects of business.[21] These papers emphasize joint ventures, but instead give examples of instances where companies have offered a First Nation a token amount of shares; they describe First Nations accepting contracts from unethical, major multi-national corporations as examples of smart business initiative; and propose bottom-feeder economic activities which legitimize resource access vastly larger than the First Nation's benefits reflect. They propose these as a sort of philosophical revolution that breaks the historical mold, and yet never acknowledge that indigenous people have always provided essential labour in settler industries; that the politics they are asking a First Nation to set aside are none other than those imposed by the Indian Act; and that there is a picture in the indigenous mind which encompasses a broader landscape than Reserve boundaries.[22] They read like indoctrination literature.

The First Nations read the doctrine more literally as saying: take down the roadblock and welcome the companies in. Separate the fact that the Band is suffering from government realpolitik, drop the outstanding issues, and climb into bed with whichever corporate industry wants the land. There is some confusion here, as such acts are not apolitical; they are poor politics. What think tanks have manufactured, however, is a coated pill: a repugnant concept sealed inside a sexy, high-rolling fantasy that is perfected by the suggestion that to swallow it is a noble deed, the mark of a leader, a sacrifice to be made by the worthy. In convincing that key man or woman of the limitless benefits to come, fairly vulgar displays of power are typical: a new car; a credit card without limit for "expenses," trips away or hockey tickets; a girlfriend. Whatever bargain is reached in these early courting routines must be sealed up tight, since no one ever gives them up or turns around to criticize the company's failures to keep its promises. Not even after the credit card is gone and they are driving their old clunker again.

Exploitation of the less powerful must call up brand name slogans like "separate business from politics," which insinuate that the shortcoming is with the weaker party. Carrying out logging on top of the angry graves of unsatisfied grandparents can hardly be seen as disinterested business sense; signing a deal which profits marginally in the short term but permits the extraction of enough timber to sustain generations in fish, clean water, berries, mushrooms and deer is not even a question of politics. Somehow the indigenous are made to feel that they are the ones being unreasonable when they take exception to such proposals. It's rarely possible to improve on the authentic view, given here by Arthur Manuel, Secwepemc, who has an extensive background in western business theory and practice to round out his traditional experiences:

> They look at the land as a resource that they put into production: that they sell through consumerism for a profit; and they produce garbage. It's a hierarchical system, and the highest participant is the billionaire. And he'll work that system right into the ground in spite of over-depletion, lack of sustainability, but somehow, like in a Hollywood movie, we're supposed to believe that some miracle will happen:

god will come down from heaven and somehow people will be able to carry on just the way they do. Indigenous peoples don't believe that. We believe that if you screw around with the earth, that's going to come back to you and bite you in the ass. And that's about as good as it gets.[23]

One of the constant refrains in the expert advice to indigenous leaders contemplating economic development is to "have an open mind."

The onus is strictly on the aboriginal parties to separate their politics from their business partnerships: the corporations are not expected to separate their politics of domination and anti-constitutional manipulation from carrying out power-plays on aboriginal communities. Perhaps the corporate world needs to remove their politics of oppression from their business models.

Landing Suspended Disbelief

> "*Making the federal government bear responsibility for improving economic conditions on Indian reservations may be good political rhetoric, but it is bad economic strategy. When tribes take responsibility for what happens on reservations and have the practical power and capacity to act on their own behalf, they start down the road to improving reservation conditions.*"
> **—Michael Chandler and Christopher Lalonde, in *Cultural Continuity as A Hedge Against Suicide in Canada's First Nations*[24]**

This type of advice recommends the indigenous will be in a better position to save their young people from depression and disaster by giving up on the struggle for justice, the restoration of a decent part of their lands and self-determination, and try harder to make ends meet, without addressing the reality of how to do so within the current confines of the Indian Act and their Reserves. It is a nasty remark, insinuating that the reason for high rates of young suicides is a function of First Nations' stubborn refusal to exert themselves on their behalf, rather than addressing the limited means at their disposal. "Business advice" spares no pressure point to chastise the indigenous into submission and cooperation.

Canada is busily cutting the legs out from under its own creature: the Indian Act. This legislation has failed to facilitate the complete transition of indigenous peoples to assimilated individuals scattered among the rest of Canadians, and has accidentally backfired and produced areas, although they are small, where lands are Reserved for Indians. It has also sustained the connection between the federal government and the welfare of the native communities. In remedy, a suite of the most extremely racist, illegal and unconstitutional Private

Member's Bills are poised to axe funds to every aspect of Band and Tribal Council administration and Indian Status life, on or off the Reserve, in 2013.

BC and Canada have been in the midst of an elaborate scheme to consolidate payments to aboriginal Bands, to maximize efficiency and save money in the Indian department. This seems sensible on the face of it, but it is also combined with an even more elaborate scheme to devolve responsibility for Indian Status programs and services to the provinces and, ultimately, to the Indian Bands or First Nations alone. The founding schedule is called the Aboriginal Horizontal Framework, and it was prepared for the Treasury Board by 2005. It is unremarkable next to such economic attempts on Indian Status as the Nielsen Report of 1985 or Trudeau's White Paper of 1969. Its timing was at one with the $5 billion Kelowna Accord, a parallel attempt to limit the obligations of the federal government to Indian people by having them accept a dollar figure in exchange for releasing the government from key fiduciary obligations.

The Horizontal Framework divides federal obligations to the indigenous into seven categories. They are housing, education, governance, land management, health care, children and families, and taxation. The plan has rolled out haltingly, subtly. It would be best known in its three most advanced forms of Education Jurisdiction, Delegated Family Services and the First Nations Land Title Act in BC, if it is known among non-natives at all. It seems the seven agendas are to be enacted separately. They are certainly not reported on in the Framework context. But each one results in responsibility for the programs coming down to the individual First Nations, in some cases Tribal Councils, which are affiliations of First Nations, in a graduated program of releasing the federal government from their fiduciary obligations.[25]

When aspects of this plan are reported, they come across as startlingly simple—in 233 words, even. Here's an excerpt containing the most solid information:

> Local Sto:lo bands will have more say in how health care is delivered to First Nations people thanks to a partnership accord signed recently. The Fraser Salish Nations and the Fraser Health Authority signed a partnership accord, the first of its kind in the province, according to a joint press release. "This agreement signals an important change, and the way ahead for how health services will be delivered to First Nations not only in the Fraser Region, but throughout British Columbia," said Grand Chief Doug Kelly of the Sto:lo Tribal Council.[26]

It is hard to imagine the average British Columbian being satisfied with this level of information if it were their health plans that were the subject of discussion. This aspect of the Framework is designed like all the others: the act of relinquishing "jurisdiction" to the Indian Act-constituted Band and its Council would snap the threads that lead to Ottawa's responsibility for aboriginal health services. The Bands will start with a five year funding agreement, and then continue negotiating five-year agreements with the province. That is the objective: to sign agreements about every aspect of Status Indian life that has a claim on federal fiduciary obligations, where the First Nations or Tribal Councils take responsibility for services, as well as the financing of them, assigning "jurisdiction" to the First Nation. This in the absence of any accompanying arrangements that might enable financial independence in order to actually be able to take on such tasks. This transfer of responsibility comes without promises, without guarantees, without matching freedoms to equal the new level of responsibility.

An extensive consultation process on the subject of delegating Child and Family Services to native service providers, the Aboriginal Peoples Family Accord, spelled out a template for having the Bands deliver the same results the provincial Ministry does in its Ministry of Children and Families, but without any specific guarantees of funding or training opportunities beyond the initial five-year interval. The "Education Jurisdiction" agreements currently in pilot mode also anticipate five year negotiated financing arrangements with the province, as well as the release of Ottawa from obligations to provide education and education monies for school-age aboriginal children and youth.[27] Criteria for accreditation and certification of First Nations Schools has been the subject of a consultation period, but final decisions will be made by the Ministry.[28]

Another Framework aspect, far more involved, is the First Nations Property Ownership Initiative. This allows Band Councils to hold a vote and have a majority agree to the scheme, which would "permit First Nations who wish to hold the legal title to their lands to do so; and... to do so without risking the loss of their governance powers... no matter what ownership rights the First Nations may themselves decide to allow."[29] The idea is that ownership of the Reserves would be severed from the crown, placed in the hands of First Nations (with underlying title subtly surrendered to BC in the process), and used as collateral for business or development ventures. What are presently Reserve lands could, under the scheme, become the property of non-native people. The Squamish nation's development of apartments on the estuary of Howe Sound is a pilot example of this Initiative. Currently, the Indian Act keeps business in check this way: "Reserves are held by Her Majesty for the use and benefit of the respective bands for which they were set apart, and subject to this Act and to the terms of any treaty or surrender, the Governor in Council may determine whether any purpose for which lands in a reserve are used or are to be used is for the use and benefit of the band."[30] The clause puts business decisions under the discretion of Ministers, previously Indian Agents.

And the real selling point for the Property Ownership Initiative made in the major dailies is apparently not what it does for First Nations. Chief Mike LeBourdais of Whispering Pines was quoted by the *Kamloops Daily News* as saying, "For the price of changing some legislation, it will probably add $4 billion to provincial coffers in terms of revenue and the jump in the gross domestic product. It makes a lot of sense."[31] Members of Parliament did not spare their high hopes for the Act's ability to get First Nations financing off their hands during the extremely brief Parliamentary debate of Bill C-24, working title: "First Nations Certainty of Land Title Act."[32]

People will hail these as overdue and clever developments, but the real dispute is not the ridiculous Reserve lands, it is traditional unceded territories. The Aboriginal Horizontal Framework, where it comes from and where it's going, remains a moot point in BC. Like the 1876 Indian Act, this federal plan is certainly in response to BC's lack of treaties. Its potential ramifications are not discussed properly, just as the those of the Indian Act never were, because British Columbians are still in denial that those foundational problems exist.

Political Migrations on Unceded Lands

No political attempt by government to resolve the outstanding land issues in BC has ever been made which was not coupled with an underlying and explicitly attached goal of assimilation and extinguishment. The migration route of successful BC politicians seems to start at an event where they prove themselves categorically hostile towards traditional indigenous peoples, and keenly aware of what part of indigenous claims they must deny. They succeed on their ability to uphold the new mythology for the new majority: life is better for Indians now than it was before contact; the ultimate goal of indigenous people is—or should be—to assimilate to the new economy; and there should be "one law for all Canadians."

In 1992, Mike Harcourt was elected Premier of British Columbia. He packed on to the existing "BC treaty process" train, somewhat less than acclimatized to the bone chilling process of extinguishment, and formalized the BC Treaty Commission. When, nearly three years into his term, indigenous sovereigntists in the interior decided to make their stand against such widely winged legal corrals as would capture wild horses, Harcourt buckled. Secwepemc protesters at 100 Mile House were adamant that being forced into a negotiations process where they couldn't win was unacceptable.[33] The Premier and his Attorney General, who was also Minister of Human Rights, gave the "green light" to shoot the protesters to death.

They signed Memoranda of Understanding with the Canadian Armed Forces for the use of six Armored Personnel Carriers. They actively denounced the "terrorists" in the media as 77,000 rounds of ammunition, some of it from

15mm Brownings, were fired on the Sundancers' camp. The only basis for their assumption of return firepower on the Defenders' side was the sighting of a few hunting rifles by an unceremoniously dismissed communications Constable, who had found the people quite hospitable and reasonable over coffee around the campfire, when he was assigned the task of visiting with them to find out their motives, and the alleged presence of an AK-47 assault rifle.

Once the camp was sealed off, negotiations between the campers and government were conducted by Mike Webster, a police psychiatrist fresh from his "communications" post at the Waco, Texas massacre of the Davidians, who had left the USA to become a Canadian citizen during his professional football career and switched to WWF professional wrestling. (He performed as Big Mike Webster or Iron Mike.) By the time he appeared back in British Columbia in 1995, he had provided his psychiatric expertise at situations in Puerto Rico, Peru and Hawaii. Over a hundred people in stand-offs have lost their lives while Webster was in charge of negotiations, only one of them on the government side. Webster has recently made an attempt to become Commissioner of the RCMP.

Harcourt's Attorney-General, Ujjal Dosanjh, doubling as Minister of Human Rights, happened to be holding the only two offices that were fully mandated to protect the lives of the people, and to receive the Sundancers' application to the Governor General for a hearing in one of the Queen's committees. His work to the contrary inspired a paper by University of Lethbridge First Nations Studies professor Anthony Hall: "Dosanjh: The Making of an Indian Fighter and Canadian Premier."

Kenneth Price, a lawyer and founding member of the Trial Lawyers' Association of BC, held Attorney-General Dosanjh largely responsible for the free rein of the police in handling the politics of the protest. He wrote, "the Attorney General never made it clear to the people of British Columbia whether in fact it was his office or the RCMP who were directing the political response to the protest... A dangerous precedent may [thus] have been set by the Attorney General. By trying so hard to distance himself from the law enforcement operation underway at Gustafsen Lake, he left the RCMP free to manipulate the politics of the situation."[34] Which, as we know, they did.

Ujjal Dosanjh recovered nicely from his outstanding conflict of interest and failure of duty as Attorney General. His sworn duties in those offices should have made him communicate the Ts'peten Defenders' notice of their wishes for an independent, impartial third-party tribunal. As AG, Dosanjh was the only living person who could have transferred that notice to the appropriate legal representative—the Governor General of Canada. As Minister of Human Rights, he was in violation of at least three BC legislative directives to protect the lives of people in his assumed area of jurisdiction—human rights. He became Premier after Glen Clark.

Mike Harcourt retired from office in 1998, quickly became the Chief

Commissioner of the BC Treaty Commission, and subsequently became an "independent advisor," mainly in the employ of the Nisga'a Lisims Government. The Nisga'a Final Agreement of 1999 was ushered in by the same government that tried to massacre the Sundancers. It inspired a legal challenge from members of the Liberal opposition government, MLAs Geoff Plant, Mike deJong and Gordon Campbell, and BC Supreme Court judge Wally Oppal. Campbell was soon after elected Premier. After the NDP lost the next election, Dosanjh crossed the floor and joined the Liberal party. The Liberals scrapped the BC Ministry of Human Rights and naturally discontinued the court action against the provincial government.

Wally Oppal was a BC judge before he formally entered politics in 2005 and formed part of Campbell's government. One of the cases he sat on, in 1994, involved deciding whether some Líl'wat roadblockers were guilty of contempt of court for disobeying an injunction against occupying a logging road into their smallpox burial grounds, or whether they were acting lawfully on their own unceded lands. Some people had built a sixty foot tripod at the entrance to the new road building site, and it was occupied by Shelagh Franklin, a non-native woman committed to Líl'wat sovereignty. Oppal stood up as he shouted down Bruce Clark, the lawyer who was attempting to register his clients' defense as being a constitutional question. Clark did not complete his opening sentence before the crown counsel, Geoff Plant, was invited to compete with it. Plant said that there was no aboriginal title in BC. Perhaps Justice Oppal was familiar with Justice Macdonald's approach to preventing Clark from mentioning that the court could not have jurisdiction in lands that had not been purchased by Canada. The following is from an earlier court date in the same hearing:

> The Court (Macdonald J.): I now ask counsel for the Attorney General to proceed with his case for contempt.
> Bruce Clark (for the Líl'wat): My Lord, I am halfway through my opening statement.
> The Court: I recognize that.
> Clark: You are refusing these people the right to have their counsel complete the opening statement?
> The Court: I am indeed.

Oppal, however less subtly, *repeatedly* interrupted Clark, the last time from a standing position and in a shout of such decibels that the court reporter could not have heard what Clark was saying even though he attempted to produce the words for the record. Oppal proceeded to become Attorney General and Minister for Multiculturalism from 2005-2009, appointed by Gordon Campbell. Geoff Plant preceded him as AG and Mike deJong succeeded him, then appointing him Commissioner of the Missing Women's Inquiry. Oppal is now Chancellor of Thomson Rivers University, where he will help start Canada's first new law school in over 30 years.

Mike deJong serves as Minister of Finance and Government House Leader, as of September, 2012. After a stint as Minister of Forests, during which term he simply removed 70,000 hectares of land claimed by two First Nations from Tree Farm License 44—the exact same action which had prompted the *Haida* result of 2004—Campbell made him Minister of Aboriginal Affairs and Reconciliation. The *Haida* case had resulted in the requirement of any crown actor to consult with and accommodate aboriginal people whose interests might be impacted by government activity, activity such as licensing logging or transferring disputed lands. As well as these posts, deJong served as Minister of Health, Minister of Public Safety and Solicitor General, and Minister of Labour and Citizens' Services.

Politicians bring the police along with them in their rise to power. The 'Integrated Security Unit' that patrolled the Sea to Sky Corridor from Vancouver to Pemberton from November 2009 to March 2010 had at least 16,500 officers. They were securing the area for the 2010 Winter Olympics. Naval forces, with a naval detachment stationed in the waters of Howe Sound; Canadian Forces officers, RCMP from across Canada, and private security personnel were headed up by policeman Bud Mercer with a $1 billion budget. Mercer told media that the greatest threat to the 2010 Games was "domestic protests," and when reporters pressed this, the RCMP media contacts sent them to Gord Hill, Kwakwakawakw, saying he was the one they were watching. Mr. Hill had never so much as been detained for questioning in relation to the Winter Games.

Mercer was present at Gustafsen Lake in 1995, where he was apparently the author of a C-4 land mine that destroyed a red truck and was clearly detonated to destroy the two people in it as well. Mercer was later charged with criminal assault by three protesters during the Elaho Valley blockades in 1999. He had cut their safety lines when they were in tripods blocking logging access roads. Bud advanced to oversee 2010 Olympic security shortly after the assault charges, which did not result in a court ruling.

These politicians in no way stray from their founding BC fathers. Amor deCosmos, second Premier of BC, published *The British Colonist,* where he supplied such editorial commentary as,

> ...proper consideration could be given to the interests of the colony, and its immediate wants satisfied.
>
> Our vast industrial resources lie hidden from the world: and the means necessary to make millions homes

and happiness, are untouched. Our fisheries remain but to be developed to prove a mine of untold wealth. Our inexhaustible coal mines—more valuable than diamonds—are scarcely opened. Our lands—the patrimony of the people—are still in the possession of the Indian, or exposed to the clutch of the land-grabber. Our vast forests—instead of making ships and homes—are unexplored and undisturbed. Our Indians—in place of being gathered into reservations—roam at large, a hindrance to settlement.[35]

deCosmos also had a chance on the provincial stage, like Dosanjh, to heighten the fervor for Indian blood. He was Premier during the chase for the Tsilhqot'in who had interrupted Alfred Waddington's road building concern through Bute Inlet. "It is a matter of self-protection and we are bound to take action against the Indian offenders in a practical manner. ...The Indian knows no law but blood for blood!" The audience at the Victoria town meeting cheered. "Any leniency only adds audacity to their crimes..."[36]

William Smithe, seventh Premier, is recalled by many indigenous keepers of history to have made some of his departing words to Nisga'a Chiefs: "When the white man came among you, you were little better than the wild beasts of the field!"[37] He certainly is on record with something similar: "to raise the Indians out of the position which they have held in the past, when they were little better than wild animals that rove over the hills,"[38] is a wish he articulated and which was transcribed in the Papers relating to the Commission on the state of the Indians of the North West Coast, 1888.

Richard McBride was the sixteenth Premier, and on his watch the advancement of Prime Minister Laurier's Supreme Court hearing into the Indian land question in BC was imminent. McBride refused to agree to the key question proposed: what was the status of the Indians' claims to their homelands? He negotiated an alternative: the McKenna-McBride Commission of 1912, the first formal Royal Inquiry in British Columbia, to consolidate the Indian Reserves. His successors Bowser, Brewster and Oliver wrapped up the Commission's findings in a legislative solution against unprecedented Indian demonstrations of dissent.

WAC Bennett flooded the Peace River Valley to create the Williston Reservoir, and the dam which displaced whole indigenous communities – without discussion, much less warning—bears the Premier's name.

In his book, *Politicians Of A Pioneering Province*, news reporter Russell Walker related the highlights of some decades of enjoying the confidence of BC's Premiers. There is not one reference to the "Indian land question," or native people at all, in his memoirs which span from Premier Richard McBride to Premier WAC Bennett.[39] A 1972 book dedicated solely to documenting early politicians' use of lands and resources for their own ends, *The Rush for Spoils,*[40] shows the heights to which the newcomer elite truly aspired. While it shows politicians robbing the settler public, its lengthy index doesn't include a single name, place or event that pertains to the indigenous nations—not even the word "Indian."

Christy Clark, the BC Premier of 2012, has made no secret of the fact that her province will do what is best for the economy, and First Nations can either take their fraction of a percentage of the profits or get out of the way. Her government was elected in 2001, and at that time they created the position of Minister Responsible for Treaty Negotiations – it was filled by Geoff Plant, one of the Plaintiffs in *Campbell,* 2000, suing the provincial government for ratifying the Nisga'a Final Agreement. After five years, they introduced the Ministry of Aboriginal Relations and Reconciliation; there were six different Ministers between the years 2005 and 2012. Premier Christy Clark cannot, at present, be bothered to stir the stagnant BC treaty process, and certainly not to clarify that it is not her government but First Nations who have abandoned it. Abandoning such sources of revenue as treaty negotiations is a substantial achievement for most First Nations. Aside from their entrapment situation with the treaty loans, they do not have the benefit of the cash flow from the lands, with which they would be able to retain advice and counsel that was actually committed to them and their interests rather than to their opponents' interests, who pay the advice and counsel for the Band: the government.

Lawyers

It is illegal in Canada for a lawyer to advise his or her clients against their own interests. But in today's climate of the gold rush for successful, and especially economical, consultations and accommodations with indigenous communities, lawyers are increasingly supportive of a wholesale liquidation scheme. The judiciary in no way impedes the legal industry's progress in processing indigenous nations and land title through the courts and producing a BC-owned landmass entirely sanitized of Other Interests.

Perhaps first a digression. A remarkable exception to the rule of judicial indifference to Indians occurred in a hunting charge case against one Tsilhqot'in, Mr. Haines, in the interior of BC. The judge actually intervened, leaving off the lawyer's arguments, and gathered evidence for himself in other places.

> I am going to dismiss the charge of having the moose carcass at your home on the reserve out of season because that is no offence if you had a right to kill the moose in the first place. In my written judgment I do not mention this charge,

> or your lawyer's interesting arguments about it, because it is
> not necessary. Your lawyer had many technical arguments
> and objections at the start of your trial. Just for the record,
> I shall say now that none of those arguments were good.[41]

The technical arguments made by Louise Mandell were of the same variety that had originally so impressed George Manuel when she got him out of a ticket for not wearing a seatbelt. Mandell has used the tools of the Canadian legal system to expand the category of aboriginal rights within that system. The expansion is checked on all sides by a Canadian government sponsored team of legal minds which is always ahead of the game—because it's their game—and whatever is won is at the discretion of the Canadians. Not a champion of indigenous sovereignty but rather a lawyer submitting to the jurisdiction of the very partial courts of British Columbia, sworn to obey the laws of the queen, Mandell did go on to make many more technical arguments on behalf of indigenous clients. It is a matter of opinion as to whether any of them were better.

Lawyers working for Bands, Tribal Councils and even individuals have never dented Canadian or BC legislation. With the exception of Sharon McIvor's case, which Canada responded to by altering the requirements for Indian Status under the Indian Act, the Canadian judiciary tells everyone to go on home and negotiate. Canada's rock-bottom position underlining such "negotiations" is, 'extinguish yourselves as a people and your accompanying title forever more.'

The majority of lawyers working for Indian Bands always make poor, but momentary fiscal use, of negotiating down from other lawyers' minor progress. Following the acknowledgment of the existence of aboriginal title, they produce benefits sharing and compensation agreements without ever establishing title—but which warrant never to bring up the matter of the particular resource again. In 2011, Mandell's firm assisted BC Hydro, the provincial utility, with the most unprecedented land acquisition (for $1 to each of eleven indigenous communities), or Settlement Agreement, and a payout to the indigenous communities that, on signing day, did not amount to the value of one year's worth of electricity from one generating station on one dam in the injured party's territory. The indigenous party waived their future right to royalties from the hydro-electric facilities, and agreed that all impacts and infringements had been settled. Mandell-Pinder was representing the indigenous parties, and negotiations were subsidized by BC Hydro. All this was helped by easily the most scandalous propaganda campaign to manufacture a yes-vote, with only the possible exception of the 2007 Tsawwassen First Nation's pro-treaty "public relations crisis management" intervention: also paid for by the BC government.

Mandell spoke at a conference in Westbank First Nation in early 2008 to discuss the meaning of the *William* decision, of Tsilhqot'in, 2007, which, as we have seen, gave the opinion that provincial legislation would be of no effect on aboriginal title land. She said, "We call it the Xeni decision." The place name "Xeni" is pronounced "honey"—of "Xeni Gwetin," the community William is from. This decision will trigger a wave of compensation and benefits sharing agreements as the government attempts to stack up sheaves of piecemeal agreements giving compensation for a plot of timber, a measure of water and a payout for new mines, which altogether will theoretically protect them from any more title claims—the much more expensive legal reality of indigenous ownership of their homelands and their right to self determination on them. While Louise Mandell has advanced as a sort of philosophical figurehead for the advancement of aboriginal rights, fighting many of the battles herself, the firm Mandell Pinder specializes in the sort of "law" which negotiates down from title to compensation and makes for a steady stream of business.

Lawyers who are more interested in a strong fiscal career than in the law are aware of what judges do and do not want to hear. One might ask them the question, why not sue the government over the entire Indian Act, instead of just one clause under one section? They might answer, *Because you want a case you can actually win.* What they are saying is: you can't fight the system—only bits of the impacts—if you want to practice law. One asks, why not bring up the issue of aboriginal title, not just rights, in a fishing case? As in, the Department of Fisheries and Oceans has no treaty with the indigenous nation that would provide for it to be making regulations here in the first place? They answer, *Because the judge will throw that part out.* They advise their indigenous clients to sue for rights or compensation provided by Canada, under Canadian law.

When Stuart Rush, Louise Mandell, Peter Grant and Michael Jackson represented Hereditary Chiefs of the Gitxsan and Wet'suwet'n in BC Supreme Court, in a case their colleagues recall having been dreamed of and prepared for a decade earlier, the first thing they did was acknowledge the sovereign jurisdiction of the Crown and of the BC court to rule on the question of indigenous sovereignty. Interestingly, the crux of the case, the first in a list of sixteen claims against the crown, was to sue for a declaration that the Gitxsan and Wet'suwet'n had a right to ownership and jurisdiction over their lands. If it is possible to imagine that a court to which plaintiffs apply, and agree has jurisdiction over them in their lands, and can act as an impartial arbiter of that very question, there still must be difficulty imagining that court would then find against itself and relinquish that control to the plaintiffs.

There is another very financially rewarding area of aboriginal law. In 2008, Micha Menczer, Counsel for Westbank First Nation, informed a summit on the implementation of the *Williams* decision that, "There are 2100 lawyers working for Canada in their justice department. 700 of them work in the area of aboriginal law." There are 650 First Nations in Canada. The lawyers Menczer refers to are working for Canada, not the Bands, and not in the Bands' interests as they are supposed to do. The Bands are, theoretically, their wards, but Canada is always working to destroy them.

Culling the Other Lawyers

Many lawyers have seen a premature death in their legal careers because they attempted to argue for indigenous sovereignty and an impartial forum in which to assert it. Bruce Clark, Jack Cram, Lyn Crompton, Renata Andres Auger and Janice Switlo are among them.

Auger, a Cree lawyer, was picked up by state intelligence when she began challenging the admission of British sovereignty which was made by lawyers for the indigenous in the *Delgamuukw* BC Supreme Court case described just above. She was suddenly brought up before the lawyers' disciplinary committee for keeping incomplete records of the trust accounts of her clients. She was not accused of any wrongdoing by her clients, no funds were missing; she was simply behind in the accounting. Auger was targeted because she was passionate and articulate and had seized on the essential point that lawyers for the *Delgamuukw* plaintiffs had, shockingly, agreed to colonial jurisdiction over a land question to which they were—and are—inarguably a party. Government agents found the only weapon available in her out of date trust records, even though this sort of infraction is scarcely cause for disbarment. Auger became the subject of other unusual inferences as disparaging assumptions as to her competence were made

Jack Cram apprehended that Auger was being treated unfairly because of her interest in the land question, and he tried to defend her. Both were dragged from the court room on the day of hearing after they tried to explain their defense. They were manhandled up the stairs to cells above the court rooms. Before it was finished, Cram was put into a psychiatric ward and disbarred. He was, at the time, also attempting to expose further and even less palatable truths of the Canadian judiciary than the denial of indigenous title.

Bruce Clark had, by 1995, many times attempted to defend clients on the basis of their rights and freedoms within their own countries which were not subject to Canada and British Columbia whatsoever. In 1995, Clark engaged in a strategy to force the legal issue with Wolverine, at Gustafsen Lake. Seventeen people ended up in Her Majesty's custody.

When Dr Clark arrived in Williams Lake to the court house where charges were to be laid and defense statements delivered, he found the door to the court room locked. There were other people inside already. As he remarked on realizing the situation, this had not happened since the Magna Carta.

Dr Clark was physically bounced off the wall from one RCMP officer to another for a few minutes until a face appeared in the strip of window next to the door. "He's ready now," the assaulting Mountie proclaimed, and the court room door was unlocked, Clark shoved inside, and the two Elders who had escorted him through a mob assembled outside the court—to prevent his entering the building in the first place—were detained outside of it. Upon composing himself, the lawyer retrieved his clients' statements from his briefcase and approached the court clerk to deliver them. Six plainclothes police officers blocked his way. At the cost of having his suit ripped to pieces by the police determined to prevent him, he succeeded in tossing the file on to the desk of the court clerk, and shouted "Served!" Finally he was dragged from the court room by the police, the court room door was unlocked, Judge Dome entered, and the session to lay charges and register defense commenced.

Clark was removed to a holding cell in the Williams Lake jail where he was deprived of sleep and subjected to unusual methods of assessing his sanity.[42] When the clinic agreed he was undeniably sane, Clark used his freedom to flee the country. He returned at the request of his Secwepemc clients, knowing he would be incarcerated for failing to appear at his hearing for contempt of court. During the ensuing trial of the Ts'epeten defenders, Clark gave three weeks of testimony, wearing a red jail-issue jogging suit and in handcuffs. Judge Josephson later instructed the jury they were not to consider it.

He was eventually disbarred by a Judge Friesen for "hectoring" the courts in Canada with the charge of judicial malfeasance in refusing to address the constitutional law of Indian territorial sovereignty. He told the judges that if they continued to refuse to hear the jurisdictional argument that they too would be complicit in fraud, treason and genocide. Friesen asserted that forty different courts had heard and considered and addressed Clark's argument. If that were true—if it were true that even one of those courts had heard and addressed the argument—there would be a record of it. There is none. Years later Clark's appointment to practice law was reinstated, but with one rather peculiar condition: if he began to practice, taxes the government wished to collect from his work in the early 1980s would be due in full; taxes he had at the time paid to his clients on Bear Island for his living on their land—untreated land, not Canadian land. Today, that tax bill exceeds some $700,000, with interest. Other employment he has since pursued was not so punished.

Dr. Clark was originally invited to assist in a case for the Lil'wat which was being advanced by BC lawyer Lyn Crompton. Once the Lil'wat were criminalized without the court having heard their defense, after thirteen court appearances in five months in the BC Supreme Court, she addressed the judge: "I'm never coming back. I will not be part of this colonial structure—I refuse to be. You made me swear when I became a lawyer to be a minister of justice, and I, for one, meant it."[43] Crompton quit law in protest.

Janice Switlo worked for the Department of Justice as legal counsel for Revenue Canada, Taxation, Customs and Excise and soon thereafter agreed to be in-house legal counsel for the Department of Indian Affairs. In that capacity, she gave advice on matters like reserve surrenders, and assisted private sector lawyers. She claims to have listened at meetings where government bureaucrats tried to choose the best indigenous person for the job of claiming to have invented the term "First Nations" as the new moniker for Indian Bands. She wrote of meetings between her clients and government staff, where they discussed the rewards offered for concluding modern day treaty negotiations in BC. In one of those meetings, one of the more successfully cooperative native treaty negotiators insisted that the reddening government treaty negotiators explain to Ms Switlo exactly how the major treaty incentives would only be received by those who finalized agreements very quickly.

In mid-career this lawyer switched teams and spent several years working for traditional indigenous clients. She argued in court for clients with hunting charges that they had a right to freedom of religion under Section 2 of the Charter of Rights and Freedoms. They believed in their people's creation story; that belief meant that they believed in their original title; and that rights to the land flowing from the Creator to the people were sufficient to make decisions about hunting and not subject to rights which flow from a Queen. During preliminary matters, the judge threatened Switlo, pointing his finger and yelling, "You will personally pay for this!" The hunting charges were ultimately dropped and did not proceed to trial.[44] In the introduction to her paper *Apple Cede,* Switlo explained her withdrawal from court:

> In 1997, Ms. Switlo did not pay her membership fees to the Law Society of British Columbia. She maintains that the Law Society exercises powers that are unconstitutional, beyond the purview of its provincial legislative authority and places Canada in breach of international conventions. She asserts that the Law Society's illegal activities and operations seriously compromise the independence of lawyers in British Columbia. Ms. Switlo concludes that the Law Society thwarts the application of the rule of law and undermines fundamental civil liberties in Canada.

One lawyer of major consequence for British Columbia was Thomas Berger. Born in Victoria the son of an RCMP officer, he married into Swedish nobility and became a lawyer and politician. His campaigns in BC provincial politics ended and he represented the Nanaimo men who were charged for being in possession of six dead deer in 1962, Clifford White and David Bob, winning judicial recognition of Governor Douglas' 1852 land purchases and promises to the indigenous as a treaty in *White and Bob.* He advanced Frank Calder's Nisga'a case from 1969 to 1973, eventually winning that pivotal minority opinion that their aboriginal title was unextinguished. Then he accepted the offer to become a judge, which silenced him for a time. He was the only lawyer with plain sympathies to the indigenous to have been made a judge.

When the Canadian Constitution was being created in 1980 and 1981, however, Berger spoke out about the importance of including aboriginal rights within it. For this he was reprimanded by the Canadian Judicial Council and he resigned in 1983. In the same year he laid out his theory that, "… if we try to force native social and economic development into moulds that we have cast, the whole process will be a failure,"[45] in a paper for *BC Studies,* a UBC quarterly. Berger went back into law practice but did not take any more indigenous rights cases. He wrote several fascinating books which sympathized with indigenous peoples in Canada and in all the Americas; as head of the Mackenzie Valley Pipeline Inquiry he sided with the indigenous; and in his role as last mediator for the settlement of the Nunavut Territory in northern Canada he wrote the Nunavut Report, 2006, which augmented the results thus far produced in the comprehensive claims process. The creation of Nunavut is meant to have replaced the indigenous titles with inclusion in the Canadian federation. Berger never pursued the matter of indigenous title past 1973.

Chapter 12

WHO ARE WE NOW?

꧁꧂

"Stewart Phillip, grand chief of the Union of B.C. Indian Chiefs
has said Canada could face an Arab Spring-style "uprising" if Prime
Minister Stephen Harper doesn't give a clear indication in his meeting
with aboriginal leaders here in Ottawa Tuesday.
Really, so now you threaten us with violence? You sure that is the way
to go, most Canadians have had enough, and that could very well be the
straw that broke the proverbial camels back.Native Spring?
Sure why not, then we can have Redneck Summer."
—**Psychodad1** commenting online under the article,
**"An aboriginal uprising is 'inevitable' if Harper doesn't listen,
chief threatens," by Peter O'Neil, Postmedia News,
The National Post, January 23, 2012,**

In the same string of online comments, sequentially:

damesbond007
What do they give us?
1. Misappropriation of tax money.
2. Rampant alcoholism and sniffing vices.
3. FAS babies.
4. Dysfunctional family life.
5. Whines, whines and more whines.
6. Uneducated people.
7. Gangs
8. Destruction of the homes we build and pay for.
9. Abject poverty on many Rez's in spite of the billions.

10. Sit on their butts, drink all day,
blame Ottawa and ask for more money.
And we're supposed to sit back and take this nonsense?

Hobbittall damesbond007
"And we're supposed to sit back and take this nonsense?"
Don't be silly. You are supposed to pay more taxes...
They deserve a raise!
(according to them at least)

Observant damesbond007
11. Generations of inbreeding and ensuing problems.

millhouse04
Start an uprising then. Just tell the Police and Military to shoot back.

ralph_cramden
This may sound racist—but I don't care

The above comments remain on display on the *National Post* website almost one year after they were posted. There are hundreds of comments posted under that article,[1] and all but a handful echo the above sentiments. The majority of editors in Canadian media agree with them as well. The following comment was taken down from their online news site sometime after a complaint to *Business in Vancouver*, but the moderator of the online discussion obviously thought it was an acceptable piece. The name of the commentator and his closing remark sound an ominous note:

sniper69714
Why not just get rid of the Native fishing all together? I understand that some of the natives do acquire the fish for food and ceremonial purposes but %95 of the fish that are caught by the natives for food and ceremonial purposes are sold to people. If you want to prove it to yourself go to Peg Leg in Chilliwack and watch how many fish the natives catch during there opening and see how many they waste! A little closer to home when there is a Native opening there are boats all the way from the mouth of the fraser up Abbotsford spaced 400' apart, and they are all claiming the fish is for personal use.

I have been an angler in the Fraser Valley for 20 years, and have seen the system abused by the natives the entire time. I applaud the people who refuse to buy fish from the natives now, but the DFO needs to step in and stop it the illegal activities by the natives, I want my grand kids to be able to catch fish the same way I am.

…If you are an angler you know they natives clean the rivers dry of all fish, lets do something to stop this.[2]

Non-native discussion of aboriginal fisheries is one of the areas which best reveals the colonial attitude and ignorance. The following is a transcription of an actual conversation held by a local, actually the author, and a visiting angler from Australia. The visitor was very well versed in the *lingua franca* of dismissing indigenous rights. His fishing buddy host jumped into the conversation once or twice.

Local: How did you enjoy your fishing trip out at Island 22?
Visitor: Ah it was lovely. Until the aboriginal fellows showed up.
L: Oh?
V: Yeah – there we were, casting our lines out, and they were going down the other side of the river in their boats. Now, that was fine. But then they started coming down our side – you know how they do. So we all had to reel in our line as fast as we could to avoid getting tangled in their nets! They could see we were all there, shoulder to shoulder with our lines out in the river, and still they took their boats right in front of us, across our lines!
L: Had you been catching the salmon there, on the edge of the gravel bar?
V: Oh yeah, it was great.
L: Maybe they crossed the river to get at the fish rather than just to upset you.
V: But we were there first!
L: Ah.
V: Well, that's not what I mean, but why should they come down the river while we were there?
L: Well, those fishermen have very limited openings. Maybe they were trying to go to where the fish were at that moment. Obviously you noticed where the fish were, that's why you were fishing there.
V: "Limited openings"? But they go fishing whenever they want!
L: Actually they have only a few openings for salmon each summer and they are very closely monitored by the Department of Fisheries and Oceans. In fact sometimes their openings are only for 12 hours at a time. They have to line up on the beach

in their boats and take turns drifting down the river, one after the other as close as possible. On the other hand, the recreational fishery is never closed.

V: It's not always open!

L: Name one time it's been posted closed to recreational fishing?

V: But it's not always open for retention. (ie, to keep the fish)

L: No, but the recreational fishery is never closed. And who monitors them? In the lower Fraser they have one or two monitors, who conduct a voluntary survey of catch history, for every 1,000 fishermen. In the interior the recreational fishery seems to have one monitor for every 10,000 square kilometers of the watershed. That's according to DFO's information, which is posted on their website. But the aboriginal fishery is closed unless posted otherwise.

V: Well, I've never heard of the aboriginal fishery being closed before. But the thing is, if they want to fish, they should just buy a license like everyone else.

L: They do have to buy licenses.

Fishing Buddy: No they don't, they get some kind of group aboriginal license and just do whatever they want.

L: It's true that each Reserve community is assigned a Communal Fishing License, but the Band has to regulate it by selling individual licenses, and they can only sell them to Band members or in some cases the husband of a Band member.

V: Well then why can't they just be regulated like we are?

L: They are fishing for food. They are practicing an economy which is culturally based. Anyway, I don't think you would like to be regulated the same way they are: their fisheries are monitored 28 days a week, by truck, foot patrol, boat and helicopter. I know a lot of people who have been arrested just for having a few fish in their possession. I know a guy who went to court with 101 charges under the *Fisheries Act*. The Chiefs advise the DFO that Elders will be fishing for a few food fish when the first sockeye run comes in, but still the officers go out and intercept them – even if it means ramming the Elder's vehicle.

FB: I've seen those guys out there when they have commercial openings for sockeye and whenever they catch pink salmon, they just kick it off the boats – it's brutal, it's disgusting. They're not fishing for food.

L: Have you ever been on a non-native commercial fishing boat when it's working?

FB: No, but they can't do that.

L: Of course they do it. Why else do you think environmental watchdogs post "bycatch statistics" from the commercial fisheries? Why do you think it's now a licensing condition in the Chinook salmon fishery to have a DFO inspector on board? It's to prevent "high grading" – that fishery is infamous for slashing the fish and throwing white meat overboard so it can fill its quota with red meat fish, which is more valuable.

V: But this is supposed to be an aboriginal fishery. They're supposed to just take what they need.

L: And how much do you think they need?

V: I don't know.

L: Well, neither does anyone else – except it's more than what they're getting right now. A few years ago, the last time there was a decent sockeye run in the 1990s, the commercial fishery took 20 million salmon; the recreational fishery took one million, and the aboriginal fisheries took half a million. But the Indian people are reluctant to bargain for some fixed number of fish because of the government's track record with numbers. I mean, for instance, they are still paying people from the Prairie Treaties $5 each year on treaty payment day.

V: Well, whatever they want, they should do it in an aboriginal way, but you see them going down the river in aluminum boats.

L: I don't think the aluminum is the issue; you're talking about people who used the rivers as highways. The old guys around here talk about roping two canoes together and ferrying cows across the Fraser River – they never lost a cow.

V: But they're using nylon filament nets!

L: So you're saying aboriginal people should only fish with cedar canoes and nets made of mesh that's spun from dog willow, like they used to?

V: Well...

L: Even if they wanted to, the Fraser Valley is so overdeveloped that they would have trouble finding enough plants to make a net. Where would they get it? And those cedars are at least as contentious as the fish these days.

V: Well, they could use cotton string, but they should have to use the traditional style of nets.

L: Our government outlawed the traditional nets over a hundred years ago.

V: Oh. What do you mean?

L: The traditional "nets" were weirs across the tributary streams, so we call that a selective fishery these days. If the run was low, they would take fish from a different stream. Incidentally, the top salmon biologists agree that kind of fishing is the only guaranteed sustainable kind of fishery, and we should be using that now instead of fishing in the ocean where the different stocks are mixed and endangered runs are being fished with abundant salmon runs. But the weir fisheries are still illegal.

V: Well then how can they have an "aboriginal right" to fish when they're using our gear, our materials, and our tools?

L: So... does that apply to me and my rights? Do you think I should only be allowed to drive a Model T Ford because that was the first car my ancestors in the USA ever had? And since then improved technologies have come from elsewhere in the world. But there is such a thing as the "right to development," you know.

V: But you can't claim a right to development AND aboriginal rights!

L: A person has to stop being aboriginal in order to use modern technology, or have the right to development?

V: Yes – if they want to be like the rest of us, fine: then be like the rest of us!

L: Does that mean I would no longer be Canadian if I used a computer made in Japan? Would I no longer be Canadian if I started to use denim jeans made in the USA out of cotton grown on plantations that were built by African slaves?

V: Well, we have trade agreements.

L: It seems to me the natives had plenty of trade agreements, not insignificantly with the first Europeans, over furs, but those went out the window when Europeans out-populated the indigenous. Then the settlers just took what they wanted. It seems to me that the government has imposed exactly the same condition on aboriginal people when it comes to trading with them that you have imposed on their fishing: they can only do it if they agree to be Canadians.

Incidentally, did you know that there is a Committee of the United Nations called "the Committee for Decolonization"?

V: No. Well, what would we do then? So we all have to go

back to Europe, all the white Australians? What would they
do with us?

L: I said the committee for "decolonization," not
"displacement."

V: Oh, no I didn't know about that committee.

After Law

> "The native agenda has taken us on a frightening journey through
> the looking glass where everything is backwards."
> —**Rafe Mair, in the Foreword to**
> ***Our Home OR Native Land?***
> **by Melvin Smith, 1995**

The relationship of the crown to the indigenous of what's now BC was proposed as one of protection from other perhaps less beneficent international forces. Two hundred years later it's hard to imagine any less beneficent influence than the one that has come to "protect" indigenous peoples here.

When lawyers like Geoff Plant don't agree that aboriginal title should be respected and further state that it does not exist and has never existed, but if it did it was extinguished by the presence of Englishmen;[3] or when they insist BC really does own it all outright, then what they are saying is that native people and their nations should die out and disappear. When people say "one law for Canadians," they are saying the same thing.

"Yeah, yeah, yeah, the courts say they have rights and title, and then they tell them to go negotiate," said former Premier Mike Harcourt, when asked to remark on the landmark decision and opinion given by Justice Vickers in 2007 regarding the Tsilhqot'in bid for a judicial declaration of Title. And that is exactly what they say every time a court rules on the presence of a right or the likelihood of title: they complete their reasons for judgment with the words "negotiate" and "reconcile."

Imagine a judge telling Rosa Parks that she did have the right to sit in the bus even if a white lady was standing, and that she should take this ruling home and negotiate with the town council for some sort of options in between, since the courts really had no way of balancing her interests with those of the white folk. What if the ruling was not enforced? Imagine a court finding that women did appear to be human beings and capable and worthy of voting in elections, but then stopped short of demanding an alteration to state voting procedures and merely recommending that women everywhere should go home and see how they could negotiate a settlement; or how they could reconcile their voting rights with the voting rights of men. What if the Constitution had affirmed "women's rights to equality" and left them undefined? Imagine a judge finds that one man is the rightful owner of land now in another man's possession, perhaps a tangle caused by some village surveyor's error, having drawn up the properties to overlap. What would happen if the judge told the two parties to go home and negotiate? They would say, the only reason we are in this courtroom, my lord, is because our case was admitted on the grounds that we can't agree on how to decide the result.

The Supreme Court is refusing to make a binding order on the government of Canada based on the constitutional law which the judge is sworn to uphold. Judges swear they will uphold the law, not the government, so their behaviour to the contrary suggests that Canada is not a rule of law society. Canadian judges have uniquely termed aboriginal title *sui generis,* anomalous, but the only thing unique about this situation is a foreign power taking over other nations' land, citizenry and governance; failing to enter into treaties or even terms of surrender; and then spending billions to invent a legal, and later historical, fiction to explain away their continued presence on unceded territories. It is not unique within the context of imperial history, but in modern times sanctions are usually placed by the international community against a state that does these things.

Many settlers have spared themselves the complicated rationalization process by simply leaping to the conclusion that assimilation and criminalization are the only avenues for native peoples, and simply maintain the original obtuse denial. Examples of this are ubiquitous throughout the province. Among British Columbians denial and dismissal of the indigenous are simply a way of life, and a static one at that. Infringement follows whatever delicately worded acknowledgment that trickles down from the Supreme Court, and indifference follows that. "Local officials have dismantled unauthorized (golf) courses at the Signal Hill Registered Archaeological Site twice this year, apparently reinstalled both times after first being decommissioned in 2010. ... The site was used as a winter home for the Wolf Clan of the Líl'wat Nation and is one of the oldest in the region..."[4] Non-native people rarely let rules about native peoples' rights get in the way of their preferred activities which might infringe those rights. In another example, Musqueam people have been protesting at one of their ancient gravesites in Vancouver for much of 2012 to try to prevent its desecration, having reached an impasse with developers, with little sympathy or result from the non-native population.[5]

Usually there isn't any press clipping to reference when discussing the active denial of indigenous rights. An instance: a landowner wishing to subdivide his property simply buries the evidence with a bulldozer when it becomes apparent that the heritage site is going to prevent the subdivision. There are a dozen or so pit-houses along the river, a traditional village—already noted by the public utility in their ancient map of heritage sites in the province. He hires a local railway engineer to produce a quasi-archaeological assessment, saying the pit houses along the river are wash basins used in early Chinese placer gold mining. A representative from the Archaeology branch visits, at the request of the local Tribal Council, and he documents the events. That includes the bulldozing which unintentionally exposed the black bits of hearth rock further confirming the buried houses below, but he never produces a report.[6] A fairly candid interview with the official who still hasn't filed was published in September, 2008. Clarifying how the BC's *Heritage Conservation Act* operates, he said:

> The Act is substantial. We have trouble with the Crown prosecutors, who won't prosecute for (contravention of) the Act. They say there is little likelihood of conviction, and that the case is not of enough public importance to go through the courts. …We have an initiative to get local governments to be more interactive with us, because Regional Districts are doing a lot of the development.
>
> We give Districts the site information we have, but most of them won't do the work. There's nothing under their Act that compels them to refer people to us. There is a legal question of whether their legislation can contradict ours. We rely on local governments to enact Heritage bylaws, but most Districts think it would inhibit development and give them more work.[7]

Ancient petroglyphs are blasted out of the way to access gravel quarries,[8] as the Arch. Branch has trouble making Regional Districts comply with the legislation. Prosecutors are sure that the issue is not of any public importance. The *Heritage Act* allows for penalties up to a million dollars and two years in jail. When points of spectacular importance are acknowledged, like the great village rock of the Sto:lo at Xáytem, the Sto:lo Tribal Council was forced to grant other concessions—in this case, the gravel quarry at Agassiz, in order to protect the heritage site which has met the proofs required by government.

It would be nice to hope that these are accidents or exceptions to the settlers' behavior: just the rare rough edge of native versus newcomer conflict. But that hope recedes before the impunity with which these acts are carried out, and the theme of repetition since contact. That hope wilts in the headlights of BC's oncoming plans and especially in the damp drizzle of non-native activism that poses no obstacle to them. The province cannot seem to get beyond insincerity.

Superiority and Schizophrenia

> "Sometimes you wake up and realize everything you think is crazy. And if you want to know the truth, you have to accept that what most people think is crazy. "
>
> **—Amiri Baraka,**
> from *The LeRoi Jones / Amiri Baraka Reader*

It is well accepted in general psychiatry that extreme denial will produce an alternative—an unpredictable and uncontrollable – signal; the double-signal response. It is regularly displayed socially, for instance when someone says "yes" while shaking their head. British Columbians give off double signals about Indians; maybe a sort of schizoid response to their denial of the indigenous.

It is not unfair to use the term *schizophrenia* in connection with BC settler behaviour. The use of indigenous artifacts, legend, artwork and so on in popular consumer culture confounds the same culture's derision of the indigenous peoples that actually created those works. There is no tourist shop in British Columbia that does not announce itself with native designs and the words "Native Art." As put best and most succinctly by Lavina White, Thowgwelth, of Haida, "They like our culture, art, dancing and songs; they like our lands—they just don't like *us*."

What effect has their media's placement of newcomer society as beyond reproach and intrinsically correct, however inconsistently and inexplicably and unsubstantially, had on that society? One result is what George Orwell observed in the 1950s: they seem not to care if they are making sense.[9] The media's portrayal of the dominating culture as democratic, "first world," advanced, even privileged, has not helped international understanding. The new people must assert perpetual righteousness, or risk lack of definition. How could they be wrong, when they clearly have the authority to make all the decisions? How could they be in that position if they were not naturally superior? If they aren't what the media tells them they are, what are they?

If they are not the beneficent and logically superior race, the triumphant race their history books describe, how are the new people supposed to understand themselves? How many British Columbians would question a quite comfortable role, no matter how stark the contrast between the popular portrayal and their witnessing of the abused, dependant, impoverished and self-destructive Indians?

What do British Columbians have to say to native people about these circumstances today? Timothy Renshaw, the editor of *Business In Vancouver,* constantly regresses to such spam as "They're still sucking the government teat." Politicians like Chuck Strahl, a Member of Parliament for two decades running, get into a media-supported you-scream-I-scream frenzy with readers and letter writers: "There should be one law for all Canadians!" This unfortunate level of ignorance is displayed in disproportionately large fervor to the very small importance aboriginal people are allowed in an otherwise racially segregated "broader society." The imbalance gives away some kind of illicit obsession, or, at best, use of a scapegoat in textbook-style addict/enabler family psychology. From *cboo44,* commenting on the online *Tyee*:

"The residential school experience has left a far-reaching and painful legacy. Its impact on parenting was one of the more serious outcomes." And worst of all, has provided a ready-made excuse for failure as parents. It has also provided the "native industry" of chiefs, elders, lawyers, advisors, etc a very lucrative income. Did you know that "claims" by residential school attendees are a very small minority of those who actually attended? Did you know that 30% of those claims are fraudulent, brought by those who NEVER attended, but have been "coached" and encouraged by others to "get free money"? Never mind the excuses, concentrate on education, self-respect and personal responsibility. That works.[10]

Commenting on the same article, *snert* gives us: "What tends to happens is that residential schooling becomes the scapegoat for everything that ails native society today and it's not." *Alive* gives us: "All I see is people dancing and chanting, evoking spirits and what not. Again let us realize that "indian problem" or not something had to be done, since you lagged centuries behind the rest of the population!"[11]

Occasionally contradictions to these prevailing attitudes are posted alongside them, but they are very outnumbered. Indigenous people cannot be heard by non-native Canadians: their voices are made crazy by the popular "sensibility" reflected in the quotes above. There can be no mistaking that the public is not listening for something more, something different.

A series of four talks was presented in early 2012 at the Vancouver Public Library by a coalition of Amnesty International, Hul'qumi'num Treaty Group and Lawyers Rights Watch—"First Nations' Rights: The Gap Between Law and Practice." Robert Morales, lawyer and chief negotiator for the Hul'qumi'num Treaty Group, opened the series to less than a one-third capacity crowd in the McKay Room, which has 240 seats in it, on a dreary Thursday night in February. Half the crowd was sponsor organizers, the speaker's entourage, and a dozen people also involved in a Petition to the Organization of American States—the subject of the talk. which was free of charge.[12]

On the third speaking date, Kenneth Deer, founder of *The Eastern Door* newspaper and surely the most successful native newspaperman of his time in Canada, spoke to an equally small audience about his twenty-five years working on the United Nations Declaration on the Rights of Indigenous Peoples.[13] The questions mustered by the humble crowds were clearly not those of an informed, opinionated elite. Deer was asked, rather brutally off-point, "Are you optimistic about the population explosion that's happening in indigenous communities across Canada?" and, "I heard some group in

Manitoba wants to talk to Iran about human rights. What's that about?" and, "Are the World Intellectual Property Organization talks going on right now just going to take another thirty years?" and, "You know, when I was out picking tobacco on the Mohawk Reserve and we parked our VW van in their field…". Morales faired perhaps worse: "Your united nations have never become part of our Constitution and I hope that never happens." "I've lived here for ten years and I never knew there was a problem like this." From one of the young legal crowd: "Why do you think the government is not implementing your rights?"

The second speaker in the lawyers' library series was not an indigenous person and was speaking about her new book, which asks the question: are Canadian courts still colonially biased? She had devised a points system to answer that question for each of the cases investigated, as if some decisions give the appearance of bias more than others. While this line of inquiry avoids the more fundamental question of whether the courts themselves are even capable of giving impartial hearings and rulings about their own competitors for legitimacy, the indigenous, that talk was full to overflowing with an up and coming legal crowd that must already knows the limit of criticism permitted in the industry.

British Columbians as a group can be less than permeable when receiving news they wish they hadn't. In early 1998, *The Vancouver Sun* ran the front page headline: *BC Indian chiefs lay claim to entire province, resources.* It was a response to the *Delgamuukw* ruling, where the Supreme Court of Canada had pointed out that British Columbia had never extinguished aboriginal title by any Constitutional means. The first lines of the article read, "The provincial government is reviewing a demand by the First Nations Summit for an immediate freeze on any development of land resources anywhere in British Columbia. BC's native Indians are laying claim to every tree, every rock, every fish and every animal in the province."[14] At the end of 2012, the same newspaper ran the front page headline: *First Nations hold veto over resource development.*[15] The article began by saying, "Governments and corporate Canada remain in denial about a new reality: aboriginal groups hold veto power over resource development." Perhaps it is also denial which allows the same news to make headlines at fifteen year intervals.

The denial of indigenous peoples' land and sovereignty rights which the newcomers have found necessary in order to benefit by taking their homelands has, however, put other valuable contributions which indigenous peoples would have probably shared, out of reach. The world views, cosmologies, languages, insight and spiritual wealth native to the indigenous must also be denied to keep up the lie, though, as the performance at the 2010 Olympics demonstrated, Canada still likes to show off the surface layer of indigenous culture to the world as part of *Canada's* unique identity. British

Columbians do not know what they are losing by extinguishing aboriginal title and the peoples dependent on respect for it—to say nothing of what the indigenous peoples themselves are losing—because British Columbians still know almost nothing about them. They could know, as Lorna Williams pointed out, and could do something to save those precious resources: "And the average Canadian must begin to see that the languages of this land exist nowhere else in the world and, when they settled here and became Canadian, all these languages became a part of their heritage."[16] Are we at the point now where such a speaker will say, "could have become"?

The cultural riches in question are undreamed of by the displaced non-native people in BC. While the Vancouver International airport is decorated with over-sized jade and cedar sculptures of creation myths, few British Columbians would be able to render a version of the stories they represent. While international travel magazines parade the beautiful regalia used in ceremonial dances, there is no regard for the grueling effort, the spiritual and personal forces, or the community investment of trust that traditionally enfranchise the wearer.

The truth of these peoples is compelling. Native people hunted whales with shell knives. They ran down deer on foot. They made canoes out of cedar trees 16 feet in diameter—by hand. Crippled old ladies could suddenly jump and dance when ceremony was in progress; there are places in the mountains where the rock bowl is hollowed because of young men who went to train as medicine people and danced there through the winter; there is an island in the lake that turns upside down when a certain wind blows. People have cured themselves of cancers using medicine from trees and roots. Some Elders will tell the story of the first time they saw a white man, as a child trading fish for some milk at a certain place while their parents paddled upriver to get a deer. Some of them will grimace and reluctantly tell you that their grandfather would instruct them to boil the water, and he would be back with a deer he spotted across the river—before the pot had begun to steam.

The people were never as desperate as they are now. Native people can revive memories of what it meant to be self-sufficient during the Dirty Thirties, hauling wood and vegetables to the white town. Some will want to note how they and their children shoveled miles of snow off the road so the school bus could get through, so important was the promise of education – and so capable the seeker.

When Judge Begbie described the St'át'imc of 1858 in his *Journey into the Interior*,[17] as even the least of them being superior to white men of better stature, he was either unwilling or incapable of identifying those good people as part of a society—organized, sophisticated, pious, independent, and in possession of their homeland: recognized by their neighbours and firm in their ability to hold it. The good people were the product of good countries. The people and leaders he met were worthy of respect, capable of cooperation, and indeed so confident and generous of spirit that they made his travels possible. These observations do not inform the public attitude.

The lethargy which characterizes human rights developments in BC has been protected from these truths and excused by now silver-haired myth-makers. The old fall-back position is, "well these people emigrated here same as us, across the Bering Land Bridge, just before us, that's all." Such wishful thinking has blurred myth and reality.

But racism and 'socio-economic mores,' are being outpaced by science however. "We're finding the opposite of what people expected. The Raven Bluff points are younger than Clovis, so it may be that they did not originate in the north, but came from the south." So says archaeologist Jeff Rasic on finding evidence contrary to the Bering Land Bridge theory in Alaska.[19]

North American creation stories and ancient histories are present in every tribe. Contradictions to every popular stereotype are readily available—if a settler would ever talk to an Indian. If they would take this simple step, even attend a native gathering or celebration or public event of any kind instead of complaining that the indigenous don't often participate in settler culture, they might learn something.

On August 25, 2010, Chief Wayne Christian, Secwepemc, spoke at the centennial anniversary of the unanswered Memorial to Sir Wilfred Laurier. The event was organized by the Shuswap Nation Tribal Council and open to all. Chief Christian laid it out as follows:

> One hundred years ago, our leaders put down a path of words for us. Today, we need to think about what it means to put down a path for the next one hundred years.
>
> At that time, the Canadian government responded to us with legislation to imprison our people if they went off the Reserve to gather food; they made it mandatory for our children to go off to residential school; they made it illegal for people to gather to meet about the land question; and they criminalized us for practicing our potlatch and singing our songs. The response today is no different.
>
> We need to go out and make a way for our people. We need to do to the government as they do to us and ignore their laws. Their laws and their customs don't apply here. We have our lands, our laws, our culture and our own people. And we will rely on those.
>
> We can no longer wait for them to respond to us. We will do what we need to do to protect our land, our children, and the fish and animals. Our children can't wait another

one hundred years with the atrocities foisted on us—we can't wait any longer.

It's time to take action, people.

If the indigenous peoples can continue to survive, and to have a chance at maintaining their land-based culture, language and knowledge, they will need the people of BC to do something different. The people of BC will need to think something different, act different, and elect a different kind of government: one that is committed to getting assistance in extricating itself from being in the conflicted position of making decisions about how to adjust the outstanding matters of jurisdiction and ownership as if they alone could decide.

Presently a wave of resistance is answering the most recent attempt of the federal government to debit Indian Status, just as it did in 1912, 1969, 1986, 1990, etcetera. The Idle No More movement has repeated the pattern of earlier expressions of resistance and attracted the support of some non-native people. The first order of business, they have discovered, is to educate those supporters. Teach-ins quickly rose to the top of the agenda among supporters, with a parallel campaign shaping up under the banner of Idle? Know More.

Post-Historic Man

"British Columbia needs no history, goes a common refrain. We are a province of the present looking to the future. To the extent that we seek out meaning, we have a geography that is bigger than life to sustain us. ... I don't agree. Some of us are recent arrivals, others have been here much longer. For those of us who are Aboriginal, that time is so far back in the mists of the past that it is lost to us as individuals and as peoples."

—*British Columbia Needs No History. Or Does It?* by Jean Barman, Professor of History at UBC[20]

Unlike the non-native BC historian quoted above, indigenous people do not say that their histories are "so far back in the mists of the past" that they are lost to them. But the world of states constructed by peoples with the written word has made countries out of their lands—member states of the United Nations – instead; in some cases out of penal colonies. The ancients are obscured and denied: the nations of Auteroa and Tasmania; the independent Ainu, Iroquois, Maasai; the several Mayan, Saami, Kuna and Igbo tribes; and so many others have been denied recognition wherever they are by invaders from near and far.

The notion of pre-historic man has been tried-on by different schools of anthropologists. Some will call the North American indigenous peoples of the Northwest Pacific Coast "pre-historic" in those times before he or she was exposed to trade in iron points with Russian fur traders—guessed to be about 250 years ago by non-native anthropologists, but an unknown time. Some would discriminately ascribe the label, aside from the iron points, to those people who did not record themselves or their history by writing on paper.

What do we call the people of today? Historic Man? But we have already called those before us by this name. And we clearly wish to separate ourselves from them, leaving any and all culpability for today's crises in their hands. What would we call ourselves, who speak of history when convenient and at other times say, "that's history": Post-Historic Man? While we are capable of writing ourselves down, we do so extremely selectively. We neither learn from history nor admit our present role in it. We don't try to heal from the past because we deny our connection to it.

Our anthropologists are not in the business of turning their scientifically rational characterizations and labels of "others" back on their own societies so methodically. Perhaps the average citizen can do it.

Canada has a clever solution to the indigenous histories and presents which compete with those of the colony: the Section 35 Solution. Section 35 of Canada's Constitution says there are aboriginal and treaty rights, but requires that each asserted right be tested in the colonizer's less-than-impartial court, at exorbitant cost to the indigenous plaintiff, that the tests be developed continually and made increasingly exclusive, and the resulting, narrowly defined practice be deposited in the otherwise "empty black box" of that Constitutional chapter.

Canada is, according to lawyer Janice Switlo,

> ...establishing new international customary law of dealing with Indigenous Peoples through a pioneered scheme of domestic/municipal aboriginal and treaty rights based on the Canadian example within the section 35 framework of the *Constitution Act, 1982* whereby justification for infringement of such a right where a valid object exists can be lawful provided the government is clear about what it is doing to the right, consults and pays compensation where it is considered fair to do so. To this end, Supreme Court of Canada justices and others are visiting other parts of the world, such as Israel, to encourage governments to come on board with Canada in order to broaden the practice so that over time it can be fully implemented internationally.[21]

Canada is trying to adjust the international standard and drag it down to its own level. Big financial support for the protracted negotiation of the United Nations Declaration on the Rights of Indigenous Peoples (UNDRIP) has afforded twenty-five years of this state's favoured "talk and log" delay tactic in the face of human rights problems. In a radical about-turn, after the whole UNDRIP had passed the Human Rights Council, Canada began mustering a little loyal opposition in the form of African representatives to the UN General Assembly—the word is that aid payments were threatened in the case of their "yes" vote to approve the Declaration.[22] And perhaps Canada will support a continuing process through the Permanent Forum on Indigenous Issues, which may remain Permanent until there are no more qualifying delegates in the country to attend it.

When Canada voted against the Declaration on September 13, 2007, its Ambassador to the United Nations, John McNee, said,

> We have stated publicly that we have significant concerns with respect to the wording of the current text, including the provisions on lands, territories and resources; free, prior and informed consent when used as a veto; self-government without recognition of the importance of negotiations; intellectual property; military issues; and the need to achieve an appropriate balance between the rights and obligations of indigenous peoples, member States and third parties.
>
> For example, the recognition of indigenous rights to lands, territories and resources is important to Canada. Canada is proud of the fact that Aboriginal and treaty rights are given strong recognition and protection in its Constitution. We are equally proud of the processes that have been put in place to deal with Aboriginal claims respecting these rights and are working actively to improve these processes to address these claims even more effectively. Unfortunately, the provisions in the Declaration on lands, territories and resources are overly broad, unclear, and capable of a wide variety of interpretations, discounting the need to recognize a range of rights over land and possibly putting into question matters that have been settled by treaty.
>
> By voting against the adoption of this text, Canada puts on record its disappointment with both the substance and process. For clarity, we also underline our understanding that this Declaration is not a legally binding instrument. It has no legal effect in Canada, and its provisions do not represent customary international law.

In an early 2008 statement delivered to a meeting of the Organization of American States Working Group to Prepare the Draft American Declaration on the Rights of Indigenous Peoples in Washington DC, the Canadian Government declared it would no longer actively participate in negotiations on that Declaration. If the final document "does not adequately address Canada's concerns", Canada has indicated that it would attempt to block consensus unless two conditions are met: the document adopted clearly indicates that Canada does not support it and that there is an explicit understanding that the text therefore does not apply to Canada.[23]

Regular visitors to international fora on indigenous issues report from Europe that when Canadians show up to tell everyone how wonderful life in Canada is for indigenous people, it seems that only the Canadian delegates themselves believe what they are saying. This is political posturing on the part of Canada, and some countries appear to be dabbling with the two-faced Canadian model. Other countries, like Bolivia, Ecuador, Venezuela and Brazil, are trying legal pluralism within their Supreme Courts and alternatively granting recognition of indigenous ownership to large tracts of land – tracts big enough to make a difference to their land-based survival, not tiny real estate packages like the ones being negotiated in the BC treaty process.

Canada has been in violation of the Genocide Convention, 1948; the International Covenant on Economic, Social and Cultural Rights, 1976; the International Covenant on Civil and Political Rights, of the same year; just to name the more modern ones. Earlier Canada was sheltered by Great Britain. For example, when a Haudenoshone delegate to the League of Nations in 1923 was planning to criticize Canada, he was prevented from speaking by The Imperial Representatives of England.

But with the winks and the nudges of the rest of the State parties to those pieces of international common law, Canada was named the number one country in the world by the UN Economic and Social Council's human development index. Canada still is a member of the UN Human Rights Council. Canadian judges, Louise Arbour for example, are propelled to and entrusted at such pinnacles of ruthless power as would make Napoleon Bonaparte whimper. Arbour named Slobodan Milosevic a war criminal, thus allowing the member air forces of NATO to bomb Yugoslavia back to the industrial revolution. Her promise to hold NATO accountable as well was derailed by an offer to serve as a Justice in the Supreme Court of Canada. The judge led the International Criminal Court and held in her hands the fate of men who, returning from American training camps, shot the President of Rwanda out of the sky and became the government of Rwanda. Canadian military men, such as Lieutenant General Charles Bouchard, lead NATO assaults to depose international leaders of states which are Members in otherwise Good Standing of the United Nations. Indigenous nations are not members of the UN, and Canada is intent on keeping it that way. States will decide what's best for them.

Is this future, this state-controlled indigenous future, tied to that of British Columbians?

The New Deal

> The province established a New Relationship policy, but details are still being worked out.
>
> In March 2005 British Columbia met with the First Nations Summit, the Union of B.C. Indian Chiefs and the B.C. Assembly of First Nations to develop new approaches to consultation and accommodation. This consultation resulted in a vision for a "New Relationship" that would include: developing a new government-to-government relationship with First Nations; and establishing new processes and structures for coordination of the management and use of land and resources.
>
> In September 2005, the Premier of British Columbia made a historical speech to the First Nations Summit. He acknowledged Aboriginal rights—the first time any British Columbia premier had done so—with the following statement: "For too long ... we did follow a path of denial. There was a denial of rights, of culture, of opportunity and equality ... The First Nations and Aboriginal people of Canada have been failed, and we must move forward to rectify that."[24]

In 2009, the provincial government had maneuvered the First Nations Leadership Council, comprised of the three provincial native organizations, into the position of conducting consultations with indigenous peoples on the proposed provincial Recognition and Reconciliation Act. The First Nations Leadership Council's work together has been uninspired, and this strange piece of legislation whose passage they attempted to grease was intercepted by traditionalists who demanded to hear what it was about before the leaders rubber stamped it for the provincial government. Initially the Leadership Council executive had no plan to inform their membership about it.[25] A total of eight public forums were eventually held to hear feedback on the very few details that were disclosed. Few people have ever read the proposed Act since it was never made public after being rejected. This response from Chief Ron West was typical of the community people's view of the Leadership Council's Act:

Dear Mr. Campbell:

I am writing this letter to give you notice that the undersigned Hereditary Chiefs of the Ned'u'ten Nation oppose any attempt by the provincial government to create legislation such as the proposed Recognition and Reconciliation Act. We are located around the Babine Lake area and we own and have jurisdiction of our traditional territories. We have not consented to this initiative. It is our opinion that the province does not have the jurisdiction to make such laws. The BC First Nation Leadership Council does not represent our clans or territories, therefore they cannot represent to you that they have our approval for the proposed legislation. Enacting such legislation would be intended Crown conduct that would interfere with our inherent rights, traditional governing and land systems. ... The majority of our Hereditary Chiefs do not know anything about the proposed legislation that the BC First Nations Leadership Council has been working on.[26]

New deals appear in fresh clothes as often as leading brand names change their commercials. The Certainty of Land Title Act promised to make individuals on Reserve the fee-simple owners of their homes and yards—so that people who have lived a good half century in abject poverty and without much of an employment record can get mortgages on their houses. This is a repetition of countless enfranchisement schemes from 1857 to the middle of the twentieth century, some of them involving the buy-out of farms that native World War One veterans had built up before the war; some simply a way out of the Indian Act—but all of them resulting in the renunciation of identity and internationally recognized legal rights.

In 2011 Premier Christy Clark announced that she would not be placing all her eggs in the BC Treaty Commission basket, and that she would be happy to simply engage First Nations in benefits sharing and impact agreements rather than get bogged down by the larger issues. We know that the appetite for dollars from any source among the impoverished communities could easily overwhelm the long-held vision of independence and dignity cherished by previous generations, who were still benefiting from healthy salmon runs, forests, wildlife and birds that weren't Blue Listed as endangered species.

Barbara Fisher, former British Columbia Treaty Commission member, in a presentation at the University of Victoria Faculty of Law in 1998, suggested that a final treaty may never actually be made if the interim agreements provide a suitable working basis for reconciling jurisdiction issues. British Columbia's interest is in business as usual—not justice.

"The New Deal" is virtually an annual event in British Columbia. Every now and then politicians forget this and get swept up in their own propaganda, thinking this year's New Deal is really it. They sometimes release pent guilt in the mistaken belief that the New Deal they are promoting will really absolve them. Former Prime Minister Brian Mulroney, in support of the 2005 Kelowna Accord, could even put it baldly: "We've existed for 140 years and we have this shameful situation…and why? Very simple. We stole their land."[27]

Mulroney might have known better than to speak too soon. When he was Prime Minister of Canada and formed the government in 1984, he pursued his election promise of tightening the budget and had Eric Nielsen make some recommendations. The report came in 1986, it recommended cuts to many areas of federal funding via the Department of Indian Affairs putting many of its costs on to provinces, and Mulroney's government presented it to media with bows on and happy enthusiasm. Indian leaders rejected it almost as loudly as the White Paper Policy of 1969. In the retractive scramble, David Crombie, Mulroney's Minister of Indian Affairs, called the report "the entrails of policies which have been found in the wastebasket of the bureaucracy."[28] That statement is of course the farthest possible from the truth.

Canada's Budget 2012 and some supporting legislation has hoved into view in nearly identical effect to the vision Mr. Nielsen laid out a quarter century before.

The indigenous continue to attempt communication while holding off government cuts with one arm and resource extraction companies with the other, as in the following press release:

> Negotiations between BC and the Tsilhqot'in came to an abrupt halt late last week when the Province of BC failed to make an interim offer for an out of court agreement as recommended by a BC Supreme Court Judge. Chief Marilyn Baptiste, Xeni Gwet'in said "We expected a substantial offer we could take to our communities starting next week. We will still be meeting with our people, but the agenda has dramatically been altered.
> Instead we will relay the message of betrayal once again."

The Supreme Court of BC ruled in *Tsilhqot'in Nation v. British Columbia* gave a non-binding judicial opinion that the Tsilhqot'in had proved aboriginal title to the Nemiah trap line area. The Justice also opined that the Tsilhqot'in had extensive aboriginal rights outside the title area.[29]

Beyond Insincerity

> *"BC is like a chronically unfaithful husband. He cheats on his wife*
> *every day and twice on Sundays, then one day comes home and says,*
> *'honey, I've changed,' while at the same time he's texting his girlfriend.*
> *They are in the business of denial. That is the basis of BC."*
> **—Lawyer Murray Brown, Woodward and Company,**
> **speaking on the possibility of sincerity in British Columbia's**
> **proposed Recognition and Reconciliation Act,**
> **at the All Chiefs Assembly, North Vancouver, August 25, 2009**

Whether we start at the beginning of this trans-planetary relationship, where the coastal people occasionally made a point of scuttling ships along with their crew who were trying to cheat them in extortionist trading practices, or go further up to the interior a few decades later where NWCo and then HBC traders were accepting furs at one five hundredth of what they would sell them for in profit and selling axes with edges nearly half an inch thick,[30] or whether we come quickly to today and see deals like the Chehalis' 3% annuity on provincial stumpage fees collected in their territory, it is time to adjust the record.

Whether it is white writers collecting and besmirching indigenous histories in Ottawa, Victoria or Vancouver; be they "academic" or wage labour in daily or weekly journals—truth needs to be let into the room so it can flush them out. Whether it is the fraud of the BC Treaty Commission or the financial satisfaction of a few privileged leaders at the expense of their communities, the pressure created by denial should be removed from this situation.

To get beyond insincerity, every deal-making and treaty-making institution now in play in the province would have to be exposed. There is no deal. There is no "modern day treaty" that is worth the paper it's written on. It requires total complicity with the neo-academics who drawl that native people never had any land claims until white people told them they did. But the Indian Industry, Francis Widdowson's "aboriginal industry," never served native peoples; just the consultants.

Those who laud the BC treaty process invariably parrot the refrain, as per Justice Lamer in the Delgamuukw ruling, and BC's New Relationship Act, that 'we are all here to stay.'[31] By this, they mean that no private property will be bargained with in satisfying the land needs of indigenous peoples. They mean: non-native society is going to maintain the standard of living to which it has grown accustomed and no human rights issues are going to stop them. This, in a phrase, is insincerity. Every single prime location in every single indigenous nation in British Columbia features privately owned settler structures, homes, ranches, towns; if not high-density low-rise condos, heavy industry, or light-footprint eco-lodges. They are not prime locations because of settler development, but because of natural assets: suited to agriculture; close to drinking water; rich in fish or wildlife; accessible by water route or trail; furnished by natural wonder such as hotsprings or agreeable winter climate – all of which were nurtured and protected by the indigenous nations who called them home.

The indigenous leaders put their openness to reconciliation more categorically. Victor Jim, a Wet'suwet'en Chief, said after the 1997 *Delgamuukw* ruling, "Our chiefs have always said that we have to live with our neighbours. We're not going to kick anybody off the land. We were here before the white man came, the sharing is going to have to continue, but we're going to have a more focused working relationship."[32] The Haida matriarch Lavina White spoke at conferences and meetings and assemblies and told thousands of listeners, "We feel that there are not enough good trees left to build enough boats to send you all home. We understand that you want to live here."

Reconciliation

> *"Brother you're right you're right you're right you're right*
> *you're... so right."*
> **—Bob Marley, Jamaica**

> *"We want restitution, reparation, restoration and compensation."*
> **—Arnold Virgil Williams, Líl'wat**

Until non-native people living in British Columbia can find affinity with native people, can find empathy or even interest, there is no chance for the 30 or so nations trapped in those borders claimed by BC and defended by Canada to assert their God-given rights to maintain their lands and peoples.

Until the seventh generation Oriental, (East) Indian and European settlers; the first generation Asian, Chinese, European, Persian and African settlers can wholeheartedly align themselves with those peoples whose country they have taken over, and cause their government to act properly, there is no hope in the world for these indigenous languages, world views, and creation stories; nor for the peoples.

How will non-natives get the chance to understand, to appreciate, to care about the indigenous nations crumpling under the wheels of their progress? As long as their popular media is subsidized by the resource extraction interests, it seems improbable. As long as their government relies on revenue from those same resource licenses—and the government controls the school curriculum and pays for it with the revenues from those licenses—it seems implausible. But do British Columbians perceive or appreciate these workings? Has that same media and "educational" indoctrination also deprived them of a sense of belonging in their own politics? Have the playwrights of the day failed to point up the most relevant challenges, subsidized as they most meaningfully are by a *Canadian* Council for the Arts? Has the Canadian Broadcasting Corporation left any window unlocked for the breeze of the times to riffle the average educated consciousness?

There is no popular British Columbian literature that lifts and falls on the pulse of an objective reality here. There is little accessible journalism that reports the human crisis of the day. There is no school curriculum in the province that registers with an accurate account of history. There are no popular works of art, no TV sitcoms, no poetic journals that remark on those few who work for others to go logging on their homelands so they can pay for their airfare to United Nations forums where Indigenous Issues are welcomed.

Some people say the token payouts of compensation—in exchange for the land itself as well going to the provincial government—are good, because it means the province acknowledges the native title. That is a strained assertion. Those payouts are seeking to assert that native title has thereby been quieted. Another says the recent settlement agreements between the province and First Nations, such as those made with BC Hydro, are a great thing, because it is better than any other settlement agreement signed so far in the province. If that sort of logic prevails, it leaves BC with hundreds of years of negotiating final agreements before it gets into serious or even reasonable reparations. But how would the indigenous survive more centuries of the Indian Act and extinguishment policies?

The Supreme Court of Canada uses the word "reconciliation" in the following context: "reconcile aboriginal titles with the crown title." Perhaps that won't be possible in Canada, as one of the parties to the reconciliation would be the judge of what is a satisfactory outcome. Perhaps the reconciliation that is required is for British Columbians to reconcile themselves with larger laws; perhaps The Golden Rule, where one does not do to another that which one would not want done to himself. The reconciliation which is really being asked of non-native people living in British Columbia, in any of the thirty unsurrendered indigenous nations, is an action of self-doubt: am I doing the right thing? They will no doubt find assistance in international courts.

It's not that the problem of a genocidal state has never happened before, never been apprehended and forced to reform. Work has been done to try to answer the problems, but the question itself has never really been raised loudly enough. There are many possible answers. Solutions tend to be less pleasant as the offending country waits longer and longer and forces other countries to intervene.

It's time that British Columbians tried some untested feasibilities. There are several suggested strategies in circulation, for native and non-native. Arthur Manuel, addressing native people, suggests:

What We Need To Do:
Stop Negotiating under the Modified Rights Model to force new policies that recognize indigenous sovereignty and Aboriginal and Treaty rights
Quit Economically Subsidizing Canada by buying into their exclusive control over our land and resources
Convert our Contingent Liability into real decision making and cash benefit to our peoples
Use International Human Rights and Economic Pressure To Achieve Recognition and Coexistence of Aboriginal and Treaty Rights.[33]

Bruce Clark, addressing non-native courts, writes:

THE REMEDIES FOR ENFORCING THE LAW

(30). The first remedy is: applications for declarations of law alone in national courts outside of North America, based upon the "universal extraterritorial jurisdiction" to prevent genocide-in-progress arguably attributable to "judicial inactivity" within North America, each declaration consisting of a finding that the national court in question shares that universal jurisdiction and a recommendation that the courts of North America address their own constitutional law. This in essence happened in relation to Guatemala in Central America in *Menchu v. Montt,* September 26, 2006, Constitutional Court of Spain, BOE Supplement, October 28, 2005, Sentence 237/2005.

(31). The second remedy is: an application by one or more Organs of the United Nations for an advisory opinion from the International Court of Justice as to whether the Organs and Agencies of the United Nations are bound by the "non-selectivity" resolution of the General Assembly, not to apply or collaborate in applying the *Convention for the Prevention and Punishment of the Crime of Genocide, 1948,* to the militarily and economically weak State Parties while at the same time neglecting to apply it to the mighty State Parties. General Assembly, A/RES/60/251, dated March 15, 2006.

(32). The third remedy is: an action in contract brought in the International Court of Justice by one or more of the State Parties to both the *Statute of the International Court of Justice* and to the international convention of the "great maritime powers of Europe" engaged in the original occupation of the Americas. *Worcester v. State of Georgia,* 6 Peters U.S. Supreme Court Reports 515 (1832).

(33).The fourth remedy is: an action in contract brought in the International Court of Justice by one or more of the State Parties to the *Nuclear Non-Proliferation Treaty* based upon the fundamental breach of that contract by the United States of America, seeking injunctive relief against the genocidally selective application of the broken contract by the breaching Party's implementation of military and/or economic sanctions.[34]

There are many resolutions promoted by academics, Conservatives, politicians and members of the public as well. They are not all so comprehensive or considered. From a UBC professor of geography:

Nonetheless, the rulings in *Haines* and, to a lesser extent, in *Quipp* recognize a degree of Indigenous control over traditional territories. Resources within those territories may be shared with others, but rights of access are to be the product of negotiation and consent. This is a model to which Canadian governments should aspire.[35]

In summary, Douglas Harris' recommendation appears to be to accept the paramountcy of the existing courts and implement their decisions; ignore Constitutional law and the rule of law and the glaring question of who has jurisdiction on unceded lands; and carry on with the political negotiations in *David v. Goliath* style, where one side is impoverished by the thieving of the other, who happens to be financing and judging the contest.

George Erasmus, National Chief of the Assembly of First Nations in 1989 suggested a formula at that time. He listed priorities as starting with re-opening the process of Constitutional reform and inviting aboriginal participation. Then fulfillment of treaties in a spirit that takes account of a land tenure system that was in play before crown title was imposed. Constitutional protection of self-government practices; increased resources to land claims negotiations and settlements; indigenous control of indigenous education; tribal courts for tribal peoples; all these are parts of his prescription.[36]

A lawyer who quit BC law on account of her view that the courts don't have jurisdiction over Indians on unceded lands, Lyn Crompton, wrote,

I urge those of us involved in the administration of justice to increase our awareness of the international human rights of Indigenous peoples in a timely fashion. This will result in the creation of an internationally overseen, mutually agreed upon, mediation style resolution process. A mechanism built on a cross cultural foundation would profoundly enhance the impartiality of the process, something that is essential for the resolution of outstanding issues between Indigenous nations and the dominant society comprising the Canadian nation.[37]

If we wish for the law to play a role in the inevitable decolonization process, each participant in the Canadian legal system must confront his or her contribution to sustaining colonialism. Practitioners and judiciary alike must undertake to increase their awareness of the breach of both domestic and international law that flows from their non-consensual usurpation of the jurisdiction of the original inhabitants over their territory.[38]

In conjunction, law schools must be required to revamp their curriculum so as to replace the current domestic colonial approach with that of an international perspective, in recognition of the inherent right of Indigenous nations to self-determination on their traditional lands.[39]

What if, in British Columbia, the people decided *not* to continue to commit crimes of genocide? What if the BC Treaty Commission admitted that it's not realistic to demand repayment of negotiating loans which often amount to half of the Settlement Transfer? What if the BC Treaty Commission insisted on negotiations which did not result in violations of international human rights law? What if the province was excluded from direct negotiations which have international stature and are therefore between nations – not between communities and provinces?

What if students graduating from high school were fluent in the history of indigenous dispossession, actual legal instruments, and the crux of the modern land debacle? What if graduates of the public school could define "the rule of law"? What if students had the opportunity to learn the local indigenous language in their public school, and funding was actually allocated to develop teaching materials and curriculum for those languages?

What if BC supported aboriginal nations' petitions for a third party, independent and impartial tribunal instead of trying to discredit them? What if stricter environmental protections were brought about so that the downward slide of species on the brink of extinction could be curbed? What if BC stopped licensing developments in the remaining salmon spawning streams, deer wintering habitat, moose swamps, and grizzly bear rearing grounds – in the remaining indigenous food supply and cultural strongholds?

What if non-native people noticed that their "socio-economic mores" are not more important than those of indigenous nations? What if non-native people stopped making decisions that belong to indigenous nations?

Who looks the other way and plugs their ears while the governments they elect carry on a policy of genocide, forcing whole peoples to sign their own death certificates? Who expects to have a victim accept the perpetrator's rules for reconciliation?

Who are we now?

ENDNOTES

Chapter 1

1   Union of BC Indian Chiefs, "A Historical Timeline," <www.ubcic.ca>

2   In separate interviews with Margaret Ann Peters of Samáhquam and Thomas Bull of Tsál'alh, both St'át'imc communities.

3   "Except where further information is desired, there will be no necessity to acknowledge receipt of this circular." Duncan Campbell Scott, Deputy Superintendent General, Department of Indian Affairs, Canada, December 15, 1921. A copy is with the author.

4   *Men of British Columbia,* by Derek Pethick, Hancock House, BC, 1975.

5   *The Decline and Fall of the British Empire, 1781-1997,* Piers Brendon, Jonathon Cape, London, The Random House Group Limited, 2007.

6   The number of miners who entered the Fraser River or came to Victoria in 1858 has been reported at varying orders of magnitude, but Charles John Fedorak, in *The United States Consul in Victoria and the Political Destiny of the Colony of British Columbia, 1862-1870,* p. 2,uses statements made by the American diplomat in Victoria at the time which put the number at over 30,000 from the USA alone.

7   *Proclamation of February 14th, 1859:* "(a) All the lands in British Columbia, and all the mines and minerals therein, belong to the Crown in fee."

8   *Journey Into the Interior of British Columbia,* 1859, Matthew Bailie Begbie J. The judge sketched the land formations, speculated as to formative geological events, and remarked on the likelihood of minerals at the various places.

9   Baptiste Ritchie, "The Smallpox Epidemic," in *Lillooet Stories* by Randy Bouchard and Dorothy Kennedy, BC Indian Language Project, 1972.

10   For examples of the considerable use of British gunboats on coastal villages, see McKelvie, *Tales of Conflict;* Hill, *War on the Coast;* Lindsay, F.W., *The BC Outlaws;* Fisher, *Contact and Conflict;* Ormsby, *British Columbia: A History;* Norcross, *The Warm Land;* Johnson, *Glyphs and Gallows,* among others.

11   *The Indians of Canada,* by Diamond Jenness, 1923, Bulletin 65, Anthropological Series No. 15, of the National Museum of Canada, published by the Minister of Supply and Services, Canada, p. 350 of the 1977 edition.

12   A recent survey found that of the 32 indigenous languages in B.C., three have no known living speakers. It also revealed that a meagre five percent of the 100,000 aboriginal people in B.C. are fluent in an ancestral tongue, and most of them are over the age of 65. Mark Cardwell, "The Right to Revitalize Canada's Indigenous Languages," *University Affairs,* November 8, 2010.

13   See Chapter 9

14   See Chapters 6 and 9.

15   This is happening in all natural resource industries, particularly in run-of-river power projects, for example, the elaborate agreement between Cloudworks Energy and Douglas First Nation made in 2009.

16   A series of papers by Janice Switlo record many tales of this from the vantage point of a

lawyer employed by Canada during those negotiations. For example, *Apple Cede,* 1999; *BC Treaty Process "Trick or Treaty?"* February 1, 1996.

17 *The British Colonist,* a front page column by the editor, Amor de Cosmos, December 18, 1858.

18 As it is worded in the Royal Proclamation of 1763 in regard to all the lands west of what is now Ontario, and this Executive Order is included in Section 25 of the Constitution Act, 1982.

19 It should also be regarded as covered by Article 1 of both International Covenants, which refers to the right of "all peoples" to self-determination, insofar as indigenous peoples are recognized to be peoples, and to exclude them from such coverage under these articles raises issues of discrimination. Why are Nicaraguans "peoples" covered by these covenants, if equally numerous and substantially more historic indigenous nations such as Cree or Sami are not?

Chapter 2

1 Committee on the Elimination of Racial Discrimination, Seventieth session, February - March 2007. "Consideration of Reports Submitted by States Parties Under Article 9 of the Convention - Concluding observations – Canada. May 25, 2007.#22: "While acknowledging the information that the "cede, release and surrender" approach to Aboriginal land titles has been abandoned by the State party in favour of "modification" and "non-assertion" approaches, the Committee remains concerned about the lack of perceptible difference in results of these new approaches in comparison to the previous approach. The Committee is also concerned that claims of Aboriginal land rights are being settled primarily through litigation, at a disproportionate cost for the Aboriginal communities concerned due to the strongly adversarial positions taken by the federal and provincial governments (art. 5 (d) (v))."

2 Opinion and Order in the United States District Court for the District of Oregon, United States of America, Plaintiff, v. James Allen Scott Pitawanakwat, Defendant. 00-M-489-ST, Opinion and Order, Stewart, Magistrate Judge.

3 *Papers Relating to the Indian Land Question* 1850-1875, Victoria, Richard Wolfenden, Government Printer, At the Government Printing Office, James Bay, 1877.

4 Section 91–24 of the British North America Act reserves to Canada against any of the provinces the responsibility to address issues concerning indigenous peoples and their Indian Reserves. BC agreed to Terms of Union with Canada in 1871, which brought the BNA Act into force in the province.

5 United Nations Committee on the Elimination of Racial Discrimination, Reports submitted by States Parties under Article 9 of the Convention, Sixteenth periodic report of States parties due in 2003 – Addendum CANADA – May 17, 2004. Article 2, Number 30, page 9.

6 *Haida Nation v. British Columbia (Minister of Forests),* [2004] 3 S.C.R. 511, 2004 SCC 73

7 The "treaty bowls" he is describing in his paper, a copy of which is with the author, are essential ceremonial tools used by many coastal peoples to produce treaties between themselves. The bowls were used in resolution of disputes regarding ownership or occupation of lands and waters, access to key resources, alliances in times of war, marriages and so on. The paper is titled, *"An extremely rare, old Indian relic is now lying in Vancouver, namely one of their most prized, colossal "Mother Treaty Bowls."* Described by Ronald Campbell Campbell-Johnston, July 1924. *"Continuation of, "The Story of the Totem Pole"*...

8 *The Lil'wat World of Charlie Mack,* Randy Bouchard and Dorothy Kennedy, Talon Press, 2010.

9 Most recently as part of the Sea-to-Sky Land Use Planning Agreement with the province, 2010.

10 *The Same As Yesterday, The Lillooet Document the Theft of their Lands and Resources,* Joanne Drake-Terry, published by the Lillooet Tribal Council, 1989.

11 See Chapter 4 of this volume under subsection "The Academic Oath."

12 *The Chilcotin War,* by Mel Rothenburger, Mr. Paperback, Langley BC, 1978.

13   *Judgement at Stoney Creek,* by Bridget Moran, Tillacum Library, Vancouver, 1990.

14   *An Error In Judgement, the politics of medical care in an Indian/white community,* by Dara Culhane Speck, Talonbooks, Vancouver, 1987.

15   "Restoration of Well-Being for Canada's First Peoples," by Bill Mussell, Skwah, Sto:lo, chair of the Native Mental Health Association of Canada, member of the Mood Disorders Society of Canada, and former chair of the First Nation, Inuit and Metis Advisory Committee to the Mental Health Commission of Canada.

16   "Message to the media: All Canadian issues are Aboriginal issues," by Maurice Switzer, Mississauga of Rice Lake First Nation, director of communications for the Assembly of First Nations, *The Globe and Mail,* March 27, 1998.

17   "Prisoners of Democracy: The Líl'wat right to an impartial tribunal. An analysis of the Lillooet Lake Roadblock Case," Lyn Crompton, PhD Thesis, UBC, 2006, p.12.

18   "Acting on What We Know: Preventing Youth Suicide In First Nations." The report of the advisory Group on Suicide Prevention, Health Canada. <www.hc-sc.gc.ca>

19   "Culture loss linked to poor health, BCMA official tells royal commission," by Gerry Bellett, *The Vancouver Sun,* June 4, 1993.

20   In her thesis "Prisoners of Democracy: The Líl'wat Right to an Impartial Tribunal," Lyn Crompton documents twelve kinds of violence, some of it with lasting effects, administered by RCMP in the arrest of the unarmed, non-violent Líl'wat protesters. Advocacy groups "Prison Justice Day" and "Sisters Inside" have extensive documentation of police violence against aboriginal people in police custody.

21   "RCMP's biggest, costliest operation ends peacefully," by Mark Hume and Lindsay Kines, September 18, 1995, *The Vancouver Sun.*

22   *The Same As Yesterday,* Drake-Terry; also *The Fourth World, An Indian Reality,* by George Manuel and Michael Posluns, Don Mills, Ontario, 1974.

23   "Urban Aboriginal Children in Canada: Building a solid foundation for prosperity and change," by Geraldine King. Published in "Aboriginal children's health: Leaving No Child Behind," Canadian Supplement to The State of The World's Children 2009, Canadian UNICEF Committee, 2009.

24   Statistics Canada, 2006, "Aboriginal Peoples in Canada in 2006: Inuit, Métis and First Nations," Ottawa, Supply and Services, 1995. Royal Commission on Aboriginal Peoples, "Choosing life: Special report on suicide among Aboriginal people."

25   "First Nations and Métis people, eastern Europeans, and poor people - were disproportionately represented amongst those subjected to eugenic ideas and practices, such as sterilization," from the study *"Living Archives on Eugenics in Western Canada,"* Community-University Research Alliance, 2011, <www.eugenicsarchive.ca>.

26   "Ottawa vows action on native school abuse," by Stewart Bell, *Vancouver Sun,* Friday June 27, 1997, page A3.

27   This activity is reported by many indigenous speakers at public meetings, such as those leading up to the interior Chiefs' protocol, "Putting Children First," in 2010.

28   "Observations on Canada's Response" to Petition 879-07, Loni Edmonds v. Canada, February, 2012. Submission to Inter-American Human Rights Commission, Organization of American States, by Diana Kly, International Human Rights Association of American Minorities.

29   This is because of the legal principle of *Nemo Potest Esse Simul Actor et Judex* (a court cannot be suitor and judge of a question), and also the inability to get a trial on this issue has been empirically proved over a history of failed attempts.

30   *This Ragged Place,* by Terry Glavin, New Star Books, 1998, from the chapter, "Last Day in Alexis Creek," pp. 134-35.

31   *Edmonds v. Canada,* submissions for admissibility to Inter-American Human Rights Commission, 2007-2012.

32   "Natives say they were targeted," *The Vancouver Sun,* February 7, 1998.

33   "Getting Children Back: one family's story of bringing two babies home from foster care," *The St'át'imc Runner* newspaper, March 2011

34   The Criminal Code of Canada, R.S.C., 1985, c. C-46, article 318.

35   As is and was the case at Cheam. "Soldiers of the salmon wars," by Rick Collins, *The*

Globe and Mail, September 18, 1999.

36   Largely American posses formed in 1858-1860 in Yale for the purpose of avenging killed miners. Written documentation of these events is predictably sparse while they live on vividly in the oral traditions of the Nlaka'pamux, or Thomson, people in BC's interior. At least reference is made to the fact that there was lethal exchange of hostilities at Grouse Creek in *British Columbia: A History,* by Margaret Ormsby, The Macmillan Company of Canada, 1958, p. 229.

37   St'át'imc men today recall attending court in Lillooet to be presented with hunting charges, where they were represented by five Chiefs who called the colonial authority into question and won relief from prosecution, effectively by mistrial, when charges were thrown out at the judge's abandonment of the case.

38   The "DIA" as it is usually referred to in this book, has recently been renamed the Ministry of Aboriginal Affairs and Northern Development, Canada. Just prior to that, it was the Ministry of Indian and Northern Affairs, Canada. The name "Department of Indian Affairs," has not been replaced in the everyday language of the people.

39   *The BC Treaty Negotiating Times,* Summer, 2007, p.6.

40   Quotation from "Indians fear police assault," by Mike Crawley, *The Vancouver Sun,* August 24, 1995. Reference to public support from, "NDP walking tightrope with hardline approach," by Justine Hunter, *The Vancouver Sun,* September 13, 1995: "Attorney-General Ujjal Dosanjh's tough stand on the Gustafsen Lake standoff is winning the beleaguered New Democratic party government some much-needed popular support. ...Dosanjh has been scoring big with his outspoken criticism of the rebels encamped on private land they say is rightfully theirs because ownership was never ceded to the crown. "The situation is fraught with danger for everyone, but Dosanjh seems to be in tune with public opinion. His stance has done wonders for the status of the Harcourt government." – Norman Ruff, political analyst and political science professor at the University of Victoria."

Chapter 3

1   British Columbia: Papers Connected with the Indian Land Question 1850-1875, Victoria, Richard Wolfenden, Government Printer, At the Government Printing Office, James Bay, 1877.

2   *The Warm land,* E. Blanche Norcross, Duncan, BC, 1959, p. 16.

3   Economic Impacts of Invasive Plants in BC, Invasive Plants Council of BC. <http://bcinvasiveplants.com>

4   "...And The Last Shall Be First," Native Policy in an Era of Cutbacks, A Discussion Paper Prepared for the Aboriginal Rights Coalition, by Murray Angus, Ottawa 1989, p. 9.

5   "...And The Last Shall Be First," p. 4.

6   "F-35 fighters: Peter MacKay aware two years ago of additional $10B cost," by Bruce Campion-Smith, April 8, 2012. <thestar.com>

7   "Sask. First Nation sues Canada, province over potash, oil properties," Kerry Benjoe, Postmedia News, Regina, January 11, 2012: "The George Gordon First Nation is suing the federal and provincial governments for $10 billion it claims it is being "cheated out of" potash and oil developments. In the suit served on the government on Tuesday, the First Nation alleges Canada and Saskatchewan improperly denied it access to billions of dollars worth of potash and oil and gas lands through misconduct by both levels of government throughout the George Gordon Treaty Land Entitlement Settlement Agreement process. The agreement was entered into by all three parties on Aug. 11, 2008."

8   Jobs, Growth and Long-term Prosperity: Economic Action Plan 2012. The Honourable James M. Flaherty, P.C., M.P. Minister of Finance, March 29, 2012.

9   "Administration gulps $1.2 billion, natives say," by Gerry Bellett, June 4, 1993, *The Vancouver Sun.*

10   Canada's Budget 2012, "Budget in Brief." <http://www.budget.gc.ca/2012/home-

accueil-eng.html>

11   *The $9 Billion Myth Exposed: Why First Nations Poverty Endures*, Assembly of First Nations, "Make Poverty History" Campaign, 2007

12   Tyrone McNeil, President of the First Nations Education Steering Committee, BC: "Making the case for adequate post-secondary support: Tyrone McNeil, FNESC President," *The St'át'imc Runner,* May 2010.

13   "Government too generous with aboriginals, Canadians tell pollster," By Teresa Smith, Postmedia News June 30, 2012. <www.canada.com>

14   Backgrounder - Aboriginal Affairs and Northern Development Canada's Financial Picture (2012-2013), March 26, 2012. <http://www.aadnc-aandc.gc.ca/eng/1332787 097473/1332787167708>

15   The First Nations Child and Family Caring Society launched a complaint with the Canada Human Rights Commission in 2007, in part over the fact of aboriginal children in care receiving an average 22% less funding than non-aboriginal children in government and foster care. The case was referred to the Canadian Human Rights Tribunal where it was stalled for four years and then rejected; at which time the CHRC put the Tribunal's ruling forward for judicial review, and the Caring Society's case is now returned to the Tribunal with its question intact, as of October 2012.

16   Tyrone McNeil, as above at 12, *The St'át'imc Runner,* May 2010.

17   "Bill for colonial past comes due," by Madeline Drohan, *The Globe and Mail,* October 22, 1999.

18   "...And The Last Shall Be First" Native Policy in an Era of Cutbacks, Murray Angus. Aboriginal Rights Coalition (Project North), 1990.

19   Grand Chief Saul Terry, former President of the Union of BC Indian Chiefs, *The St'át'imc Runner,* November 2009, UBCIC 40th Anniversary Special Edition, p.22.

20   "Retiring MLAs to get $13.7 million in pensions," Glen Korstrom, *Business in Vancouver,* August 31, 2012.

21   *The Income Gap Between Aboriginal Peoples and the Rest of Canada*, by Daniel Wilson and David Macdonald, Canadian Center for Policy Alternatives, April 2010.

22   Commodities charts 2012, <www.mongabay.com>; and, *The History of the Northern Interior of British Columbia,* A. G. Morice, John Lane London, 1906.

23   "McLeod Lake Indian Band divided over mine deal," by Arthur Williams, *The Prince George Citizen,* May 26, 2012.

24   See endnote 23.

25   "No Protocol," *The St'át'imc Runner* newspaper, May 2007; see also *The St'át'imc Runner,* July 2007, p.2.

26   "Some of the members of INET have been involved in the Softwood Lumber Dispute, since the initiation of the investigation on Softwood Lumber from Canada, in April 2001. Joint submissions of Aboriginal peoples and environmental groups, who were given special standing, were made to the US Department of Commerce on May 15th, 2001. Aboriginal peoples from the Interior of British Columbia, the heartland of softwood lumber extraction, were the first indigenous peoples ever to make substantive filings to the World Trade Organization. Their amicus curiae brief was officially accepted by the WTO Panel on the US DoC Preliminary Determination on Softwood Lumber on April 26th, 2002, and circulated to all parties and third parties for comment. Since then filings have been made under INET and joined by the Nishnawbe Aski Nation and the Grand Council of Treaty 32. These filings to both the WTO and NAFTA panels on CVD have also been officially accepted." – Excerpted from "Comments regarding US and Canadian Tribal Interests," Submitted by the Indigenous Network on Economies and Trade on the Proposed Policies Regarding the Conduct of Changed Circumstances Reviews Under the Countervailing Duty Order On Softwood Lumber From Canada (C 122 839).

Also see, "International Trade Law and Indigenous Peoples: *A New Direction in Human Rights Advocacy,"* by Megan Davis, based on a paper given to the Australian New Zealand Society of International Law Annual Conference in Canberra, Australia, 18-20 June 2004. Printed in the Australian Indigenous Law Reporter, Volume 9, Number 2,

January 2009.
27   *Settlers, Prospectors and Tourists Guide*, or *Travels Through British Columbia*; Newton H. Chittenden, London, 1882.
28   *A World Geography For Canadian Schools*, by V L Denton and A R Lord., Toronto, 1936, p. 66.
29   *Supra*, p. 47.
30   Conference hosted by Westbank First Nation: "Implementing the Tsilhqotin Decision," March 12-13, 2008.
31   Indigenous Language Instructors' Certificate Elders Circles - How Indigenous Knowledge informs and directs the development of an instructors' certificate in Indigenous languages. Report on findings by Diana Steinhauer, Anna-Leah King, Heather Blair, and James Lamouche, January 2010.
32   *West Moberly First Nation v British Columbia (Chief Inspector of Mines)*, 2011 BCCA 247 (CanLII). The animals referred to are the Burnt Pine caribou in West Moberly.
33   Prime Minister Pierre Trudeau referring in a speech in Vancouver, supporting his white paper, to the indigenous and why they should no longer be recognized as Status Indians in Canada with distinct rights. August 8, 1969.
34   Chehalis Forest and Range Consultation and Revenue Sharing Agreement, 2010.

Chapter 4

1   Quotation from "We Are Not O'Meare's Children," Hamar Foster, 2003.
2   Michael A. Dorris, from *Through Indian Eyes: The Native Experience in Books for Children.* AmerIndian Studies Center; 4th edition, 1998.
3   *Reel Injun*, 2009, Director Neil Diamond.
4   *Chronicles of Pride,* Richardson Logie, 1990. The quote is inside the cover jacket.
5   *Canadian Pioneers, Scholastic Canada Bibliographies.* Maxine Trottier, Scholastic Canada Ltd, 2003.
6   *The Elders Are Watching,* by David Bouchard. Illustrations by Roy Henry Vickers. Raincoast Books, Vancouver, 1997.
7   *Tales The Totems Tell,* Hugh Weatherby. Macmillan Company of Canada Limited, 1962.
8   For example, Robert James Challenger's series of fables, published by Heritage House, BC.
9   *British Columbia Almanac*, Mark Forsythe, Arsenal Pulp Press, Vancouver, 2000. Page 13. Emphasis added.
10   MMII Denali Music Canada (A division of King Motion Picture Company) SOCAN. 1981, www.thislivingworld.com
11   *The Taming of the Canadian West,* Frank Rasky, McLelland and Stewart Limited, 1967.
12   *The Fall of the British Empire 1781–1997,* Piers Brendon, London 2007.
13   James Latham, 2012 interview.
14   *Assessing the effectiveness of the Chilliwack School District's First Nation Kindergarten program,* by Tracy L. Wagner; A paper presented to the Gordon Albright School of Education in partial fulfillment of the requirements for the Degree of Master of Education, June 2009.
15   This mandate is made explicit by the BC Ministry of Education and in each of the preambles to the Agreements themselves.
16   Abbotsford School District #47, September 2012 parent newsletter.
17   *History of the Canadian Peoples, Volume 1, Beginnings to 1867*; Conrad and Finkel, 2009. Page 220.
18   *The History of the Northern Interior of British Columbia,* A.G.Morrice;1904. (1978 edition)
19   *The Taming of the Canadian West*, by Frank Rasky. McLelland and Stewart Limited, 1967. Page 61.

20   *Ibid*

21   *History of the Canadian Peoples, Volume 1*, by Margaret Conrad and Alvin Finkel, Pearson Longman Editions, 2009, p. 219.

22   *Disrobing the Aboriginal Industry,* by Albert Howard and Frances Widdowson. McGill-Queen's University Press, 2008.

23   An 18th century essay by Jonathan Swift proposed that the Irish should eat their babies instead of going hungry.

24   *The Warm Land,* E. Blanche Norcross, Duncan, BC, 1959, p. 34.

25   *British Columbia: A History,* by Margaret Ormsby, The Macmillan Company of Canada, 1958, p.168

26   *Beyond the Nass Valley: National Implications of the Supreme Court's Delgamuukw Decision; edited by* Owen Lippert. The Fraser Institute, Vancouver, 2000. Biographies of contributing writers.

27   *The Nature of Aboriginal Title*, Brian Slattery, in "Beyond the Nass Valley" by the Fraser Institute. Vancouver, 2000.

28   From the text of the Royal Proclamation of King George III, 1763.

29   Judge John Marshall, Chief Justice of the American Supreme Court, gave this opinion in *Worcester v. State of Georgia*, 6 Peters Supreme Court Reports 515 (1832), clarifying a statement made in *Johnson vs. McIntosh*, 8 Wheaton's Rep., 543 (1823). The particular quotations from his reasons appear in Chapter 8.

30   The name Ntsínlemqen is held by a Líl'wat man today, and it is the name of the man —something of a metaphysicist—who anticipated the flood and followed heavenly instructions to save his people from it.

31   The name of the Sacred Rock, Seymelst (Black Dome), comes from that mountain and is carried today.

32   See, among others, *The Warm Country*, by E. Blanche Norcross, 1959

33   *The Claim Based on Native Title,* Appendix "B", The Land Question, by Chief William Scow for delivery to the Annual General Meeting of the Union (of BC Indian Chiefs), Victoria, November 17, 1971, p. 7. "An additional facet of the Douglas policy was that the title of the reserved lands of the Indians remained with the crown and was inalienable."

34   Examples of this type are numerous - they result, for instance, in such accepted practices as the Forest and Range Agreements and all kinds of modern day settlements which do not reflect the cost of infringement but rather a sort of amnesiac desire to "move forward." See Chapter 9, *The Role of Law.*

35   *The Fort Victoria Treaties,* by Wilson Duff. BC Studies No. 3, Fall 1969

36   *Aboriginal Peoples and Politics: The Indian Land Question in British Columbia,* by Paul Tennant, UBC Press, 1989, *p.* 81.

37   From an interview with Arthur Dick of Dog Creek, printed in *The St'át'imc Runner*, August 2010 p. 22; and confirmed by other Elders such as Desmond Peters Senior, Pavillion, and Albert Joseph, Bridge River.

38   Professor Hamar Foster biography, <http://www.uvic.ca>

39   *Essays in the History of Canadian Law: The Legal History of British Columbia and the Yukon,* Edited by Hamar Foster and John McLaren, Osgoode Society, University of Toronto Press, 1995.

40   Foster, Hamar,. Berger, Benjamin L, and Buck, A.R.,*The Grand Experiment: Law and Legal Culture in British Settler Societies*, The Osgoode Society, UBC Press, 2008

41   Parks and Recreation in Sonoma County document the March, 1812, building of Fort Ross by Russian traders. http://www.parks.sonoma.net/rosshist.html

42   *The Resettlement of British Columbia*, Cole Harris, UBC Press, 1997. Page 4, re. smallpox epidemic c. 1782.

43   *Gold Creeks and Ghost Towns: East Kootenay, Boundary, West Kootenay, Okanagan and Similkameen,* by N.L. Barlee, 1970 first printing, Canada West Magazine, Summerland, BC, p. 35.

44   *The Warm Land,* by E. Blanche Norcross, Duncan, BC, 1959. Chapter 3.

45   James Teit's maps of tribal trade routes, in the BC Archives, Victoria, Boas microfilm

collection: MS 1425 372 Roll 1.

46   *British Columbia Disasters,* by Derek Pethik, 1975, Hancock House, BC

47   *'Take precautions against the natives': Life as a sick Indian at Lytton, BC, 1910-1940.*
      Helen Bromley, Simon Fraser University, Geography, in partial fulfillment of Master
      of Arts Degree. July, 1994, p. 75.

48   *Disrobing the Aboriginal Industry,* by Frances Widdowson and John Howard, McGill-
      Queen's University Press, 2008.

49   *On the Path of the Explorers:Tracing the expeditions of Vancouver, Cook, Mackenzie,
      Fraser and Thompson,* by Steve Short and Rosemary Neering, Whitecap Books,
      Vancouver/Toronto, 1992. Page 88

50   *Glyphs and Gallows, The Rock Art of Clo-oose and the Wreck of the John Bright,* by
      Peter Johnson, Heritage House Publishing Company Ltd., Surrey, BC, 1999, p. 9.

51   *Glyphs and Gallows,* p. 35.

52   For example, *I Have Lived Here Since the World Began,* Arthur J. Ray, 1996, p.239;
      Paul Tennant, *Aboriginal Peoples and Politics;* John Lutz, *Makúk;* Hamar Foster, *We
      Are Not O'Meara's Children.*

53   Aside from many interviews on this subject, one can refer to *Breaking the Silence.
      An Interpretive Study of Residential School Impact and Healing as Illustrated by the
      Stories of First Nations Individuals,* 1994, Assembly of First Nations.

54   Private sources.

55   "Litigation and the BC Treaty Process - Some Recent Cases in a Historical Perspec-
      tive," Speaking Notes for Professor Hamar Foster, University of Victoria Faculty of
      Law, at the BC Treaty Commission conference "Speaking Truth to Power III: Self-
      Government:Options and Opportunities," March 14 – 15, 2002.

56   *The Chilcotin War,* by Mel Rothenburger, published by Mr. Paperback of Langley, BC,
      p. 33.

57   *Take precautions against the natives;* 'Helen Bromley, Page 74; *List of Bella Coola
      Villages,* Archives of the American Bureau of Ethnography, Smithsonian Institute,
      #4178; Bill Mussell, *Restoration of Well-Being for Canada's First Peoples.*

58   Charlie Mack's story called "The Route to Cariboo Country," in *Lillooet Stories,*
      1977. Recorded by Dorothy Kennedy and Randy Bouchard. BC Provincial Archives,
      Victoria.

59   Chapter One, *The Resettlement of British Columbia,* Cole Harris, UBC Press, 1997.

60   *The Indians of Canada,* by Diamond Jenness, 1923, Bulletin 65, Anthropological Series
      No. 15, of the National Museum of Canada. Page 347 of the 1977 edition, published
      by the Minister of Supply and Services, Canada.

61   For example, *Raven's Village:The Myths, Arts and Traditions of Native People from
      the Pacific Northwest Coast.* by Nancy Ruddell, Canadian Museum of Civilization,
      1995, 1996.

62   *Guests Never Leave Hungry, The Autobiography of James Sewid, a Kwakiutl Indian;*
      Edited by James P. Spradley, McGill-Queen's University Press, 1972. (Copyright by
      Yale University Press 1969).

63   *White Slaves of Maquinna: John R. Jewitt's Narrative of Capture and Confinement
      at Nootka,* by John Jewitt. First published 1815. Heritage House Publishing Co. Ltd.;
      Surrey, BC edition, 2000.

64   *The Real Poverty Report,* Ian Adams; M. G. Hurtig, 1971, pp. 68, 227.

65   By Hugh and Karmel McCullum, Toronto, 1975.

Chapter 5

1   *British Columbia Ghost Town Series 3 – Fraser Canyon;* by T.W. Paterson, Sunfire
     Publications Limited, Langley BC, 1985.

2   As in the case of the Soowahlie of the Sto:lo in 1864.

3   These exiles are not well documented in archives or scholarly publications. My sources
     include, for Kitsilano, Dr Peter Cole; Pemberton, Harold Pascal, Rosalin Sam, James
     Louie; Squamish, the location of the Reserve and city today; Musqueam, exhaustive

litigation by the Musqueam against the City of Vancouver and the province; Katzie, Reserve location under the Golden Ears bridge and excavations of village during the building of the bridge; Bulkley Valley, the Gitxsan web archives; Neskonlith, Arthur Manuel and Chief Judy Wilson and actions against Sun Peaks and the province, as well as a map of the 1862 Reserve which is still in their possession; Lillooet, Ceda Scotchman; Bella Coola, BC Archival documents of the village sites; Saanich, recent court action for compensation; Kwikwitlem, fishing rights to collect from the Albion test fishery and miniscule fishing Reserves on the Fraser. "Penticton," means in Okanagan, "people always there" (Thomson, Duane; The Response of Okanagan Indians to European Settlement). This list is by no means exhaustive or even in number to be representative.

4   "In Time Immemorial, " by Daisy Sewid-Smith, *BC Studies,* No. 89, Spring 1989.

5   PABC, B.C., Colonial Despatches, 1860: Douglas to Newcastle, 9 October and 25 October 1860. Registering to be Free Miners was a process designed to alleviate the men of their identity in the same way as the *Act for the Civilization of the Indian Tribes of Canada,* 1857.

6   Geo. A. Walkem; Chief Commissioner of Land and Works to Superintendent of Indian Affairs, December 5, 1872; *Papers Related to the Indian Land Question in British Columbia* 1850-1875, page110.

7   To the Editor of the Victoria Standard, by C. J. Grandidier, Okanagan Mission, August 28th, 1874. *Papers Related to the Indian Land Question in British Columbia 1850-1875.*

8   *Confidential Report of the Royal Commission on Indian Affairs for the Province of British Columbia,* Victoria, B.C., June 30, 1916.

9   Geo. A. Walkem to AG of Superintendent of Indian Affairs, December 29, 1873.

10   *Papers Related to the Indian Land Question in British Columbia 1850-1875*, Report of the Governor of BC on the Survey of Indian Reserves, page 2.

11   The petition of the Chiefs of Douglas Portage, of Lower Fraser, and of the other tribes on the seashore of the mainland to Bute Inlet, to the Indian Commissioner for the Province of British Columbia, 1874.

12   *The Lands We Lost - A History of Cut-off Lands and Land Losses from Indian Reserves in British Columbia,* by Reuben Ware, for the *Union of BC Indian Chiefs,* 1974.

13   Appellants' Factum, by Thomas Berger, Counsel, on appeal from the Supreme Court of British Columbia from Gould J., October 17, 1969, signed by Berger, February 27, 1970.

14   Naas Harbor, October 19th, 1887, para. 436 "REPORT OF COMMISSION N. W. COAST INDIANS, 1888."

15   Papers Relating to the Commission appointed to enquire into the state and condition of the Indians of the North-West Coast of British Columbia. By Command. Jno. Robson, Provincial Secretary. Provincial Secretary's Office, 22nd February, 1888. (Great Seal) Hugh Nelson. Canada. Province of British Columbia.

16   Letter of resignation from Chairman of Royal Commission on Indian Affairs for the Province of British Columbia, E L Wetmore, dated November 29, 1913 at Victoria. The original is with the Commission Reports in the BC Archives, Victoria.

17   The *Memorial to Sir Wilfred Laurier*, August 25, 1910.

18   The *Memorial to Frank Oliver, Minister of the Interior and Superintendent of Indian Affairs*, May 10, 1911.

19   Statement from the BC Indian Conference, Vancouver, June, 1916.

20   Letter of resignation from Chairman of the Royal Commission on Indian Affairs for the Province of British Columbia, E L Wetmore, November 29, 1913. The original is with the Commission Reports in the BC Archives, Victoria.

21   *Our Homes are Bleeding : a Short History of Indian Reserves,* by Reuben Ware, Union of British Columbia Indian Chiefs. Land Claims Research Centre, 1975.

22   As reported in the North American Indian Brotherhood paper on Jurisdiction and the Indian Claims Commission, apparently written in or about 1964. A copy is with the author.

23 "Aboriginal Rights Position Paper - Resource Kit," Indian Government Portfolio, Union of B.C. Indian Chiefs, October 15, 1979. Part F. Alliance for Assimilation 1944-1969.

24 This memo is undated but a copy is with the author.

25 This brief is with the author.

26 *Gov't to appeal Indian Hunt case,* Nanaimo (Staff), *The Sun*, March 5, 1964.

27 Memo, David Munro, Assistant Deputy Minister (Indian Consultation and Negotiation) April 1, 1970. A copy is with the author.

28 Statement of the Government of Canada on Indian policy (the "White Paper Policy") Presented to the First Session of the Twenty-eighth Parliament by the Honourable Jean Chrétien, Minister of Indian Affairs and Northern Development, 1969.

29 "Aboriginal Rights Position Paper - Resource Kit," Indian Government Portfolio, Union of B.C. Indian Chiefs, October 15, 1979. Part II, pp. 22, 23, 33.

30 A Position Paper, Aboriginal Rights and Title Resource Kit, National Indian Brotherhood, 1979.

31 St'át'imc Chiefs Support St'át'imc-Hydro Agreement, youtube video, posted April 6, 2011.

32 *Corbiere v. Canada (Minister of Indian and Northern Affairs).* [1999] 2 S.C.R. 203.

33 *The St'át'imc Runner*, November, 2009 Special Edition on the UBCIC; interviews with Rose Charlie and Bill Lightbown.

34 See "The Role of Law," Chapter 9, re. The Frozen Right.

35 H.B. Hawthorn, "A Survey of the Contemporary Indians of Canada," Vol. I and II, Ottawa, Indian Affairs Branch, 1966-1967.

36 *McIvor v. The Registrar*, Indian and Northern Affairs Canada, 2007 BCSC 827.

Chapter 6

1 Minister of Indian and Northern Affairs, Chuck Strahl, in a letter to the First Nations Summit dated October 25, 2007. Emphasis added in the quotation above.

2 According to Professor Marvin Stark, business law, at Simon Fraser University. "SFU professor points to ways to settle Indian land claims," by Terry Glavin, *The Vancouver Sun*, May 14, 1990.

3 In June 1991, the Task Force reported. It made nineteen recommendations, all of which were accepted by Canada, the Province and the Summit. These recommendations are the genesis of the British Columbia treaty process, proposing that:

1. The First Nations, Canada, and British Columbia establish a new relationship based on mutual trust, respect, and understanding—through political negotiations.

2. Each of the parties be at liberty to introduce any issue at the negotiation table which it views as significant to the new relationship.

3. A British Columbia Treaty Commission be established by agreement among the First Nations, Canada, and British Columbia to facilitate the process of negotiations.

4. The Commission consist of a full-time chair-person and four commissioners - of whom two are appointed by the First Nations, and one each by the federal and provincial governments.

5. A six-stage process be followed in negotiating treaties.

6. The treaty negotiation process be open to all First Nations in British Columbia.

7. The organization of First Nations for the negotiations is a decision to be made by each First Nation.

8. First Nations resolve issues related to overlapping traditional territories among themselves.

9. Federal and provincial governments start negotiations as soon as First Nations are ready.

10. Non-aboriginal interests be represented at the negotiating table by the federal and provincial governments.

11. The First Nation, Canadian, and British Columbian negotiating teams be sufficiently funded to meet the requirements of the negotiations.

12. The commission be responsible for allocating funds to the First Nations.

13. The parties develop ratification procedures which are confirmed in the Framework Agreement and in the Agreement in Principle.

14. The commission provide advice and assistance in dispute resolution as agreed by the parties.

15. The parties select skilled negotiators and provide them with a clear mandate, and training as required.

16. The parties negotiate interim measures agreements before or during the treaty negotiations when an interest is being affected which could undermine the process.

17. Canada, British Columbia, and the First Nations jointly undertake public education and information programs.

18. The parties in each negotiation jointly undertake a public information program.

19. British Columbia, Canada, and the First Nations request the First Nations Education Secretariat, and various educational organizations in British Columbia, to prepare resource materials for use in the schools and by the public.

In September of 1992, the three parties executed the British Columbia Treaty Commission Agreement. In this document, Canada agreed to introduce legislation to establish the Commission referred to in recommendation #3, as did the Province. The role of the Commission was stated to be "... to facilitate the negotiation of treaties ..." and the Agreement set out in detail criteria for assessing the readiness of the parties to commence negotiations. The Agreement also mandated the Commission to report annually to Parliament and the Legislative Assembly, and stated specifically that the 1991 Task Force Report could be used as an aid to the interpretation of the Agreement.

4   Report of the Auditor General of British Columbia, 2005.

5   Politicians spend a considerable amount of time debating this point, the question of whether negotiations are based on aboriginal title. They say, like Chuck Strahl: "the parties recognize that Aboriginal title exists ... where Aboriginal title exists in British Columbia it is a legal interest in land and is a burden on Crown title." This excerpt is from a letter by Strahl to the Union of BC Indian Chiefs, also dated October 25, 2007.

6   Professor Anthony Hall, University of Lethbridge, Alberta, Canada, testifying at the *Pitawanakwat* extradition trial, Oregon County, USA, 2000: Opinion and Order in the United States District Court for the District of Oregon, *United States of America, Plaintiff, v. James Allen Scott Pitawanakwat, Defendant*. 00-M-489-ST, Opinion and Order, Stewart, Magistrate Judge.

7   See Chapter 9.

8   "The NDP takes some comfort in land claims decision," by Vaughn Palmer, *The Vancouver Sun,* December 12, 1997.

9   *The BC Treaty Negotiating Times,* Summer, 2007

10   Memo, Deputy Minister, Department of Indian Affairs, April 1 1970. A copy is with the author.

11   "Why Canada's comprehensive claims process will never work for First Nations," an open letter to Chief Doug White, Chief Beverly Clifton Percival and AFN Ad Hoc Committee Members, from Arthur Manuel, April 5, 2011.

12   *"Treaty Negotiations in British Columbia: An Assessment of the Effectiveness of British Columbia's Management and Administrative Processes,"* Report of the Auditor General for Canada, Sheila Fraser, 2006.

13   UBCIC Open Letter to Governments of Canada and BC: Canada's Comprehensive Claims Policy; updated letter, July 25, 2007.

14   UN Committee for the Eliminaton of all forms of Racial Discrimination, response to Canada's report, 2002.

15   Tim Koepke, provincial treaty negotiator, interview for *The St'át'imc Runner*, May 2007.

16   "Glossary of Treaty-Related Terms As Used by the Province of British Columbia" BC Treaty Commission website, 2007. Before it was removed, these two definitions were

re-printed in *The BC Treaty Negotiating Times,* Summer 2007.

17   May, 2011; Baird was a panel member on a discussion of treaty rights sponsored jointly
     by Canada and USA.

18   Presentation by Point to In-SHUCK-ch (treaty group) General Assembly, May 26,
     2007, in Mission.

19   Terry Glavin, quoted by Alex Rose in *Spirit Dance at Mediazin, Chief Joseph Gosnell
     and the Nisga'a Treaty,* Harbour Publishing, BC, 2000, pp. 131-32.

20   "Native leaders challenge Ottawa: Letter from Indian and Northern Affairs Minister
     misrepresents principles of treaty negotiation, chiefs say," by Cathryn Atkinson, *The
     Globe and Mail,* December 3, 2007.

21   "In historic judgment, top court strengthens Indian land claims," by Stewart Bell, Peter
     O'Neil and Jim Beatty, *The Vancouver Sun,* December 12, 1997.

22   *Spirit Dance at Mediazin, Chief Joseph Gosnell and the Nisga'a Treaty, supra,* p.
     214.

23   "Settle BC's Indian land claims first, economist says," by Stewart Bell, *The Vancouver
     Sun,* March 31, 1998.

24   *Luuxhon v. The Queen (*1999), C981165 S.C.B.C.

25   "'Negotiate with us,' chief tells conference," by Dianne Rinehart, *The Vancouver Sun,*
     March 27, 1998.

26   Attributed to Elder M.A. Peters by Hereditary Chief Kakila, Clarke Smith, Tenas
     Lake, interview 2006.

27   *Stolen Lands, Broken Promises. Researching the Indian Land Question in British
     Columbia* (Second Edition) UBCIC, 2004.

28   Nisga'a Final Agreement, Tsawwassen Final Agreement, Maa-nulth Final Agreement.

29   Tsawwassen Final Agreement.

30   "Treaty Making in the Spirit of Co-existence: An Alternative to Extinguishment;"
     Royal Commission on Aboriginal Peoples, Ottawa: Canada Communication Group,
     1995.

31   Select Standing Committee on Aboriginal Affairs, Lillooet public forum, November
     14, 1996.

32   Tsawwassen Final Agreement, Chapter 2, section 13.

33   *Municipal Government Act,* British Columbia, 1998.

34   "Nisgaa Treaty - Final Agreement Act - Bill C51 - Committee Stage" - the Provincial
     Government's debate televised on CPAC and recorded on the Government's website/
     Hansard, January 19,1999.

35   Union of BC Indian Chiefs, News Release, February 20, 2007.

36   Hamar Foster, *Litigation and the BC Treaty Process —Some Recent Cases in a His-
     torical Perspective*, March 15, 2002, speaking notes for "Speaking truth to power,
     Session III: Self Government: Options and Opportunities," an event held by the BC
     Treaty Commission.

37   From a full page advertisement by the Interior Alliance in *The Vancouver Sun,* Sep-
     tember 16, 1999.

38   Rose Doolan, Kincolith, Nisga'a; interview 2007, "Nisga'a Now," *The BC Treaty
     Negotiating Times,* Summer 2007.

39   *Supra.*

40   Chief Harry O'Donnaghy, N'Quátqua, interviewed in *The St'át'imc Runner,* July,
     2007, p.14.

41   Private source.

42   *The St'át'imc Runner,* December 2009, p. 28.

43   "Maa-nulth First Nations Practice Standards for Ratification of the Treaty, August
     –September 2007," p.13.

44   Bertha Williams to Stephen Harper in an open letter, July 2007.

45   *A Neutral framework for modeling and analyzing aboriginal land tenure systems,* Mele
     Estella Rupou Rakai, January 2005, University of New Brunswick.

46   An Open Letter To Huu-ay-aht Regarding the Maa-nulth Final Agreement, July 24,
     2007, from David Dennis.

Chapter 7

1   *They Came Before Columbus: The African Presence in Ancient America,* by Ivan Van Sertima, Random House, Inc., 2003; Copyright 1976 by Ivan Van Sertima.
2   *Pagans In The Promised Land, Decoding the Doctrine of Christian Discovery,* by Steven Newcomb, Fulcrum Publishing, 2011.
3   *Scenes and Studies of Savage Life*, G.M. Sproat, London, 1868.
4   Lyn Crompton, speaking at *The Gathering of The Clans: A Conference Addressing "New World" Claims to Empire Across the Non-compliant "Barbarous Nations" of North America,* Vancouver, September 7, 2012.
5   Instances of native communities erecting the first churches in BC span Vancouver Island, the lower mainland of BC and the Interior, according to the local historians listed in the bibliography, especially James Teit, E. Blanche Norcross, and A.G. Morice.
6   *The Fourth World*, by George Manuel and Michael Posluns; Collier-Macmillan Canada, 1974.
7   Recorded in the *Journal of American Folklore*, no. 36, 1923.
8   *A Village Journey, The Report of the Alaska Native Review Commission,* by Thomas Berger. Hill and Wang, for the Inuit Circumpolar Conference, 1985, p. 1.
9   *I am prepared to die*, by Nelson Mandela, International Defense and Aid Fund for Southern Africa, Canon Collins House, London, 1979, p. 26.
10   *Papers Connected to the Indian Land Question in British Columbia, 1850-1875.* Government Printer, James Bay, 1877, p. 150.
11   Colonial Land Ordinance of 1870, Section3: "3. From and after the date of proclamation in this Colony of Her Majesty's assent to this Ordinance, any male person being a British Subject, of the age of eighteen years or over, may acquire the right to pre-empt any tract... Provided that such right of pre-emption shall not be held to extend to any of the Aborigines of this Continent, except to such as shall have obtained the Governor's special permission in writing to that effect." Note: the Governor's permission was never obtained by a Status Indian in BC.
12   This was first written as a defense for BC by Justice Gould, rejecting the Nisga'a claim in *Calder,* citing "overt acts by the Crown Imperial by way of proclamation, ordinance, and proclaimed statute." *Calder,* SCBC, 1969.
13   In 1996, the journal *BC Studies* published an article which included in its opening mission statement, "the importance of the blockade and the paucity of other academic analyses suggest the need to offer an initial survey." Blomley, Nicholas; "SHUT THE PROVINCE DOWN": *First Nations Blockades in British Columbia, 1984-1995. BC Studies*, no. 111, Autumn 1996. No further survey has been conducted.
14   *The B.C. Outlaws: The Saga of Ah-Chee-Wun*, by F.W. Lindsay. Regatta City Press Ltd., Kelowna, 1963.
15   There are occasional exceptions. For instance, a Chief of the Mount Currie Indian Band allegedly sold a field to a white man sometime in the 1950s. He was raising funds for a criminal defense for a Band member.
16   *The 500 Years of Resistance Comic Book*, Gord Hill, Arsenal Pulp Press, Vancouver, 2009.
17   As in note 16, also, *Tales of Conflict*, B.A. McKelvie, 1949.
18   "The Drifters," told by Sam Mitchell in *Our Stories are Written on the Land*, Trefor Smith, Upper St'át'imc Language, Culture and Education Society, 1998.
19   *An Error In Judgement: The politics of medical care in an Indian/White community,* by Dara Culhane Speck, Talonbooks, Vancouver 1987, p. 168.
20   *Colonizing Bodies. Aboriginal Health and Healing in British Columbia 1900-50,* by Mary Ellen Kelm, UBC Press, Vancouver, 1998
21   Between 1910 and 1976, this school was home to eleven male dormitory supervisors who have recently been charged with sexual and physical abuse of the children who lived in the dormitories for ten months of the year. The school curriculum seems to have been focused primarily on the Bible, while the major activity was farm work required to keep the institution running and self-supporting. <www.irsr.ca>

22   "The Sharpshooter's Grudge," *BC Provincial Police Stories, Volume 2, by Cecil Clark, Heritage House Publishing, 1986, p.64.*

23   Larry Narciss, 2010 interview, Lillooet; *Haines,* 1981, BCCA; *Bob* and *White,* 1964, SCC.

24   "B.C. Indians Reject Government Fund," *The Province,* July 8, 1970

25   Brian Grandbois, participant at Cache Creek, from Cold Lake Alberta, 2010 interview.

26   Arnold Williams, Líl'wat, unpublished journals.

27   By Lynda Jean Crompton, LL.B., A Thesis submitted in partial fulfillment of the requirements for the Degree of Master of Laws; University of British Columbia, December 2006.

28   *confidential* First Nation accounts, BC Treaty Commission filing cabinets.

29   *B.C. Native Blockades and Direct Action From the 1980's to 2006,* Warrior Publications, Vancouver, 2006.

30   A Conference organized by the Association of Multicultural Societies and Service Agencies of BC, with the United Native Nations, Sal'I'shan Institute, Canadian Anti-Racism Education and research Society, and Vancouver Multicultural Society. Vancouver, January 25-26, 1991.

31   Rebecca Sommers, film maker, took the photo that was later published in *The St'át'imc Runner* newspaper, October 2008, p. 3.

32   The indigenous peoples – as peoples – should have their complaints reviewed by the Human Rights Committee of the International Covenant on Civil and Political Rights – if that body would only do so. But it has backed away on this, and not just for indigenous plaintiffs. Nonetheless, the limitations of CERD are clear, and that may be the reason for focusing on it – it is no danger to the status quo.

33   "'Indian Time' doesn't cut it for innovative chief with on-the-edge humour", Roy Macgregor, *The Globe and Mail,* Thursday, September 21, 2006.

34   China News, November 6, 2008.

35   "Real warriors hold jobs," by Kevin Libin, *National Post,* Saturday, January 19, 2008.

36   *The BC Treaty Negotiating Times,* Fall, 2007.

37   Bertha Williams speaking at *The Gathering of The Clans: A Conference Addressing "New World" Claims to Empire Across the Non-compliant "Barbarous Nations" of North America,* Vancouver, September 7, 2012.

38   Several phone-calls and e-mails were made making and confirming the request for this information between the author and the Trust administration, but the information was never provided. The request was made for the purposes of completing a news article for *The St'át'imc Runner* about the progress of the Trust.

39   A Summary of the Complaint, pertaining to the imminent ratification of a Final Agreement between the St'át'imc Chiefs Council, BC Hydro and British Columbia, was submitted by the International Human Rights Association of American Minorities, an NGO in consultative status with the Economic and Social Council of the United Nations, on behalf of Pau Tuc La Simc, James Louie, in May of 2011. The letter and 22 supporting documents were received by the Special Rapporteur's office, which replied with interest and forwarded the request for a meeting to Canada. Canada refused to meet, forming a procedural stonewall in the application to a United Nations committee of review.

40   Article by Robert Freeman in the *Chilliwack Progress,* March 4, 2008.

41   Burston-Marstellar might be best remembered in British Columbia for the work it did for the Macmillan Bloedel logging company in the 1990s, when Bloedel was outed for clearcutting massive areas up and down the old growth coastal rainforest, leading 850 people to block their operations in Clayoquot Sound with their bodies, and be arrested for it.

42   Interview with Bill Lightbown, 2011.

43   The Plaintiffs in the *Calder* Appeal: "On appeal from the Supreme Court of British Columbia from the Judgment of the Honourable Mr. Justice Gould pronounced October 17th, 1969, and entered February 6th, 1970.
       Between:

Frank Calder, James Gosnell, Nelson Azak, William McKay, Anthony Robinson, Robert Stevens, Hubert Doolan, Henry McKay, suing on their own behalf and on behalf of all other members of the Nishga Tribal Council, and James Gosnell, Percy Tait, Jacob Davis, Gordon McKay, Roy Azak, Joseph Gosnell, , Peter Clayton and Cecil Mercer, suing on their own behalf and on behalf of all other members of the Gitlakdamix Indian Band, and Maurice Nyce, Jacob Nyce and Eddie Azak, suing on their own behalf and on behalf of all other members of the Canyon City Indian Band, and W.D. McKay, William Leeson, Kelly Stevens, Henry McKay, Wilfred Tate, Louis McKay and Alvin McKay, suing on their own behalf and on behalf of all other members of the Greenville Indian Band, and Anthony Robinson, Graham Moore, Chester Benson, Nathan Barton, Nelson Clayton, William Angus, William Stanley and Harold Barton, suing on their own behalf and on behalf of all other members of the Kincolith Indian Band."

AND

Attorney General of British Columbia"

Those account for all of the four Nisga'a communities, or Indian Reserves, at that time.

44   "Health Nutz," Aboriginal Peoples' Television Network

45   Rose Doolan, interview 2010; Chief James Mountain, *The BC Treaty Negotiating Times*, Fall 2007.

46   One tour included Lake Babine First Nation, home of longtime BCTC Commissioner Wilf Adam. *The St'át'imc Runner,* June 2008.

47   "Steve's Roadshow," *The BC Treaty Negotiating Times*, Summer 2007.

48   As in the case of Nkwala, who in "1858, a year before his death, confronted a party of California gold miners who had massacred a body of unarmed Okanagan Indians. Dressed in his company-issue uniform and stove-pipe hat, with imperial medals on his chest, the chief cautioned the miners regarding the Okanagan Lake massacre, stating that "he did not think much of Bostons, or Americans, who would do the like." On the advice of the Hudson's Bay Company officials he did not retaliate, but instead referred the incident to the colonial authorities, who at this time had no presence in the area and could take no action." Duane Thomson, "The Response of Okanagan Indians to European Settlement," *BC Studies* no. 101, Spring 1994, p. 96-117.

49   From The Provincial Residential School Project's publication "Information Package," probably published in 1997 but undated. 911-100 Park Royal South, West Vancouver, BC.

50   These Grade 12 enrolment statistics are from Dr. E. Richard Atleo's doctoral dissertation at UBC: "Grade 12 Enrolments of Status Indians in British Columbia: 1949-1985". Dr. Atleo was born at Alert Bay in 1939. He was the first indigenous man in British Columbia to achieve a Doctorate level of education, in 1988.

51   "The Children of Tomorrow's Great Potlatch," by Ernie Crey, *BC Studies* No. 89, Spring 1991.

52   These and other observations are made regularly by former students, whenever discussing the schools. A number of books documenting the schools have included such stories, see this book's bibliography.

53   Lorna Williams, speaking at a Power of Place conference, Lillooet, 2008.

54   The practicing teachers who recounted these events prefer to remain anonymous sources.

55   Press release printed in Bridge River Lillooet News, November 2010.

56   Private source.

57   This event occurred in the author's kitchen.

Chapter 8

1   *The Illustrated History of British Columbia,* Terry Reksten, Douglas & McIntyre, 2001, p. 11.

2   Isaac Beshara, Maori, interview at the International Indigenous Leadership Gathering,

2010, Xaxl'íp (near Lillooet, BC). Printed in part in *The St'át'imc Runner,* September, 2010.

3   *Tales of Conflict,* by B.A. McKelvie, published by The Vancouver Daily Province, 1949.

4   *The Journey to Canada,* David Mills, Saxon House Canada, Toronto, 1996, p. 44.

5   *The Journey to Canada,* p.58.

6   Almost no European women lived in BC until the 1860's, when "Brideships" were sent, full of women, to adjust the imbalance. Most of the passengers, the "King's daughters," did wed quickly.

7   *Songs of the Pacific Northwest,* by Philip J. Thomas, Hancock House, Vancouver, 1979.

8   An address by former McLeod Lake Chief Alec Chingee on September 29, 2000, when the McLeod Lake Indian Band signed the adhesion to Treaty 8.

9   *The Chilcotin War,* by Mel Rothenburger, published by Mr. Paperback of Langley, BC, p. 13.

10 *The Illustrated History of British Columbia,* p. 42.

11 Matthew MacFie, *Vancouver Island and British Columbia,1865.* From, *"a few acres of snow" Documents in Canadian History, 1577-1867,"* edited by Thomas Thorner, Broadview Press, 1997.

12 *Frontier Theatre*, Chad Evans, Sono Nis Press, Victoria, 1983.

13 The *Illustrated History of British Columbia,* p.56.

14 *The B.C. Outlaws,* by F.W. Lindsay, Regatta City Press, Ltd., Kelowna, 1963.

15 *The B.C. Outlaws, supra.*

16 *The Chilcotin War,* by Mel Rothenburger, published by Mr. Paperback of Langley, BC in 1978. Rothenburger also authored *The Wild McLeans* about his family. He had a career as a daily newspaper editor in Kamloops, and was involved in politics, writing a biography for his friend in the Social Credit government, Phil Gaglardi who, Rothenburger says, "literally paved the wilderness and opened the way for the wheels of industry."

17 *Men of British Columbia*, Derek Pethick, Hancock House, BC, 1975.

18 At Skátin, Church of the Holy Cross; among others.

19 *The Warm Country,* by E. Blanche Norcross, Duncan, BC, 1959, p. 30.

20 Confidential Report of the Royal Commission on Indian Affairs for the Province of British Columbia; June 10, 1913. Royal Museum of BC, BC Archive, Victoria; GR 672 6.5 f.1.

21 *The Fourth World: An Indian Reality*, by George Manuel and Michael Posluns, Don Mills, Ontario, 1974.

22 *The Douhkhobors,* by George Woodcock and Ivan Avakumovic; Oxford University Press (Canadian Branch), 1968.

23 London. Printed by Mark Baskett, Printer to the King's most Excellent Majesty; and by the Assigns of Robert Baskett. 1763. As found in the Report of the Royal Commission on Aboriginal Peoples, 1986.

24 After Marshall's judgment in *Cherokee Nation v. The State of Georgia.*

25 *The Warm Land*, p. 33, quoting an 1859 issue of the *Times Colonist.*

26 *The Warm Land,* p.15.

27 James Williams, Frog Clan, Nadleh Whuten, Carrier Sekani. He addressed the people in his language and asked a translation of Chief Patrick at the *Recognition and Reconciliation Act* consultation meeting hosted by the First Nations Leadership Council, May 28, 2009, Prince George.

28 *Worcester v. State of Georgia,* 6 Peters Supreme Court Reports 515 (1832). *In* A legal opinion on legal remedies to prevent global eco-genocide, by Dr. Bruce Clark, December 10, 2006, Oslo.

29 Steven Newcomb, speaking at *The Gathering of The Clans: A Conference Addressing "New World" Claims to Empire Across the Non-compliant "Barbarous Nations" of North America,* Vancouver, September 7, 2012.

30 Indian Law Resource Center. *United States Senate Committee on Indian Affairs, Hear-*

ing on *"Setting the Standard: Domestic Implications of the UN Declaration on the Rights of Indigenous Peoples."* Testimony of Robert T. Coulter, Executive Director, Indian Law Resource Center, June 9, 2011; Attachment, written and edited by the Native Land Law Project, Indian Law Resource Center, Sponsored and published by the Indian Land Tenure Foundation. February, 2010.

31 *Connelly v. Woolrich,* (1867), 11 LCJ 197, 205-07 (SC Quebec), affirmed (1869), RLOS 356-7 (CA Quebec).

32 See Brian Slattery, "The Nature of Aboriginal Title," in *Beyond the Nass Valley, National Implications of the Supreme Court's* Delgamuukw *Decision,* Fraser Institute, Vancouver, 2000.

33 The Company was licensed to trade for furs with the Indians, and officially was not allowed to trade with alcohol. The Royal African Company's charter, two years later, by comparison and contrast, was licensed to trade in human slaves.

34 Simon Fraser, "Journal of a voyage from the Rocky Mountains to the Pacific Ocean performed in the year 1808," Sunday [Saturday], July 9, p. 136.

35 *The History of the Northern Interior of British Columbia,* A.G. Morice. John Lane London, 1904.

36 This according to Daniel Manuel, Secwepemc, and mentioned by professor Keith Carlson in this article by Sandra Shields, *Long Road to a Treaty,* April 20, 2007, TheTyee.ca: "The promise went like this: when lands outside their reserves were sold, the Sto:lo would receive a third of the proceeds, B.C. would receive a third, and the Queen would receive a third. "One of the things that I think is impressive about the oral history is the consistency of it," Carlson says. "A couple of different families have slightly different versions -- one says a quarter, one says a third -- but that's not important, all the basic parts are consistent and unchanging.""

37 *The Illustrated History of British Columbia, supra.*

38 *The Journey to Canada,* David Mills, p. 148.

39 "The Fort Victoria Treaties," Wilson Duff, *BC Studies,* No. 3, Fall 1969, UBC.

40 These descriptions of the giveaway items are documented in *The Chilcotin War,* by Mel Rothenburger, published by Mr. Paperback of Langley, BC, p. 80.

41 This sentence is repeated as written – perhaps the unusual use of "could would" just lacked the word "and" in the middle. Leon J. Ladner; *The Ladners of Ladner:By Covered Wagon to the Welfare State,* Mitchell Press Limited, Vancouver, 1972, p. 59.

42 *The Ladners of Ladner,* p. 127.

43 Treaty of Peace, League of Nations, as reprinted in *Historical Documents of Canada, Volume V. "The Arts of War and Peace, 1914-1945;* General Editor C.P. Stanley, The Macmillan Company of Canada Limited, Toronto, 1972.

44 Winston Churchill, Mansion House, London, 4 September 1941, at a luncheon in honour of Mackenzie-King, Prime Minister of Canada.

45 *Wilfred Laurier: A Pledge for Canada,* by Roderick Stewart; 2002, XYZ Publishing, Montreal.

46 *The Journey to Canada,* David Mills.

47 *Class and Race in the Social Structure of British Columbia, 1870-1939,* edited by W. Peter Ward. In *British Columbia: Historical Readings,* p. 590.

48 Submission, April 14, 2008, by St'át'imc Tribal Women to the Indigenous Women's Caucus, United Nations Permanent Forum of Indigenous Peoples.

49 *British Columbia Almanac,* Mark Forsythe, Arsenal Pulp Press, Vancouver, 2000, p. 10.

Chapter 9

1 Wolverine, William Ignace of Secwepemc and the Gustafsen Lake stand-off, attempted with lawyer Bruce Clark to access that court in a petition dated January 3, 1995. It was stonewalled by the Attorney General of BC, as is described later in this chapter.

2 *Regina v. Jack et al.* [1975] W.W.D. 135 British Columbia Provincial Court, Heard

Prov. J.

3   Justice Hall, page 223, *Calder v. Attorney-General of British Columbia*, [1973] S.C.R.

4   *Regina v. Dennis and Dennis,* (1974), 56 D.L.R. (3d) 379 (also reported: [1975] 2 W.W.R. 630, 28 C.R.N.S. 268, 22 C.C.C. (2d) 152) British Columbia Provincial Court.

5   *Westar Timber Ltd. v. Gitksan Wet'suwet'en Tribal Council* (B.C.C.A.), 1989, BCJ No. 1077, Locke J.

6   Chief Justice Antonio Lamer of Supreme Court of Canada, in *Delgamuukw v. British Columbia* [1997] 3 S.C.R. 1010 at paragraph 165

7   *R. v. Van der Peet,* [1996] 2 S.C.R. 507, 23 B.C.L.R. (3d) 1

8   *With or Without You: First Nations Law in Canada,* John Borrows, McGill Law Journal,1996, 41 McGill Li. 629.

9   As of 2011, over $5 million in fines against forestry companies in British Columbia was outstanding.

10   *R. v. Adams,* [1996] 3 S.C.R. 101.

11   "The first remedy is: applications for declarations of law alone in national courts outside of North America, based upon the "universal extraterritorial jurisdiction" to prevent genocide-in-progress arguably attributable to "judicial inactivity" within North America, each declaration consisting of a finding that the national court in question shares that universal jurisdiction and a recommendation that the courts of North America address their own constitutional law. This in essence happened in relation to Guatemala in Central America in *Menchu v. Montt,* September 26, 2006, Constitutional Court of Spain, BOE Supplement, October 28, 2005, Sentence 237/2005." Excerpted from, Clark, Dr. Bruce; *A legal opinion on legal remedies to prevent global eco-genocide*, December 10, 2006, Oslo.

12   The precedent wasn't carried through to meaningful consequence in *The Guatemala Case.* In *Menchu v. Montt,* Rigoberta Menchu charged the Guatemalan government with genocide and insisted that Spain must make itself judicially available in the absence of its former colony's impartiality towards the victims of genocidal assaults there.

13   "Deal or leave forest, Tsilhqot'in say, Spring breakup deadline, incursion warning issued over resource-use negotiations," by Gordon Hamilton, *The Vancouver Sun,* February 19, 1998.

14   *Haida Nation v. British Columbia (Minister of Forests),* [2004] 3 S.C.R. 511, 2004 SCC 73.

15   *Forest and Range Agreement Act,* BC, Ministry of Forests, 2004.

16   *Huu-Ay-Aht First Nation et al. v. The Minister of Forests et al.,* 2005 BCSC 697.

17   *Supra.*

18   *Lax Kw'alaams Indian Band v. Canada (Attorney General)* [2008], BCSC 447.

19   *R. v. Sparrow,* [1990] 1 S.C.R. 1075

20   Cohen Commission testimony, Barry Huber, Aboriginal Fisheries Liaison, Kamloops Department, DFO Pacific Region.

21   *Taku River Tlingit First Nation v. British Columbia (Project Assessment Director),* [2004] 3 S.C.R. 550, [2004] SCC 74 ; *R v. Douglas et al* [2007], BCCA (265); *Halfway River First Nation v B.C.* [1999] BCCA 470.

22   The only historical numbered treaty to take place between the crown and an indigenous nation in British Columbia was the adhesion to Treaty 8 (which extends to Saskatchewan), of several Bands in the northeastern corner of the province in 1899.

23   *Tsilhqot'in Nation v. British Columbia* [2007] BCSC 1700.

24   *Uukw v. British Columbia* (1987), 16 B.C.L.R. BCCA.

25   *Skeetchestn Indian Band et al. v. Registrar of Land Titles,* Kamloops, unregistered, CA026838, September 26, 2000.

26   *Westar Timber Ltd. v. Gitksan Wet'suwet'en Tribal Council* (B.C.C.A.) [1989], BCJ No. 1077.

27   *Proclamation of February 14th, 1859:* (a) All the lands in British Columbia, and all the mines and minerals therein, belong to the Crown in fee.

28   *Lax Kw'alaams Indian Band v. Canada* (Attorney General), 2008 BCSC 447 [124].

29   *Ordinance of March 31ˢᵗ, 1866:* "the aborigines of this colony (BC) or the territories

neighbouring thereto" could not pre-empt or hold land in fee simple without obtaining special permission of the Governor in writing.

30   *On the Path of the Explorers:Tracing the expeditions of Vancouver, Cook, Mackenzie, Fraser and Thompson;* Steve Short and Rosemary Neering, Whitecap Books, Vancouver/Toronto, 1992

31   *Native People and Explorers of Canada,* Daniel Conner, Prentice-Hall Canada Inc., 1984.

32   *R. v. Gladstone,* [1996] 2 S.C.R. 723, line 41.

33   Heltsiuk press statement, August 25, 2009, delivered at the All Chiefs Assembly in North Vancouver.

34   I met a Haida man who had 104 charges under the *Fisheries Act.* That is, 104 charges at one time.

35   Bill Lightbown, October 2011 interview.

36   Private source.

37   *Making Native Space,* Cole Harris, p. 323

38   The opening entry on this subject in the Canadian Encyclopedia online is:
     Royal commissions, once described by a member of Parliament as costly travelling minstrel shows, are a form of official inquiry into matters of public concern. They descend from the British monarch's prerogative power to order investigations, said by some to have been exercised first by King William I when he commanded the preparation of the Domesday Book, though the Commission on Enclosures initiated by Henry VIII in 1517 is a more likely prototype of contemporary royal commissions.
     Closely related to the royal commissions and often hard to distinguish from them are several other kinds of public inquiry; eg, commissions of inquiry, task forces and investigations established by departments and other agencies under statutory powers of the Inquiries Act, first passed by Parliament in 1868. <http://www.thecanadianencyclopedia.com/articles/royal-commissions>

39   These original documents produced by the 1912-1916 Reserve Commission are stored in the BC Archives in Victoria.

40   "Student wants skills she can bring home to Skátin," front page, *The St'át'imc Runner,* April 2006.

41   *The Same As Yesterday,* Joanne Drake-Terry, p.228.

42   Chief Jack Mussel of Skwah, Sto:lo; Fred Shields, Tsal'álh, St'át'imc, among others.

43   *First Nations in Canada,* Ministry of Indian and Northern Affairs, 1997, p. 114.

44   The $350 million Fund was finally discontinued in 2009, during the Indian Residential Schools Survivors Settlement Agreement.

45   *Cost of reforms $30-billion, report on aboriginal says,* by Scott Feschuk, November 22, 1996, *The Globe and Mail.*

46   Chief Fred Samson, Siska, Nlaka'pamux.

47   Statement by Strahl during a scheduled meeting with Salmon Talks Lillooet during an official visit to the town of Lillooet, 2010.

48   "Missing Women Commissioner wants answers to RCMP officer's sexually explicit photos," Ian Mulgrew, *The Vancouver Sun.* Friday, July 6, 2012.

49   "Missing Women inquiry has no credibility with aboriginal community: Grand Chief," By Neal Hall, *The Vancouver Sun,* March 7, 2012.

50   "'I saw I couldn't do my job,' says lawyer who quit missing women inquiry," Judith Lavoie, <timescolonist.com> March 21, 2012.

Chapter 10

1   *Our Home OR Native Land,* by Melvin Smith, Stoddart Publishing Co. Ltd., 1996.

2   *Rafe, A Memoir,* Rafe Mair, 2004.

3   *Politicians Of A Pioneering Province,* by Russell Walker, Mitchell Press Limited, Vancouver, 1969.

4   "Ottawa, B.C. put dealing back on," by Ian Austin, *The Province,* September 17, 1995.

5   "Bloodshed can be avoided: Gitxsan," by Suzanne Fournier and Jason Proctor, *The Province*, September 17, 1995.

6   "MILITANCY, Beat the drum loudly," by Rudy Platiel, *The Globe and Mail*, September 16, 1995, and the companion article, "The strange sojourn of Bruce Clark," by Peter McFarlane and Wayne Haimila.

7   "Rebel Indians 'fanatics,'" by Peter O'Neil and Mike Crawley, *The Vancouver Sun*, August 24, 1995.

8   "The thugs of Gustafsen and our moment of truth," Editorial Staff, *The Province*, August 23, 1995.

9   "B.C. standoff ends peacefully," Canadian Press and Staff, *The Globe and Mail*, September 18, 1995.

10   "All the news that's fit to… be manipulated," Editorial, *The Province*, September 22, 1995.

11   Kenneth A. Price in *The Verdict*, a publication of the Trial Lawyers' Association of British Columbia, October 1995.

12   "Ottawa, B.C. put dealing back on," by Ian Austin, *The Province*, September 17, 1995.

13   "Treaty touted as good deal," *The Vancouver Sun*, February 16, 1996.

14   "How to know aboriginal title and rights when you see 'em," *The Vancouver Sun*, December 12, 1997.

15   "Natives win on land rights, Top court rules that oral history gives bands constitutional claim in absence of treaties," front page of *The Globe and Mail*, December 12, 1997.

16   By Owen Lippert (Fraser Institute), *The Vancouver Sun*, December 19, 1997.

17   "A distant court, an imprudent decision," by Terry Morley, president of the consulting firm Negotiated Solutions, teacher of Canadian politics at UVic, *The Vancouver Sun*, December 20, 1997.

18   "Nisga'a get a state within in a state," (sic), *The Globe and Mail*, February, 1998. Mair was defending his friend Gordon Gibson's sustained attacks on the Nisga'a deal in his regular column.

19   Lillian Moyer, Tahltan, 2008 interview. The Chief in question was Jerry Asp, later to become the founding President of the Canadian Aboriginal Minerals Association.

20   The *Vancouver Sun*,

21   Tahltan Elders' press release, January 31, 2005.

22   *The St'át'imc Runner*, August, 2007.

23   Private source, 2011.

24   It's unlikely that a single First Nation was unscathed by the lump-sum payment, but the media did not acknowledge or document connections between the IAP or CEP and deaths at the time. A survey report titled, *Common Experience Payment and Healing: A Qualitative Study Exploring Impacts on Recipients*, was prepared for the Aboriginal Healing Foundation in 2010. It included many revealing quotations about such deaths by survivors of the IRSSSA, recipients of the lump-sum compensation.

25   She now is associated with Idle No More, and an intern with IHRAAM.

26   Shuswap Nation Tribal Council study, 2002.

27   "Truth and Native Abuse:How one man's wild claims threaten success of Truth and Reconciliation," by Terry Glavin, <thetyee.ca>, April 30, 2008.

28   *Stolen From Our Embrace*, by Suzanne Fournier and Ernie Crey, Douglas and McIntyre, 1997, p. 78.

29   *The Circle Game – Shadows and Substance in the Indian Residential School Experience in Canada*, by Roland Chrisjohn, with Sherri Young and Michael Maraun. Theytus Books Ltd., Penticton, 1997.

30   Private source.

31   CBC *The Current*, Saturday, December 22, 2012.

32   In a call to Mark Hume over his report in *The Vancouver Sun* of the March 8 seasonal plenary planning session between DFO and First Nations at Richmond, 2008.

33   "The Newspaper's View," editorial column, "Court ruling challenges Victoria to move faster on native treaties," *The Vancouver Sun*, November 22, 2007.

34   "Judgment presents serious challenge to B.C. forestry regime," by Vaughn Palmer,

	The Vancouver Sun, November 22, 2007.
35	"Court gives band a boost in quest for title to land," by Jonathon Fowlie and Gordon Hamilton; "Legal odyssey ends with advice to get a treaty," by Ian Mulgrew; both from *The Vancouver Sun*, November 22, 2007. "Band awarded partial victory," by Justine Hunter, November 22, 2007; "A complicated victory," by Justine Hunter, November 24, 2007, both from *The Globe and Mail.* "Court ruling's implications 'huge': Tetrault," by Jennifer Miller, *The Question*, November 29, 2007.
36	"Gitxsan Treaty Society doesn't have authority to sign deals with Enbridge, " By Neil J. Sterritt, *The Vancouver Sun*, January 6, 2012.
37	A two page paid ad from *The Spirit of The North* magazine, November 2009.
38	Press Release: "Heiltsuk Demand Recognition of Commercial Fishing Rights," November 9, 2009, posted by the First Nations Fisheries Council online < http://www.fnfisheriescouncil.ca/>.
39	Okanagan Nation Alliance Press Release: "Okanagan Nation rebuffed by owners of Spotted Lake, Chief Clarence Louie repeats requests for meeting with Christine Smith in order to prevent further escalation of conflict," Westbank, December 13, 2000.
40	"Native blockade evokes varied response," by James MacKinnon, *The Martlet*, February 14, 1991.
41	The Cedar Project: Historical trauma, sexual abuse and HIV risk among young Aboriginal people who use injection and non-injection drugs in two Canadian cities; Margo E. Pearce, Wayne M. Christian et al; 2008 Elsevier Ltd.
42	CBC Radio *Early Edition* with Hal Wake, October 19, 1995.
43	CBC TV Newsworld, Tuesday September 12, 1995, 10:15 AM PST.
44	"Savage or chieftain? Six Nations reclaims its history." CBC Broadcast Date: August. 11, 1960.
45	"Why treaty rights are worth fighting for." CBC Broadcast Date: April 19, 1971.
46	"Loggers confront Haida blockades." CBC Broadcast Date: Nov. 2, 1985.
47	*British Columbia Almanac*, by Mark Forsythe, Arsenal Pulp Press, Vancouver, 2000, p. 44.
48	"Group aims to change policy on Indian affairs," *Canadian Press*, September 26, 1995.
49	First Nations Unity Protocol Agreement, News Release, January 18, 2007.
50	Arthur Manuel, Secwepemc, speaking at *The Gathering of The Clans: A Conference Addressing "New World" Claims to Empire Across the Non-compliant "Barbarous Nations" of North America*, Vancouver, September 7, 2012.
51	"First Nation's treaty deal historic first for B.C;" Peter O'Neil, CanWest News Service; *The Vancouver Sun*, August 2, 2006.
52	*This Ragged Place – Travels Across the Landscape,* Terry Glavin, New Star Books, Vancouver, 1996.
53	1865 is possibly the first time when the Secwepemc picked up rifles and barricaded their fishing grounds against the Game Warden, a photograph of which is included in the magazine *B.C. Native Blockades and Direct Action*, by Warrior Publications, 2006.
54	*The Autobiography of Dacajeweiah, Splitting the Sky,* By John Boncore, p. 96.
55	*The Autobiography of Dacajeweiah*, p.96.
56	"RCMP's biggest, costliest operation ends peacefully," by Mark Hume and Lindsay Kines, *The Vancouver Sun*, September 18, 1995.
57	"Renegade lawyer sees nationwide conspiracy against Indians; Fighting for native rights," by Stewart Bell, *The Vancouver Sun*, August 26, 1995. And "Rebel group's lawyer petitioning Queen to intervene," by Peter O'Neil, Sun Ottawa Bureau, *The Vancouver Sun*, August 31, 1995.

Chapter 11

1	*Scenes and Studies of Savage Life,* Gilbert Malcolm Sproat, 1864.
2	Report of the Commission on N.W. Coast Indians, 1888, p. 454.
3	*Confidential* Report of the Royal Commission on Indian Affairs for the Province of British Columbia, 1913.

4   Statement of the Government of Canada on Indian policy (The White Paper), 1969.

5   "Power to the People" Celebration, Port Douglas, November 12, 2010, on the occasion of having their community connected to the BC Hydro electrical supply grid. Reported in *The St'át'imc Runner,* December, 2010.

6   *Scenes and Studies of Savage Life,* Gilbert Malcolm Sproat, 1864.

7   Statements posted to "Conservative Thoughts" online, Tuesday, June 7, 2011, by Alan Forseth. <http://kamloopsthompsonbcconservatives.blogspot.ca>

8   At an August 26 meeting reported in the *100 Mile House Free Press* August 31, 2011.

9   Randy Hawes, Junior Minister for Mines, statement reprinted in a press release issued by the Carrier Sekani Tribal Council: *First Nations in BC Call for Resignation of Junior Mines Minister Hawes,* October 1, 2010.

10   "Judith Sayers joins UVic Law," by UVic Communications: Law News and Events, 2009-10-13.

11   "BC Treaty Commission: Keeper of the Process" advertisement in the Vancouver Sun, March 20, 2012.

12   Pricewaterhouse Coopers, *"Financial and Economic Impacts of Treaty Settlement in BC,"* 2009.

13   *Delgamuukw,* 1997, SCC, par. 128.

14   A Global Assessment of Salmon Aquaculture Impacts on Wild Salmonids, by Jennifer Myers and Ransom Ford, *PLOS Biology,* February 2008.

15   This activity was described by the previous Chief, Darren Blaney, an anti-fish farm advocate who led court action against the local salmon farm, in public talks in Lillooet seeking support to fight the expansion of the farms.

16   *Blaney et al v. British Columbia (The Minister of Agriculture Food and Fisheries) et al,* 2005 BCSC 283.

17   Siska Traditions Society runs the berry and plant-based product manufacturing. The Siska fishwheel supplies their processing and salmon-smoking business as a road-side outlet, working in agreement with the Department of Fisheries and Oceans. The Yale First Nation has a similar business. These models are labour intensive, producing a value-added product, and appear to be sustainable.

18   Economic Development in First Nations, An Overview of Current Issues; by The Public Policy Forum, Ottawa, January 2005, p. 16.

19   "Options for Commercial Enterprises in First Nations," by John Graham and Heather Edwards Institute On Governance, Institute On Governance, Ottawa, February 10, 2003, p. 5

20   Economic Development Toolkit for First Nations Economic Development Officers, Chiefs and Councils and Community Members – *Basic Information and Guide;* Prepared for the Industry Council for Aboriginal Business by Kekinsuqs, Dr. Judith Sayers, With Funding from Indian and Northern Affairs Canada, May, 2011, p. 20

21   One Nation Economic Forum Round Table Discussions, October 2007, Vancouver. Forum Report, by BDO Dunwoody LLP, Chartered Accountants and Advisors, for the Aboriginal Leadership Institute.

22   A vast selection of papers exist which do not defy the key qualities listed. To mention two more: *Sharing Canada's Prosperity – A Hand Up, Not A Hand Out;* Final Report on the Special Study on the involvement of Aboriginal communities and businesses in economic development activities in Canada, by The Honourable Gerry St. Germain, *Chair,* Standing Senate Committee on Aboriginal Peoples, March 2007. *Accountability and the Separation of Business and Politics in Corporate – Aboriginal Partnerships.* By Matthew Bourke, a project submitted to partially fulfill the requirements of a Degree in Master of Public Policy, Simon Fraser University, Spring 2005. *Higher Performing First Nations Separate Business and Politics,* The Frontier Centre for Public Policy, February 18, 2008.

23   Manuel was speaking at *The Gathering of The Clans: A Conference Addressing "New World" Claims to Empire Across the Non-compliant "Barbarous Nations" of North America,* Vancouver, September 7, 2012.

24   A recent Canadian study which found a strong correlation between First Nations in

British Columbia with low suicide rates and those with significant interests and activities relating to self-government, *Transcultural Psychiatry*, V. 35, June 1998.

25   "Art and Russell's Roadshow," *The St'át'imc Runner,* November 2006.

26   "Sto:lo bands sign health accord", The Abbotsford Times, December 27, 2011.

27   *The St'át'imc Runner,* August, 2006.

28   First Nations Schools Association Annual Report 2008-2009, as well as confirmations with the Association to identify the status of First Nations Schools teacher certification guidelines.

29   The First Nations Property Ownership Initiative and Alternatives, November 1, 2010, Woodward & Company

30   *Indian Act* (R.S.C. 1985) Section 18, paragraph 1.

31   "First Nation property ownership gains momentum," By Mike Youds, *Kamloops Daily News*, January 24, 2011.

32   Parliamentary Debate, CPAC, June 15, 2010.

33   The question remains whether the army incident at Gustafsen Lake was preconceived or not. Superintendent Len Olfert supplied in his trial testimony that police had started to prepare for the incident command in April – three months before the conflict between Lyle James and the Sundancers broke out physically.

34   Kenneth A. Price in *The Verdict*, a publication of the Trial Lawyers' Association of British Columbia, October, 1995.

35   *The British Colonist*, Vol. 1 Victoria. VI., Saturday, Dec 18, 1858. No.2. Front page, by Amor DeCosmos, Editor.

36   A full account of the meeting was printed in *The British Colonist,* deCosmos' newspaper, on June 2, 1864 and June 7, 1864. That record was later reproduced in *The Chilcotin War,* by Mel Rothenburger, published in 1978 by Mr. Paperback in Langley, BC.

37   This legendary comment was attributed to Smithe by Joseph Gosnell, Nisga'a, in his speech in the BC Legislature, December 2, 1998. *Spirit Dance at Meziadin: Chief Joseph Gosnell and the Nisga'a Treaty,* by Alex Rose. 2000, Harbour Publishing, Vancouver, p. 18.

38   Premier William Smithe, Victoria, B. C., 29th July, 1887. 51 Vic. REPORT OF COMMISSION N. W. COAST INDIANS. 461.

39   *Politicians Of A Pioneering Province,* Walker, Russell R.; Mitchell Press Limited, Vancouver, 1969.

40   Martin Robin, *The Rush for Spoils, The Company Province 1871-1933.* McLelland and Stewart Limited Toronto, 1972.

41   *Regina v. Haines* (1978), 44 C.C.C. (2d) 162 (also reported: 8 B.C.L.R. 211).

42   *Justice in Paradise,* Dr. Bruce Clark, McGill-Queen's University Press, Toronto, 2007.

43   Lyn Crompton, speaking at *The Gathering of The Clans: A Conference Addressing "New World" Claims to Empire Across the Non-compliant "Barbarous Nations" of North America,* Vancouver, September 7, 2012.

44   "Apple Cede: First Nations Land Management Regime," by Janice G.A.E. Switlo, B.Com., LL.B, June 9, 1999

45   "Native History, Native Claims and Self-Determination," by Thomas R. Berger, in *BC Studies,* no.57, Spring 1983.

Chapter 12

1   <http://news.nationalpost.com/2012/01/23/canada-could-face-aboriginal-uprising-if-harper-doesnt-listen-chief-threatens/>

2   "Food fishery tangled in native net profits: BC Supreme Court lawsuit claims damages after band prevented from fishing for food in 2010 while other First Nations conducted commercial harvest," Nelson Bennett Tue Jun 12, 2012, *Business in Vancouver*, online edition.

3   As he did in all the cases where he represented British Columbia in court against aboriginal plaintiffs or appellants or defenders, in cases such as *Delgamuukw.*

4   *The Whistler Question,* Pemberton edition, October 13, 2011

5   "Musqueam, developer continue wrangling over Vancouver land," By Mike Howell, *The Vancouver Courier,* September 6, 2012.

6   The only government authority on heritage sites and archaeology in British Columbia is the Archaeology Branch of the Ministry of Tourism, Sports and the Arts. The subdivision in this example was to happen near Lillooet. In spite of two site visits and a verbal confirmation that there was an outstanding problem, five years ago, the Archaeology Branch official has neither produced a report nor withdrawn permission to subdivide the property. Newspaper reports from the time of the incident were only published in *The St'át'imc Runner*, the Lillooet Tribal Council's newspaper. See October, 2008 and May, 2009.

7   "What Happened at Cwíten Xelíten X7ilh," *The St'át'imc Runner,* May 2009.

8   For example, in Líl'wat at the industrial park.

9   *Why I Write,* by George Orwell, 1946.

10   *Comment posted under, Talking to Native Teens about School: What First Nations kids say keeps them going, and what pulls them away. Second in a series.* By Jacqueline Windh, 27 July 2010, <*TheTyee.ca*>

11   *Supra.*

12   "Seeking Justice Elsewhere: The Hul'qumi'num Treaty Group case before the Inter-American Commission on Human Rights," first in the Series *First Nations' Rights: The Gap Between Law and Practice.* The talk was sponsored by Lawyers Rights Watch Canada and Amnesty International, February 23, 2012.

13   "Indigenous Rights in the UN System: Development of the UN Declaration on the Rights of Indigenous Peoples," Kenneth Deer, March 19, 2012, at Vancouver Public Library.

14   By Rick Ouston, *The Vancouver Sun,* February 2, 1998.

15   By Barbara Yaffe, *The Vancouver Sun,* November 12, 2012.

16   "Hupacasath First Nation fears its language may die," *The Vancouver Sun,* December 18, 2009.

17   *Journey into the Interior of British Columbia*, by Begbie, Matthew Bailie, Esq. Justice; 1859. Communicated by the Duke of Newcastle, F.R.G.S., H.M. Secretary for the Colonies.

18   *In the Dawning. A Story of Canada*, MMII Denali Music (A division of King Motion Picture Company) SOCAN. www.thislivingworld.com

19   *Frontier Scientists* University of Alaska Fairbanks, article posted by "liz" June 2011.

20   *British Columbia Needs No History. Or Does It?* By Jean Barman, *British Columbia Almanac*, by Mark Forsythe, Arsenal Pulp Press, Vancouver, 2000, p. 168.

21   *The River Forks Here.* Janice G.A.E. Switlo, 2002.

22   Kenneth Deer, Mohawk, speaking at the Lawyers' Rights Watch series at Vancouver Public Library, February, 2012.

23   *The St'át'imc Runner,* May 2008.

24   *Report of the Auditor General of British Columbia,* 2005, page 26.

25   *The BC Treaty Negotiating Times,* Summer 2009, interview with Stewart Phillip.

26   The letter was read and distributed at the All Chiefs Assembly on August 25, 2009, in North Vancouver.

27   The *Times Colonist* newspaper, March 22, 2007.

28   *Surviving as Indians,* by Menno Boldt, p.296.

29   Tsilhqot'in National Government Press Release, October 31, 2008, Williams Lake.

30   *A History of the Northern Interior of British Columbia*, A.G.Morice, 1904, p. 194.

31   *BC New Relationship Act,* 2004, preamble.

32   "Gitxsan history set right," by Ken MacQueen, *The Vancouver Sun,* December 12, 1997.

33   Arthur Manuel, on a Sovereignty Speaking Tour, Lillooet, November 2006.

34   *A legal opinion on legal remedies to prevent global eco-genocide*, Dr. Bruce Clark, December 10, 2006, Oslo.

35   *Indigenous Territoriality in Canadian Courts* by Douglas Harris, in *Box of Treasure or Empty Box?* Ed. Ardith Walkem and Halie Bruce, Theytus Books, 2003.

36   *Drum Beat – Anger and Renewal in Indian Country,* edited by Boyce Richardson, 1989 Assembly of First Nations, Summerhill Press Ltd.

37   *Prisoners of Democracy: The Lil'wat right to an impartial tribunal*, by Lyn Crompton, Master's Thesis, UBC, 2006, p. 25.

38   *Prisoners of Democracy,* p. 186.

39   *Prisoners of Democracy,* p. 195.

INDEX

A

Aboriginal Horizontal Framework 47, 272, 274
Aboriginal Native Rights Committee of the Interior Tribes 157
Aboriginal Peoples Family Accord 273
Ah-Chee-Wun 153
Ahousat 151, 163, 221
Alexis 155
Allied Tribes 66, 105, 110-12, 119, 133, 193, 224
Arbour, Louise 303
Assembly of First Nations 36, 45, 65, 129, 151, 163, 166, 236, 241-42, 304, 311
Atleo, Shawn 151, 163
Auger, Renata Andres 282

B

Babine 109, 199, 305
Baird, Kim 126, 166, 172
Baptiste, Ethan 175
BC Association of Non-Status Indians 157, 160, 65
BC Special 112,
BC Business Council 267
BC Treaty Commission (BCTC) 19, 25, 28, 54, 56, 65, 75, 87, 119-39, 152, 161, 163, 166, 169, 172, 220, 235, 240, 252, 254-261, 266-67, 274, 276, 305, 307, 312
benefits sharing 49, 53, 251, 280-81, 305
Bennett, William A.C. 157, 278
Begbie, Justice Matthew Bailie 14-17, 90, 184, 200, 228, 298
Berger, Thomas 284-85
Bering land bridge theory 61, 299

Biko, Steven 85
Black Dome 72, 76
Boas, Franz 101
Brazeau, Patrick 162
British Colonist, The 277
British Columbia Indian Rights Association 101
"British liberalism" 60, 185
British navy 17, 153, 181
Business in Vancouver 171, 251, 287, 295

C

Calder, 1973 court ruling 29-30, 67, 75, 123-24, 169, 191, 207, 209
Calder, Frank 29, 69, 113, 172, 204, 284
Campbell, Gordon 139, 168, 239, 276
Campbell Scott, Duncan 39, 104, 120, 245
Canadian Broadcasting Corporation (CBC) 246, 249-253
Canadian Constitution
    British North America Act 71, 94, 200, 210; development and powers 74, 98, 125, 129, 203-04, 285; Section 25, Royal Proclamation of 1763 18, 71-73, 76, 105, 188-91, 192, 207, 210, 217-18, 228; Section 35 25, 27, 68, 123, 215, 301
Carrier 40, 91, 159, 199
Carrier Sekani 137, 193
Cashore, John 123
Chehalis 54, 307
Chilcotin War 34, 39
Christian, Wayne 299
Christianization 148, 182, 187
Claims of the Allied Tribes 119, 193
Clark, Bruce 168, 194, 236, 250, 261, 276, 282-83, 310
Clark, Christy 279, 305

Cohen Commission 227
Coleman, Rich 265
Comprehensive Claims Policy 120, 121, 123, 124, 128, 132, 235, 252, 256
Conference of Berlin 193
Constitution Express 159
Coppermoon Communications 167
Corbiere 116, 118
Cowichan 42, 76, 92, 101, 109-10, 152, 156, 183, 187, 192-93, 199, 202
Cowichan Petition 101, 202
Cram, Jack 282
Crey, Ernie 162, 246, 328 – 7/51, 333 – 10/28
criminalization 13, 36, 37, 49, 142, 151, 158, 227, 254, 293
Crompton, Lyn 147, 282-83, 311

D

Daily Colonist 149
Deer, Kenneth 296
Delgamuukw 29-31, 73, 122, 125, 127-29, 133, 159, 208, 211, 214, 216-19, 238, 248, 267, 282, 297, 307-08
deCosmos, Amor 277-78
deJong, Mike 120, 131, 139, 276-77
Dennis, David 140, 161
Derrickson, Ron 211
Dickason, Olive 61
doctrine of discovery 194-96
Dosanjh, Ujjal 236-37, 275-76, 278
Douglas, James
    BC Governor 14-15, 59, 90, 198, 200, 202, 217-18
    HBC Chief Factor 14, 63, 183, 265
    Reserve selection 16, 92-94, 105
    treaty purchases 17, 42, 72, 78, 79, 92-93, 199, 206-07, 284
Douglas 2007, court ruling 214-15
Douglas Lake roadblock 257

E

Education Jurisdiction Agreements 272-73
Elliot, A C 43
Empowered Residential School Survivors 241
extinguishment 22, 27, 74, 75, 118, 123-25, 132, 163, 210, 254, 267, 274

F

Federation of Saskatchewan Indians 157
fiduciary obligation 42, 130, 189, 272-73
First Nations Certainty of Land Title Act 274, 305

First Nations Leadership Council 166, 168, 304, 305
First Nations Summit 65, 120, 127, 137, 162-63, 166, 252, 255, 258, 297, 304
First Nations Unity Protocol 133, 257-59
Fisheries Act 206, 213, 257, 289
flag of BC 26, 199, 204-05
Forest and Range Agreements 42, 53, 54, 212-13
Foster, Hamar 77, 133
Four Host First Nations 171
Fraser, Simon 77, 90, 154, 197, 265
Friends of the Indians 102
frozen rights 73, 218-21
fur trade
    commercial value 59; dependence on indigenous 265, 60, 65; exploitation of indigenous 48, 63, 173; forming government 199; "partnership" 62, 63; violence towards indigenous 33, 63

G

Gabereau, Vicki 251
Garrett, Reverend Alex C. 43
genocide 18, 20, 25, 27, 32, 40, 90, 146, 148, 161, 181, 210, 226, 232, 244-45, 251, 283, 310, 312-13
Genocide Convention 37, 40, 243, 303, 310
Gitxsan 30-31, 133, 138, 159, 208, 217, 235-36, 239, 248, 281
Gladstone, William 221
Gladstone, 1996 court ruling 221
Glavin, Terry 235, 245, 260-63
gold rushes
    Cariboo 50, 92, 184, 186; Fraser 14, 184, 186; Yukon 184
Gosnell, James 128
Gosnell, Joseph 140, 153, 172, 238
Gorsline, Ken 49
Grouse Creek War 15
Gustafsen Lake stand-off, 21, 26, 29, 37, 42, 61, 121-22, 133, 152, 154, 160, 168, 236-38, 251, 252, 260-63, 275, 277, 282

H

Haida 93, 100, 109, 110, 120, 135, 156, 159, 168, 229, 252, 295, 308
Haida, 2004 court ruling 31, 54, 211-13, 277
Haines 279, 311
Halfway River 214
Hall, Anthony 121, 275
Harcourt, Mike 119, 236, 274-75, 292

Harris, Douglas 87, 311
Hawes, Randy 265
Hawthorn Report 117
Helin, Calvin 164-65
Heltsiuk 221
Hill, Gord 174, 277
Home Children 24
Hudson's Bay Company
    forming BC government 14, 15, 18, 33,
    63, 79, 92-3, 173, 181, 183, 185, 198-99
    charter, 41, 183, 190, 196-97, 218
    land claims 79, 93, 190, 192
    trade with indigenous 17, 41, 63, 65, 82
Hul'qumi'num Treaty Group 133, 258-59, 296
Hume, Steven 235
Huu-ay-aht 212
hydroelectric production
    compensation agreements 53, 167, 175,
    280, 309; impacts to indigenous 33, 38,
    216, 208, 280

I

IHRAAM 39
Indian Act
    imposed governance 19, 37, 42, 46-47, 73,
    89, 101, 111, 115, 158, 225, 229, 236, 248,
    251, 253, 265, 270-74, 305, 309; offenses
    under, 37, 39, 41, 66, 89, 110-11, 148-
    49, 158, 200, 207, 219, 222
Indian Homemakers Association of BC 157
Indian Residential Schools
    Aboriginal Healing Fund 226; attendance
    compulsory 18, 39, 110; educational
    impact 76, 85, 126, 156, 173; genocidal
    impact 17, 18, 34, 38, 41, 53, 87, 89,
    170, 241-43, 245-46; government
    apologies 226, 243; Survivors' Settlement
    Agreement, 2008 170, 241-42, 244; Truth
    and Reconciliation Commission 34, 37,
    244
Indian Rights Association 65, 101, 106-08,
    156
Indigenous Network on Economies and Trade
    49, 125
Inter-American Commission on Human Rights
    39, 209
International Human Rights Association of
    American Minorities (IHRAAM) 39
Indian Reserves
    administration of 19, 45, 114-16;
    conditions of life on 37-38, 41, 45,
    91, 215, 221-22, 226; conversion to
    First Nations 91; conversion to Treaty
    Settlement Lands 27, 56, 130, 138;

original surveys of 16, 66, 91, 94, 108-09;
    ownership of 72, 100; reduction or
    removal of 16, 27, 94-100, 130, 224-26,
    278; indigenous resistance to 100-113
Indian Status
    attempts to eliminate 114, 120, 130, 135,
    137, 252, 255, 272-73, 300; eligibility
    and registration 117-18, 157, 280;
    entitlements of 44-45, 47-48, 156, 160,
    173, 177, 222, 244, 272-73
Inter Tribal Fishing Treaty 65, 159-60, 256
Ipperwash 21, 122, 236

J

James, Lyle 260-62
Jenness, Diamond 17
Joe, Clarence 112
John, Edward 127-28, 162-3, 245, 252
Joint Committee of the Privy Council 79,
    111-12
Joseph, Tewannee 171

K

Kelly, Peter 79, 90, 112,
Kelowna Accord 61, 272, 306
King George III of England 188-92, 198, 205
King George Men 17
Koepke, Tim 125
Kootenay 92
Kwakiutl / Kwagiulth 89, 93, 156, 163

L

Ladner, Leon 201
Lamer, Justice Antonio 208, 307
Lampert, Jerry 267
language loss 18, 20, 28, 52, 61, 76, 86, 117,
    147, 161, 167, 175, 176, 241, 243, 245,
    297, 300, 308, 312
Laurier, Wilfred 76, 102, 104, 107, 171, 204,
    224, 299
Liberal (government of BC) 167, 235, 239-40,
    253, 255, 276,
Liberal (government of Canada) 113, 233
Lightbown, Bill 168
Líl'wat 17, 33, 39, 61, 94, 159, 160, 171, 175,
    209, 226, 227, 250, 253, 276, 283, 293,
    308
logging
    commercial value 48, 50, 53, 54, 128, 208,
    222, 232, 245, 267; impacts of clearcutting
    38, 128, 210, 251, 268; legal challenges to

210-12, 238, 247-48, 277; roadblocks of 159, 160-61, 210, 250, 252, 276, 277
Louie, Clarence 163-64, 172, 266
Louie, James 61
Louie, Robert 44, 137
Loring, Kevin 169
Luggi, David 137
Lutz, John 80, 133

M

McBride, Richard 102-05, 278
McEachern, Justice Alan 30, 235
McIvor, Sharon 118, 280
McLeod Lake Band 268
Maa-nulth 42, 138, 140, 163, 172
Mair, Rafe 233, 235, 239, 292
Malloway, Richard 112
Mandell, Louise 227, 280-81
Manuel, Arthur 49, 123, 158, 270, 309
Manuel, George 65, 104, 157-9, 171, 174, 187, 280
Maquinna 64, 149
Martin, Paul 61
Matthias, Joe 251
measles 155, 266
Memorial to Frank Oliver 76, 91, 103-04
Memorial to Wilfred Laurier 76, 102-03, 299
Menczer, Micha 281
Ministry of Children and Families, BC 39-40, 166, 273
missionaries
    advocacy for indigenous rights 228, 76, 78, 90; at Metlakatla, 228; impact on indigenous 37, 67, 148
Moccasin Walk of 100 Miles 157
modified rights 27, 125, 132, 310
Morales, Robert 258, 296
Morice, Father A.G. 63, 90, 198
Mulroney, Brian 306
municipalization 25, 75, 126, 129, 132, 139, 166, 253, 255, 301
Musqueam 92, 154, 171, 213, 293

N

National Indian Brotherhood 65-66, 157, 166
Native Brotherhood 66, 110, 156
National Post, The, 286-87,
Neskonlith 16, 49, 92, 94, 123, 157, 187
New Relationship Agreement, "the new relationship", 121, 137, 167-68, 304, 307
New Relationship Trust 167

Newcomb, Steven 146
Nielsen Report 44, 272, 306
Nisga'a, 29-30, 42, 69, 100, 120, 124, 128-41, 153, 156, 172, 192, 199, 204, 209, 224, 228, 233, 238-39, 254-56, 260, 276, 278-79, 284
Nisga'a Final Agreement 30, 128, 131, 153, 172, 255, 276, 279
Nlaka'pamux 59, 148, 158, 169, 199
North American Indian Brotherhood 112, 156
North West Company 62, 65, 154, 196-98,
Nunavut Territory 132, 285
Nuu-chah-nulth 64, 88, 219-21
Nuu-chah-nulth, 2009-11 court rulings 73, 219-21
Nuxalk 88, 147, 161

O

Obyerodhyambo, Oby 206
Oka 160, 226, 235, 252
Okanagan 76, 91, 92, 102, 109, 158, 175, 199, 211, 249
Olympic Games, 2010 169, 171, 229, 253, 277, 297
O'Meare, Edward 77, 193,
Oppal, Wally 229-30, 276-77
Oregon Territory 63, 80, 93, 197, 198, 199
Osgoode Hall 69, 78
Osoyoos 121, 163, 266

P

Papal Bulls
    dominion 195; Inter Caetera 143-45; Sublimus Dei 146
Paull, Alex 112
Pemberton 16, 92, 94, 176, 277
Penner, Barry 265
Phillip, Stewart 254-55, 286
Piapot 42
Pierre, Sophie 169, 254-55
Pitawanakwat, "OJ" James 26, 29, 121-22
Plant, Geoff 135, 240, 254, 276, 279, 292
Point, Steven 127, 172, 240
Pontiac 188, 192
Posluns, Michael 174
Potlatch
    ceremony 89, 148, 150, 93; criminalization of 32, 89, 148-51, 156, 158, 200, 223, 299
poverty 21, 35, 42, 45-46, 49, 53, 90, 114, 117, 126, 133-34, 179, 221-22, 250, 266, 305
Privy Council of England 70-73, 96, 102,

104-6, 112, 120, 189-95, 206, 224

Q

Queen Anne of England 206, 262
Queen Victoria of England 204
Qwatsinas 119

R

Rasky, Harry 252
Recognition and Reconciliation Legislation
    168, 304-05, 307
Red Paper Policy 114
Rejection of Funds, 1975 47-48, 158
reparations 244
Reserve Commissions
    McKenna-McBride Commission 66,
    95, 105-10; Commission on the state
    of the Indians of the North West Coast,
    228, 265, 278
Richardson, Miles 120
roadblocks 33, 37, 52, 120, 153, 156, 158-
    62, 211, 235, 247-48, 250, 252, 257,
    260, 276-77
Robin, Martin 68
Rosette, Percy 260-62
Rothenburger, Mel 88
Royal Commission on Aboriginal Peoples,
    1996   36, 130, 226
Royal Commission on Indian Affairs for
    the Province of British Columbia,
    1912, see "McKenna-McBride" under
    "Reserve Commissions"
Rupert's Land 192, 196, 218

S

salmon
    canneries 155, 187, 201; commercial
    value 20, 33, 50; decimation of 20, 73,
    210, 214, 227-28, 312; farms 51, 161,
    173, 256, 268; indigenous dependence
    on 33, 73, 150, 155, 159, 220-22, 227,
    288-91, 305
Satanove, Madame Justice 213, 218, 219
Sechelt 112, 137, 158, 173, 246
Secwepemc 29, 49, 56, 76, 91, 98, 102,
    104, 121, 123, 156, 158-59, 161, 174-
    75, 199, 204, 246, 249, 260-62, 270,
    274, 283, 299
Sewid, James 89
Seymour, Frederick 199, 205
Simon Fraser University 64
Slattery, Brian 69-74, 85
smallpox 17, 33-34, 80, 82, 88, 266, 276

Sparrow, 1990 court ruling 73, 160, 213-14
Spain
    colonization of "BC" 59, 80
    extradition of political prisoners, 29
Spanish Constitutional Court 247, 310
    "Catholic Monarchs" 143, 145
Spintlum 59
Sproat, Gilbert Malcolm 90, 147, 182-83,
    264-65
Squamish 171, 273
Standard and Poor's 259
St'át'imc 61, 158, 163, 176-77, 231, 241,
    249, 298
Sto:lo 60, 94, 162, 199, 208, 228, 272, 294,
sui generis 30, 70, 74, 293
suicide 35-36, 242, 248, 271
Switlo, Janice 282-84, 301

T

Tachie Barricade Agreement 156
Tahltan 156, 161, 164, 240
Taku 211, 214, 227
Teit, James 55, 86, 101, 110, 148
terra incognita 192, 216, 218
terra nullius 72, 148, 183
Thevarge, Edward 112
Times Colonist 257
Tom, Alaina 231
Treaty 8 42, 82, 214
Trudeau, Pierre Elliott, 29, 113-14, 123,
    132, 172, 252, 265, 272
Trutch, Joseph 55, 94, 100, 200, 265
Tsawwassen 42, 126, 132, 138-39, 166,
    172, 201, 280
Tsawwassen Accord 166
Tsilhqot'in 31, 34, 39, 51, 79, 127, 155,
    158, 160, 169, 199, 211, 215, 247, 266,
    278-80, 292, 306
Tsimshian 64, 100-01, 156, 218, 228-29,
    265
Tsleil-Waututh 171
Ts'peten Defenders 21, 275
tuberculosis 14, 38, 155, 266

U

Union of BC Indian Chiefs (UBCIC) 47,
    65, 117, 120, 124, 157-60, 166, 172,
    254-55,
United Nations
    Committee for the Elimination of all
    forms of Racial Discrimination 125,
    163; Declaration on the Rights of
    Indigenous Peoples 22, 163, 296, 302,

303; Permanent Forum on Indigenous
    Issues 25, 162, 204, 253, 302
United Native Nations 34, 65, 160, 162
University of British Columbia 64, 201
University of Victoria 77, 80, 239, 266, 305
usufructuary rights 71, 74, 113

V

Vancouver Sun, The 128, 238-40, 248, 260,
    297
Van derPeet 208, 214
Victoria 14, 17, 59, 67, 82, 99, 100, 102-03,
    116, 156, 186, 198-99, 247, 265, 278
vital statistics, indigenous 38, 45-46

W

Waddington, Alfred 155, 185-86, 278
Walker, Russell 234, 278
Wake, Hal 250
West, Ron 305
Westbank 44, 51, 137, 211, 280, 281
Wet'suwet'n 30-31, 34, 129, 133, 159, 208,
    235, 281
White, Lavina 135, 168, 295, 308
White and Bob 75, 113, 207, 284
White Paper Policy 114, 123, 132, 157,
    252, 272, 306
Widdowson, Frances 84, 307
William, Roger 215
Williams, Arnold 308
Williams, Bertha 139, 166
Williams, James 193
Williams, Lorna 175, 298
Wilson, Dan 211
Wilson-Raybould, Jody 163
Wolverine, 152, 262, 282
World Council of Indigenous Peoples
    158-59
World Trade Organization 49

X

Xeni Gwetin 215, 248, 281

Y

Yale 92, 186, 258
Yukon Settlement Agreement 75, 132, 235